Rea ̶ ̶ ̶JS with ⦿ WebLinks

Issues in

Human Sexuality
98/99

*Current and controversial readings
with links to relevant Web sites*

Readings and World Wide Web Sites
Edited and Selected by

Richard Blonna, Ed.D., C.H.E.S.

Morton Publishing Company
925 W. Kenyon Avenue, Unit 12
Englewood, CO 80110

800/348-3777

http://www.morton-pub.com

About the Editor: Richard Blonna is an Associate Professor of Community Health at William Paterson College. He teaches classes in Human Sexuality, Epidemiology, Stress Management, and Personal Health. Dr. Blonna has a doctorate in Health Education from Temple University and a Master's Degree in Counseling from Seton Hall University. He has written several articles on Human Sexuality, Sexually Transmitted Disease Prevention, and Stress Management. Prior to becoming a professor, Dr. Blonna worked for 15 years in public health in the areas of STD Control, Reproductive Health & Family Planning, and HIV/AIDS Control. He has lectured extensively around the country, presenting a variety of papers on these and related subjects. On a personal note, Dr. Blonna has been married to his wife Heidi for 26 years and has two sons, William and Michael.

Credits:
Interior Design: Joanne R. Saliger
Cover Design: Bob Schram, Bookends
Typography: Ash Street Typecrafters, Inc.
WebLinks Logo: Laura Patchkofsky

For Morton Publishing Company:

Douglas N. Morton, President and Publisher
Mimi Egan, Publisher, Series Publishing
Maureen Owen, Senior Editor, Series Publishing

ReadingsPLUS with WebLinks: Issues in Human Sexuality, 98/99
Copyright © 1998, Morton Publishing Company
925 W. Kenyon Avenue, Unit 12
Englewood, Colorado 80110
800/348-3777

ISBN: 0-89582-388-8

5   4   3   2   1

WebAdvisory Board

Members of the WebAdvisory Board provide feedback on readings and World Wide Web sites, and generally advise the editor and the publishing staff. WebAdvisory Board Members are drawn from colleges and universities throughout the United States and Canada. They are academics with a variety of specialties and teaching experiences.

Because Morton Publishing Company also values the perspective students bring to course materials, student advisors are instrumental in shaping *ReadingsPLUS with WebLinks*.

Janell Campbell
California State University - Chico

Deb Goodman
University of Oklahoma

Carolyn O'Drobinak
Austin Peay State University

Kyran Owen-Mankovich
Student Advisor
University of Colorado

Jerry Strouse
Central Michigan University

Preface

Why another book about human sexuality? When I was asked to edit this edition of *ReadingsPLUS with WebLinks*, I had to ask myself that same question. Do we, students and professors, really need another book about human sexuality? After much serious contemplation, my answer is a resounding "Yes!"

Obviously, our culture is fascinated by the subject. People talk about sex and sexuality all the time. It is a favorite subject of the media. In fact, some conservatives criticize our society for being overly concerned with sexual matters. They argue that sex dominates advertising and the media and that the government has gone too far in protecting the free expression of sexuality and sexual themes. On the other hand, some liberals argue that our society is sexually restrictive and even downright puritanical. They cite the lack of uniform standards for sex education in the schools and the discrimination faced by gays and lesbians as examples to support their claim. Still others argue that our society is filled with mixed messages about sex: sex is used to market and sell almost everything, so sex it seems is everywhere, yet many schools are not allowed to teach about the fundamentals of sex, and most Americans lack basic knowledge about human sexuality and reproduction.

The truth is that as a society we embrace all three of these positions. We are liberal about some sexual issues, conservative on others, and downright confused about the rest. All of this leads us right back to the question, "Why another book about sexuality?" We need another book about human sexuality to help make sense of the continual onslaught of sexual information—to build a solid knowledge base and to learn how to think critically about issues in human sexuality.

While many people think human sexuality refers just to sexual behavior (what people do, how often they do it, etc.), sexuality is much more complex than that. It involves our genetic inheritance, our anatomy and physiology, and the reality of being sexual creatures in a biological sense. It also includes our thoughts and feelings about our bodies and what it means to be men and women. It involves our ethics, values, and the cultural traditions we've assimilated through our families, ethnic groups, and religious affiliations. Our sexuality extends beyond the self to encompass our friendships, intimate relationships, and sexual relationships. Lastly, our sexuality doesn't exist in a vacuum. It is influenced by and influences our environment. Our neighborhoods, communities, campuses, states, and countries help shape who we are and our options as sexual beings.

ReadingsPLUS with WebLinks: Issues in Human Sexuality is an attempt to capture the essence of what it means to be sexual in our society right now and to impart up-to-date information on research and topics in human sexuality. It does this by offering you a selection of very current readings, some very serious, some not-so-serious, some scholarly and full of research details, others controversial, which add up to a complete and current examination of the key aspects of human sexuality. These readings were chosen for their quality, divergent points of view, and the timeliness of their themes. Also, *ReadingsPLUS with WebLinks: Issues in Human Sexuality* connects you to the World Wide Web (see Part 7: Working With the World Wide Web), which can provide updated information on all aspect of this ever changing subject.

The organization of the parts of the book follows that of the majority of the textbooks currently available. This makes its easy to assign the readings in a systematic way that makes sense to the students. For a complete discussion of all the features of *ReadingsPLUS with WebLinks*, please read "A Note from the Publisher."

I hope you enjoy the readings and are challenged by their ideas.

—Richard Blonna

A Note from the Publisher

Welcome to *ReadingsPLUS!*

Alert and adventurous readers are important to us in keeping this volume up-to-date and accurate. So if you would like to recommend a timely reading on an important topic in human sexuality, or if you happen upon a great World Wide Web site with compelling resources, or even if you discover an error (it happens), we'd appreciate hearing from you. Our phone number is 1-800-348-3777. Or just drop us a line at:

Morton Publishing Company
925 W. Kenyon Avenue, Unit 12
Englewood, Colorado 80110

Fax: 303-762-9923

E-mail: morton@morton-pub.com

Web address: http://www.morton-pub.com

What You Will Find in This Book

This book contains **34 current and controversial readings** on topics in human sexuality. The readings are drawn from a mix of professional journals and popular, high-quality magazines and newsletters. The readings that are controversial carry the label *A Reading for Critical Thinking*. In addition, you will find:

Reading Review Form

(See Appendix A at the back of the book.) The Reading Review Form is designed to assist you as you reflect on the readings that have been assigned and to enhance your critical thinking skills. Use it for extra credit for assigned readings, for writing class papers or exercises, or to generate classroom discussion. You are encouraged to tear out the Reading Review Form and make photocopies of it and use it for each reading in whatever way works best for you.

"Health Information On-Line"

This introductory reading at the front of the book will provide you with a general overview of the World Wide Web (what it is and how to use the Web as a resource). This reading also contains excellent suggestions for how to evaluate online sources of information on any topic.

WebLinks: A Directory of Annotated World Wide Web Sites

At the back of the book in **Part 7: Working with the World Wide Web**, you will find Web sites that contain information and resources relevant to the issues discussed in the readings. The Web addresses have been fully verified, and all the sites are briefly described. The Web sites are organized alphabetically by site name, and each site has been numbered for easy reference and referral. **The Quick Reference Guide to Topics/Readings/World Wide Web Sites** (which is described in detail below) will let you quickly match a reading with the Web sites that are relevant to it. However, please note that the Guide, while extensive, is not exhaustive in linking readings with Web sites, and you may want to explore sites on your own and make your own connections between readings and Web sites. The brief description of each Web site can also assist you in deciding which sites to consult.

Web Site Evaluation Form

In Part 7 at the back of the book you will find a Web Site Evaluation Form, which you can use in any of a number of ways: to evaluate Web sites that are assigned for extra credit, as a tool to assist you if you are preparing a research assignment, or simply for your own reference. Even if your instructor does not require you to use the Web Site Evaluation Form, we encourage you to photocopy it and use it to direct your work on the Web.

Web Journal

(See Part 7 at the back of the book.) Use these pages to make note of sites you have visited. You could record your reactions to a site, or briefly note what information you found there. Is the site worth a repeat visit in your opinion? Could you use it for personal reference? Could you use it for a research assignment? Who runs the site? Where is it located? You may want to develop the habit of evaluating both the content at a site and how well the site operates. Ask yourself, is the site easy to navigate? Are the graphics odd or are they appropriate? Are there any special features that you particularly like? How does the information at a site compare with what you have learned in a reading? If you write up your visit to a site, you will have a record of where you have been on the Web. Use these pages as you would any journal or lab manual. It is a place for you to make personal observations about your Web experiences, and to raise issues you would like to discuss in class about a site. (Should you run out of Web Journal pages, you may photocopy the Web Journal for your own personal use.)

Quick Reference Guide to Topics/Readings/World Wide Web Sites

The Quick Reference Guide correlates topics on human sexuality with the readings and World Wide Web sites found in the book. It can be used for easy reference to locate readings and Web sites. In addition, the Quick Reference Guide makes it possible to integrate readings and Web sites with any course syllabus or textbook. The Guide can also be used to make class assignments. Although it is not comprehensive in its scope (i.e., there may be topics addressed in the readings and Web sites that are not listed in the Quick Reference Guide), it can still serve as a convenient starting point.

Other Features

Updates to WebLinks (http://www.morton-pub.com/updates/updates.stml)

Using the Web as an academic resource is not without its frustrations and limitations! You type the complete address for a site into the Location bar and, to your dismay, you don't get the results you are

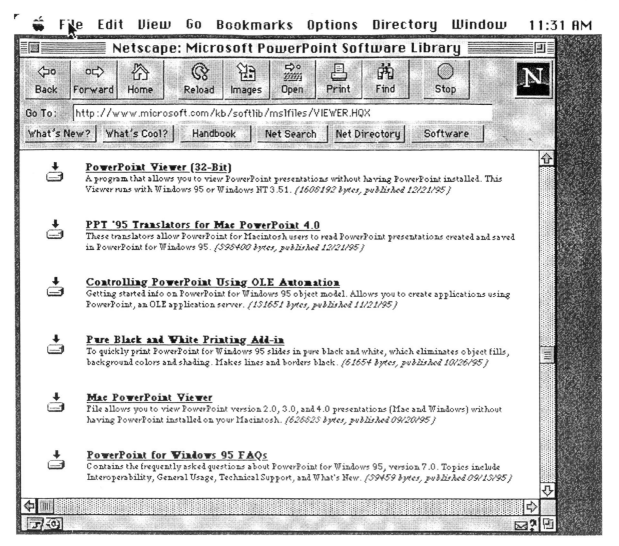

expecting. The site doesn't load, or it no longer exists, or the site has moved to a new location but no forwarding address or link has been provided. It is like going to the library to check out a book that is supposed to be on reserve for your course only to discover that it is not there. At our Morton Publishing Company Web site, we are developing a section dedicated to keeping you updated about the Web addresses listed in our books that we discover are no longer operational for one reason or another. Although we carefully verify all Web addresses just prior to a book's publication, and although the publishing staff and academic editor select reputable, stable sites that will in all likelihood exist for some time, Web addresses can change or go out of service. It's the nature of the technology. Should you be unable to access a site and think that the problem is not with the server, time of day, how you entered the address, etc., go to the **Updates to WebLinks** section of the Morton Web site (http://www.morton-pub.com/updates/updates. stml), scroll down to the title of the book you are using, and click on the *Update!* icon to see if we have recommended a replacement site or a new address.

You will also find that *ReadingsPLUS with WebLinks* is fully indexed.

Suggestions for Accessing a Web Site

WebLinks: A Directory of Annotated World Wide Web Sites contains sites that relate to the topics covered in the readings. You will see that each Web site has been assigned a descriptive heading and a number. For each site, the exact address, or Universal Resource Locator (URL), is provided. Here is an example of a site's descriptive heading with its assigned number: *The Safer Sex Page, No. 110.* Its address or URL is http://www.safersex.org/. To access a Web site, you will need to be at a computer that is hooked to the Internet and has a graphical browser—that is the software that allows you to access the World Wide Web. (Two popular browsers are Netscape and Mosaic.) Once you have opened Netscape or Mosaic, delete the address that appears in the Location bar. Then, *carefully* type the address or URL of the Web site into the Location bar (or Go To bar) on the screen and press the Enter key.

The screen may look something like the one page vi after you have typed in the address.

There are many ways to visit cyberspace, and the WebLinks Directory is designed to be a guide to academically appropriate Web sites on issues related to human sexuality. Use it for research for class assignments, or to follow your own interests.

A Word About Critical Thinking

ReadingsPLUS with WebLinks: Issues in Human Sexuality introduces you to a wide variety of current and controversial readings, and there are over 100 World Wide Web sites for you to consult as well. All the readings have been selected with care to provide you with a wide range of perspectives on important topics in human sexuality. The readings that are labeled "A Reading for Critical Thinking," however, are ones that are especially designed to encourage your critical thinking skills. To arrive at a thorough understanding of a topic, you will need to think critically about what you are reading (both in print and on screen). Critical thinking skills are increasingly important, particularly as the amount of information available to the average person keeps expanding. To be a critical thinker, you will need to learn how to ask questions, and to consider not only what is said (or written) but what is not said (or implied). You may want to consider taking a course in critical thinking. And we recommend the following print and online resources:

In Print

M. Neil Browne and Stuart M. Keeley, *Asking the Right Questions: A Guide to Critical Thinking,* 2nd ed. (Prentice-Hall, 1986).

Vicent Ryan Ruggiero, *Becoming a Critical Thinker,* 2nd ed. (Houghton Mifflin, 1996).

Glen Thomas and Gaye Smooth, "Critical Thinking: A Vital Work Skill," *Trust for Educational Leadership* (February/March 1994), pp. 34–38.

Online

Effective Learning: Study Skills/Critical Thinking

http://www.cdtl.nus.sg/UFM/Effect/Es4_3_7.html

The National University of Singapore has a portion of its Web site devoted to student study skills, including critical thinking skills. This address will take you to several lively pages that define critical thinking, explain the characteristics of a critical thinker, and review fallacies to avoid. Although there are no links, the straightforward, practical text is well-designed and the guidelines are useful. (You might also want to check out the entire orientation section, which offers advice on how to make a smooth transition to higher education and on how to develop communication skills and time management skills, among other suggestions.)

The Critical Thinking Community

http://www.sonoma.edu/CThink/

This site is maintained by Sonoma State University's Center for Critical Thinking. Site provides educators, students, and the public with a wealth of information about the theory and practice of critical thinking, concepts and definitions, techniques for learning and teaching, and classroom exercises that implement the principles. Other features include weekly updates, an Educator's Resource Guide for integrating critical thinking into the curriculum, a collection of critical thinking articles, and a list of conferences. Links to online discussion groups. The site is directed by Richard Paul, Ph.D., and comments are invited through E-mail addresses provided. Also offers links to a sampling of critical thinking offices nationwide.

Mission: Critical

http://www.sjsu.edu:80/depts/itl/

This site is produced by the Institute for Teaching and Learning at San Jose State University. Its goal is to create a "virtual lab" capable of familiarizing users with the basic concepts of critical thinking in a self-paced, interactive environment. Comments and reactions are encouraged, and an E-mail address is provided. Site includes links to each step in the process plus exercises for the student to do. A good online way to become a critical thinker.

Your Thoughts Are Important to Us

Our mission in developing *ReadingsPLUS with Web-Links* is simple: to make the resources of the popular press and the World Wide Web accessible and usable within a course specific context. By carefully selecting current, academically appropriate readings from high-quality popular press sources, and by filtering and organizing World Wide Web sites, we can help you keep up-to-date and current, and we can assist you in incorporating new technology into your courses. We sincerely welcome your feedback, and please contact us with your suggestions and recommendations.

Contents

Marilynn Larkin, *FDA Consumer* (June 1996), pp. 21–25.

PART 1 *Biological and Research Perspectives on Human Sexuality, 1*

PART 2 *Gender and Sex Roles, 16*

Please note: Indicates a reading on a controversial topic, to encourage critical thinking.

PART 7   *Working With the World Wide Web, 174*

Quick Reference Guide to Topics / Readings / WWW Sites

For a complete description of the Web sites that appear in this Guide, please consult *WebLinks: A Directory of Annotated Web Sites,* which is located at the back of the book in **Part 7: Working With the World Wide Web.** There you will find in detail all the Web sites referred to in the Quick Reference Guide, and more.

Topic Area	Treated in: Reading	Treated in: Web Site
Abortion	20. Birth Control Failure	Alan Guttmacher, No. 2 National Abortion Rights League, No. 71 National Right to Life, No. 77 National Women's Health, No. 79 Planned Parenthood, No. 88
Attraction/Love	14. "Love" and the Mental Health Professions	American Psychological Assoc., No. 5 Female Sexual Disorder Screening, No. 41 National Institute on Mental Health, No. 75 The New Male Sexuality, No. 81
	16. Joy . . . What Is Most Human	Association for Couples, No. 10
Biological Differences	1. Puberty May Start at 6	The Kinsey Institute for Research, No. 55 SIECUS, No. 102
	2. Male Hormone Molds Women, Too	American Psychological Assoc., No. 5 SIECUS, No. 102 Women's Health Resources, No. 113
	6. Man's World, Woman's World?	Feminism and Women's Resources, No. 42 Men's Issues, No. 68 The New Male Sexuality, No. 81
Birth Control/ Contraception	18. Still Waiting for the Contraceptive Revolution	Ann Rose's Birth Control Links, No. 7 Assoc. of Voluntary & Safe Contraception, No. 11 Birth Control Pills, No. 13 Birth Control Trust, No. 14 Contraceptive Contemplation, No. 28 Planned Parenthood, No. 88
	19. On the Needless Hounding of a Safe Contraceptive	American Civil Liberties Union, No. 3 SIECUS, No. 102 Thrive @ Sex, No. 108
	20. Birth Control Failure	DepoProvera, No. 31 Natural Family Planning, No. 80 A Primer on Natural Family Planning, No. 89
	21. How Reliable Are Condoms?	Condommania, No. 26 Condoms, No. 27 Sex Directory, No. 97 Trojan, No. 109
Communication Skills/Sexual Communication	13. Back Off!	Dr. Feelgood, No. 35 Dr. Ruth's Homepage, No. 93 The Student Counseling Virtual Pamphlet Collection, No. 104 Suggestions for Improving Communication Skills in Relationships, No. 105

Topic Area	Treated in: Reading	Treated in: Web Site
	17. Silent Sperm	Male Infertility, No. 57 Male Sexual Disorder Screening, No. 58 Medic's Impotence Information Center, No. 61 Men's Health, No. 65
	24. Truth or Consequences	Man's Guide to Sexuality, No. 59 Men's Health Issues, No. 66 The New Male Sexuality, No. 81
Obscenity/ Pornography	29. The End of Obscenity	ACLU, No. 3 The Cyberporn Debate, No. 29 People for the American Way, No. 86 Sex, Censorship and the Internet, No. 96
Prostitution	30. Prostitution and the Case for Decriminalization	National Task Force on Prostitution, No. 78 Prostitution Issues, No. 90
Relationships	11. A Peace Plan for the Gender Wars	Assoc. for Couples, No. 10 Divorce Source, No. 33 Man's Guide to Sexuality, No 59 Marriage Encounter, No. 60 WWWomen, No. 114
	14. "Love" and the Mental Health Professions	American Psychological Assoc., No. 5 Female Sexual Disorder Screening, No. 41 National Institute on Mental Health, No. 75 The New Male Sexuality, No. 81
	15. Celibate Passion	Lifelines @ Work, No. 56 Thrive@Sex, No. 108
	16. Joy . . . What Is Most Human . . . Is Our Capacity for Intimacy	Dr. Feelgood, No. 35 Dr. Ruth's Homepage, No. 93
Research in Human Sexuality	5. Review: . . . Sexual Practices in the U.S.	The Kinsey Institute for Research in Sex, Gender and Reproduction, No. 55 Survey: Informed Concent, No. 106
Safer Sex	21. How Reliable Are Condoms?	Condommania, No. 26 Condoms, No. 27 Sex Directory, No. 97 Trojan, No. 109
	22. Bringing the Fundamentals of Gender Studies into Safer Sex Education	CDC Division of STD Prevention, No. 18 Does Sex Education Work?, No. 34 The Safer Sex Page, No. 94
	27. The Safest Sex	Coalition for Positive Sexuality, No. 24 Dr. Feelgood, No. 35
Sexual Coersion	33. Why Is Date Rape So Hard to Prove?	Men Against Domestic Violence, No. 62 M.A.L.E., No. 63 Northern Centre Against Sexual Assault, No. 84 Rape, Abuse, and Incest, No. 92 Sexual Assault Information, No. 98
Sexual Harassment	28. Is This Sexual Harassment?	ACLU, No. 3 Equal Employment Opportunity Commission, No. 38 Minnesota Center Against Violence and Abuse: Rape, Sexual Assault & Harassment, No. 70 Student Counseling Virtual Pamphlet Collection, No. 104 WWWomen, No. 114

Topic Area	Treated in: Reading	Treated in: Web Site
Sexuality and Advertising	8. Toy Story	Feminist Internet Gateway, No. 44 Voice of the Shuttle: Gender Studies Page, No. 111
	10. Advertising, Sexuality, and Sexism	Feminism and Women's Resources, No. 42 Feminist Internet Gateway, No. 44 National Organization for Women, No. 76
	32. Sexuality and Television Advertising	Feminist Internet Gateway, No. 44 Selected Women and Gender Resources on the World Wide Web, No. 95
Sexually Transmitted Diseases	22. Bringing the Fundamentals of Gender Studies into Safer-Sex Education	Alan Guttmacher Institute, No. 2 American Social Health Assoc., No. 6 Assertive Communication, No. 9 CDC Division of STD Prevention, No. 18
	25. Confronting a Hidden Epidemic	American Journal of Public Health, No. 4 Johns Hopkins Univ. STD Research Group, No. 54 The Safer Sex Page, No. 94 STD Homepage, No. 103 Trojan: HIV/AIDS/STDs, No. 109
	26. STDs in Women	Forum on Women's Health, No. 45 HealthGate, No. 52 Women's Health Resources On-line, No. 113
Women's Sexual Health	2. Male Hormone Molds Women, Too, in Mind and Body	HealthGate, No. 52
	26. STDs in Women	Feminist.com, No. 43 Forum on Women's Health, No. 45 PAP Test, No. 85 Women's Health Resources, No. 113
	31. Female Circumcision Comes to America	Circumcision Issues, No. 23 The Female Genital Multilation Research Homepage, No. 40

Health Information
On-Line

By Marilynn Larkin

Consumers are using the Internet to get information about health. How reliable is this information? That's not an easy question to answer.

It's no secret that the Internet — especially its graphics portion, the World Wide Web — is enjoying unprecedented popularity in business and professional communities, and in homes across America. A recent survey by the Times Mirror Center for the People & the Press revealed that the number of Americans subscribing to on-line services jumped from 5 million at the end of 1994 to nearly 12 million in mid-1995, while an additional 2 million people have direct connections to the Internet.

Among people with home offices, approximately one-third have access to the Internet, and, of these, about 10 percent have a home page on the Web, according to a survey conducted by the Gallup Organization and reported in the Dec. 19, 1995, issue of *PC Magazine*.

Another survey, by CDB Research & Consulting, indicates that consumers are showing a growing interest in obtaining information about health and beauty aids on-line as a means of supplementing traditional medical counsel. The company speculates that the discretion and convenience of the on-line environment may hold special appeal to people with disabilities and chronic illnesses.

However, easy access to virtually limitless health and medical information has pitfalls, experts caution. "My advice to consumers about information on the Internet is the same as it is for other media: You can't believe everything you see, whether it's in a newspaper, on TV, or on a computer screen," says Bill Rados, director of FDA's Communications Staff. Since anyone — reputable scientist or quack — who has a computer, a modem (the device that permits a computer to dial and connect to the Internet or an on-line service), and the necessary software can publish a Web page, post information to a newsgroup, or proffer advice in an on-line chat room, "you must protect yourself by carefully checking out the source of any information you obtain."

> *The FDA home page provides an excellent jumping off point for those who want to learn more about the agency and the drugs, food supplements, and medical devices it regulates.*

WORLD WIDE WEB

By far, the most consumer-friendly part of the Internet is the World Wide Web. It is also the newest part of the Internet, having become accessible only in the past couple of years, with the wider availability of browsers such as Mosaic and Netscape Navigator. While the rest of the Internet displays text only, the Web, as it has come to be called, has the ability to display colorful graphics and multimedia (sounds, video, virtual reality) to complement text-based information. For example, sites that offer medical information on neurological diseases, such as stroke, may also contain images of the brain showing which areas are affected by disease or may have downloadable (files that can be copied from one computer to another) "movies" of actual magnetic resonance imaging (MRI) exams pinpointing blockages in blood vessels.

From *FDA Consumer* (June 1996), pp. 21–25.

Many legitimate providers of reliable health and medical information, including FDA and other government agencies, are taking advantage of the Web's popularity by offering brochures and in-depth information on specific topics at their Web sites. Material may be geared to consumers as well as industry and medical professionals (see "Sources of Internet Health Information").

But con artists have also infiltrated the Web. "A physician was browsing the Web when he came across a site that contained a fraudulent drug offering. He called us to report it," says Roma Jeanne Egli, a compliance officer in FDA's division of drug marketing. "The person who maintains the site claimed he had a cure for a very serious disease, and advised those with the disease to stop taking their prescription medication. Instead, they were told to buy the product he was selling, at a cost of several hundred dollars."

More details can't be released because FDA has a case pending against the Web site owner who, according to Egli, has a history of marketing bogus cures. She advises consumers to be skeptical when someone advocates a purported "cure" to be purchased and taken in lieu of prescribed medicine.

If you come across a suspected fraudulent offering on the Internet, alert FDA by E-mail: *otcfraud@cder.fda.gov.*

If con artists and scientists have equal publishing rights on the Internet, what's to keep a health-conscious consumer from getting sidetracked by an official looking page offering unsound advice?

"This is a real concern," says Valencia Camp, of FDA's Office of Information Resources Management. "Although the Internet can be a reliable source of information, it is important to be aware that what is found there is only as good as the quality and integrity of the original information. What you find cannot be taken as gospel. It should be checked out and supported by other sources." (See "Is This Site Reliable?")

FDA ON-LINE

The FDA home page provides an excellent jumping off point for those who want to learn more about the agency and the drugs, food supplements, and medical devices it regulates. "Twenty-five cents of every dollar spent by consumers goes for something that FDA regulates," Rados notes. These products "could be used more safely and more effectively if people know more about them." Because it is expensive to print and mail materials, FDA offers many of its publications on the Internet.

FDA material can be downloaded to a home or office computer and then printed out. Those who don't have a personal computer can try accessing the Internet from their local library or from a community organization. If you have a computer but do not have Internet access, you can receive text from FDA's site (no graphics) by dialing by modem the agency's bulletin board service (BBS): (1-800) 222-0185; type "bbs" and select the information you want from the menu.

If you come across a suspected fraudulent health or medical offering on the Internet, alert FDA by E-mail: otcfraud@cder.fda.gov

---

"Our goal is to have virtually all consumer education material available on the Internet," says Rados. "Every new piece we publish is immediately placed on our Web site. We now have more than a hundred different publications to choose from." FDA also has a "comments" button on many of its Web pages so that visitors can offer suggestions and feedback. However, questions about specific drugs, devices, or food supplements should be addressed to the agency in writing at FDA (HFE-88), Rockville, MD 20857, or by calling your local public affairs specialist listed under "FDA" in your local phonebook, Rados adds. Before beginning any particular therapy, however, consult with your doctor or pharmacist.

In addition to providing consumer education materials, the FDA site also offers technical information to help industry professionals file regulatory materials.

EXCHANGING INFORMATION

In Internet "newsgroups," such as Usenet groups, people post questions and read messages much as they would on regular bulletin boards. Through "mailing lists," messages are exchanged by E-mail, and all messages are sent to all group subscribers. In "chat" areas on some services and on the Internet's IRC (Internet Relay Chat) users can communicate with each other live.

Assessing the value and validity of health and medical information in news and chat groups demands at least the same — and maybe more — discrimination as for Web sites, because the information is more ephemeral and you often can't identify the source. Although these groups can provide reliable information about specific diseases and disorders, they can also perpetuate misinformation.

"Around Christmas time last year, I saw a whole bunch of messages implying that mistletoe has anti-cancer properties," recalls Serena Stockwell, editor of the medical trade publication *Oncology Times* and longtime user of various cancer-related forums and resources on one of the commercial on-line services. "I wondered where this was coming from, since it seemed a little odd."

Stockwell did some digging and discovered that in an announcement of a new drug to treat lung cancer, "one of the researchers had a slip of the tongue and said the drug was derived from mistletoe instead of periwinkle. As a result, the word soon spread to the newsgroups, where people inadvertently perpetuated the mistake."

In another instance, Stockwell saw that the herbal tea Essiac was being touted in a newsgroup as a cancer remedy. "Doctors were being questioned about it, so I assigned a reporter to cover the story," she says.

As it turned out, there is no evidence to support this claim.

As with all health and medical information in cyberspace, advice in newsgroups "should not be taken by itself," Stockwell says. "As a writer and editor, I find newsgroups useful for keeping in touch with topics of conversation among patients, doctors and researchers. But to determine whether the information is trustworthy, I'd want to document it in the usual ways."

Other information services are commercial on-line services, fee-charging companies that provide vast amounts of proprietary information. They often include health and medical databases, electronic versions of popular newspapers and magazines, and

Is This Site Reliable?

FDA staff and others familiar with Internet medical offerings suggest asking the following questions to help determine the reliability of a Web site:

- Who maintains the site? Government or university-run sites are among the best sources for scientifically sound health and medical information. Private practitioners or lay organizations may have marketing, social or political agendas that can influence the type of material they offer on-site and which sites they link to.

- Is there an editorial board or another listing of the names and credentials of those responsible for preparing and reviewing the site's contents? Can these people be contacted by phone or through E-mail if visitors to the site have questions or want additional information?

- Does the site link to other sources of medical information? No reputable organization will position itself as the sole source of information on a particular health topic.

  On the other hand, links alone are not a guarantee of reliability, notes Lorrie Harrison of FDA's Center for Biologics Evaluation and Research. Since anyone with a Web page can create links to any other site on the Internet—and the owner of the site that is "linked to" has no say over who links to it—then a person offering suspect medical advice could conceivably try to make his or her advice appear legitimate by, say, creating a link to FDA's Web site. What's more, health information produced by FDA or other government agencies is not copyrighted; therefore, someone can quote FDA information at a site and be perfectly within his or her rights. By citing a source such as FDA, experienced marketers using careful wording can make it appear as though FDA endorses their products, Harrison explains.

- When was the site last updated? Generally, the more current the site, the more likely it is to provide timely material. Ideally, health and medical sites should be updated weekly or monthly.

- Are informative graphics and multimedia files such as video or audio clips available? Such features can assist in clarifying medical conditions and procedures. For example, the University of Pennsylvania's cancer information site, called OncoLink, contains graphics of what a woman can expect during a pelvic exam.

  Bear in mind, however, that multimedia should be used to help explain medical information, not substitute for it. Some sites provide dazzling "bells and whistles" but little scientifically sound information.

- Does the site charge an access fee? Many reputable sites with health and medical information, including FDA and other government sites, offer access and materials for free. If a site does charge a fee, be sure that it offers value for the money. Use a searcher (see "Sources of Internet Health Information") to see whether you can get the same information without paying additional fees.

  If you find something of interest at a site—say, a new drug touted to relieve disease symptoms with fewer side effects—write down the name and address of the site, print out the information, and bring it to your doctor, advises Valencia Camp of FDA's Office of Information Resources Management. Your doctor can help determine whether the information is supported by legitimate research sources, such as journal articles or proceedings from a scientific meeting.

  In addition, your doctor can determine if the drug is appropriate for your situation. Even if the information comes from a source that is reputed to be reliable, you should check with your doctor to make sure that it is wise for you to begin a certain treatment. Specific situations (such as taking other drugs) may make the therapy an inadvisable choice. Your doctor can decide whether the drug is suitable for you and may be able to offer more appropriate alternatives.

— M. L.

Sources of Internet Health Information

There are literally thousands of health-related Internet resources maintained by government agencies, universities, and non-profit and commercial organizations. Following are the addresses of Usenet groups (newsgroups), mailing lists, and reputable sites that link to other sites with medical information. This list is by no means complete; it is offered as a jumping-off point.

Usenet Groups

(Access is through the Internet provider)

bionet. immunology
(immunology research and practice)

bionet.aging
(issues related to aging theory and research)

misc.health.diabetes
(discussion of diabetes management in daily life)

sci.med diseases.cancer
(cancer treatment and research)

sci.med. vision
(treatments for vision problems)

Mailing Lists

(to subscribe, send an E-mail message to the address given; in the message area type "subscribe," followed by the name of the list and then your name)

Alzheimer's Disease
List name: ALZHEIMER
Subscribe:
listserv@wubois.wustl.edu

Breast Cancer
List name: BREAST-CANCER
Subscribe:
listserv@MORGAN.UCS.MUN.CA

Stroke
List name: STROKE-L
Subscribe:
listserv@UKCC.UKY.EDU

Geriatrics
List name: GERINET
Subscribe:
listserv@UBVM.CC.BUFFALO.EDU
(Source: *A Guide To Healthcare and Medical Resources on the Internet* by Michael S. Brown)

World Wide Web Sites

American Cancer Society:
http://charlotte.npixi.net/acs/.facts.html

American Heart Association:
http://www.amhrt.org/ahawho.htm

American Medical Association:
http://www.ama-assn.org/

Centers for Disease Control and Prevention: *http://www.cdc.gov/*

Department of Health and Human Services: *http://www.os.dhhs.gov/*

Food and Drug Administration: *http://www./fda.gov/*

National Cancer Institute: *http://www.nci.nih.gov/*

National Institutes of Health: *http://www.nih.gov/*

National Institute for Allergies and Infectious Diseases: *http://www.niaid.nih.gov/*

National Library of Medicine: *http://www.nlm.nih.gov/*

Oncology Data Base/University of Pennsylvania (ONCOLINK): *http://cancer.med.upenn.edu/ about_oncolink.html*

SEARCH PROGRAMS

Because the Internet contains no central indexing system, getting the information you want quickly can be a major challenge. That's where search engines come in. These powerful tools can help narrow the field if you have a specific topic to pursue, or the name of a specific organization but no address for its site. Input a few words that describe what you're looking for, and the searcher returns a list of sites related to your query.

Be aware, however, that although a searcher can point the way, it does not evaluate the information it points to. For example, a search on the words "breast cancer" is just as likely to point to a page advertising a reconstructive surgeon or a health food store's article on the purported benefits of phytochemicals as it is to the National Cancer Institute. The reason? Scott Stephenson, production engineer and spokesman for Webcrawler, one of the popular searchers, explains. "Webcrawler scans documents and counts the number of times a particular word or expression searched for appears on a Web page. That alone determines whether the page is listed in our results and where it appears on the list." This means that by mentioning, say, breast cancer many times in the Web page copy, a savvy marketer of bogus medicinals could draw a lot of people to his or her site. It is up to the visitor to evaluate the information the site contains. Here are a few of the many search engines:

Alta Vista:
http://www.altavista.digital.com/

Excite: *http://www.excite.com/*

Lycos: *http://www.lycos.com/*

Webcrawler:
http://www.webcrawler.com/

Yahoo:
http://www.yahoo.com/Health/ Medicine/

— M. L.

their own chats and newsgroups, as well as Internet access.

The fact that information may be screened by a commercial service does not necessarily make it more reliable than other sources. And most services do not verify what is posted in their newsgroups, nor control what is "said" in chat rooms. Health and medical material obtained through services also should be corroborated by your physician or other medical sources.

REGULATORY CONCERNS

The fact that it is easy to publish health and medical information and reach vast audiences without having the information verified by other sources presents potential issues for FDA and other government agencies, according to Melissa Moncavage, a public health advisor in FDA's division of drug marketing, advertising, and communications. FDA has created a working group from each of its divisions to address the issues that fall within the agency's purview.

"We are working together to determine the scope and type of product information that is going directly to consumers. Product information on the Internet is unlike traditional forms of advertising and labeling. Current regulations on prescription drug advertising differ between print and broadcast media. The Internet presents additional challenges," Moncavage says.

While regulatory agencies try to devise ways of ensuring that accurate and well-balanced health and medical information is presented on the Internet, consumers "will have to use a lot more discretion in evaluating what they see," Moncavage says. "A Web page can be changed very quickly. It is easy to put up, and easy to take down. There is no guarantee that what you see one day will be there the next." So on the Internet, as elsewhere, "caveat emptor" — let the buyer beware — are watchwords for the foreseeable future.

Marilynn Larkin is a medical writer whose Web site links to the Web sources of health information listed in this article: http://members.gnn.com/mlco

PART I

Biological and Research Perspectives on Human Sexuality

We seem to have come full circle recently concerning our views about the influences of biology on sexuality. Before the 1960s, researchers generally assumed that male and female sexuality was fundamentally different because of the genetic, hormonal, anatomical, and physiological differences between men and women. Male and female sexuality was believed to be driven primarily by biological differences, and men were viewed as aggressors and women as nurturers.

The sexual revolution of the 1960s and the impact of the women's movement of the 1970s contributed to a revision of this sexual determinism by asserting that men and women were fundamentally equal. This new viewpoint concerning male and female sexuality emphasized the importance of psychosocial conditioning and cultural opportunity as the key determinants of male and female sexuality.

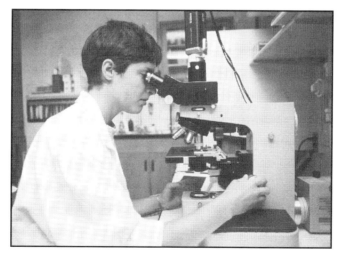

The 1990s ushered in a new climate of curiosity and acceptance concerning male and female sexual differences. This has reopened the dialog concerning the importance of biological influences on our sexuality and has sparked the reemergence of research into the biological basis of sexuality. Recent studies have uncovered some interesting findings regarding the effects of genetics, brain structure, and hormones on male and female sexuality.

The readings in Part 1 examine new evidence concerning the effects of genetics, brain differentiation, and sex hormones on our sexual orientation, behavior, and gender identity. The readings also reveal much about how research into human sexuality is conducted.

A Reading for Critical Thinking

Puberty May Start at 6 As Hormones Surge

By Hara Estroff Marano

Puberty, usually considered to be the bane and also the thrill of early adolescence, may actually be almost over just when most accounts of human development have it beginning.

In fact, two University of Chicago researchers, Dr. Martha K. McClintock, a biopsychologist, and Dr. Gilbert Herdt, an anthropologist, say that puberty may actually begin around the age of 6. And the hormones that kick off puberty this early come not from the ovaries and testes roaring to a start but from the much more mundane adrenal glands, which huddle around the kidneys and are perhaps better known for turning out stress hormones. Still, the adrenal sex steroids do what sex hormones typically do, influence behavior as well as the body.

In a recent issue of the journal Current Directions in Psychological Science, the two researchers marshaled evidence that this early hormonal activity is responsible for the behavioral hallmark of puberty, sexual attraction. Using data from three separate studies, they said that sexual attraction first manifested itself in the fourth grade, from the ages of 9 to 10. The report, published in the December issue of the journal, reached subscribers only in April because of a delay in publication.

The evidence also indicates that attraction is far different from action. In fact, there are several steps: attraction, actual desire and finally a readiness to act on the desire.

"That's the crucial point," Dr. McClintock said. "Sexuality is a process of development" that begins in middle childhood, she said, not "a precipitous psychological event" that emerges at a single moment in time.

"Our culture regards middle childhood as a time of hormonal quiescence," said Dr. McClintock, who is also a MacArthur Foundation Fellow. "Freud called it 'latency.' But actually a great deal of activity is going on."

The hormone charged with stirring things up so early is dihydroepiandrosterone (DHEA), a weak adrenal androgen that appears to reach a critical level at the age of 10. Synthetic DHEA is marketed in health-food stores as a miracle anti-aging substance, but no such functions have ever been medically documented. Scientists do know that in both boys and girls, levels of this hormone are substantial at birth, decline sharply, then begin a slow but steady ascent at the age of 6, reaching adult levels around 18, before beginning a long, slow descent. The turning on of adrenal androgen activity at 6 is called adrenarche.

One bodily effect of adrenal androgens is the instigation of changes in complexion. Around the age of 6, oil-producing sebaceous glands begin to develop in children's skin. DHEA also appears to be responsible for a growth spurt that occurs around 6.

And while DHEA is an androgen, Dr. McClintock took pains not to call it a male hormone, pointing out that androgens are an important part of female puberty. "Women's pubic hair comes from androgen," she said. "People don't think of the adrenals as a sex organ, but they certainly are a puberty organ."

What drew the attention of both Dr. McClintock and Dr. Herdt to the hormonal happening of adrenarche were the results of three separate studies of

Puberty may begin at 6, contrary to Freud's view.

people reporting their sexual history. All three are part of the growing literature on development of sexual orientation.

Dr. Herdt, who specializes in the development of sexual identity, was the co-author of one study, which involved the collection of detailed histories of 146 young men and 55 young women who were homosexual. Their histories were examined in the context of

From the *New York Times* (July 1, 1997), pp. C1, C6. Reprinted with permission from the *New York Times*.

the effect of their sexual identity on their families. All were 14 to 20, with a mean age of 18, and all lived in Chicago.

The two other studies, conducted by researchers at the National Cancer Institute, examined genetic influences on homosexuality. Both those studies gathered retrospective data, one from 144 men, and another from 358 women. In both cases the subjects were 18 to 55, mostly in their mid 30's, drawn from all over the United States. Both samples were split equally between homosexuals and a comparison group of heterosexuals of the same age. The study of 144 men was first reported in 1993 in the journal Science, and the study of women was reported in 1995 in Behavior Genetics.

In Dr. Herdt's study, the mean age of first-recalled sexual attraction was 9.6 for men, 10.1 for women. In the cancer institute's studies, the mean age of first sexual attraction was 10 to 10.5.

Dr. Herdt recalled "being struck by the significant number of teens in our study who made remarks about attractions" occurring at 9 or 10. "I thought that was strange, certainly inconsistent with the literature," Dr. Herdt said. "But many of the teens specifically placed their experiences in the fourth grade."

The reports were strikingly at odds with the collective wisdom on sexual development. Furthermore, the researchers said, the strong cultural stigma that homosexuality still carries should have inhibited recognition of same-sex attraction. And, in fact, in the institute's study of 358 women, those who were heterosexual recognized their sexual stirrings, on average, a year and a half sooner (not quite 9½) than the homosexual women did (closer to 11).

Dr. McClintock and Dr. Herdt, in their new paper, proposed the existence of a powerful, hormonally driven developmental sequence of sexuality starting with attraction. The best way to describe attraction, Dr. McClintock, said is this way: "Suddenly you notice. With a capital N. It's like Mel Brooks's Thousand-Year-Old Man. He wakes up and says 'I think there's ladies here.' A boy or a girl suddenly starts noticing people with a vaguely sexual valence, with a little libido, a little juice behind it, whereas before, the figure didn't stand out from the background."

Dr. Herdt's interviews of homosexual teen-agers, conducted with Dr. Andrew Boxer, a psychiatrist at the University of Chicago, also indicated two further stages of psychosexual development. About a year and half after they became aware of attraction to another person, the adolescents recognized a sense of sexual desire for the first time. Desire kicked in at a mean age of 11.2 years for males, 11.9 for females.

An adrenal hormone kicks off physical changes.

"At this stage people aren't just reacting to what they see, which is what attraction is all about," said Dr. McClintock. "They start developing a sense of fantasy and wish."

The first sexual activity came two years later in males (mean age of 13.1) and more than three years later in females (age 15.2). Only then had they reached anatomical maturity, usually considered the landmark event of puberty.

Commenting on the report by her colleagues at the University of Chicago, Dr. Susan Fisher, a clinical professor of psychiatry, emphasized that children were not asexual beings, although the culture regards them as such.

"There is a state of being before there is a condition of doing," she said. "The early Freudians thought there was a period where sexual fantasy was latent. There is no latency. There may not be activity, but everybody, always has something on the brain."

"We can't ignore the possibility that things are going on at age 10 that may be due to subclinical puberty," said Dr. Robert Rosenfield, a professor of pediatrics and medicine and head of pediatric endocrinology at the University of Chicago's Pritzker School of Medicine. "The average girl begins breast development at 10½. There is evidence that at age 9 the pituitary hormones associated with puberty are already being produced. There are secretions from the ovaries."

He also considers it "a real possibility" that the androgen-related hormones of adrenarche may be exerting effects on behavior. It is known from animal research and studies of various clinical anomalies in humans that androgens are taken up by neurons in the brain, and alter the way that neurons function.

Although no receptor for DHEA has yet been identified, its close biochemical cousin DHEA sulfate is known to interact with brain receptors for the neurotransmitter GABA. "This suggests there is a place for DHEA at a neuroactive site," Dr. Rosenfield said.

Just where that site might be has not been established. But androgen receptors have been identified in the cortex, the thinking part of the brain, as well as in areas known to regulate sexual-hormone activity, such as the hypothalamus.

Despite its obvious importance "the neurobiology of puberty is a remarkably underinvestigated area," Dr. Bruce McEwen of Rockefeller University said. Dr. McEwen, a neurobiologist who studies the effect of hormones on the brain, believes that "what is currently recognized as puberty may be only the most noticeable sign of a whole series of physical and psychosocial events beginning early in life."

Dr. McEwen said adrenal androgens might account for an array of cognitive, emotional and social changes others have documented around age 10, as well as "a continuing evolution of what we later call sexuality." For example, the age of 10 brings a qualitative leap in abstract reasoning skills. Researchers have reported a developmental shift in the ability to categorize, recognize relationships between things and understand sameness and difference.

If there is a hallmark in the social functioning of fourth and fifth graders, it is the sudden emergence of boy-girl teasing. "Something new is in the air," Dr. McClintock notes. "It isn't sexual in the adult sense, but it has some sexualized quality. There is both a consciousness of liking and a recognition of vulnerability." Other researchers document a new capacity for embarrassment.

Until now, Dr. McClintock said, no biological explanation has been offered for the emotional and behavioral changes that occur in fourth and fifth graders. The hormonal changes she has reported may offer such an explanation, she said.

"I'm saying adrenarche is a major biological event that has been totally overlooked by psychology," Dr. McClintock said. "We at least ought to be investigating how it affects behavior in middle childhood."

Male Hormone Molds Women, Too, in Mind and Body

By Natalie Angier

Try as humans may to appreciate life's complexities and half-tones, we often resort to good old-fashioned dualism, dividing the world into conservatives and liberals, rich and poor, straights and gays, somebodies and nobodies, and, of course, men and women, with their complementary genitalia and their characteristic hormones. Men have androgens, most notably testosterone, while women have estrogens.

Even the words have a binary spin: "androgen" comes from the Greek "maker of males," and "estrogen" signifies the maker of the estrus cycle, the boss of ovulation and menstruation, the essence of womanhood.

But nature abhors absolutes, and it turns out that men and women each have a fair amount of the opposite sex's hormones coursing through their blood. Scientists have known this for years, yet they have long played down the implications of that hormonal kinship, particularly when it came to studying how testosterone and other androgens work in a woman's body.

They knew estrogen to be indispensable to the growth of all embryos, regardless of sex. By contrast, testosterone has been viewed as a luxury, needed mainly to shape a male's form and sexual function, and only vestigially and irrelevantly present in women. But these dismissive assumptions were made in the absence of any research or evidence.

Now, with the explosion of interest in women's health issues generally, physicians and scientists from a broad cross section of disciplines at last have begun to consider the role of so-called male hormones on the making of a female. They are trying to determine how closely testosterone is linked to a woman's sex drive, and whether the hormone is necessary to maintain female muscle mass and bone density into old age.

These preliminary and often conflicting investigations already have physicians sharply divided over the wisdom of giving post-menopausal women small doses of testosterone along with the estrogen-replacement therapy they may receive. Doctors in Britain and Australia are much more likely to prescribe low-dose testosterone pellets or injections for women complaining of flagging libido and depression than are their colleagues in the United States, who are hesitant to begin treating women with a potent hormone that is linked to men's comparatively early death.

With even greater trepidation, some scientists are seeking to learn the extent to which androgens influence a woman's personality, energy levels, relative aggressiveness or assertiveness, and any other traits commonly described as masculine.

Debate rages over the wisdom of replacing male hormones.

"The borders between classic maleness and femaleness are much grayer than people realized," said Dr. Robert A. Wild, professor and chief of the section on research and education in women's health at the University of Oklahoma Health Sciences Center, in Oklahoma City. "We're mixed bags, all of us."

THE RISE AND FALL OF TESTOSTERONE

One reason researchers have neglected the study of androgens in women is a simple matter of quantity:

From the *New York Times* (May 3, 1994), pp. C1, C13. Reprinted with permission from the *New York Times*.

women have, on average, much less of them than men do. There are many androgens, but the major hormone circulating freely is testosterone.

Men have between 300 and 900 nanograms of testosterone for every deciliter of blood, much of it generated by the testes but some originating in the adrenals, the little hat shaped glands abutting the kidneys. (A nanogram is a billionth of a gram.) In women, a high measurement of testosterone is 100 nanograms, but the average is around 40, said Dr. Geoffrey P. Redmond, president of the Foundation for Developmental Endocrinology and a physician at Mount Sinai Hospital in Cleveland.

But the testosterone level varies significantly with the menstrual cycle, as do the more stereotypically female hormones, estrogen and progesterone. That is because a woman's testosterone comes not only from her adrenal glands (which are fairly steady from week to week in their hormonal productivity), but also from her ovaries, with each organ contributing about half. And as the estrogen production in the ovaries falls and soars, so, too, does testosterone output, meaning that a woman's maximum androgen secretion corresponds with her estrogen spike and hence with her ovulation.

Thus, in women with normally high testosterone levels, the ovulatory spike may bring them into androgen ranges approaching those of a low-testosterone male.

The impact of that fluctuating testosterone on the body is not clear. Researchers have a good idea of what testosterone does to males. During fetal development, it shapes the growth of the male genitals and possibly influences brain circuitry. When a boy reaches puberty, androgen production in the testes swings into gear to sculpt the secondary sexual characteristics: the thickening of muscles and vocal cords, the widening of the shoulders, the growth of the penis and the beard and the sudden obsession with sex.

In girls? Well, scientists know testosterone contributes to their adolescent development as well. It makes pubic and underarm hair grow. It could help their muscles and bones develop, although how it interacts with estrogen—which is known to be necessary for calcium absorption and bone strength—is unclear. "I wouldn't be surprised if female athletes have higher testosterone levels than nonathletes, although that's not well defined," said Dr. Roger S. Rittmaster, an associate professor of medicine at Dalhousie University in Halifax, Nova Scotia.

Girls with high androgen levels may also end up with comparatively small breasts, he added, for in males the presence of testosterone is known to prevent a man's circulating estrogen from prompting the breast tissue to swell. Androgens can also cause a teen-age girl's skin to become oily and break out, just as the hormones do to luckless boys.

A DEBATE OVER TREATMENT

The question would be merely of titillating interest were it not for a fierce debate over the use of testosterone replacement therapy in post-menopausal women. Dr. John Studd of the department of obstetrics and gynecology at Chelsea and Westminster Hospital in London said that besides estrogen-replacement therapy, about 25 percent of his post-menopausal patients receive testosterone pellets inserted under the skin. Among those recipients are women who have had their ovaries removed, as well as non-ovariectimized women who complain that their sex drive and energy levels are not what they used to be.

The degree to which testosterone levels ordinarily decline with age in either women or men is not known, but the atrophying of the ovaries post-menopausally can, in some cases cut down a woman's testosterone production. Dr. Studd says the pellets clearly help his patients.

"They may have their lives transformed," he said. "Their energy, their sexual interest, the intensity and frequency of orgasm, their wish to be touched and have sexual contact—all improve."

Dr. Studd insisted that the doses used in his patients are so low that they have no adverse health affects. But many American physicians remain reluctant to prescribe the testosterone therapy for women.

"I have not seen women who need testosterone, except those who have had their ovaries removed," Dr. Redmond said. Other American scientists said there was a strong need to do a solid clinical trial of testosterone therapy in women.

Dr. Redmond and others believe that excess androgens are a far more pressing health problem than their diminution. By far, the bulk of the new research is focused on disorders that arise when a woman's body generates too much testosterone, resulting in everything from cosmetic problems like acne, balding and the growth of facial hair so abundant that the woman must shave twice a day to more severe complications like infertility, diabetes, high blood pressure, heart disease and cancer of the uterus. Even some cases of breast cancer, a disease normally associated with too much estrogen, may in fact be the result of excess testosterone, several experts said, although the data on this remain sketchy.

Researchers said the incidence of androgen disorders in women has been grossly underestimated, and that as many as 15 to 30 percent of all women may have problems caused by the overproduction of testosterone, an excessive sensitivity to the influence of circulating androgens, or both. They suggest that doctors should be on the lookout for women—and even young girls—who may be suffering from excess androgen secretion, so that the patients can be treated early enough to prevent the onset of serious and possibly fatal complications of a lifetime of androgen overdosing.

The signs of high androgen output sometimes are obvious: a tendency to put on weight in the upper body, particularly the stomach, rather than on the thighs and buttocks, as most women do; irregular periods; and hair sprouting in great abundance on the face, the thighs, in a woolly stripe from pelvis to belly button. Doctors can also perform blood tests to check for anomalous hormone secretions.

"It's not healthy for women to have abnormalities of androgen production, and these patients ought to be identified and treated as early as possible," said Dr. Philip D. Darney, a professor of obstetrics, gynecology and reproductive medicine at the University of California at San Francisco. "We've got a lot of work ahead of us educating physicians and patients on how to identify these states."

Among the treatments used to suppress or counteract androgen production are birth control pills; spironolactone, an anti-androgen drug, and dexamethasone, a synthetic steroid hormone that suppresses adrenal activity.

SO, WHAT LEVEL IS ABNORMAL?

But scientists concede that the line between normal and abnormal levels of androgens in women is blurry and somewhat arbitrarily assigned. The dark mustache that may be considered unacceptable on women in this country—and thus a symptom of a hormone imbalance—is often viewed as ordinary and even sexy on women in Mediterranean countries. Some critics argue that the new emphasis on androgen excess is just another attempt to pathologize variations on a theme, turning traits once considered relatively normal into diseases that must be treated with potent medications taken over a lifetime.

"What society says is normal and what is normal for women can be very different," said Dr. Rittmaster. "Women can have a full beard and still be breastfeeding."

Many of the issues surrounding androgen disorders in women were discussed at a recent conference in Rockville, Md., sponsored by the National Institute of Child Health and Human Development. The meeting was organized by Dr. Florence Haseltine, a surgeon, gynecologist and firebrand for the study of women's health.

Dr. Haseltine said she has been shown to have elevated levels of androstenedione, a precursor to testosterone. And though she admits she has no proof for her assumptions, she believes this hormonal excess explains why she becomes quite aggressive when under stress.

One common androgenic disorder in women is polycystic ovarian syndrome, when, for reasons that remain mysterious, the ovaries produce excess testosterone, resulting in infertility and problems with insulin that can prompt the onset of diabetes. Women with the disorder often are very hairy on the face and body but balding, and on an ultrasound test their ovaries may appear to be bulging in the middle, in the stromal tissue that produces androgens. The disease sometimes can be treated with anti-androgen drugs, but it must be caught early if diabetes is to be averted.

Other scientists are fascinated by a hereditary disorder called congenital adrenal hyperplasia, in which a person lacks one of the five enzymes needed to produce cortisol, an important hormone in responding to stress. As a result of the defect, precursors to cortisol released by the adrenal glands build up in a budding fetus and act like male hormones.

Girls with congenital adrenal hyperplasia may emerge from the womb looking like boys, with an enlarged clitoris and even a scrotal sac, although they have fully formed ovaries and uterus. In the worst cases, the girls may need genital surgery to give them a more characteristically female appearance.

In other instances of the disorder, said Dr. Maria I. New, chairman of pediatrics at New York Hospital–Cornell Medical Center in Manhattan, girls are born with normal genitals but masculinize later in life, becoming hairy, acned and suffering from reduced fertility. For both severe and mild cases of hyperplasia, patients are given dexamethasone to inhibit adrenal overactivity.

Dr. New and her colleagues are completing a study of the psychology, sexuality and gender identity of women who have congenital adrenal hyperplasia, to see whether the high androgen levels in the womb influenced in any measurable way the women's neurological development. Dr. New will not yet say what their results are, other than to hint that "there are definitely effects of androgens on the brain."

But whether the women are said to be more mathematical, more aggressive, more sexually active, more enamored of guns and computers, or any number of traits commonly attributed to men, the results are sure to arouse the perennial quarrel over the nature of human nature: how much is head, how much hearth and how much a few simple hormones.

A Reading for Critical Thinking

The Veil Torn:

Ethics Over the Possibility That a Gene Might Cause Homosexuality

Abstract: *Dr. Dean Hamer's discovery that a gene might be responsible for homosexuality caused much controversy when his findings were announced in 1993. The findings are paramount in research pertaining to genetic causes of behavior patterns. Use of such findings is the base of an ethics debate.*

When he is interviewing people, Dean Hamer asks them whether they can curl their tongue so that the tip makes a little U, or even an O. He thinks there may be a genetic basis for the ability.

This is a good idea. If you want to show a genetic basis for behaviour, it makes sense to choose something in which no one has any great emotional investment. But it is not the main thrust of Dr Hamer's field of inquiry—just a sort-of-frivolous side show. Dr Hamer is looking at a question which has a lot of emotion invested in it; the genetic basis for homosexuality.

Two years ago, in a flourish of controversy, he published his initial findings. Every man receives one of his mother's two X chromosomes; any two brothers should have a 50–50 chance of having the same X chromosome. However, he found that gay brothers seemed often to share the same X chromosome. Particularly implicated was a region called Xq-28; it might harbour a gene that had helped make the brothers gay. The media announced the discovery of a gay gene.

But there is no such thing—at least, not in the sense that such an announcement would suggest. If Dr Hamer's studies bear fruit, he will not have found a gene that all gays have, nor one that no heterosexuals have. He will not have found a gene devoted to disposing male desires towards male bodies. Among other things, a gene that did nothing but promote such behaviour would have trouble moving from generation to generation. It may well turn out that the gene moderately increases female fertility, giving its female carriers enough advantages to outweigh any reproductive drawbacks it may produce in a boy.

Dr Hamer's gene, if it is found, will mark a predisposition, not a destiny. That is still controversial, though, and some of the dimensions of the debate are surprising. Dr Hamer always knew that some people would want to develop a test allowing fetuses feared to be "gay" to be aborted—wrongly, in his opinion. He did not expect that reprints of his paper would be sent by gay men to their mothers as Christmas presents, evidence that their sexuality was inherited, not acquired.

In this, the fuss cut across traditional lines of argument. The right has, in the past, typically favoured the idea of innate characteristics while the left has stressed the influence of the social environment on the tabula rasa of the human soul. Yet here were liberal gays happy to be able to say that they did not choose their life, that it was their biological nature. Alongside that, though, and especially in Europe, people feared that appeals to biology might bring with them risks of medicalisation. It is not long since the World Health Organisation listed homosexuality in its registry of diseases.

THE NATURE THAT HAS BEEN SELECTED

Homosexuality; romantic love; violence; intelligence; tongue-curling: all are aspects of human nature.

Anyone who thinks that humans and their nature have evolved through natural selection will expect to find genes linked to these traits, or for almost anything that seems like a human universal. Scientists working with the tools of the genome project are bound to unearth some of them soon; in time, they may find many.

This marks a significant change in human genetics. As Dr Hamer points out, until recently human geneticists were not interested in particular genes; they were interested in statistics that showed a trait was inheritable. Now that they can study the specific genes involved, they may develop a biological understanding of how the trait works. From that should flow an understanding of the possibilities of environmental enhancement or mitigation. Even before getting down to the level of individual genes, the new biology is discovering things old human genetics could not. The variation between two people's genotypes can be measured (this is, among other things, the basis of genetic fingerprinting). These measures show that the amount of variation within groups is far greater than the variation between groups. Races do not differ very much in genetic terms; nothing like as much as individuals within a racial group may. The new genetics is a study of individuals.

Yet at the same time it is a study of groups of genes. Like the genetic basis of common diseases, which the genome companies are teasing out, the genetic basis of behaviour will depend on the complex interaction between many different genes and the environment. Among these genes, scientists expect to find many that play a part in the development of the body's behaviour organ—the brain. These developmental genes are likely to be highly interrelated, and each of them will have multiple effects. Proteins that regulate complicated developmental systems are likely to have slightly different effects at different times and in different parts of the body. To call any such gene a gene for one thing is to miss the point.

As an illustration, consider recent changes in neurology. At one point, it was thought that visual images from the eye were processed in a hierarchy of nerve cells. At the bottom there would be cells that responded to general information—lines, circles and so on. At the top there would be cells that responded to very specific images, such as grandmothers. Though there is some truth in this, the idea of a grandmother cell is out of date. Memories are seen as patterns of activity, rather than things stored in cells. There is no single cell without which you would not recognise your grandmother. Similarly, complex behaviours may be due to patterns of genes. Very similar patterns will have different effects; some

quite different patterns may add up to much the same thing.

THE CHOICES YET TO BE MADE

For all this difficulty, some behaviour patterns will be linked to some genes. Dr Hamer may find his gene. Another group of scientists has found a gene associated with some forms of dyslexia. The field of behavioural genetics is strewn with retracted findings, and others that turned out to be only narrowly applicable: a mutation that seemed to cause unwarranted aggression among some men in a Dutch family is turning out to show little variation in the population at large. In general, the variation in an evolved trait may not be closely linked to the genes, even though the biological underpinning is.

Where there is behaviour-linked variation, though, there will be tests. They could be helpful on the phenylketonuria principle, where knowing the gene lets you adapt the environment to compensate. A child with a genetic predisposition to dyslexia may be far better served by his educators if that predisposition is known. An informed, supportive environment makes a huge difference: just compare the abilities of people with Down's syndrome brought up in worlds adapted to their needs and those written off as idiots.

Yet for all that, many people with Down's syndrome are not born at all. Fetal tests are, and will continue to be, used to inform choices about abortion. Attempts to allow such choices only on purely medical grounds are hampered by the nature of the dividing line: a broad swathe of grey. In general, people should be able to choose what they want for their child—individuals' religious convictions permitting—and that includes a degree of genetic choice. Any rules limiting this choice would, in effect, force women to bear children that they do not want. If, as may happen, some deaf families want deaf children, it may be right to allow them that choice. Some observers worry that certain choices could not be economically accommodated within a society's health-care system, giving rise to a new eugenics based on the rationing of health care. But the overall effect of choice will undoubtedly be a decline in gene-linked disorders. Choice will be influenced by social pressures, and perhaps even by public policy. If people were choosing boys in excessive numbers, social disapproval or even tax regimes favouring girls might stop them. In principle choice is desirable. If the range of choice is to be wide, then abortion, even abortion made much easier and less stressful than it is today, is an unsatisfactory way of choosing. Instead, in-vitro fertilisation may become quite common; among the affluent, it could be the norm. In effect, it allows the choice to be made in parallel from among an array of embryos open to inspection, rather than forcing selections to be made one at a time in the womb. Birth has, in many places, moved from the bedroom to the hospital. Conception—already divorced from sex by contraception—could easily follow it. People could thus be allowed to choose among a range of different combinations of their genes, representing a range of children they might have.

But what of children who would never be born without the test tube—children with genes present in neither parent? The gene therapies that put new genes into cells can be applied to egg cells and sperm cells or to embryos; in laboratories they are routinely used on animals such as the goats mentioned at the beginning of this survey. So such children are possible, but for various reasons they are unlikely. Very few medical applications of genetics would call for the genetic manipulation of an embryo; choice provides sufficient remedy. Why engineer a replacement cystic fibrosis gene into an embryo when you can simply choose an embryo that does not need such treatment? Few couples will be so unlucky in the genetic draw that some combination of their genes will not look pretty healthy.

An altogether more perplexing reason for genetic manipulation of the embryo might be the desire to give the child certain traits absent from the parents.

Such manipulation might become technologically possible, but it would raise profound moral issues. Axel Kahn, a French gene therapist, speaks for many when he rejects it on the basis that it requires human beings to be treated as means, rather than as ends in themselves. This would be particularly true of experimental people on whom such a technology would need to be developed—embryos who had genes added to them in order to see what the effect might be. There is no other way of finding out. Any such experiment is far beyond the ethical pale, and there it should remain.

The technologies offered by genetics are best used as a source of information allowing people to achieve a better fit between environment and genome. A person's genome should, perhaps, be seen as something akin to the Freudian notion of the subconscious: a strong influence on a person's life, but normally hidden. With help it is at least partially inspectable and explainable, and such explanations can provide helpful insights into how that life might be led. To use genetic technology as a way of trying to control what other people will become is not only immoral; it is also to miss the point. The true significance of genetic technology, and the power that it is delivering over life, is not that people can be designed from scratch, but that they can break free from some of the limitations imposed by their inbuilt genes.

A Reading for Critical Thinking

Focus on Only Two Sexes Is Narrow

Anne Fausto-Sterling

In Western culture, every adult is either man or woman, and the difference is not trivial. It means being available for, or exempt from, draft registration, as well as being subject to laws governing marriage, the family and human intimacy. But the state and legal system's interest in maintaining a two-party sexual system defies nature, for biologically speaking there are many gradations running from female to male: Along that spectrum lie at least five sexes—perhaps even more.

The field of medicine uses the term "intersex" as a catchall for three major subgroups with some mixture of male and female characteristics: the so-called true hermaphrodites, whom I call "herms," who possess one testis and one ovary (the sperm- and egg-producing vessels, or gonads); male pseudo-hermaphrodites ("merms"), who have testes and some aspects of female genitalia but no ovaries; and female pseudo-hermaphrodites ("ferms"), who have ovaries and some aspects of the male genitalia but lack testes.

THE BIOLOGICAL MAKEUP

In some true hermaphrodites, the testis and the ovary grow separately but bilaterally; in others, they grow together within the same organ, forming an ovo-testis. Not infrequently, at least one of the gonads functions well, producing either sperm cells or eggs, as well as functional levels of the sex hormones: androgens or estrogens.

In contrast with true hermaphrodites, pseudo-hermaphrodites possess two gonads of the same kind along with the usual male (XY) or female (XX) chromosomal makeup. But their external genitalia and secondary sex characteristics do not match their chromosomes. Thus, merms have testes and XY chromosomes, yet they also have a vagina and a clitoris and at puberty they often develop breasts. They do not menstruate, however. Ferms have ovaries, XX chromosomes and sometimes a uterus, but they also have at least partly masculine external genitalia.

While it is difficult to estimate the frequency of intersexuality, John Money of Johns Hopkins University, a specialist in the study of congenital sexual organ defects, suggests that intersexuals may constitute as many as 4 percent of births. However, medical advances enable physicians to catch most at birth. Such infants are entered into a program of hormonal and surgical management so that they can slip quietly into society as "normal" heterosexual males or females. The aims of the policy are humanitarian. The assumptions behind that wish—that there be only two sexes, that heterosexuality alone is normal—have gone virtually unexamined.

WHY SUPPRESS INTERSEXUALITY?

Ironically, a more sophisticated knowledge of sexuality led to the repression of intersexuality. In 1937, Hugh H. Young, a urologist at Johns Hopkins, published *Genital Abnormalities, Hermaphroditism and Related Adrenal Diseases*. In this unusually even-handed study, Young drew together case histories to demonstrate and study the medical treatment of such

Reprinted with permission of Manisses Communications Group, Inc. Originally published in *The Brown University Child and Adolescent Behavior Letter* (1994, Vol. 10, No. 7). Contact: 800/333-7771.

"accidents of birth." Yet even as Young was illuminating intersexuality with the light of scientific reason, he was beginning its suppression. His book is also a treatise on surgical and hormonal methods of changing intersexuals into either males or females.

By 1969, when Christopher J. Dewhurst and Ronald R. Gordon wrote *The Intersexual Disorders*, intersexual infants were almost always subject to surgery and hormonal treatment. The condition, they wrote, "is a tragic event which immediately conjures up visions of a hopeless psychological misfit doomed to live always as a sexual freak in loneliness and frustration." Though there are few empirical studies to back up such near-hysterical assertions, scientific dogma has held fast to the theory that without medical care hermaphrodites are doomed to a life of misery.

THE POLICY DESERVES QUESTIONING

The treatment of intersexuality in this century demands scrutiny. Society mandates the control of intersexual bodies because they challenge traditional beliefs about sexual difference. Hermaphrodites have unruly bodies. They do not fall into a binary classification: only a surgical shoehorn can put them there.

What if things were different? Imagine a world in which medical knowledge used to intervene in the management of intersexual patients had been placed at their service. Thus, hermaphrodites would be concerned primarily not about whether they conform to society but about whether they might develop the life-threatening conditions that sometimes accompany their development: hernias, gonadal tumors, adrenal malfunction. Medical intervention would take place only rarely before the age of reason; subsequent treatment would be a cooperative venture between physician, patient and, perhaps, a gender adviser.

No doubt the most troublesome arena would be the rearing of children. Parents, at least since the Victorian era, have fretted over the fact that their children are sexual beings. But would rearing children as intersexuals be that fraught with peril? Modern investigators tend to overlook numerous case histories, such as those collected by Young, that describe children who grew up knowing that they were intersexual and adjusted to their status.

With remarkable unanimity, the scientific community has avoided contemplating the alternative route of unimpeded intersexuality. Perhaps it will begin now.

Anne Fausto-Sterling, a geneticist and professor of medical science at Brown University, is author of Myths of Gender: Biological Theories about Women and Men *(NY: Basic Books, 1992).*

Review

The Social Organization of Sexuality: Sexual Practices in the United States

Edward O. Laumann, John H. Gagnon, Robert T. Michael, Stuart Michaels.
Chicago, Ill: The University of Chicago Press; 1994. 718 pages.

Sexual Attitudes and Lifestyles

Anne M. Johnson, Jane Wadsworth, Kaye Wellings,
Julia Field. Oxford, England: Blackwell Scientific
Publications; 1994. 499 pages.

The publication of *The Social Organization of Sexuality Practices in the United States* may have raised more questions than it has answered. From the beginning, this sex survey—titled the National Health and Social Life Survey—has been dogged by controversy. The first source of controversy had to do with the federal government's role in funding sexuality studies of the US population. Initiated in 1988 as a contract to the University of Chicago and the National Opinion Research Center (NORC) to design a survey of adult sexual behavior (with support from the National Institute of Child Health and Human Development [NICHD]), the project quickly attracted the attention of congressional conservatives. Despite successive modifications of the questionnaire and very intensive efforts by National Institutes of Health officials to persuade Congress of the scientific and public health importance of the survey, congressional language was used to prohibit the further release of government funds for this project. The assistance of a national advisory board of prominent scientists and the support of a variety of US Public Health Service agency heads and officials were insufficient to persuade the Office of Management and Budget to allow the project to proceed under federal sponsorship. Fortunately, a consortium of major foundations came through with support, enabling the team to go into the field in 1992. However, a major problem was that the survey's sample was reduced from its originally intended size of 10 000–20 000 to only 3432.

While the most obvious impetus of the survey, and the one of most interest to public health, was the use of its findings for sexually transmitted disease intervention and education, the survey's roots are in other scientific traditions. Despite 40 years of attempts at comprehensive studies of sexuality, there had been no national survey of adult sexual behavior. Most studies of sexuality, especially of what would now be called high-risk behavior, used limited non-probability samples. No matter how insightful these were, they could provide neither national estimates of behavior nor clear guidelines for intervention. Thus *The Social Organization of Sexuality* is a landmark study in the sexual behavior field.

A second impetus for the study was the longstanding tradition of fertility-related research in the Public Health Service, primarily at the National Center for Health Statistics and the NICHD. Lack of knowledge about sexuality has limited our ability to understand demographic phenomena such as adolescent pregnancy, household and family formation, divorce, and contraceptive use. The introduction of sexuality into demography reflects a broadening theoretical perspective. Phenomena such as fertility are seen in the context of other aspects of human behavior and social life and not as mere observations.

A third impetus for the project was the increasing threat of acquired immunodeficiency syndrome (AIDS) and the surge in other sexually transmitted diseases during the 1980s. It quickly became clear that certain forms and parameters of sexual behavior (such as anal intercourse and high numbers of partners) placed individuals—particularly gay and bisexual men and their female partners—at high risk of infectious disease. Without accurate estimates of the population

From *American Journal of Public Health* (July 1996, Vol. 86, No. 7), pp. 1037–1039. Reprinted by permission of The American Public Health Association (APHA). © 1996.

prevalence of homosexuality and bisexuality, of patterns of partner selection, and of the association of sex with behaviors such as alcohol and drug use, it was difficult to forecast accurately the spread of the epidemic and hence the likely numbers of new human immunodeficiency virus (HIV) or other infections. The extent to which those infections might be contained within certain social networks or migrate beyond them was equally difficult to estimate. In the absence of such understanding, agencies should not have been expected to design realistic and efficient intervention campaigns. In particular, all three traditions—sexuality, fertility and family and household formation, and public health—had often in the past ignored the fact that sexual and demographic behavior occurs in the context of social networks, the area of expertise of *The Social Organization of Sexuality*'s first author, Edward O. Laumann.

The *Social Organization of Sexuality* is organized into four parts: an orientation to the study's theoretical framework and design; a series of chapters on sexual preferences and experiences, including number of partners, sexual networks, homosexuality, and forced sex; a section on sexual happiness and dysfunction, sexually transmitted diseases, and fertility, cohabitation, and marriage; and extensive technical appendices that include the text of the questionnaire. Findings with implications for the public health community are found in every section, but those that have received widespread attention include the prevalence of monogamy and of same-gender sexual activity. Not surprisingly, married people were far less likely than the never- or once-married to have had more than one partner during the previous 12 months (93.7% of married persons had had only one sexual partner in the last year, compared with 38% of those never married and not cohabiting). About 79% of married individuals had had only one partner in the past 5 years, and married people were much more likely than singles to report being extremely or very happy. These data about monogamy help explain another of the book's key findings: the lack of overlap between sexual networks. A high prevalence of enduring monogamous partnerships and segregated networks must obviously curb the sexual transmission of infection.

The report's analysis of the prevalence of homosexuality distinguishes between age-specific homosexual behavior, desire, and identity. About 9.1% of men and 4.3% of women reported engaging in any same-sex activity since puberty. For nearly half of these men (about 4% of the total sample), this behavior occurred only before the age of 18. By contrast, only about 1.4% of the women and 2.8% of the men reported a homosexual *identity*.

These results are relatively similar to the data from the population-based survey of sexual behavior in the United Kingdom, *Sexual Attitudes and Lifestyles*. The British study reported rates of same-gender sexual experience that ranged up to 6.1% for men and 3.4% for women. By contrast, the Kinsey study,[1,2] which used convenience rather than random samples, found a much higher prevalence of homosexuality.

Both the US and British studies found regional differences in the prevalence of same-gender sexual behavior. In the United States, homosexual behavior appeared to be far more common in the 12 largest cities; in the United Kingdom, male homosexual contact appeared to be two to three times as prevalent in London as elsewhere, especially for recent, rather than lifetime, exposure. In Britain, regional differences in the prevalence of homosexual orientation were far more striking for men than for women. These regional differences occur because of the selective migration of individuals with same-gender sexual identity into more accepting environments and because of social environmental effects on individuals in urban settings. Opportunities for same-gender sexual behavior are greater and sanctions are fewer in big cities than in smaller places.

The British and US surveys were also similar in their sampling techniques and in their reliance on face-to-face interviews with self-administered questionnaires. But the sample size of the former (18 876 residents of Great Britain aged 16 to 59 years) was considerably larger than that of the latter, and the British response rate of 64.7% was smaller than the US study's 78.6%. And the books differ very much in style. The British book, written by a team of epidemiologists and public health specialists, has almost none of the theoretical language of the US study with its use of concepts such as master status, sexual script, and network and economic choice theory. Thus the British book is a much more straightforward, less conjectural description of sexual and fertility-related practices. The readability of the British survey—both visually and stylistically—makes it very accessible to public health and lay audiences.

The Social Organization of Sexuality (but not *Sexual Attitudes and Lifestyles*) has recently become the cynosure of a debate on the accuracy of responses to the survey, on the survey's validity as science, and on whether in fact the social sciences are science at all (survey authors Laumann and Gagnon are sociologists, Michael an economist, and Michaels a survey methodologist). An editorial in *The Economist* titled "74.6% of Sociology is Bunk"[3] charged that insecurity about professional identity drove the Chicago team to a quantitative analysis. In a *New England*

Journal of Medicine review of the popular version of the survey,[4] the reviewer complained of tendentiousness and overinterpretation.[5] A review by Harvard University biologist R.C. Lewontin is the most extensive.[6] Lewontin attacks the survey methodology on which the US survey is based, including the use of a population probability sample and the validity of self-reports of sexual behavior. But Laumann et al., like the British team, went to great lengths to test both the internal and the external validity of their findings.

Lewontin is more on target with his theoretical objections to *The Social Organization of Sexuality*. The problem is this: Most of the behavioral findings are analyzed and reported according to a set of what Laumann et al. refer to as master statuses. These are fundamental demographic characteristics about which it is quite easy to gather data: gender, race/ethnicity, age, education, marital status, and religious affiliation. Lewontin's concern is that relying on these variables and inflating them by attempting to read into them undue theoretical importance misses where the real touchstones might be for public health. For example, a household sample survey necessarily ignores those institutionalized populations—prisoner, soldier, homeless person, college student—whose master statuses and living situations place them at particular risk of sexually transmitted disease. (The sampling frame of the British survey also excluded some elements of the institutionalized population such as the homeless but included unspecified others.) Thus the very strength of the US survey from the point of view of social science is also its weakness, particularly from the point of view of public health. This leads to the question of to what extent the book's reiteration (despite the initial fears of conservatives) of the strong relationship between traditional heterosexual marriage, personal happiness, religiosity, and monogamy is a product of the way the sample was constructed, the survey methodology, the response rate, and the way that questions were framed and analytic categories employed. Has the US study given us the best possible data and the most accurate picture of the population?

The absence in the US survey of any discussion of the real-life conditions under which people engage in sexual behavior is also striking: Are there children around? How old are the children? Is the household crowded? What are the respondents' sleep and vacation patterns? Attention to the context of daily life in which sexual behavior occurs, beyond the use of alcohol and drugs, might have made the data more interpretable. Additionally, despite its underpinnings in

network analysis, the US study does not provide the comprehensive network-based approach found in many smaller studies of sexual and drug use behavior. More significant, given the stated public health goals of the study, is the survey's omission of a physician, a biologist, or an epidemiologist from the research team. Many of the speculative, theoretical explanations in the book would have been better grounded with data about biological and medical factors that might affect sexuality, such as hormone use (including use of oral and topical medications), menstrual cycles and discomforts, nursing, pregnancy and postpartum conditions, and prostate problems; such information is quite limited in the book.

The goals of the British survey were much more overtly related to public health. In fact, the authors state, "The research instrument was designed to provide data which would assist health care professionals working in many areas of sexual health: psychosexual counselling, the prevention of STD and family planning"; the authors also hoped to stimulate further social inquiry into this area of human behavior. The public health-related data they present seem more accessible than that of the US volume, perhaps because there is much less social science theory.

Some of the questions raised by the British and US sexual behavior surveys are still to be answered: Is it possible to obtain reliable data about sexual behavior, preferences, and identification? From whom will the data be most and least accurate? What kind of survey techniques are most likely to provide truthful data? Can policymakers be better educated about the public health importance of understanding sexual behavior? And finally, what admixture of public health and social science is most likely to produce data useful to advancing our understanding of this most fundamental of social relationships?

Nancy Moss, PhD, Behavioral and Social Research Program, National Institute on Aging, Bethesda, MD

REFERENCES

1. Kinsey AC, Pomeroy WB, Martin CE. *Sexual Behavior in the Human Male*. Philadelphia, PA: Saunders; 1948.
2. Kinsey, SC, Pomeroy WB, Martin CE, Gebhard PH. *Sexual Behavior in the Human Female*. Philadelphia, PA: Saunders; 1953.
3. 74.6% of sociology is bunk. *The Economist*. May 13, 1995:15. Editorial.
4. Michael RT, Gagnon JH, Laumann EO, Kolata G, eds. *Sex in America: A Definitive Survey*. Boston, MA: Little, Brown; 1994.
5. Money J. Sex in America: a definitive survey. *N Engl J Med.* 1995;332:1452–1453.
6. Lewontin RC. Sex, lies and social science. *NY Rev Books.* April 20, 1995; XLII (7):24–29. [Letters May 25, 1995; June 8, 1995.]

PART 2

Gender and Sex Roles

Twenty years ago, the advent of the modern women's movement compelled us to begin to examine our attitudes, values, and beliefs about men and women—what it means to be a man or woman and how we talk about masculinity and femininity. Today, some social commentators now argue that this dualistic way of discussing gender is too confining, that being either male or female doesn't embrace the full scope of gender possibilities. The transgender movement celebrates a diversity of gender that includes transsexuals, transvestites, and intersexual people.

With the enactment of laws that prohibit discrimination based on gender, there have been sweeping changes in the way we do business, raise our sons and daughters, educate our school children, and provide for equal opportunity in all facets of life. There have been fundamental changes in the way men and women view themselves and in their relationships with like and opposite genders.

In Part 2 we will examine some of these changes, highlighting some of the more controversial gender-related issues of the 1990s.

A Reading for Critical Thinking

Man's World, Woman's World? Brain Studies Point to Differences

Gina Kolata

D r. Ronald Munson, a philosopher of science at the University of Missouri, was elated when Good Housekeeping magazine considered publishing an excerpt from the latest of the novels he writes on the side. The magazine eventually decided not to publish the piece, but Dr. Munson was much consoled by a letter from an editor telling him that she liked the book, which is written from a woman's point of view, and could hardly believe a man had written it.

New scanner finds more evidence of how the sexes differ in brain functions.

It is a popular notion: that men and women are so intrinsically different that they literally live in different worlds, unable to understand each other's perspectives fully. There is a male brain and a female brain, a male way of thinking and a female way. But only now are scientists in a position to address whether the notion is true.

The question of brain differences between the sexes is a sensitive and controversial field of inquiry. It has been smirched by unjustifiable interpretations of data, including claims that women are less intelligent because their brains are smaller than those of men. It has been sullied by overinterpretations of data, like the claims that women are genetically less able to do everyday mathematics because men, on average, are slightly better at mentally rotating three dimensional objects in space.

But over the years, with a large body of animal studies and studies of humans that include psychological tests, anatomical studies, and increasingly, brain scans, researchers are consistently finding that the brains of the two sexes are subtly but significantly different.

Now, researchers have a new noninvasive method, functional magnetic resonance imaging, for studying the live human brain at work. With it, one group recently detected certain apparent differences in the way men's and women's brains function while they are thinking. While stressing extreme caution in drawing conclusions from the data, scientists say nonetheless that the groundwork was being laid for determining what the differences really mean.

"What it means is that we finally have the tools at hand to begin answering these questions," said Dr. Sally Shaywitz, a behavioral scientist at the Yale University School of Medicine. But she cautioned: "We have to be very, very careful. It behooves us to understand that we've just begun."

The most striking evidence that the brains of men and women function differently came from a recent study by Dr. Shaywitz and her husband, Dr. Bennett A. Shaywitz, a neurologist, who is also at the Yale medical school. The Shaywitzes and their colleagues used functional magnetic resonance imaging to watch brains in action as 19 men and 19 women read nonsense words and determined whether they rhymed.

In a paper, published in the Feb. 16 issue of Nature, the Shaywitzes reported that the subjects did equally well at the task, but the men and women used different areas of their brains. The men used just a

From the *New York Times* (February 28, 1995), pp. C1, C7. Reprinted with permission from the *New York Times*.

small area on the left side of the brain, next to Broca's area, which is near the temple. Broca's area has long been thought to be associated with speech. The women used this area as well as an area on the right side of the brain. This was the first clear evidence that men and women can use their brains differently while they are thinking.

Another recent study, by Dr. Ruben C. Gur, the director of the brain behavior laboratory at the University of Pennsylvania School of Medicine, and his colleagues, used magnetic resonance imaging to look at the metabolic activity of the brains of 37 young men and 24 young women when they were at rest, not consciously thinking of anything.

In the study, published in the Jan. 27 issue of the journal Science, the investigators found that for the most part, the brains of men and women at rest were indistinguishable from each other. But there was one difference, found in a brain structure called the limbic system that regulates emotions. Men, on average, had higher brain activity in the more ancient and primitive regions of the limbic system, the parts that are more involved with action. Women, on average, had more activity in the newer and more complex parts of the limbic system, which are involved in symbolic actions.

Men have larger brains; women have more neurons.

Dr. Gur explained the distinction: "If a dog is angry and jumps and bites, that's an action. If he is angry and bares his fangs and growls, that's more symbolic."

Dr. Sandra Witelson, a neuroscientist at McMaster University in Hamilton, Ontario, has focused on brain anatomy, studying people with terminal cancers that do not involve the brain. The patients have agreed to participate in neurological and psychological tests and then to allow Dr. Witelson and her colleagues to examine their brains after they die, to look for relationships between brain structures and functions. So far she has studied 90 brains.

Several years ago, Dr. Witelson reported that women have a larger corpus callosum, the tangle of fibers that run down the center of the brain and enable the two hemispheres to communicate. In addition, she said, she found that a region in the right side of the brain that corresponds to the region women used in the reading study by the Shaywitzes was larger in women than in men.

Most recently, Dr. Witelson discovered, by painstakingly counting brain cells, that although men have larger brains than women, women have about 11

percent more neurons. These extra nerve cells are densely packed in two of the six layers of the cerebral cortex, the outer shell of the brain, in areas at the level of the temple, behind the eye. These are regions used for understanding language and for recognizing melodies and the tones in speech. Although the sample was small, five men and four women, "the results are very, very clear," Dr. Witelson said.

Going along with the studies of brain anatomy and activity are a large body of psychological studies showing that men and women have different mental abilities. Psychologists have consistently shown that men, on average, are slightly better than women at spatial tasks, like visualizing figures rotated in three dimensions, and women, on average, are slightly better at verbal tasks.

Dr. Gur and his colleagues recently looked at how well men and women can distinguish emotions on someone else's face. Both men and women were equally adept at noticing when someone else was happy, Dr. Gur found. And women had no trouble telling if a man or a woman was sad. But men were different. They were as sensitive as women in deciding if a man's face was sad—giving correct responses 90 percent of the time. But they were correct about 70 percent of the time in deciding if women were sad; the women were correct 90 percent of the time.

"A woman's face had to be really sad for men to see it," Dr. Gur said. "The subtle expressions went right by them."

Studies in laboratory animals also find differences between male and female brains. In rats, for example, male brains are three to seven times larger than female brains in a specific area, the preoptic nucleus, and this difference is controlled by sex hormones that bathe rats when they are fetuses.

"The potential existence of structural sex differences in human brains is almost predicted from the work in other animals," said Dr. Roger Gorski, a professor of anatomy and cell biology at the University of California in Los Angeles. "I think it's a really fundamental concept and I'm sure, without proof, that it applies to our brains."

But the question is, if there are these differences, what do they mean?

Dr. Gorski and others are wary about drawing conclusions. "What happens is that people overinterpret these things," Dr. Gorski said. "The brain is very complicated, and even in animals that we've studied for many years, we don't really know the function of many brain areas."

This is exemplified, Dr. Gorski said, in his own work on differences in rat brains. Fifteen years ago, he and his colleagues discovered that males have a comparatively huge preoptic nucleus and that the area in females is tiny. But Dr. Gorski added: "We've been studying this nucleus for 15 years, and we still don't know what it does. The most likely explanation is that it has to do with sexual behavior, but it is very, very difficult to study. These regions are very small and they are interconnected with other things." Moreover, he said, "nothing like it has been shown in humans."

And, with the exception of the work by the Shaywitzes, all other findings of differences in the brains or mental abilities of men and women have also found that there is an amazing degree of overlap. "There is so much overlap that if you take any individual man and woman, they might show differences in the opposite direction" from the statistical findings, Dr. Gorski said.

Dr. Munson, the philosopher of science, said that with the findings so far, "we still can't tell whether the experiences are different" when men and women think. "All we can tell is that the brain processes are different," he said, adding that "there is no Archimedean point on which you can stand, outside of experience, and say the two are the same. It reminds me of the people who show what the world looks like through a multiplicity of lenses and say, 'This is what the fly sees.'" But, Dr. Munson added, "We don't

know what the fly sees." All we know, he explained, is what we see looking through those lenses.

Some researchers, however, say that the science is at least showing the way to answering the ancient mind-body problem, as applied to the cognitive worlds of men and women.

Dr. Norman Krasnegor, who directs the human learning and behavior branch at the National Institute of Child Health and Human Development, said the difference that science made was that when philosophers talked about mind, they "always were saying, 'We've got this black box.'" But now, he said, "we don't have a black box; now we are beginning to get to its operations."

Dr. Gur said science was the best hope for discovering whether men and women inhabited different worlds. It is not possible to answer that question simply by asking people to describe what they perceive, Dr. Gur said, because "when you talk and ask questions, you are talking to the very small portion of the brain that is capable of talking." If investigators ask people to tell them what they are thinking, "that may or may not be closely related to what was taking place" in the brain, Dr. Gur said.

On the other hand, he said, scientists have discovered that what primates perceived depends on how

Approaches to Understanding Male-Female Brain Differences

Studies of differences in perception or behavior can suggest how male and female thinking may diverge; studies of structural or metabolic differences can suggest why. But only now are differences in brain organization being studied.

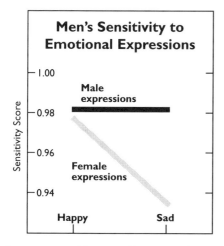

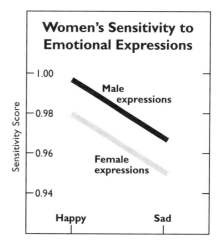

A study compared how well men and women recognized emotions in photos of actors portraying happiness and sadness. Men were equally sensitive to a range of happy and sad faces in men but far less sensitive to sadness in women's faces.

The women in the study were generally more sensitive to happy faces than to sad ones. They were also better able to recognize sadness in a man's face. For both sexes, sensitivity scores reflected the percent of the time the emotion was correctly identified.

their brains function. Some neurons fire only in response to lines that are oriented at particular angles, while others seem to recognize faces. The world may well be what the philosopher Descartes said it was, an embodiment of the workings of the human mind, Dr. Gur said. "Descartes said that we are creating our world," he said. "But there is a world out there that we can't know."

Dr. Gur said that at this point he would hesitate to baldly proclaim that men and women inhabit different worlds. "I'd say that science might be leading us in that direction," he said, but before he commits himself he would like to see more definite differences in the way men's and women's brains function and to know more about what the differences mean.

Dr. Witelson cautioned that "at this point, it is a very big leap to go from any of the structural or organizational differences that were demonstrated to the cognitive differences that were demonstrated." She explained that "all you have is two sets of differences, and whether one is the basis of the other has not been shown." But she added, "One can speculate."

Dr. Witelson emphasized that in speculating she was "making a very big leap," but she noted that "we all live in our different worlds and our worlds depend on our brains."

"And," she said, "if these sex differences in the brain, with 'if' in big capital letters, do have cognitive consequences, and it would be hard to believe there would be none, then it is possible that there is a genuine difference in the kinds of things that men and women perceive and how these things are integrated. To that extent it may be possible that in some respects there is less of an easy cognitive or emotional communication between the sexes as a group because our brains may be wired differently."

The Shaywitzes said they were reluctant even to speculate from the data at hand. But, they said, they think that the deep philosophical questions about the perceptual worlds of men and women can eventually be resolved by science.

"It is a truism that men and women are different," Dr. Bennett Shaywitz said. "What I think we can do now is to take what is essentially folklore and place it in the context of science. There is a real scientific method available to answer some of these questions."

Dr. Sally Shaywitz added: "I think we've taken a qualitative leap forward in our ability to ask questions." But, she said, "the field is simply too young to have provided more than a very intriguing appetizer."

A Reading for Critical Thinking

Throwing style is not determined by biology—
anyone can learn to throw like an athlete

Throwing Like a Girl

By James Fallows

Most people remember the 1994 baseball season for the way it ended—with a strike rather than a World Series. I keep thinking about the way it began. On opening day, April 4, Bill Clinton went to Cleveland and, like many Presidents before him, threw out a ceremonial first pitch. That same day Hillary Rodham Clinton went to Chicago and, like no First Lady before her, also threw out a first ball, at a Cubs game in Wrigley Field.

The next day photos of the Clintons in action appeared in newspapers around the country. Many papers, including *The New York Times* and *The Washington Post*, chose the same two photos to run. The one of Bill Clinton showed him wearing an Indians cap and warm-up jacket. The President, throwing lefty, had turned his shoulders sideways to the plate in preparation for delivery. He was bringing the ball forward from behind his head in a clean-looking throwing action as the photo was snapped. Hillary Clinton was pictured wearing a dark jacket, a scarf, and an oversized Cubs hat. In preparation for her throw she was standing directly facing the plate. A right-hander, she had the elbow of her throwing arm pointed out in front of her. Her forearm was tilted back, toward her shoulder. The ball rested on her upturned palm. As the picture was taken, she was in the middle of an action that can only be described as throwing like a girl.

The phrase "throwing like a girl" has become an embattled and offensive one. Feminists smart at its implication that to do something "like a girl" is to do it the wrong way. Recently, on the heels of the O.J. Simpson case, a book appeared in which the phrase was used to help explain why male athletes, especially football players, were involved in so many assaults against women. Having been trained (like most American boys) to dread the accusation of doing anything "like a girl," athletes were said to grow into the assumption that women were valueless and natural prey.

I grant the justice of such complaints. I am attuned to the hurt caused by similar broad-brush stereotypes when they apply to groups I belong to—"dancing like a white man," for instance, or "speaking foreign languages like an American," or "thinking like a Washingtonian."

Still, whatever we want to call it, the difference between the two Clintons in what they were doing that day is real, and it is instantly recognizable. And since seeing those photos I have been wondering, Why, exactly, do so many women throw "like a girl"? If the motion were easy to change, presumably a woman as motivated and self-possessed as Hillary Clinton would have changed it. (According to her press secretary, Lisa Caputo, Mrs. Clinton spent the weekend before opening day tossing a ball in the Rose Garden with her husband, for practice.) Presumably, too, the answer to the question cannot be anything quite as simple as, Because they *are* girls.

A surprising number of people think that there is a structural difference between male and female arms or shoulders—in the famous "rotator cuff," perhaps—that dictates different throwing motions. "It's in the shoulder joint," a well-educated woman told me recently. "They're hinged differently." Someday researchers may find evidence to support a biological theory of throwing actions. For now, what you'll hear if you ask an orthopedist, an anatomist, or (especially) the coach of a women's softball team is that there is no structural reason why men and women should throw in different ways. This point will be obvious to any male who grew up around girls who liked to play baseball and became good at it. It should be obvious on a larger scale this summer, in broadcasts of the Olympic Games. This year, for the first time, women's fast-pitch softball teams will compete in the Olympics. Although the pitchers in these games will deliver the ball underhand, viewers will see female shortstops, center fielders, catchers, and so on pegging the ball to one another at speeds few male viewers could match.

Even women's tennis is a constant if indirect reminder that men's and women's shoulders are "hinged" the same way. The serving motion in tennis is like a throw—but more difficult, because it must be coordinated with the toss of the tennis ball. The men in professional tennis serve harder than the women, because they are bigger and stronger. But women pros serve harder than most male amateurs have ever done, and the service motion for good players is the same for men and women alike. There is no expectation in college or pro tennis that because of their anatomy female players must "serve like a girl." "I know many women who can throw a lot harder and better than the normal male," says Linda Wells, the coach of the highly successful women's softball team at Arizona State University. "It's not gender that makes the difference in how they throw."

So what is it, then? Since Hillary Clinton's ceremonial visit to Wrigley Field, I have asked men and women how they learned to throw, or didn't. Why did I care? My impetus was the knowledge that eventually my sons would be grown and gone. If my wife, in all other ways a talented athlete, could learn how to throw, I would still have someone to play catch with. My research left some women, including my wife, thinking that I am some kind of obsessed lout, but it has led me to the solution to the mystery. First let's be clear about what there is to be explained.

At a superficial level it's easy to tick off the traits of an awkward-looking throw. The fundamental mistake is the one Mrs. Clinton appeared to be making in the photo: trying to throw a ball with your body facing the target, rather than rotating your shoulders and hips ninety degrees away from the target and then swinging them around in order to accelerate the ball. A throw looks bad if your elbow is lower than your shoulder as your arm comes forward (unless you're throwing sidearm). A throw looks really bad if, as the ball leaves your hand, your wrist is "inside your elbow"—that is, your elbow joint is bent in such a way that your forearm angles back toward your body and your wrist is closer to your head than your elbow is. Slow-motion film of big league pitchers shows that when they release the ball, the throwing arm is fully extended and straight from shoulder to wrist. The combination of these three elements—head-on stance, dropped elbow, and wrist inside the elbow—mechanically dictates a pushing rather than a hurling motion, creating the familiar pattern of "throwing like a girl."

It is surprisingly hard to find in the literature of baseball a deeper explanation of the mechanics of good and bad throws. Tom Seaver's pitching for the Mets and the White Sox got him into the Hall of Fame, but his book *The Art of Pitching* is full of bromides that hardly clarify the process of throwing, even if they might mean something to accomplished pitchers. His chapter "The Absolutes of Pitching Mechanics," for instance, lays out these four unhelpful principles: "Keep the Front Leg Flexible!" "Rub Up the Baseball," "Hide the Baseball!" "Get it Out, Get it Up!" (The fourth refers to the need to get the ball out of the glove and into the throwing hand in a quick motion.)

A variety of other instructional documents, from *Little League's Official How-to-Play Baseball Book* to *Softball for Girls & Women*, mainly reveal the difficulty of finding words to describe a simple motor activity that everyone can recognize. The challenge, I suppose, is like that of writing a manual on how to ride a bike, or how to kiss. Indeed, the most useful description I've found of the mechanics of throwing comes from a man whose specialty is another sport: Vic Braden made his name as a tennis coach, but he has attempted to analyze the physics of a wide variety of sports so that they all will be easier to teach.

Braden says that an effective throw involves connecting a series of links in a "kinetic chain." The kinetic chain, which is Braden's tool for analyzing most sporting activity, operates on a principle like that of crack-the-whip. Momentum builds up in one part of the body. When that part is suddenly stopped, as the end of the "whip" is stopped in crack-the-whip, the momentum is transferred to and concentrated in the next link in the chain. A good throw uses six links of chain, Braden says. The first two links involve the lower body, from feet to waist. The first motion of a throw (after the body has been rotated away from the target) is to rotate the legs and hips back in the direction of the throw, building up momentum as large muscles move body mass. Then those links stop—a pitcher stops turning his hips once they face the plate—and the momentum is transferred to the next link. This is the torso, from waist to shoulders, and since its mass is less than that of the legs, momentum makes it rotate faster than the hips and legs did. The torso stops when it is facing the plate, and the momentum is transferred to the next link—the upper arm. As the upper arm comes past the head, it stops moving forward, and the momentum goes into the final links—the forearm and wrist, which snap forward at tremendous speed.

This may sound arcane and jerkily mechanical, but it makes perfect sense when one sees Braden's slow-mo movies of pitchers in action. And it explains why people do, or don't, learn how to throw. The implication of Braden's analysis is that throwing is a perfectly natural action (millions and millions of people can do it), but not at all innate. A successful throw involves an intricate series of actions coordinated among muscle groups, as each link of the chain is timed to interact with the next. Like bike riding or skating, it can be learned by anyone—male or female. No one starts out knowing how to ride a bike or throw a ball. Everyone has to learn.

Readers who are happy with their throwing skills can prove this to themselves in about two seconds. If you are right-handed, pick up a ball with your left hand and throw it. Unless you are ambidextrous or have some other odd advantage, you will throw it "like a girl." The problem is not that your left shoulder is hinged strangely or that you don't know what a good throw looks like. It is that you have not spent time training your leg, hip, shoulder, and arm muscles on that side to work together as required for a throw. The actor John Goodman, who played football seriously and baseball casually when he was in high school, is right-handed. When cast in the 1992 movie *The Babe*, he had to learn to bat and throw left-handed, for realism in the role of Babe Ruth. For weeks before the filming began, he would arrive an hour early at the set of his TV show, *Roseanne*, so that he could practice throwing a tennis ball against a wall left-handed. "I made damn sure no one could see me," Goodman told me recently. "I'm hard enough on myself without the derisive laughter of my so-called friends." When *The Babe* was released, Goodman told a newspaper interviewer, "I'll never say something like 'He throws like a girl' again. It's not easy to learn how to throw."

What Goodman discovered is what most men have forgotten: that if they know how to throw now, it is because they spent time learning at some point long ago. (Goodman says that he can remember learning to ride a bicycle but not learning to throw with his right hand.) This brings us back to the roots of the "throwing like a girl" phenomenon. The crucial factor is not that males and females are put together differently but that they typically spend their early years in different ways. Little boys often learn how to throw without noticing that they are learning. Little girls are more rarely in environments that encourage them to learn in the same way. A boy who wonders why a girl throws the way she does is like a Frenchman who wonders why so many Americans speak French "with an accent."

"For young boys it is culturally acceptable and politically correct to develop these skills," says Linda Wells, of the Arizona State softball team. "They are mentored and networked. Usually girls are not coached at all, or are coached by Mom—or if it's by Dad, he may not be much of an athlete. Girls are often stuck with the bottom of the male talent pool as examples. I would argue that rather than learning to 'throw like a girl,' they learn to throw like poor male athletes. I say that a bad throw is 'throwing like an old man.' This is not gender, it's acculturation."

Almost any motor skill, from doing handstands to dribbling a basketball, is easier to learn if you start young, which is why John Goodman did not realize that learning to throw is difficult until he attempted it as an adult. Many girls reach adulthood having missed the chance to learn to throw when that would have been easiest to do. And as adults they have neither John Goodman's incentive to teach their muscles a new set of skills nor his confidence that the feat is possible. Five years ago Joseph Russo, long a baseball coach at St. John's University, gave athletic-talent tests to actresses who were trying out for roles in *A League of Their Own*, a movie about women's baseball. Most of them were "well coordinated in general, like for dancing," he says. But those who had not happened to play baseball or softball when they were young had a problem: "It sounds silly to say it, but they kept throwing like girls." (The best ball-field talents, by the way, were Madonna, Demi Moore, and the rock singer Joan Jett, who according to Russo "can really hit it hard." Careful viewers of *A League of Their Own* will note that only in a fleeting instant in one scene is the star, Geena Davis, shown actually throwing a ball.)

I'm not sure that I buy Linda Wells's theory that most boys are "mentored" or "networked" into developing ball skills. Those who make the baseball team, maybe. But for a far larger number the decisive ingredient seems to be the hundreds of idle hours spent throwing balls, sticks, rocks, and so on in the playground or the backyard. Children on the playground, I think, demonstrate the moment when the kinetic chain begins to work. It is when a little boy tries to throw a rock farther than his friend can, or to throw a stick over a telephone wire thirty feet up. A toddler's first, instinctive throw is a push from the shoulder, showing the essential traits of "throwing like a girl." But when a child is really trying to put some oomph into the throw, his natural instinct is to wind up his body and let fly with the links of the chain. Little girls who do the same thing—compete with each other in distance throwing—learn the same way; but whereas many boys do this, few girls do. Tammy Richards, a woman who was raised on a farm in central California, says that she learned to throw by trying to heave dried cow chips farther than her brother could. It may have helped that her father, Bob Richards, was a former Olympic competitor in the decathlon (and two-time Olympic champion in the pole vault), and that he taught all his sons and daughters to throw not only the ball but also the discus, the shotput, and the javelin.

Is there a way to make up for lost time if you failed to invest those long hours on the playground years ago? Of course. Adults may not be able to learn to speak unaccented French, but they can learn to ride a bike, or skate, or throw. All that is required for developing any of these motor skills is time for practice—and spending that time requires overcoming the sense of embarrassment and futility that adults often have when attempting something new. Here are two tips that may help.

One is a surprisingly valuable drill suggested by the Little League's *How-to-Play* handbook. Play catch with a partner who is ten or fifteen feet away—but do so while squatting with the knee of your throwing side touching the ground. When you start out this low, you have to keep the throw high to get the ball to your partner without bouncing it. This encourages a throw with the elbow held well above the shoulder, where it belongs.

The other is to play catch with a person who can throw like an athlete but is using his or her off hand. The typical adult woman hates to play catch with the typical adult man. She is well aware that she's not looking graceful, and reacts murderously to the condescending tone in his voice ("That's more like it, honey!"). Forcing a right-handed man to throw left-handed is the great equalizer. He suddenly concentrates his attention on what it takes to get hips, shoulder, and elbow working together. He is suddenly aware of the strength of character needed to ignore the snickers of onlookers while learning new motor skills. He can no longer be condescending. He may even be nervous, wondering what he'll do if his partner makes the break-through first and he's the one still throwing like a girl.

Toy Story:

A Look Into the Gender-Stereotyped World of Children's Catalogs

Debra W. Haffner, M.P.H., SIECUS President
with Megan Casselman

As many of you know, I am the proud mother of a two-year-old son and a ten-year-old daughter. In our home, we strive to raise our children with a strong sense of their gender identity while at the same time not limiting them with stereotypes about what is masculine or feminine.

This Christmas, our home was deluged with toy catalogs. As I flipped through them, I was struck by the outdated images of boys and girls. Pink pages featured toys for girls; blue pages, toys for boys. In most, girls played with dolls while boys constructed buildings or drove trucks and cars. I was both amused and amazed that such images are at the center of marketing strategies.

It was at this point that I decided to conduct a simple analysis of toy catalogs. I enlisted the help of Megan Casselman, a friend who works with pre-school children. First, we selected catalogs from nine toy companies.* Then we used the photographs in each catalog to tabulate the total number of children, their demographic composition, the pairing of playmates, and the types of toys they were enjoying.

CATALOGS INCLUDED CHILDREN FROM MANY RACIAL/ETHNIC BACKGROUNDS

A total of 566 children—275 boys and 291 girls—were in the catalogs, with an average of 63 children per catalog. They were from a variety of racial/ethnic backgrounds. In fact, such diversity was evident in 7 to 26 percent of all photos. As far as we could ascertain from the photos, a total of 10 percent were African-American, 6 percent were Asian-American,

"Play helps children prepare for their future adult roles."

and 2 percent were of Hispanic heritage. No catalogs showed a boy or girl with a noticeable physical disability. One catalog (*Sensational Beginnings*) had one picture of a child with Downs Syndrome.

We were pleasantly surprised to find a large number of pictures where girls and boys played together. When more than one child was in a picture, 15 percent were of girls playing with other girls; 15 percent were of boys playing with other boys; and 69 percent were of boys and girls playing together. Boys and girls were most often shown playing together with toys not classified by gender stereotypes (balls, puppets, outdoor play equipment, mazes, and trampolines). Pairs of girls usually played with dolls, dress-up clothes, and art projects; pairs of boys with cars, trains, building equipment, and traditional dress-up clothes. Children of differing ethnic backgrounds rarely played together. In fact, only 18 percent of all pictures of children playing together were of children from different ethnic backgrounds.

ALL CATALOGS REINFORCED GENDER STEREOTYPES

Girls and boys were shown playing with very different toys. Dolls, household items, and shopping toys were almost exclusively for girls while cars, trucks, and trains were almost exclusively for boys. No girls played with erector sets. The only toy which was used equally by boys and girls were toy musical instruments. Two of the catalogs (*Childcraft* and *Lilly's Kids*) actually color coded their pages: pink for girls and primary colors for boys.

From *SIECUS Report* (Sexuality Information and Education Council of the United States), (April/May 1996, Vol. 24, No. 4), pp. 20–21.

Girls were overwhelmingly shown with dolls and household toys. In fact, 95 percent of the pictures of dolls showed a girl. A boy played with a doll in only one catalog (*Hearth Song*). Girls were shown in 65 percent of the photos of household items such as irons, vacuums, and shopping carts. Boys were shown in 35 percent. Girls were also predominant in photographs showing children playing with art-related toys. They were in 81 percent of the pictures while boys were in 46 percent.

Both boys and girls were shown in "dress-up" clothes, although the type of clothing was very much based on gender stereotypes. Boys wore cowboy suits, safari outfits, pirate costumes, and firefighter/police uniforms while girls dressed up as glamorous women, princesses, and nurses. Girls were, however, given a little more flexibility than boys. They wore less traditional clothes—doctor and firefighter uniforms—in 22 percent of the "dress-up" photos while boys were never shown in anything but traditional male outfits.

Eighty-one percent of the sports pictures depicted boys. In fact, only boys were shown playing basketball, hockey, soccer, baseball, and boxing. When shown (35 percent of the photos), girls jumped rope or exercised on a gym mat or pull-up bar. The only sports featuring boys and girls were tennis, swimming, and jumping on a trampoline.

Boys dominated in many of the categories where both genders were represented. They were in 62 percent of the photos marketing academic toys; girls were in 51 percent. They were in 72 percent of the photos of outdoor equipment (swings, jungle gyms, and bouncers); girls were in 57 percent. They were in 65 percent of the photos of building sets and blocks; girls were in 53 percent.

Of interest, adults, by and large, did not appear in the toy catalogs with their children. There were only three photos of adults playing with children. The *Childcraft* catalog did include a photo of a mother and son using a cooking kit and a photo of a father and daughter working on an art project.

CONCLUSION

Play helps prepare children for their future adult roles. In today's (and, one hopes, tomorrow's) world both men and women will not only nurture their children but will also shop, cook, and take care of their homes. Both men and women drive cars, design buildings, excel at sports, and succeed in careers not limited by gender. Everyone has a part in helping make certain that today's parents prepare their children for that world and not the gender-stereotyped world of the toy catalogs. *Caveat emptor!*

*LIST OF SURVEYED CATALOGS

Adventures for Children
Childcraft
Constructive Playthings
Hand in Hand
Hearth Song
Lilly's Kids
Toys To Grow On
Troll Learn & Play
Sensational Beginnings

Megan Casselman works with pre-school children and is a specialist in communication disorders.

Sex
and the Soldier

By Stephanie Gutmann

February 4, 1997, and an all-too-familiar looking headline—"TOP ENLISTED MAN IN THE ARMY STANDS ACCUSED OF SEX ASSAULT"—occupies a prime corner of the front page of *The New York Times*. Just a few weeks earlier, the papers had been reporting charges of inappropriate hazing of female cadets at the Citadel. And just a few months before that, several female recruits at the Army's Aberdeen Proving Ground had accused drill instructors of rape and sexual harassment, unleashing a torrent of similar accusations from female soldiers around the country. In this latest case, as in so many of the others, blame will be difficult to affix. Once more it will come down to "he said, she said." Once more there will be op-eds, hand-wringing and counselors; once more the Army will have to deploy its investigatory troops. This, just as the Army digs out from Aberdeen—where there are still over 200 criminal charges to investigate, and a hot-line brings in new complaints every day.

What no one is publicly saying (but what everyone in the military knows) is that incidents like these are bound to recur. In a military that is dedicated to the full integration of women, and to papering over the implications of that integration as best it can, sex and sexual difference will continue to be a disruptive force. And regulating sex will become an ever more important military sideline, one whose full costs in money, labor and morale we will not really know until the forces are called on to do what they are assembled to do: fight.

The military's sex problems begin with the simple anatomical differences between men and women. Racial integration, to which the integration of women is ceaselessly compared, took the military about a century to achieve (quite successfully in the end) and that involved differences that are only skin deep. An effective fighting force depends on a steady supply of known quantities; it needs "units" made up of interchangeable elements called soldiers. Once one got over skin color, racial integration was still about integrating the same body.

But what happens when you try to absorb a population that is not, in unit terms, interchangeable? What happens when you try to integrate into a cohesive whole two populations with radically different bodies? In the elemental, unremittingly physical world of the soldier, sex differences—masked by technology in the civilian world—stand out in high relief. Consider the female soldier not in political terms, but in the real, inescapable terms of physical structure. She is, on average, about five inches shorter than the male soldier, has half the upper-body strength, lower aerobic capacity and 37 percent less muscle mass. She has a lighter skeleton, which may mean, for instance, that she won't be able to "pull G forces" as reliably in a fighter plane. She cannot pee standing up, a problem that may seem trivial, but whose impact on long marches was the subject of an entire Army research study; under investigation was a device called the "Freshette Complete System," which would allow women to pee standing up in places where foliage doesn't supply ample cover. She tends, particularly if she is under the age of 30 (as are 60 percent of military personnel) to get pregnant.

One would expect that such a sweeping social experiment (and one so expensive—just refitting the *U.S.S. Eisenhower* to accommodate 400 new female sailors cost $1 million, for example) would hit some rough patches. But don't expect to hear about them from the military brass. Afflicted by a kind of "Vietnam syndrome" about the possibility of winning an ideological battle against the civilians who increasingly influence military policy, the brass now seem mostly concerned with trying to prove how well, as one officer put it, they "get it" where women are concerned. This week, when Army Chief of Staff General Dennis J. Reimer said he thought the service should re-examine whether the advantages of jointly training men and women outweigh the drawbacks, it was something of a bombshell. In general, the military has maintained a virtual silence about problems with the new influx of female soldiers, and, in the ranks, negative comments about integration are considered "career killers." Those who don't "get it" talk about it in the barracks and on the Internet, which has become a haven for military samizdat about sex and other dicey matters. As one soldier wrote in a typical online exchange, "examples of these latest 'revelations' [about sex between subordinates and their immediate superiors] are known to nearly everyone who has served. But we were never allowed to discuss . . . our concerns openly because it would raise issues about the efficacy of mixing girls and boys and that was politically incorrect, a career-ending taboo."

In general, the military's response to the problems of gender integration has been to recruit more women. The more women, the more feminized the culture, the fewer problems with sex, goes the thinking. (One corollary of this may be the recent decline in male enlistment. In focus groups, young men tend to cite, among other reasons for not joining up, fear of purges like the one after Tailhook and the increased presence of females in the ranks.)

The big recruitment drive has brought the percentage of women in the force to 14 percent, which may not seem like much but is up from 2 percent at the close of the Vietnam War. Women now make up 20 percent of new recruits—compared to 12 percent a decade ago. And the effort to recruit still more women is relentless. In 1991, when the Marines replaced their slogan "A Few Good Men" with "The Few, The Proud, The Marines," the idea was to sound more female-friendly. Nowadays, much of a military recruiter's time is consumed with trying to cajole women to enlist. And in practice, unfortunately, this often means adapting—which is to say, lowering—standards without exactly admitting to doing so.

The goal for a young Marine recruiter named C.J. Chivers, for example, became just "'Get 'em on the plane.' If there were any problems, boot camp could sort it out." Chivers, whose stint as a recruiter lasted

from 1992–94, adds that "invariably we would fill up the white male quotas almost immediately. So it became any woman that came in there that met the minimums, we gotta hire. What that did was take all the subjectivity out of it, an enormous part of the evaluation process. I couldn't say 'I got a bad vibe' the way I could with a guy." A recruiter also had to work hard to maintain what Chivers calls an "informal double standard" on strength differences: "Invariably the guys went down to Officer Candidate School with a near-perfect physical score while the women just cleared the minimum"—even using what military brass call "gender-normed" test results and "dual," i.e. lower, standards: for example, in the Marines, fitness for women is tested with a flexed arm hang instead of pull-ups, half the number of sit-ups and a slower run.

Women have also been lured into the service with the promise of a more important role. Since 1994 more than 80,000 new jobs have been opened in positions that were formerly off-limits. Rescinding the combat exclusion law and the risk rule has allowed women to qualify to fly combat planes and to serve on combat ships. Women are still not allowed to serve on submarines, but *Navy Times* reports that "a review underway to examine future submarine designs may include a study on including women crew members."

And ever since the Gulf war, when women served in combat support roles, the possibility of taking that last step—of knocking down barriers to the infantry—has been very much in the air. Ground combat, considered the most potentially brutal, the most physically demanding and certainly the grubbiest form of combat, is seen as a crucial piece of turf by the Old Guard and plenty of the young old guard, too. Opponents of integrating ground combat tend to argue that mixed-sex units won't achieve the right kind of "cohesion," that women on the whole aren't strong enough to, say, effectively lob grenades or load tanks, and that there is, at bottom, something repugnant about a male officer ordering women barely out of their teens into harm's way. The opposing argument has been pointedly made by N.O.W. President Patricia Ireland, who maintains that exclusion promotes the view that women are weak, inferior and in need of protection. (With Patricia Schroeder, the great pro-combat warrior, in retirement, the next pro-combat push may come from a commission appointed by Army Secretary Togo D. West Jr. after the rape charges surfaced at Aberdeen. The commission's official mandate is to look at causes of sexual harassment, but the many pro-women-in-combat appointees are expected to argue the familiar exclusion-equals-lower-status-equals-harassment line when they make their recommendations.)

To understand why gender integration became such an unquestionable in the military culture, we have to return to 1992, the year of the Clarence Thomas hearings, the trial of Mike Tyson, "They just Don't Get It"—and the Tailhook investigations. Tailhook was officially declared a symptom of a larger problem—not an isolated event involving at most about six men—when investigators were ordered to scrutinize the "cultural" context. Through the prism of Tailhook and of sexual harassment, the culture that had long prepared men for battle suddenly looked, as then-acting Navy Secretary J. Daniel Howard put it, "diseased and decaying." "What happened at Tailhook," he told reporters, "was not just a problem with the integration of men and women in our ranks. It was just as much a problem with the toleration of Stone Age attitudes about warriors returning from the sea . . . ."

Somewhere in the committees and hearings charged with studying this "cultural problem" a remedy swam into focus: men harassed women because they did not see them as equals. If women were brought in in great numbers, "the warrior culture" would be diluted. After Tailhook, the military made recruitment of women a top priority; barriers toppled, policies changed, promotions were spirited through the pipelines.

The new thinking also held that, if you got to them early enough, all kinds of "sexist attitudes" could be nipped in the bud. And early enough meant starting with boot camp. Enter Gender Integrated Basic Training. In 1992 the Navy began training all new female recruits at one of three integrated boot camps—a way, as Captain Kathleen Bruyere put it, to give recruits "a chance to make mistakes, say stupid things, and tell them we don't do that here." At Bruyere's camp in Orlando, Florida, recruits did "everything but sleep together in the same compartment"—including physical training and bunk and dress inspections. They also spent a good deal of time watching films about sexual harassment, while questionnaires like the one that stated "The Navy is a man's world. True? or False?" gave the new troops ample opportunity to "say stupid things."

By the end of 1993, and into 1994, the Army followed suit with its own gender-integrated training. The Army may have been slower on the uptake because it had already experimented with the process in the early '80s and found that when the sexes, say, ran obstacle courses together, the women tended to have a high injury rate from trying to keep up, and the men complained that they weren't challenged.

To avoid dealing with the problems posed by differences in physical strength between men and women, the proponents of sexual integration have increasingly favored a movement to "re-evaluate" the way soldiers are trained. As Barbara Pope, then assistant secretary of the Navy for manpower and reserve affairs, put it in the early '90s, "We are in the process of weeding out the white male as norm. We're about changing the culture." And so, in some boot camps, the fundamental character of training is changing. Fort Jackson, the camp where gender-integrated training was thought to have failed in the early '80s, began to evaluate "soldierization skills" by putting more emphasis on skills like "map-making and first aid" at which female recruits excel. The result has been a kind of feel-good feminization of boot camp culture, with the old (male) ethos of competition and survival giving at least partial way to a new (female) spirit of cooperation and esteem-building.

At the instigation of a Navy weekly called *Soundings*, a group of middle-aged officers revisited their old basic training camp last fall to see how "the kinder, gentler Navy" was doing things. The oldsters were greeted by a commander—one Captain Cornelia de Groot Whitehead—who used her opening briefing to inform them that 40 percent of new recruits have at some time been victims of serious physical or sexual abuse, while 26 percent have contemplated suicide. Accordingly, de Groot Whitehead said, "We've decided we needed to do something different." The tourists from the "Old Navy" were bemused to learn that the infamous obstacle course of yore had been renamed the "confidence course" and moved indoors to comprise "an indoor labyrinth of pipes to crawl through, monkey bars to swing from, ladders to climb up and balance beams to sidestep over."

And at Fort Jackson, South Carolina—where, in 1995, boys and girls shared barracks—an *Army Times* reporter recently found that grunts no longer have to do push-ups to a count. Instead, they are asked to perform "a timed exercise in which soldiers do the best they can in a set period." One drill instructor has solved the male/female strength discrepancy problem by putting young recruits in "ability groups" for their morning run. "You're not competing with the rest of the company," Colonel Byron D. Greene, the director of Plans, Training and Mobilization, told *Army Times*. "You are competing against yourself and your own abilities."

But life—especially military life—does not ignore physical differences. When young soldiers leave training, they are assigned jobs (called Military Occupational Specialities or MOSs), and the physical requirements of these jobs are not nearly as forgiving as a "New Army" drill instructor. A typical Army MOS, the kind of combat support MOS a young woman might request, could involve lots of lifting and loading, of shell casings, for instance. Pat Schroeder can say what she likes, but "a shell casing," groused an Army physiologist, "is always gonna weigh ninety pounds. There's nothing we can do about that."

Female soldiers themselves know this. A 1987 Army Research Institute survey found that women are more likely than men to report that insufficient upper body strength interferes with their job performance. Twenty six percent of female light wheel vehicle mechanics, for example, said they found it "very difficult" to do their job, as opposed to 9 percent of the men in that speciality who were polled.

And, according to Army physiologist Everett Harman, "[Command Reports] have indicated that many soldiers are not physically capable of meeting the demands of their military occupational specialities. Unfortunately women fall disproportionately into this category." Attrition is particularly high, Harman said, in "heavy" (requiring 100-pound lifting) and "very heavy" (over 100 pounds) MOSs like Food Service Specialist, Motor Transport Operator and Unit Supply Specialist. Retraining and reassigning a soldier has been estimated to cost about $16,000, but advising a female soldier that she may have trouble with an MOS she is considering is, sources say, one of those "career-killing" statements that bureaucratically wise officers have learned to avoid.

There have been two attempts made in the past fifteen years to establish "gender-neutral" strength standards and a qualifying pre-test for each MOS, but as *Army Times* reported, "on both occasions, the requirements were eventually abandoned when studies showed most women couldn't meet the standards proposed for nearly 70 percent of the Army specialities." In 1995, a group of military researchers were set to try again, but this time the project didn't even reach the partial implementation stage because funding was denied. Funding was also recently denied to Harman, who had applied for a grant to do a second study of "remedial strength training for women," after his first had shown promising results. Harman believes the brass do not like his approach because it admits that female soldiers are not strong enough to perform basic military tasks, which is contrary to the military's line. "At the highest level, I think they feel that if we show that women can get stronger, then the onus would be on the women to get stronger," he says, "while it is the jobs that should be made easier."

But can the jobs be made easier? Can weapons get lighter (as some advisers are urging)—without reducing lethality? Proponents of the change-the-equipment-not-the-people view point to the highly automated Air Force. But the Air Force is not the Army, and it is not the Marines. "If you have a plane sitting on the runway and you have to load it with supplies—bombs, whatever, you can have machines that drive out there, that raise the stuff on a little elevator," Harman points out. "But out in the woods and fields a lot has to get done by hand. Even in the kitchen there are big pots weighing about 100 pounds or so. It would take a tremendous amount of research to make certain jobs lighter, because you're talking about re-engineering the whole thing. Carrying a tool box, changing a truck tire; there are certain jobs, for instance, where you have to carry a toolbox that might weigh a few hundred pounds and put it up on the wing of a plane."

Online, where military folk often say impolitic things, there is a sense of foreboding about the danger of ignoring the strength issue: "Nothing is more demoralizing," wrote one Marine, "than to have to turn your formation around to go pick up the females. This is only training. I can even put the females on remedial training and they still hold up my formations. I would hate to see how many Marines I would lose if we were in combat and had to be somewhere fast."

There is one respect, though, in which the stubborn physical realities of integrating women cannot be easily denied—and that is their capacity for childbearing. A recent article in *Stars and Stripes* reported that a woman had to be evacuated for pregnancy approximately every three days in the Bosnian theater from December 20, 1995, when the deployment began, until July 19, 1996. Army public relations people in Bosnia don't dispute that claim, but they also say pregnancy is no particular problem for the Army, "no different than appendicitis."

It is clearly not a problem anymore in a career sense. All branches and some of the service academies have softened policies on pregnancies and made it clear that their official stance is now completely accepting. Unfurling one such policy in February, 1995, Navy Secretary John H. Dalton told reporters that "Navy leadership recognize that pregnancy is a natural event that can occur in the lives of Navy servicewomen . . . and is not a presumption of medical incapacity." The Army has followed suit, stating that "Pregnancy does not normally adversely affect the career of a soldier."

In fact, pregnancy is now so "non-adverse" that soldiers say it's sometimes used to get out of "hell tours" like Bosnia, to go home. "I know other females that have done things . . . probably to get out of going somewhere," Specialist Carrie Lambertus told *Army Times*. "It happens all the time."

A woman who turns up pregnant in Bosnia is shipped in short order to the U.S. or Germany. Then, according to an Army spokesman, "female soldiers have the option of either staying on active duty or applying for release [with an honorable discharge] from active duty." Those who decide to stay in the military get six weeks maternity leave. The new Navy policy also provides for help in locating a runaway dad and in establishing paternity.

In the Navy, pregnancy rates run about 8 percent of the force at any given time. A pregnant woman is allowed to stay onboard ship up to her fifth month; then she gets reassigned to shore duty to avoid the heavy lifting that is a sailor's lot, not to mention the hazardous chemicals in engine rooms. Of the 400 women on the first gender-integrated warship the *U.S.S. Eisenhower*, twenty-four were "non-deployable" due to pregnancy at the start of a Persian Gulf tour and another fifteen were evacuated once on the water. On the *U.S.S. Acadia*—dubbed "the Love Boat" by the press—thirty-six out of a total 360 female sailors aboard had to be evacuated during a Gulf tour.

And no matter how determinedly the military defines pregnancy as a non-issue, the facts of pregnancy cannot be altered. A pregnant soldier is—or soon will be—a non-deployable soldier. A General Accounting Office study of soldiers called up to go to the Persian Gulf showed that women were four times more non-deployable than men—because of the pregnancy and recovery numbers. As Lambertus puts it, "If you're in a platoon where they're moving equipment or digging, setting up tents, [pregnant soldiers] are not going to be doing anything, except maybe sitting there and answering the phone all day. That really does cause some resentment." If her commanders had wanted to make sure the unit was truly deployable "they'll have to reclassify me and send me somewhere else, which would take more money, more time. So actually, it would be cheaper for them just to wait and keep me [here] ."

Then there is the matter of how one gets pregnant in the first place—the matter of what happens when you take men and women, aged on average 18 to 25, away from what are generally small town homes, ship them to exotic ports of call, house them in the catacomb-like berthing areas of ships, in coed tents or in crowded barracks and then subject them to loneliness, boredom and high stress. The fantasy of civilian activists like Pat Schroeder is that the result will look something like the bustling, efficient bridge of the *Starship Enterprise*. The reality is apt to look more like "a big high school"—which is the way a sailor named Elizabeth Rugh described her ship, the newly integrated *U.S.S. Samuel Gompers*.

Troops in Bosnia and Herzegovina (there were 1,500 female troops in the first deployment) generally live in coed tents with eight to ten people. Ranks are mixed, privates bedded down next to superiors. Troops are not allowed to drink alcohol or eat in restaurants, but they are allowed to have sex—as long as they are single and not doing it with a subordinate (or superior) in their chain of command. In a solemn statement provided to *Stars and Stripes*, Army spokesman Captain Ken Clifton wrote that "the Army does not prohibit heterosexual relations among consenting single soldiers . . . but it does not provide facilities for sexual relations."

Lack of official facilities does not seem to be a great obstacle. "Where there's a will there's a way!" Captain Chris Scholl told *Stars and Stripes*. Favorite locations, he said, include the backs of Humvees parked on a deserted air strip, tents, latrines, even underground bunkers—if you can hack standing up to your ankles in icy water. "It's going on all over the place," said Scholl. "They've locked us down so what else is there to do?"

And there is, of course, the problem of nonconsensual sex. A Defense Department spokesman says "there is no way to get a good number" on the frequency of rapes and sexual assaults in the armed forces, because each service keeps its own numbers and defines things slightly differently. Still, it is clear that the Aberdeen case was not an isolated incident. The Army recorded twenty-four incidents it categorized as "sexual assaults" involving U. S. soldiers in the Gulf war; these cases range from that of a 24-year-old specialist who had been on overnight guard duty in the desert with a male soldier and awoke to find him fondling her under the blanket they had shared for warmth to that of a 21-year-old private who was raped at knifepoint by a sergeant.

The making of a soldier is a rough, hands-on, invasive process—a preparation for what may be a very rough end. "[T]he training, the discipline, the daily humiliations, the privileges of 'brutish' sergeants, the living en masse like schools of fish," wrote James Jones in his essay "The Evolution of a Soldier," "are all directed toward breaking down the sense of sanctity of the physical person, and toward hardening the awareness that a soldier is the chattel (hopefully the proud chattel but a chattel all the same) of the society he serves."

Soldiers abuse each other—in training, in command, in hazing rituals. It is a self-regulating mechanism; finding the weak links, then shaming them or bullying them to come up to par, is one way a unit ensures, or tries to ensure, its own survival, since on the battlefield one's life depends on one's buddies' performance.

Meanwhile, the brass attempt to operate on both tracks, to honor the standards of both the civilian and the military world. They know they must encourage "cohesion" in their mixed-gender units, but they know, too, that they must avoid the wrong kind of cohesion—the kind that could stimulate jealousies, lovers' spats and . . . babies. So they end up sending a rather scrambled message, something like "Women are different but they're not different"; "We have the same expectations for women but you cannot treat them the same."

"Cry havoc and let slip the dogs of war," roared Shakespeare's Marc Antony. Something tells me he wasn't talking about 19-year-old girls. "Let the dogs loose," read a piece of locker-room samizdat (observed by writer Kathy Dobie) at a coed basic training program in Florida. Men ache to unleash their dogs of war. Women generally have to be exhorted or trained to—then, good students and employees that they are, they can probably manage a semblance of dogginess at least for a while. But do we really want them to? Can a man of say, 35, be trained not to stay his hand when he needs to send a 20-year-old girl onto a mortar-strafed field? Can the impulse which, still, impels men to try to protect women be overridden? Do we want it to be? Won't sex always gum up the works? Would we really prefer if it didn't?

Stephanie Gutmann is a writer living in New York.

Advertising, Sexuality, and Sexism: A Slide Show Spotlights Gender Issues

Robert Jensen, Ph.D.

Participants in my classes and workshops about sexuality and the media often make comparisons between pornographic materials and advertising. Why pick on the sexually explicit, some ask, when mainstream advertising is so similar?

There are lots of reasons to "pick on" the intentional eroticization of domination and submission.[1] But the point is well taken. Misogyny is obvious in advertisements even if it is not as intense. The pornographic continuum in American culture is definitely alive and well in mainstream media—particularly in advertisements.

These discussions sparked me to develop a slide show about gender and sexuality in advertising for classes and public presentations to illustrate how the feminist critique helps us understand not only contemporary advertising in the United States but also the larger patriarchal sexual system.

MEDIA, GENDER, AND CULTURE

I introduce my slide show by making a few basic assertions about gender and the role of media in contemporary culture:

- **Advertisers do not have exceptional powers to influence people.** They are taken seriously because they take their image-making seriously enough to spend billions of dollars each producing and circulating their messages.

- **Advertisers did not invent sexism.** But some advertisers (as well as some producers of television programs, movies, and erotica) keep sexist images and ideas in circulation, and help maintain a male dominant system.

- **There is no conspiracy among the producers of media products to produce oppressive images of women.** Advertisers simply use codes and conventions that have developed over time, drawing on an existing ideology that is institutionalized (and replicated through widely accepted institutions and practices).

- **Photographs, like any form of human communication, require interpretation, and people's readings of advertisements may differ.** One person may suggest that a photograph carries a certain meaning. Another may read it differently. Both can be right. The goal is a conversation about meaning, not an imposition of a definitive judgment about meaning.

- **The meaning of any single image is formed in part by that image's place in a wider system.** Advertisements, like any cultural artifact, must be analyzed in context. Images of women, men, and sexuality are viewed in a patriarchal world. The wider cultural meaning of sexuality and gender is crucial to understanding any single image.[2]

I conclude my introduction by making it clear that the slide show is based on a feminist critique, which asserts that cultural aspects of sexuality are a key site for the dominance of males and the subordination of females (which is part of a larger system of social, political, and economic subordination[3]). The most important components are compulsory heterosexuality, the eroticization of domination and submission, the normalization of aggression, and the sexualization/objectification of women.

From *Siecus Report* (Sexuality Information and Education Council of the United States) (June/July 1996, Vol. 24, No. 5), pp. 10–12.

CODES AND CONVENTIONS FOR DEPICTING WOMEN

The thesis of my slide show—which is based on an analysis of images from a variety of news and opinion, fashion, lifestyle, and women's magazines—is not that every representation of women in advertising is sexist, but that there are ways in which women are depicted that men are not. There is a pattern to the way in which gender and sexuality are represented; all images don't fit the pattern, but the pattern exists.

The show moves from the subtle to the more blatant, beginning with an analysis of codes and conventions of advertising photography borrowed in part from Erving Goffman[4] and informed by the work of Jean Kilbourne[5]:

- *the feminine touch:* women touching themselves in a delicate manner that can suggest fragility, daintiness, or sexiness;
- *unstable and/or vulnerable positions:* women standing on one foot with the knee bent and/or with arms above their heads;
- *subordinate or provocative body positions:* women on their knees or lying down;
- *facial expressions:* women striking the sultry, seductive look or the staring-off-into-space look of psychological withdrawal.

The slides themselves also show how women are placed within the frame of the photograph, often constructed as objects to be viewed, either by men in the photograph or implicitly by the reader. They also show more blatant ways in which women's bodies are used in advertisements as little more than props for selling products. Witness the common photograph of a half-naked woman posing provocatively to sell jeans, cars, alcohol, and a host of other products.

The show also includes slides of men in advertisements to remind the audience that the photographic conventions commonly used to depict women are rarely used for men. In fact, the images of men convey strength, competence, and control. These gender differences are made clear through slides of pairs of advertisements for the same product or company, one showing a woman and one showing a man. The routine objectification and sexualization of women provide a stark contrast to the depictions of men. The slides go on to illustrate the more explicit sexualization of women, including standard pornographic depictions of them as animal-like, as nymphomaniacs, as prudish (requiring male prodding to be sexual), or

"Ideas about what is sexy are . . . cultural constructions open to critique and challenge."

as physically controlled (by men). In many of these slides, women are in various stages of undress or in positions that suggest sexual availability.

These depictions of gender and sexuality often go unnoticed; the patterns are commonplace and often invisible unless viewed with a critical eye. Here are some detailed examples from the slide show:

- An advertisement for Johnnie Walker Red liquor shows two men in casual clothing sitting on a sand dune, talking about a woman not in the frame. The caption reads, "She looks even better when she's walking toward you. And she drinks Johnnie Walker Red." The men are the sexual subjects who watch an object, the woman off camera. Her prime attribute, in addition to her choice of alcohol, is her appearance. In another advertisement in the same series, two women in long dresses sit at a bar, giggling, with their faces partly obscured as they lean toward each other. The cut of the dresses allows their legs to be prominently displayed. The caption reads, "He's not married or anything. And he drinks Johnnie Walker Red." Here, the women again are the sexual objects, posed in a manner that displays their bodies. The man's body is not discussed; his prime attribute is that he is available for marriage.

- In an advertisement for Jordache clothing, three men clown around with a woman in a convertible sports car. The woman is reclining in the back seat with her legs up over the front seat. One of the men sits behind her on top of the back seat, holding her arms above and behind her head. The other two men sit on the top of the windshield looking down. The positions of the people are important. The woman's legs are spread and she is restrained from behind. She appears to be laughing, although sunglasses make it hard to read her expression. The men are laughing or grinning. She looks off into the distance while the men gaze directly at her. While this is not a picture of a gang rape, the position of the participants in a gang rape might look very similar. The role and status of each person in the advertisement is cued by expression, body position, and position within the frame.

- The main photo in an advertisement for Lagerfeld, "the sexy new men's fragrance," shows a man photographing a woman who holds a towel around herself, her breasts nearly exposed. She has the standard sultry expression. Three smaller photos at the bottom of the advertisement show her running through the room, still wrapped in the towel, as if she is being pursued; fully dressed and applying makeup in front of a mirror with the man watching; and cornered by the man as his arms pin her against the wall. The themes of pursuit, voyeurism, and the threat of violence give the advertisement, in the words of a woman who saw the slide show, a "creepy feel." Though these images are not overtly violent and do not depict sexual activity, they are encoded with male dominance, female submission, sex as conquest, and sex as the acquisition of pleasure.

- The slide show concludes with a series of close-ups of women's facial expressions, some taken from advertisements and some from pornography. The first time through the slides, I don't label the source of the image. The second time, I reveal the magazine in which each appeared (*Cosmopolitan, Vanity Fair,* and *The New York Times Magazine;* and *Playboy* and *Gallery*). This leads to a discussion of the pornographic continuum: mainstream advertisements don't look exactly like sexually explicit pornography, but they often draw on the same concept of women as objects to be used for sex. So, the sultry facial expression that conveys sexuality works just as well in an advertisement as in a pornographic magazine.

MAKING SENSE OF THE IMAGES

Two responses to this slide show are common.

First, some women get angry. Seeing these advertisements in a critical framework sparks a recognition of the way the images have affected their lives. Women talk about being tired of men treating them as sexual objects and about spending their lives trying to achieve a certain beauty standard.[6]

Second, others—both male and female suggest that I am reading too much into the advertisements or, if my reading of them is sensible, that I am making too big of a deal out of it. They say: sexual attraction is normal; men like to look at women; women like for men to look at them. In short, it's no big deal, so lighten up. My response is that the issue is not whether human beings are sexual but how a society constructs the meaning of sexuality and channels sexual desire. Specific sexual practices and ideas about what is sexy are not "natural" but are cultural constructions open to critique and challenge.

Another point often raised is that men's sexuality and men's bodies increasingly are being exploited in advertisements, especially by such companies as Calvin Klein. While that is true, the slide show is based on a pattern, not a few rogue images. Some advertisers are using men in non-traditional ways, but such depictions are not the norm. Also important is the societal context in which those images appear. If men and women do not have the same power in society, similar depictions of men and women will not necessarily mean the same thing or have the same effect. In patriarchy, men in the world are not sexual objects, and the objectification of them in advertisements does not change that. Beyond that, I point out that a radical feminist critique of sexuality helps us understand why treating men like women in this context is not progress. Objectifying men and commodifying male sexuality does not lead us away from a patriarchal sexual system that eroticizes domination and submission. Nor does it help us move toward the eroticization of equality.

This slide show offers a critique of our existing sexual ethic. I ask people not just to accept an analysis of particular images in advertisements, but to ask difficult questions about their own sexuality and how it has been shaped by a patriarchal society.[7] That is a question that this society is generally not comfortable answering, but one that people cannot afford to ignore.

REFERENCES

1. A. Dworkin, *Pornography: Men Possessing Women* (New York: Plume, 1989).
2. G. Dines and J. M. Humez, eds., *Gender, Race and Class in Media: A Text-Reader* (Thousand Oaks, CA: Sage, 1995).
3. M. Frye, *Willful Virgin* (Freedom, CA: Crossing Press, 1992); S. Jeffreys, *Anticlimax: A Feminist Perspective on the Sexual Revolution* (New York: New York University Press, 1990).
4. E. Goffman, *Gender Advertisements* (New York: Harper & Row, 1976).
5. J. Kilbourne, *Still Killing Us Softly: Advertising's Image of Women* (Cambridge: Cambridge Documentary Film, 1987).
6. N. Wolf, *The Beauty Myth* (New York: William Morrow, 1991).
7. R. Jensen, "Patriarchal Sex," *International Journal of Sociology and Social Policy* (in press).

A Peace Plan for the Gender Wars

By Mark B. White, Ph.D., and Kirsten J. Tyson-Rawson, Ph.D.

Do you and your mate argue (covertly) over who is right?
Do you have unspoken expectations about how affection should be expressed?
Say hello to the Gendergram. It's not something you send.
It's a way to uncover the hidden beliefs that make you struggle as you do.

It's 6:00 P.M. in the Barnett household. Alex and Susan have been home from work for about 15 minutes. It's Alex's turn to cook dinner. But the only thing steaming in the kitchen is Susan.

Alex has just hung up from ordering a pizza—for the third time this month. When it's her turn for dinner, Susan tries to prepare something nutritious, varied, and low in fat. She wants their five-year-old daughter, Eliza, to learn to eat healthy at a young age. Alex scoffs at her concern: "Eating pizza for dinner is not going to warp her for life!"

After arguing the point for minutes, Susan realizes there is more to it than meets the eye. "Its not the pizza—its just that you always take the easy way out when you have to help out around here."

Alex snaps back: "Why are you always criticizing how I do things? Practically all I ever hear from you is that I never do enough around here and the things I do do are never good enough. I do plenty around here that I never get any credit for!"

More than likely, this interchange sounds familiar. We live in a time where gender-based roles are changing and few pathways are marked as we try to figure out the right way to make our lives work in relationships. What complicates gender relations is that the world we inhabit today would have been almost impossible to envision even 40 years ago.

Gender relations in contemporary society present a seemingly paradoxical picture. On one hand, we are told that women and men are rapidly becoming equal partners at home and in the workplace. With women and men moving into each other's traditional spheres, it would seem logical that we would finally be able to understand each other's experiences. Women have now had to compete day in and day out to financially support their family. They have set their sights on many of the same goals as their male counterparts; today there are, for example, more women than men in many university professional schools. Surely women can now understand the societal pressures to succeed that have always burdened their husbands.

As wives have moved in even greater numbers into the workforce, husbands have had to take on more of women's traditional responsibilities for child care and homemaking It would seem they can now understand the magnitude of these responsibilities, the never-ending routine of care and crisis.

On the other hand, we are told that our social experiences are separated by light years and we need a manual to decode what we say to one another. At the same time, the media delivers daily body counts in the gender wars in stories of spouse abuse, divorce, child custody battles, and disputes over affirmative action.

What has not changed, apparently, over the past 40 years is the desire of men and women to figure out what is appropriate for their own and the other gender—and to find ways to live together. What has

From *Psychology Today* (March/April, 1996), pp. 51–54, 74, 78, 80, 82. Reprinted by permission of Mark B. White, Ph.D., a marriage and family therapist, and faculty member in the Dept. of Human Development and Family Studies at Auburn University and Kirsten J. Tyson-Rawson, Ph.D., Assistant Professor, Clinical Faculty, Marriage and Family Therapy Program, Dept. of Child Development and Family Relations, East Carolina University, Greenville, NC.

Questions for the Gendergram

1. In what ways have these people had a lasting influence on how you view yourself as a woman or man?

2. How did changes in your physical appearance, whether due to maturation, accidents, or illness, influence how you felt about yourself as a man or woman?

3. What did you learn about your sexuality during this time? How did you learn it?

4. In what ways did what you learn impact your definition of yourself as a woman or man?

5. What spiritual/religious influences were important to you at this time and how have they informed your feelings about yourself as a man or woman?

6. Describe the emotional climate of your home during this time?

7. How was affection expressed between women? Between men? Between women and men? Between parents/adults and children?

8. How was conflict handled?

9. Did men and women express the same emotions differently?

10. How secure did you feel when you were at home?

11. How was conformity to your family's gender norms rewarded? How was nonconformity punished?

12. What did men/women in your family do at this time in the family? At work? In the community? For recreation? As disciplinarians? In general?

changed is that we are now less sure about what is the right way to be a man or a woman.

And so you, both of us, and Alex and Susan all wrestle with gender issues on a daily basis. At the end of last year, Susan was promoted to vice president of the bank for which she works. She now makes more money than Alex, who is a chemist with a large producer of agricultural products. Under intense pressure to maintain the profitability of the bank's investments, Susan often works long hours. She drives herself hard to exceed expectations for her. Alex has had to pick up the slack at home. When he was under considerable pressure in the first few years of his career, Susan pulled the heavier load at home. Accordingly, both he and Susan have greater empathy for each other's worlds, although at times empathy isn't enough to bridge the gulf between reality and expectations.

To a large degree, the ambiguity everyone's feeling about gender is part of a greater uncertainty about what is real, true, and right in general. Human relations and the search for identity, which translates into ways of believing and being, have grown particularly complicated courtesy of the technological explosion and information saturation we all now experience. Through it, we are exposed to much information and many people in fragmented contexts. As Kenneth Gergen points out in *The Saturated Self* (Basic Books, 1992), we each have multiple selves—the person we are with our boss, the person we are with our peers or subordinates, the roles we play at home, the image we communicate over the telephone, or via anonymous contacts on the Internet.

The Gendergram Form

Name:_____   **Date:**_____   **Same / Other**

Relevant Information   **Life Cycle Stage**   **Roles / Patterns / Themes**

Childhood

Adolescence

Adulthood I

Adulthood II

This process is further compounded by the challenges in society to many of the beliefs that we have held as self-evident for so long about gender differences, religion, boundaries between the races, to name a few. As Gergen observes, "Gender is but one of the traditional categories of self-identification that now deteriorates." That encompasses not only the belief in two genders but in notions of masculinity and femininity. Result: rampant confusion about how men and women are supposed to act in the 90s.

Recently, the Barnetts went shopping for a new car for Susan. Once it became clear who would be driving the car, the salesperson spoke almost exclusively with her. Although it made perfect sense to Alex, it irritated him to no end. He was fuming as they left the dealership but couldn't really give Susan a good reason why. For him, the act of buying a car has gender-role expectations attached to it that he did not even recognize.

HOW ROLES ARE BRED

What we call "gender" encompasses biological sex but goes beyond it to the socially prescribed roles deemed appropriate for each sex by the culture in which we live. Complicating the issue is that only the broad outlines of gender roles are drawn by the larger society. The gender roles we each carry out are highly individualistic, built on our biological and physical makeup, appearance and personality, life experiences such as work and education, and history of sexual and romantic interactions. Each element influences how others perceive us as a man or a woman and how we perceive others' intentions and expectations for us.

What's more, the religious beliefs we do—or do not—espouse, our ethnic inheritances, the degree to which experiences with peers affect us, and the role models to which we are exposed, as well as personal factors, are all filtered through and shaped by our experiences in the most complex club to which we each belong, our family of origin. If we ever hope to untangle the gender-role beliefs that today tie our relationships in knots, we must examine our experiences in the primary context of socialization, the nuclear family.

One of the first things we ask when a child is born is "Is it a girl or a boy?" Most of us find it extremely difficult to talk about another person—even an infant—without referring to "he" or "she." Gender is one of the first things each of us learns about ourself as a young child, and the gender roles that we learn in

Susan's Childhood

Name: Susan Barnett	Date: 11/30/95	Same/<u>Other</u>
Relevant Information	**Life Cycle Stage**	**Roles/Patterns/Themes**

- Born in Sacramento, CA.
- Mom worked part-time three evenings/week; Dad managed house then.
- Both parents took care of house and yard. Dad taught me how to cook.
- Loved brother, James, four years older; nice to me most of the time.
- Grandpa Richards lived across the country; he and Grandma visited every year; he spoiled me.
- Had good friend, Ricky. After age eight, other kids teased us for spending time together; we stopped doing things together.
- Too private trumpet lessons. Teacher, Mr. Cosini, was very strict, really pushed me to excel. I did.
- My parents, especially Dad, were proud of me when I did well, disappointed when I didn't. So I tried to do my best to please him.

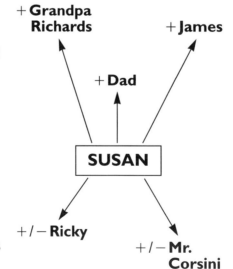

- Men share in managing household responsibilities and child care.
- Men are nurturing.
- Men treat women as equals and with respect.
- Beyond a certain age, boys and girls tend not to get along.
- Men encourage women to do their best.

our families continue to develop as we grow. We begin taking in elements of gender roles from significant others from the time we're born. These ideas are incorporated into our individual sense of self and assumptions about how men and women—both ourself and others—ought to believe and behave. We learn what is expected of each of us not only from what others teach us directly but also from how we are treated, disciplined, nurtured, and loved.

What we learn about gender organizes our behavior, our beliefs, and our relationships, including our expectations of how our partner should behave. We judge whether or not we are loved by whether our partners love us in the way we believe love ought to be shown, which is based on what we experienced in our family of origin. In a recent marital therapy session, Susan remarked that she was unsure some days whether Alex really loved her. He shot back, "Of course I do, I'm here, aren't I?" "Yes," Susan said, "but you don't seem to enjoy being with me unless you want sex." Hurt and frustrated, Alex sighed, "I go to work, I help with the house and Eliza, I'm faithful to you—all that means I love you!" Life experiences have given each of them unspoken scripts, highly idiosyncratic, defining how men and women should, and do, express love to their partners.

Solving the Barnett's problems would be easier if all men behaved one way and all women another. But no one can predict how any two people will react to each other's ideas about gender until they interact with each other. It is the interaction of roles and expectations that creates all the heat.

Despite their struggles over housework, Susan and Alex are compatible in their approach to parenting. They each had nurturing adults of both genders in their life. Each provides Eliza with ample expressions of love and affection. Their gender-role expectations for fathers and mothers fit.

TOO CLOSE TO SEE

Gender is so basic to our assumptions about who we are and how we and others should behave that we are seldom aware that gender-related experiences influence and shape the ways we think about others and ourselves. Our beliefs—typically experienced as "oughts" and shoulds"—nevertheless guide our behavior, establishing the nature of the interaction in intimate relationships without our conscious awareness.

Into our basic sense of ourself as man or woman, our so-called gender-role identity, we also incorporate boundaries, experienced as "dos" and "don'ts" as in "I could never do that." The oughts and shoulds and the dos and don'ts of gender beliefs are played out as hidden forces in intimate relationships, invisible because they are so central to our sense of who we are. Yet they typically act up in emotionally volatile situations—those times when what we are really doing is fighting to enforce our role beliefs in the relationship. The heat is intense because to give up the fight is to give up a part of the self. We look to our partners to meet our needs in the ways we each think they should be met because that is what each of us feels we need to have our perception of self validated.

Gender beliefs carry special power because couples don't talk about the assumptions that fuel arguments. To a large degree we may not really understand what the passion is all about. As therapists, we believe it crucial that couples do understand what the passion is all about. That allows partners to discuss the deeper issues—rarely the content of arguments but the process, the patterns by which they air or do not air mismatched gender beliefs.

Of course not all the issues that arise between partners are gender-related. But gender-role beliefs, being so primary to our identity, are the axis along which we organize what we perceive about our own and our partner's behavior. Gender is typically such an obvious characteristic, and one so basic to the ways we interact with others, that we not only look at our partner as an individual but, at times, as a prototypical member of the Other Gender; we attach to the individual what we have come to believe about the group.

As the intimate representative of the Other Gender in our lives, our partners routinely ignite in us old loves, desires, hurts, fears, and traumas. These surface especially in issues related to who is in control, who makes decisions about sex, money, children, and housework, and whether or not we are each loved by the other. But they could show up anywhere, depending on the unique gender-socialization histories of the two parties. Any issue, for a particular couple could be a gender issue—say, who cleans up after dinner—while that same problem would not be a gender issue for another couple.

We typically don't ask what it means to our partner that the dishes aren't done or that one earns more money than the other or that one is responsible for finding baby-sitters. But even if we did, our partner might not know how to respond, so embedded are gender influences in a sense of self. A woman may assume that because she is the mother, and therefore primarily responsible for the children, she will need to find a baby-sitter if neither spouse is available to take care of the children. A man may not share his fears about financial problems because he assumes that the man is the person who should solve financial problems.

Alex's Childhood

Name: Alex Barnett   **Date: 11/30/95**   <u>Same</u>/Other

Relevant Information	Life Cycle Stage	Roles/Patterns/Themes
• Born in Columbus, OH. • Family moves soon after to Cleveland because of Dad's new job. • Spent a lot of time with Grandpa Barnett as we lived just down the street from them. We were very close. • Dad very busy with his new job, didn't see him much. • Enjoyed visits by Uncle Karl; he was so crazy, although I didn't get to spend as much time with him as I would have liked. • My cousin Michael was my hero; he died when I was nine in an automobile accident. He tried to outrun a train in his sports car.	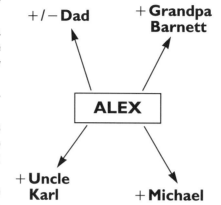	• Men aren't home much. • Men contribute to their family by working hard and providing for them. • Men don't do housework. • Older men are free to be nurturant and care for children. • Men take risks. • Sometimes men's risk taking is fun, other times stupid and dangerous. • Men are often rowdy, loud, and fun to be with.

Even harder to discuss are gender-related experiences that have more to do with emotions than behavior. Couples often fight about who does what, but the fights may really be about feelings—what doing or not doing the tasks, spending time together or not spending time together, making love or not making love means to each partner emotionally.

Susan and Alex struggle with communicating affection and love. Alex is sometimes insecure in the relationship, requiring lots of verbal and physical expressions of affection. His parents did not have a good marriage and his romantic relationships prior to marriage were not very satisfying. Although Susan has no problem being expressive, she has come to realize that she expects men in relationships not to be so emotionally needy; she is in fact irritated when Alex acts this way. But the minute they try to talk about it, they usually end up fighting about the proper way to show affection, rather than discussing what giving and affection means to them.

Indeed, gender beliefs—dos and don'ts, oughts and shoulds—may actively prevent us from expressing what we want. A man who feels sad and lonely may hesitate to ask his partner to hold and comfort him because he may fear she will see him as less of a man. And he may be right; she may hold beliefs dictating that a man does not require comforting. Still, because of his fears he may be cutting himself off from needed nurturance that is readily available.

A woman may be angry with her partner but fear that he will see her as offensive if she expresses that anger directly. He might, but he also might be relieved to know precisely what he did to upset her rather than feel he has done something wrong—if only he could figure out what it is.

ENTER THE GENDERGRAM

As family therapists facing couples with seemingly insurmountable differences, and as individuals dealing with colleagues, friends, and our own intimate partnerships, we have struggled with these issues. No matter the content or the setting, what we have come to call the "bloody gender wars" always seemed to involve beliefs and expectations about what men and women should do.

We came to believe that what we needed was not only to find a way to identify gender beliefs that influenced interaction but to create awareness of why these beliefs were so important to the person who held them. That is, by making gender influences overt and therefore open to scrutiny we could be more objective about the struggles of both genders and pass this attitude or understanding on to our clients. Instead of arguing covertly over who was right, we wanted our clients to understand the process through which deeply held, but often latent, beliefs drove arguments about the way things ought to be.

To do this, we needed to find a way each partner could explore personal beliefs without fearing judgment. We wanted to help people understand the role of these beliefs in their lives, not debate the validity of these beliefs. We developed the Gendergram, a do-it-yourself exercise for making overt the hidden values, beliefs, role expectations, and assumptions about gender that we absorb during life and deploy in intimate relationships.

In the classic Frank Capra film *It's a Wonderful Life*, Jimmy Stewart's character, George Bailey, gets the opportunity to observe how other's lives would have been had he not been there. The Gendergram allows the reverse: you examine the impact significant others have had on you and your gender identity.

Your (Fill in the Blank) Life

A look at the Gendergrams of Alex and Susan suggest how to complete your own.

Step One: Divide a blank sheet of paper into three columns:

Relevant Information
Life Cycle Stage
Roles/Patterns/Themes.

Step Two: Separate your life into meaningful stages: childhood, adolescence, and one or more adult stages. The number of stages is entirely personal, depending on the events of your life.

Step Three: Beginning with the first stage of your life, write your name in the center of the middle column. Next, place around you the names of significant same-sex individuals in your life at that stage (it's important to examine relationships with people of the same gender before those of the other gender). You can represent their importance to you by how close to your name you put them.

Connect each of these people to you with a line. Place a plus sign (+) by the connecting line if the person had a positive influence on you, a negative sign (−) if the person had a negative influence, both signs (+/−) by the line if the person's influence on you was essentially neutral.

When Alex filled out the same-sex Gendergram for his childhood (see box), he identified four significant males: his father, grandfather Barnett, uncle Karl, and cousin Michael. The latter three had a more positive effect on him; his father's impact he cited as essentially neutral.

Step Four: Under Relevant Information, list the significant life events that occurred during that stage of your life. What happened to you and your family—births, deaths, moves, divorce?

Briefly describe the nature of your relationships with each of the key people named in the center column.

Step Five: Reflect on what each of the significant people in your life at this stage taught you about being a woman or a man. Responding to the following questions about each person should help:

What explicit "gendered" rules did this person share with you ("Good girls act like this . . .", "Boys don't do that!," "Young ladies don't do that!")?

What did you learn about men and women from watching this person (men do this, women do that, men don't do this, etc.)?

By observing how this person functioned in relationships, what did you learn about men and women (such as, who takes greater emotional responsibility for the relationship, who initiates activities, who has the final say in mutual decisions)?

How did the way this person treated you influence your beliefs about men and women (for example, men are noncommunicative, women are nurturing, women are seductive, men are playful and boisterous)?

Summarize the information in the Roles/Themes/Patterns column. Based on your experiences with these people at this stage of life, what did you learn about the roles of men and women? What themes were present in your beliefs about men and women? What patterns were present in your significant relationship at that time?

In childhood, Alex had pretty traditional male role models and thus was exposed to predictable themes and patterns: Men's work absorbs their time and attention; men are not actively involved in their children's lives; men are rough, fun to be with, daring. Such roles can be dangerous, as Alex learned through the death of his cousin. But through his relationship with his grandfather, he experienced a caring, nurturing man. He has relied on what he learned in that relationship for his role as a father.

The questions (in the Gendergram box) can help you flesh out the information. Remember to focus only on same-sex information right now.

Step Six: Repeat steps three through five for the remaining stages of your life, again focusing only on same-sex individuals. Use additional sheets of paper as necessary.

Step Seven: Complete steps one through six for the significant other-sex individuals in your life. In Susan's other-sex Gendergram (see box), we can see the somewhat nontraditional arrangement her parents had and its impact on her expectations for the division of labor in the home. She expected that her husband would take an active role in household tasks and child care.

Step Eight: This is likely the single most important step. Examine the Roles/Patterns/Themes column for both your same-sex and other-sex Gendergrams.

As you reflect on the gendered messages you learned across the stages of your life, note those roles, patterns, and themes that are operating in your life and relationships today. What are the consequences of each for your own well-being and for your relationship(s)? Which aspects of your gender identity and functioning in relationships do you want to continue? Which aspects do you want to modify or discontinue? How will you do so? Make a plan of action today.

As we developed the Gendergram, one of our basic assumptions was that we were not the experts on other people's gender-role expectations and behavior in relationships, they are. However, we did want people to examine the benefits and costs of the beliefs they hold and the behaviors they demonstrate.

GENDER MENDING

The bottom line is really What is working for you, and what isn't? What changes will you need to make so that your relationship works for you? As Alex completed his Gendergram, he was more aware of the impact of his significant relationships on his gender-role behaviors and expectations. He and Susan have tried to create a marital relationship that is very different from the one his parents had. Lacking close experience with an egalitarian partnership, he struggles at times to do his share. The Barnetts have a part-time housekeeper for the deep cleaning, but they share the light housework, cooking, and laundry.

Alex has since agreed to do all the grocery shopping and to prepare healthy meals when it's his turn to cook. He has also struggled to do his part in the emotional maintenance of the relationship. His usual response to conflict is to take distance and then wait for Susan to seek reconciliation. He set a goal to take more responsibility for making up after arguments and to nurture the relationship by not allowing conflicts to drag on into the next day, initiating two dates a month, and spending more time with Susan by watching one less television program each evening.

After examining her Gendergram, Susan realized that her drive to excel at work was in part a vestige of trying to please her father. Her brother James has not been successful in his chosen career, and it seems as if her father has transferred his aspirations for the success of his children onto her. He was extremely pleased when she was promoted to VP. Susan has begun to wonder if she is driving herself harder than necessary to succeed, She is feeling physically stressed and believes it is compromising the quality of her marriage and her parenting. Accordingly, she has decided to begin an exercise program two days a week, to leave work one hour early whenever possible, to take a couple of afternoons off per month to

spend with Eliza, and to plan a weekend getaway with Alex as soon as possible.

TWO CAN PLAY

If you are currently in a relationship, then the critical portion of the Gendergram exercise involves discussion of the results with your partner. We know from our clinical experience that couples find the Gendergram very useful. As partners discuss each other's Gendergram, they gain a better understanding of why their partner acts as he or she does.

Much research on marital interaction focuses on the role of attribution—our personal theories or explanations for why our partner does as he or she does. Couples who make neutral or positive attributions about each other's behavior generally enjoy greater marital satisfaction than those who make negative attributions. The Gendergram can aid and abet this process. Understanding the messages our partner received while growing up and their lasting impact allows us to make more benign attributions of their behavior.

Take, for example, a situation marital therapists commonly encounter. Suppose that your partner frequently pursues you when you "need space." You may think he or she is overly needy, insecure, a "control freak." But if the Gendergram reveals that your partner has been abandoned by several significant people in life and believes that "men/women get close to you and then abandon you," he or she is probably experiencing distressing feelings that have been associated with abandonment in the past. The next time your partner pursues, you may want to ask him/her what he/she is feeling at the time and how the two of you can handle it differently.

When Susan and Alex sat down to discuss their Gendergrams, they were able to point to several sources of current difficulties. They each had different role expectations for husbands and fathers that crept into their struggle over the division of labor. The men and women in their respective families of origin expressed emotion and affection in differing ways. Yet in both of their families the emotional management of relationships was a task for the women—something Susan and Alex wanted to change in their own house. As a result of their discussion, they were less hostile to each other the next time they hit a snag on household tasks or making up after a fight. They agreed to view each other as having had different life experiences and different expectations. This helped them refrain from viewing the other as being difficult and negative on purpose. They divided up the household chores and agreed on standards of completion.

They settled on creating a role of "conflict manager," whose job it was to call time out when arguments heated up and ask what the other was thinking—without attacking the conflict manager. It was awkward at first, but they decided to alternate this role—Alex was conflict manager on even-numbered days, Susan on odd days.

The Gendergram lets spouses work as a team at deciding what roles/patterns/themes are good for the relationship and which are destructive. This helps a couple address difficult issues proactively, when they are calm, rather than react in the middle of an argument.

Of course, knowledge alone is insufficient to change behavior; otherwise no one would smoke and we'd all exercise and eat a healthy diet. More often than not it takes a pivotal experience to convince us to change. Nevertheless, gaining knowledge about our behavior is an important first step. The Gendergram gives couples information about their gender-related assumptions and behavior that they can examine, poke and prod, and make decisions about.

AFTERPLAY

We hope that after completing the Gendergram, people probe each gender-related assumption, value, and behavior and ask: Do I want to continue believing and/or acting this way? If not, what will I do to change? If so, how can I enhance this part of my life?

We should make clear that, despite the current ambiguity about gender roles—and their pervasiveness in our lives—clashing gender-role expectations are not the only underlying factor in marital strife, and each couple's assortment of gender-related challenges is unique. Nor can the Gendergram help individuals or couples up against forces of the larger society—like sexual harassment at the workplace. Nevertheless, we believe there is room for optimism. If men and women are willing to invest in their own personal growth and in their relationships, things will get better. We introduced the Gendergram as a means to this end.

Men's Perceptions of Their Roles and Responsibilities Regarding Sex, Contraception and Childrearing

William R. Grady, Koray Tanfer, John O. G. Billy and Jennifer Lincoln-Hanson

Data from the 1991 National Survey of Men examine men's perceptions about their roles in relation to those of women in a couple's decision-making about sex, contraception and the rearing of children. A majority of men (61%) perceive that there is gender equality in sexual decision-making, and more than three-quarters (78%) believe that men and women share equal responsibility for decisions about contraception. However, men are three times as likely to say that women play a greater role in a couple's decisions about sex as they are to believe that men have the greater voice (30% compared with 9%). In contrast, men are more than twice as likely to perceive that men have a greater responsibility in contraceptive decisions as they are to say that women do (15% compared with 7%). Finally, 88% of men strongly agree that a man has the same responsibilities as a woman for the children they have together.

(Family Planning Perspectives, 28:221–226, 1996)

Men's involvement in decisions about sex, contraception and childrearing strongly influences sexual and contraceptive behavior,[1] significantly strengthens and reduces discord in relationships,[2] and reinforces a man's responsibility for the children he fathers.[3] Few studies, though, have investigated men's perceptions of their roles and responsibilities regarding decisions about sex, contraception and the raising of children. Furthermore, only recently has such research been identified as being important. High levels of nonmarital childbearing, growing concern about the spread of AIDS and other sexually transmitted diseases (STDs) and the concomitant increase in the prophylactic use of condoms has led developers of social policy to include men in efforts to prevent pregnancy and STDs. However, most investigations of men's perceptions about their roles and responsibilities have targeted adolescents and other groups of young, unmarried males. Thus, we have little understanding of how married or older men perceive their roles in these decisions.

Current trends in contraceptive method choice suggest that male-controlled methods are increasingly popular. Indeed, the recent rise in contraceptive use among young, unmarried couples is due almost entirely to an increase in the rate of condom use.[4] By 1988, about one-third of married couples were using male methods of contraception, including sterilization,[5] while in a 1991 study, 39% of single men aged 20–39 reported using a condom in the four weeks prior to being interviewed.[6] Clearly, men have an important role in decision-making regarding contraception and family planning.

Research indicates that there has been an increase in the extent to which family planning is considered a joint responsibility. In a study conducted during the 1970s,[7] only about one-third of adolescent males thought that men and women should be equally responsible for contraception. However, by the late 1980s, more than two-thirds of young men endorsed this belief.[8] Moreover, in the later study, substantially more males thought contraception was solely a male

---

*For a detailed description of the survey and its design, see K. Tanfer, "National Survey of Men: Design and Execution," Family Planning Perspectives, 25:83–86, 1993.

responsibility than thought it a female responsibility. While several other studies have shown that adult males tend to view contraception as a shared decision,[9] only one examined factors that predict such a view: Married men who were older and those who held more egalitarian attitudes were more likely to think that men and women have a shared responsibility for contraception.[10]

There is currently renewed interest in the role of the father in family life, and this is especially so for men raising children outside the context of a marital relationship.[11] Men's attitudes toward parenting responsibilities have a direct bearing on contraceptive behavior:[12] A man is less likely to take responsibility for effective contraception if he lacks a sense of obligation for the children that may result from his sexual behavior.[13] While a very high proportion of adolescent males think that men and women have equal responsibility for the children they have together,[14] there is growing evidence that the fathers of infants born to adolescent mothers are likely to be adults.[15]

In this study, we use data from the 1991 National Survey of Men (NSM) to examine men's perceptions about their role in a couple's decision-making about sex and contraception, as well as their beliefs about the relative responsibility of men and women for the children that they have together. We explore how a man's individual characteristics may affect his perceptions and beliefs, and identify those men who are likely to feel that they have roles and responsibilities that are greater than, less than, or equal to those of women. Examining the effects of couple characteristics on men's perceptions helps us to understand how men's views are shaped by both the nature of the relationship in which such decisions are made (e.g., marital or cohabiting) and the characteristics of their partner in that relationship.

DATA AND METHODS

Sample

The 1991 NSM is a nationally representative household survey of men aged 20–39 living in the coterminous United States. The survey was based on a stratified and clustered area probability sample design.* Black households were oversampled to ensure adequate representation. The sampling frame

contained 17,650 housing units, of which 93% were successfully screened for eligibility. A total of 3,321 in-person interviews were completed (70% of the eligible men). The sample was weighted on the basis of population statistics to account for stratification, clustering and disproportionate sampling, as well as for differential nonresponse.

Since our goal is to examine men's perceptions regarding a man's roles within a sexual relationship, the analyses are restricted to the 2,526 respondents who were in a heterosexual relationship at the time they were interviewed; furthermore, only these men were asked to provide detailed information about their partner's characteristics. Thus, the analyses that follow are based on a sample of 958 black and 1,568 white men.

Measurement

One purpose of the NSM was to develop an understanding of factors influencing a man's decisions about sex, contraception (particularly the use of condoms) and fertility. Thus, men were asked a series of questions regarding their perceptions about both men's and women's roles in these decisions. The analyses presented in this article are based on responses to the following five statements: It is generally the man who decides whether or not the couple will have sex; it is generally the woman who decides whether or not the couple will have sex; it is a woman's responsibility to make decisions about using birth control; it is a man's responsibility to make decisions about using birth control; and men have the same responsibilities as women for the children they father.

When presented with these statements, the respondents were handed a card that displayed a five-point scale (with one representing "strongly disagree," three representing "neutral" and five representing "strongly agree") to indicate their level of agreement with the statements. We cross tabulated responses to the first two statements to create a combined, three-category measure of perceptions about whether decisions about sex were male-oriented, egalitarian, or female-oriented. Men who indicated a higher level of agreement with the male-focused statement than with the female-focused statement were considered to have a male-oriented perception. Men who indicated a higher level of agreement on the female-focused statement were considered to have a female-oriented perception. Those who registered equal levels of agreement on both items were considered to have an egalitarian orientation. Thus, a respondent who disagreed with the statement that it is generally the man who decides when a couple has sex, and also disagreed

---

* The characteristics of the standard population, used for comparison purposes only, were set for the continuous variables at age 30 and 12 years of education (for both the man and his partner). For the other variables the modal categories were used. For male characteristics, these were white, non-Hispanic, not previously marred and "other Protestant" religion. For partner characteristics, these were non-Hispanic, not previously married and Protestant.

that it is generally the woman who decides, was considered to have an egalitarian orientation on the contraceptive measure. A similar procedure was used with the third and fourth statements to assess perceptions about contraceptive decision-making.

The item capturing beliefs about responsibility for the children that men and women have together is not based on a combination of two separate questions. Thus, it is not exactly comparable to the combined measures used to examine the other dimensions. Moreover, a very high proportion of men (87%) strongly agreed with the statement that men and women have the same responsibilities for their children. Thus, in the multivariate analyses, this item was collapsed into a dichotomous outcome variable (strongly agree vs. not strongly agree).

Statistical Approach

A multinomial logit regression approach was used to analyze the two combined measures.[16] This procedure provides the likelihood of being in any one category of the dependent variable for respondents in a given category of the predictor variable, relative to respondents in the reference category of that predictor. The regression models included the demographic and socioeconomic characteristics of both the men and their partners that were considered likely to influence a man's perceptions regarding sex and contraceptive decision-making. The age and education of the man and his partner, although shown as discrete categories, were included in the multivariate analyses as continuous variables. Because racial homogamy is so extensive in our sample, partner's race (black vs. white) could not be entered into the models that included the man's own race. Variables capturing couple homogamy with respect to ethnicity, education and religion were also tested for inclusion, but as none were found to be statistically significant, they were not included in the final models.

Since it is difficult to interpret the coefficients from multinomial logit models, we used the estimated coefficients to calculate standardized probabilities that men would fall into each of the three cells of either of the composite measures. Thus, for example, to examine the effect of race on perceptions of whether the man or the woman makes the decision to have sex, we show the probabilities that black men and men of other races would fall into each category of the composite measure if they did not differ with respect to the other characteristics in the model. In the analyses, we accomplished this by setting the other characteristics in the model to those of a "standard population."*

The probabilities reported in this article are therefore not the average probabilities exhibited by a group. Rather, they demonstrate how a factor such as race affects the relative scoring of the two measures when the other factors in the model are statistically controlled. For the nominal variables included in the analyses, standardized probabilities were calculated for each category of the variable. For the two age variables (man's age and partner's age), probabilities were calculated for ages 20, 30 and 40. Education variables for both the man and his partner were calculated for eight, 12, and 16 years of education.

We used a binomial logit regression to analyze the dichotomous statement regarding responsibility for children. Again, to simplify the analysis of the effects of the covariates in the model, we used the estimated coefficients to calculate the probability of strongly agreeing with the statement. These calculated probabilities were also standardized so that the independent effect of each covariate is shown.

RESULTS

The characteristics of the men and their partners are shown in Table 1. Eighty-eight percent of the men in the sample were white and 12% were black; 8% were of Hispanic origin. Thirty percent of the men were 35 and older, and 19% were in the 20–24 year age-group. Two-thirds of the men were married and living with their spouse, while 11% were cohabiting and 23% had a regular partner. Only 11% of the men in the sample had not completed high school, and 22% had completed college. One-third of the men were Catholic, 36% were nonconservative Protestant and 16% were conservative Protestant. Partners were somewhat younger than the men; 21% were 35 and older, and 25% were younger than 25. However, partners were more likely to have had a previous marriage: Twenty-one percent of the partners had been previously married, compared to only 9% of the male respondents.

Only 9% of men registered stronger agreement with the statement that it is generally the man who decides whether the couple will have sex than with the statement that it is generally the woman who decides this. In contrast, 30% reported stronger agreement with the female orientation than with the male orientation. Sixty-one percent of men registered equal levels of agreement with both statements.

Fifteen percent of men registered stronger agreement with the statement that it is a man's responsibility to make decisions about contraception than with the statement that it is a woman's responsibility to make these decisions. This is significantly higher than the 7% who indicated greater agreement with the statement that it is a woman's responsibility, and is consistent with recent research examining the perceptions

TABLE I

Percentage distribution (and unweighted Ns) of U.S. men aged 20–39 currently in a heterosexual relationship, by demographic and socioeconomic characteristics, 1991

Characteristic	%	Unweighted N
Race		
Black	12.3	958
White	87.7	1,568
Hispanic origin		
Yes	8.2	165
No	91.8	2,361
Age		
20–24	18.5	474
25–29	23.3	554
30–34	28.2	723
>35	29.9	775
Previously married		
Yes	8.7	221
No	91.3	2,305
Relationship status		
Married, living with spouse	66.0	1,602
Cohabiting	11.3	274
Regular partner	22.7	650
Education		
<high school	10.7	276
High school graduate	44.1	1,024
Some college	23.6	709
College graduate	21.6	517
Religion		
Catholic	32.6	593
Conservative Protestant	16.4	582
Other Protestant	35.9	1,006
Other/none	15.1	345
Partner's origin		
Hispanic	7.8	164
Non-Hispanic	92.2	2,362
Partner's age		
<25	25.0	638
25–29	26.1	668
30–34	27.7	677
>35	21.2	543
Partner previously married		
Yes	21.1	517
No	78.9	2,009
Partner's education		
<high school	9.9	246
High school graduate	44.0	1,060
Some college	24.7	676
College graduate	21.4	544
Partner's religion		
Catholic	33.1	615
Protestant	52.5	1,563
Other/none	11.7	254
Unknown	2.7	94
Total	**100.0**	**2,562**

of male adolescents.[17] Seventy-eight percent of respondents reported an egalitarian orientation on this measure.

Shown below are the weighted percentage distributions of responses to the two composite measures of men's perceptions:

Measure	Female oriented	Egalitarian	Male oriented
Decisions about sex	29.9	60.8	9.3
Contraception	6.5	78.2	15.2

A very high proportion of men (87%) strongly agreed with the statement that men have the same responsibility as women for the children they father, a finding that is also consistent with prior research with adolescents.[18] An additional 8% of men indicated that they somewhat agreed with the statement. In contrast, 5% of men disagreed with the statement or were neutral (not shown).

Decisions About Sex

Table 2 presents the standardized probabilities derived from the multinomial logit analysis of the composite measure on decisions about sex. Men's race, age and prior marital history had no significant impact on the relative scoring of the male and female orientations. Hispanic origin, in contrast, had a large impact. Specifically, Hispanic men were substantially more likely than non-Hispanic men to have a male-dominant scoring pattern (.20 vs. .10). They were also less likely than other men to endorse a female dominant scoring pattern (probabilities of .20 and .36, respectively).

Cohabiting males were more likely than either married men or single men with a regular partner to have a female-dominant scoring pattern (.43 vs. .36 and .35, respectively) and were less than one-half as likely to exhibit a male-dominant scoring pattern. Education was negatively related to the likelihood of scoring the two orientations equally (.61 for men with eight years of education compared with .48 for men with 16 years of education) and was positively related to the likelihood of scoring the male orientation higher: The probability that men with 16 years of education indicated greater agreement with the male orientation was twice that of the probability among those with only eight years of education (.14 vs. .06). Nonetheless, for all levels of education, men with nonegalitarian perceptions were more likely to endorse a female than a male orientation.

Among religious subgroups, Conservative Protestants had the highest probability of scoring both orientations equally (.66) and the lowest probability of

TABLE 2
Standardized probabilities, by men's orientations regarding decisions about sex and contraception, according to demographic characteristics of the respondent and his partner

Characteristic	Decisions about sex			Decisions about contraception		
	Female	Egalitarian	Male	Female	Egalitarian	Male
RESPONDENT						
Race†						
Black	.354	.570	.076	.164	.732	.105
White	.355	.550	.095	.060	.747	.194
Hispanic origin†**						
Yes	.199	.599	.202	.035	.854	.111
No	.355	.550	.095	.060	.747	.194
Age at Interview†						
20	.373	.551	.076	.033	.802	.165
30	.355	.550	.095	.060	.747	.194
40	.335	.546	.118	.106	.674	.220
Previously married†						
Yes	.338	.552	.110	.039	.838	.123
No	.355	.550	.095	.060	.747	.194
Relationship status*,‡						
Married, living with spouse	.355	.550	.095	.060	.747	.194
Cohabiting	.427	.532	.040	.056	.756	.188
Regular partner	.346	.557	.097	.028	.718	.253
Completed education (in years),‡**						
8	.326	.610	.063	.172	.682	.146
12	.355	.550	.095	.060	.747	.194
16	.376	.484	.140	.019	.747	.253
Religion,†**						
Catholic	.313	.606	.081	.048	.775	.177
Conservative Protestant	.238	.662	.099	.046	.773	.181
Other Protestant	.355	.550	.095	.060	.747	.194
Other/none	.258	.627	.116	.046	.850	.104
PARTNER						
Hispanic origin‡						
Yes	.425	.500	.075	.178	.645	.177
No	.355	.550	.095	.060	.747	.194
Age at Interview‡						
20	.358	.532	.110	.122	.668	.210
30	.355	.550	.095	.060	.747	.194
40	.351	.567	.083	.028	.801	.171
Previously married*						
Yes	.427	.493	.079	.060	.747	.192
No	.355	.550	.095	.060	.747	.194
Completed education (in years),‡**						
8	.362	.502	.136	.038	.703	.259
12	.355	.550	.095	.060	.747	.194
16	.342	.593	.066	.091	.769	.140
Religion						
Catholic	.308	.609	.083	.065	.778	.157
Protestant	.355	.550	.095	.060	.747	.194
Unknown	.288	.670	.043	.103	.616	.281
Other/none	.282	.591	.126	.108	.684	.208

Note: For decisions about sex, *=p≤ .01; for decisions about contraception, †=p≤ .01.

having a female-dominant scoring pattern (.24). For other Protestants, this pattern was reversed: These men had a probability of .55 of scoring both orientations equally, compared to a probability of .36 of having a female-dominant response pattern. Catholics were the least likely to have a male-dominant scoring pattern (.08), and those men whose religion was categorized as "other or none" were the most likely to have this pattern (.12).

Whether a man's partner was Hispanic had no significant impact on his scoring patterns. However, partner's previous marriage did influence the pattern of scores. Men with a previously married partner were less likely than men with a never-married partner to score both orientations equally (.49 compared with .55) and were more likely to have a female-dominant scoring pattern (.43 compared with .36). Men with highly educated partners were more likely than those with less educated partners to score the measures equally and less likely to exhibit a male-dominant scoring pattern. The effects of partner's religion were not statistically significant.

Decisions About Contraception

Table 2 also presents results of the analysis of the composite contraceptive responsibility measure. Black men were significantly more likely than white men to have a female-dominant scoring pattern (.16 vs. .06) and were less likely than white men to have a male-dominant scoring pattern (.11 vs. .19). Hispanic origin, in contrast, was associated with an elevated probability of egalitarian scoring and a reduced likelihood of either a male-dominant or female-dominant scoring pattern.

Older age was associated with a less egalitarian scoring pattern: The probability of scoring the two measures equally was .80 at age 20 compared with .67 at age 40. This was due primarily to an increase in the likelihood of female-dominant scoring among older men. A prior marriage was associated with an increased likelihood of having an egalitarian scoring pattern and with a decreased likelihood of a male-dominant scoring pattern. Currently married and cohabiting men were more than twice as likely as unmarried, noncohabiting men to have a female-dominant scoring pattern.

Education was positively related to the likelihood of a male-dominant scoring pattern and was negatively related to the likelihood of a female-dominant scoring pattern. For example, men with 16 years of education were much less likely than men with eight years of education to have a female-dominant scoring pattern (.02 vs. .17). Additionally, men in the category

of "other or no religion" had the lowest probability male-dominant scoring pattern.

Having a partner of Hispanic origin significantly increased the likelihood of a female-dominant scoring pattern, while having an older partner decreased the likelihood of a female-dominant scoring pattern: Thus, a man with a 40-year-old partner was only about one-fourth as likely as a man with a 20-year-old partner (.03 compared with .12) to display a female-dominant scoring pattern. Partner's age was also positively related to egalitarian scoring. Partner's education, in contrast, was positively associated with a female-dominant scoring pattern among respondents and negatively associated with a male-dominant scoring pattern.

Finally, men with Catholic partners had the highest probability of an egalitarian scoring pattern (.78), and those who did not know their partner's religion had the lowest probability of such a pattern (.62). These men also had the lowest and highest probabilities (.16 and .28, respectively) of exhibiting a male-dominant scoring pattern.

Responsibilities for Children

Table 3 presents the results of the binomial logit analysis of men's beliefs regarding responsibility for the children they father. Hispanic origin was significantly and positively related to the belief that both sexes have an equal responsibility for their children (p.<.01). Men with Hispanic partners, however, had a lower probability of strongly agreeing with the statement about equal responsibility than those whose partners were not Hispanic (.73 compared with .87, p<.01).

Men who were previously married were more likely than other men to strongly agree that both sexes have equal responsibility for their children (.94 vs. .87, p<.05). In contrast, men with previously married partners were less likely to have a strong level of agreement (.82 vs. .87, p<.05). No other characteristic of either the man or his partner had a significant impact on this belief.

Discussion

Most men perceive a couple's decision-making regarding sexual behavior and contraception as an egalitarian process. Sixty-one percent of men currently in a heterosexual relationship view decisions about sex as a shared responsibility and 78% view decisions about contraception in this way. Moreover, men are highly likely to perceive that the responsibility for children is a shared effort: Nearly 90% of men strongly endorse such a belief.

Among men who are not egalitarian in their views, decisions about sex are likely to be perceived as

TABLE 3
Standardized probabilities of men strongly agreeing that they have the same responsibility as women for their children, by demographic characteristics of the respondent and his partner

Characteristic	Probability
RESPONDENT	
Race	
Black	.844
White	.869
Hispanic origin**	
Yes	.950
No	.869
Age at interview	
20	.856
30	.869
40	.881
Previously married	
Yes	.939
No	.869
Relationship status	
Mamed, living with spouse	.869
Cohabiting	.901
Regular partner	.878
Completed education (in years)	
8	.858
12	.869
16	.879
Religon	
Catholic	.859
Conservative Protestant	.858
Other Protestant	.869
Other/none	.890
PARTNER	
HIspanic origin**	
Yes	.725
No	.869
Age at Interview	
20	.833
30	.869
40	.899
Previously married	
Yes	.818
No	.869
Completed education (in years)	
8	.861
12	.869
16	.877
Religion	
Catholic	.874
Protestant	.869
Unknown	.907
Other/none	.831

*p ≤ .05.   **p ≤ .01.

a woman's domain, whereas decisions about contraception are likely to be perceived as a man's responsibility. Men with nonegalitarian perceptions are three times as likely to have a female-dominant orientation towards sexual decisions as to express a male-dominant one, but they are twice as likely to register a male-dominant orientation toward contraceptive responsibility as to have a female-dominant view.

Race, while unrelated to the perception of either male dominance or female dominance in the sexual decision-making process, is significantly related to perceptions of relative responsibility for contraception. Black men are more likely than men of other races to view the decision to practice contraception as a woman's responsibility and less likely to view it as a man's responsibility. In comparison, men of Hispanic origin are more likely than non-Hispanics to perceive men as dominant in sexual decision-making and are also more likely than non-Hispanics to indicate that men and women have an equal responsibility regarding contraception. Being black has no significant effect on the level of agreement that both sexes share responsibilities for their children, where as Hispanic origin is related to stronger agreement in this area. Having a Hispanic partner has no impact on a man's perception of who makes decisions about sex, but it is associated with a perception that women bear a greater responsibility for the decision to use contraceptives and with lower levels of agreement that men and women have the same responsibilities for their children.

Age is unrelated to perceptions of male or female dominance in sexual decision-making. However, older men are more likely than younger men to view women as governing contraceptive decision-making. Men with older partners, in contrast, are less likely than those with younger partners to view women as controlling these decisions. This may reflect a shift by women, as they age, away from the use of oral contraceptives and toward either coitus-dependent methods or male sterilization.[19]

A man who has been previously married is more likely than other men to have egalitarian views about the responsibilities of parenthood. However, if a man's partner has been previously married, he is less likely to hold these views. This may reflect perceived differences between men and women in the kinds of experiences they have in dealing with former spouses who are the parents of their children or differences in their expectations about these experiences. Such expectations may be more salient for men who have already experienced a marital dissolution. Previously married men are also more likely to feel that there is joint responsibility in contraceptive decision-making, a relationship that may reflect prior cooperative involvement in such decisions.

Cohabiting men are less likely than their married or noncohabiting peers to view either men or women as primarily responsible for sexual decision-making. This is consistent with research indicating that those in cohabiting relationships have a less traditional sexual ideology, and that cohabiting women initiate sex more often than women in marital relationships.[20] Cohabiting men are also most likely to indicate perceived gender equality in the responsibility for contraceptive use. Unmarried, noncohabiting men, in contrast, are more likely than men in coresidential unions to indicate male dominance in contraceptive decision-making, a pattern that may reflect the greater use of condoms for disease prevention among such men.

A man's educational attainment is positively associated with his perceptions of dominance in decisions regarding both sex and contraception. Men whose partners are highly educated, however, are more likely to perceive that decisions about sex are egalitarian, and they are also more likely to perceive that women have greater responsibility in contraceptive decision-making. These findings are consistent with a relative power hypothesis that suggests that the higher the status of the man, the more likely he is to view himself as the dominant decision-maker, while the higher the status of his partner, the more likely he is to adopt a view of her as either an equal or as the dominant decision-maker.[21]

Conservative Protestants are the most likely to perceive men and women as egalitarian and the least likely to adopt a female-oriented view concerning whether a couple will have sex. This is consistent with a conservative view of gender roles and of the family, a view that increasingly accepts sexuality as a positive, mutual aspect of a marital relationship, yet still tends to favor patriarchal authority.[22] That men who are affiliated with a Christian denomination are more likely than non-Christians and those with no religious affiliation to adopt a male-dominant orientation toward contraceptive decisions may derive from proscriptions against abortion that lead such men to take greater responsibility over contraceptive decisions, to insure that an unintended pregnancy does not occur.[23]

Men who do not know their partner's religious affiliation are very likely to perceive that contraceptive use is a male responsibility. Not knowing the religious affiliation of one's partner may be an indicator of poor communication in the relationship, which also reduces the likelihood of joint decision-making.

Several issues should be kept in mind when interpreting the results presented here. The data are based on perceptions about the behaviors and responsibilities of men and women in general; men's responses therefore reflect ideology more than actual behaviors or the true division of responsibilities in their own relationships. Thus, while about 30% of the men in our sample indicated that the woman generally decides whether or not a couple will have sex, it cannot be assumed that the partners of these men actually exert greater decision-making power regarding sex. Similarly, although a very high proportion of men indicated that men and women have equal responsibility for decisions about contraceptive use, it seems unrealistic to assume that they are all involved equally with their partners in those decisions. Yet, it is likely that such attitudes and perceptions are strongly influenced by an individual's own behavior.

Personal attitudes and perceptions shape sexual and contraceptive decisions. Numerous studies have shown that a woman's partner has a major effect on her sexual, contraceptive and fertility behavior.[24] Yet partners may have appreciable differences in their sexual values, and more importantly, one partner's perception of the other's values may be inaccurate.[25] Effective contraceptive behavior may depend on joint decision-making to minimize the consequences of such misperceptions.[26]

The impact of such misperceptions extends beyond their implications for unintended pregnancy to other issues of reproductive health, including the risk of STD and HIV infection. The importance of partner influence underscores the need to include men in interventions to reduce unintended pregnancies and STDs. Yet the prevailing policy and program emphasis on women as the key figures in these decisions often unjustly and unwisely excludes men.

The results reported in this article add to our knowledge about how men perceive their role in decisions about sex and contraception, as well as how they view their parental responsibilities. They also show how men's perceptions and views are shaped by their own characteristics, the characteristics of their partner and the nature of their relationship. Despite the limitations discussed above, the information provided here is useful for understanding the sexual and contraceptive behavior of men, and instrumental for efforts to increase their participation in family planning and reproductive health decisions.

REFERENCES

1. J. Burger and H. Inderbritzen, "Predicting Contraceptive Behavior Among College Students: The Role of Communication, Knowledge, Sexual Anxiety and Self-Esteem," *Archives of Sexual Behavior*, 14:343–350, 1985; W. B. Miller, "Why Some Women Fail to Use Their Contraceptive Method: A Psychological Investigation," *Family*

Planning Perspectives, 18:27–32, 1986; J. Inazu, "Partner Involvement and Contraceptive Efficacy in Premarital Sexual Relationships," Population and Environment, 9:225–237, 1987; and M. Gerard, C. Breda and F. X. Gibbons, "Gender Effects in Couple Sexual Decision Making and Contraceptive Use," Journal of Applied Social Psychology, 20:449–464, 1990.

2. I. L. Reiss, *Journey Into Sexuality*, Prentice-Hall, Englewood Cliffs, N. J., 1986, pp. 235–236; and P. Blumstein and P Schwartz, *American Couples*, William Morrow, New York, 1983.

3. L. J. Beckman, "Husband's and Wive's Relative Influence on Fertility Outcomes," *Population and Environment*, 7:182–197, 1984.

4. F. L. Sonenstein and J. H. Pleck, "The Male Role in Family Planning: What Do We Know?" unpublished manuscript, The Urban Institute, Washington, D. C., 1994.

5. W. D. Mosher and W. F Pratt, "Use of Contraception and Family Planning Services in the United States, 1988," *American Journal of Public Health*, 80:1132–1133, 1990.

6. K. Tanfer et al., "Condom Use Among U. S. Men, 1991," *Family Planning Perspectives*, 25:61–66, 1993.

7. J. H. Pleck, F L. Sonenstein and S. O. Swain, "Adolescent Male's Sexual Behavior and Contraceptive Use: Implications for Male Responsibility," *Journal of Adolescent Research*, 3:275–284, 1975.

8. S. D. Clark, Jr., L. S. Zabin, and J. B. Hardy, "Sex, Contraception and Parenthood: Experience and Attitudes Among Urban Black Young Men," *Family Planning Perspectives*, 16:77–82, 1988; and F. L. Sonenstein and J. H. Pleck, 1994, op. cit. (see reference 4).

9. W. Marsiglio, "Husband's Sex Role Preferences and Contraceptive Intentions: The Case of the Male Pill," *Sex Roles*, 12:22–31, 1985; W. Marsiglio and E. G. Menaghan, "Couples and the Male Birth Control Pill: A Future Alternative in Contraceptive Selection," *Journal of Sex Research*, 56:278–284, 1987; and F. L. Sheean, S. K. Ostwald and J. Rothenberger, "Perceptions of Sexual Responsibility: Do Young Men and Women Agree?" *Pediatric Nursing*, 12:17–21, 1986.

10. W. Marsiglio and E. G. Menaghan, 1987, op. cit. (see reference 9).

11. S. K. Danzinger and N. Radin, "Absent Does Not Equal Uninvolved: Predictors of Fathering in Teen Mother Families," *Journal of Marriage and the Family*, 52:536–642, 1990; H. P. Gershenson, "Redefining Fatherhood in Families with White Adolescent Mothers," *Journal of Marriage and the Family*, 45:591–599, 1983; and A. D. Greene, C. Emig and G. Hearn, "Improving Federal Data on Fathers: A Summary of the Town Meeting on Fathering and Male Fertility, March 27, 1996, Washington, D. C.," Child Trends, Inc., Washington D. C., unpublished report, 1996.

12. B. Major et al., "Male Partners' Appraisals of Undesired Pregnancy and Abortion: Implications for Women's Adjustment to Abortion," *Journal of Applied Social Psychology*, 22:599–614, 1992; and W. Marsiglio, "Male Procreative Consciousness and Responsibility: A Conceptual Analysis and Research Agenda," Journal of Family Issues, 12:268–290, 1991.

13. Ibid.

14. .L.Sonenstein and J. H. Pleck, 1994, op. cit. (see reference 4).

15. D. J. Landry and J. D. Forrest, "How Old Are U. S. Fathers?" *Family Planning Perspectives*, 27:159–161 & 165, 1995.

16. G. S. Maddala, *Limited-Dependent and Qualitative Variables in Econometrics*, Cambridge University Press, Cambridge, U. K., 1983; and S. D. Hoffman and G. J. Duncan, "The Effects of Income, Wages, and AFDC Benefits on Marital Disruption," *Journal of Human Resources*, 30:19–41, 1988.

17. S. D. Clark, Jr, L. S. Zabin and J. B. Hardy, 1988, op. cit. (see reference 8); and F. L. Sonenstein and J. H. Pleck, 1994 op. cit. (see reference 4).

18. Ibid.

19. W. R. Grady et al., "Contraceptive Switching Among Currently Married Women in the United States," *Journal of Biosocial Science*, Vol. 11, Supplement, 1989, pp. 114–132.

20. P. Blumstein and P. Schwartz, 1983, op. cit. (see reference 2).

21. I. L. Reiss, 1986, op. cit. (see reference 2); C. Saflios-Rothschild, "The Study of Family Power Structure: A Review 1960–1969," Journal of Marriage and the Family, 32:522–539, 1970; and —Love, Sex, and Sex Roles, Prentice-Hall, Englewood Cliffs, N. J., 1977.

22. W. V. D'Antonio, "Family Life, Religion, and Societal Values and Structures," in W. V. D'Antonio and J. Aldous, eds., Families and Religions, Sage Publication, Beverly Hills, Calif., 1983, pp. 81–108.

23. Ibid.

24. S. S. Brown and L. Eisenberg, eds., *The Best Intentions: Unintended Pregnancy and the Well-Being of Children and Families*, National Academy Press, Washington, D. C., 1995.

25. L. J. Severy, "Couples' Contraceptive Behavior: Decision Analysis in Fertility," address delivered at the annual meeting of the American Psychological Association, Toronto, Aug. 28, 1984.

26. L. J. Severy and S. E. Silver, "Two Reasonable People: Joint Decision-Making in Contraceptive Choice and Use," in L. J. Severy, ed., *Advances in Population Psychosocial Perspectives Vol. 1*, Jessica Kingsley Publishers, London, 1994, pp. 207–227.

William R. Grady, Koray Tanfer and John O. G. Billy are senior research scientists, and Jennifer Lincoln-Hanson is a research assistant, at Battelle Human Affairs Research Centers, Seattle. This research is partially supported by the National Institute of Child Health and Human Development (NICHD), under grant ROI-HD26288. The views expressed in this article are those of the authors and do not necessarily reflect the views or policies of NICHD or the Battelle Memorial Institute.

Establishing and Maintaining Relationships

What is love? People from all cultures, races, and religions, from the dawn of recorded history, have pondered that question. Love is one of the most profound of all human experiences and even transcends the self. People profess not only a love of each other but also love of country, flag, and God.

In Part 3 we'll examine aspects of love and intimate relationships. Regardless of the myriad of changes that have occurred over the the past 20 years in men's and women's roles, in our understanding of how gender identity is formed, and in research into sexual orientation, forming and nurturing loving relationships is still a central concern for most people. The readings in this part explore intimacy, love, and relationships, as well as the current understanding of adult love from the point of view of researchers and therapists.

A Reading for Critical Thinking

BACK OFF!

We're putting way too many expectations on our closest relationships. It's time to retreat a bit. Consider developing same-sex friendships. Or cultivating a garden. Whatever you do, take a break from the relentless pursuit of intimacy.

By Geraldine K. Piorkowski, Ph.D.

Y ou can't miss it. It's the favorite topic of Oprah and all the other talk shows. It's the suds of every soap opera. And I probably don't have to remind you that it's the subject of an extraordinary number of self-help books. Intimate relationships. No matter where we tune or turn, we are bombarded with messages that there is a way to do it right, certainly some way of doing it better—if only we could find it. There are countless books simply on the subject of how to communicate better. Or, if it's not working out, to exit swiftly.

We are overfocused on intimate relationships, and I question whether our current preoccupation with intimacy isn't unnatural, not entirely in keeping with the essential physical and psychological nature of people. The evidence suggests that there is a limit to the amount of closeness people can tolerate and that we need time alone for productivity and creativity. Time alone is necessary to replenish psychological resources and to solidify the boundaries of the self.

All our cultural focus on relationships ultimately has, I believe, a negative impact on us. It causes us to look upon intimate relationships as a solution to all our ills. And that only sets us up for disappointment, contributing to the remarkable 50 percent divorce rate.

Our overfocus on relationships leads us to demand too much of intimacy. We put all our emotional eggs in the one basket of intimate romantic relationships. A romantic partner must be all things to us—lover, friend, companion, playmate, and parent.

We approach intimate relationships with the expectation that this new love will make up for past letdowns in life and love. The expectation that this time around will be better is bound to disappoint, because present-day lovers feel burdened by demands with roots in old relationships.

We expect unconditional love, unfailing nurturance, and protection. There is also the expectation that the new partner will make up for the characteristics we lack in our own personality—for example, that he or she will be an outgoing soul to compensate for our shyness or a goal-oriented person to provide direction in our messy life.

If the personal ads were rewritten to emphasize the emotional expectations we bring to intimacy, they would sound like this. "WANTED: Lively humorous man who could bring joy to my gloomy days and save me from a lifetime of depression." Or, "WANTED: Woman with self-esteem lower than mine. With her, I could feel superior and gain temporary boosts of self-confidence from the comparison."

From my many years as a clinical psychologist, I have come to recognize that intimacy is not an unmitigated good. It is not only difficult to achieve, it is treacherous in some fundamental ways. And it can actually harm people.

The potential for emotional pain and upset is so great in intimate relationships because we are not cloaked in the protective garb of maturity. We are unprotected, exposed, vulnerable to hurt; our defenses are down. We are wide open to pain.

Intuitively recognizing the dangers involved, people normally erect elaborate barriers to shield themselves from closeness. We may act superior, comical, mysterious, or super independent because we fear that intimacy will bring criticism, humiliation, or betrayal—whatever an earlier relationship sensitized us to. We develop expectations based on what has happened in our lives with parents, with friends, with a first love. And we often act in anticipation of these expectations, bringing about the result we most want to avoid.

The closer we get to another person, the greater the risks of intimacy. It's not just that we are more vulnerable and defenseless. We are also more emotionally unstable, childish, and less intelligent than in any other situation. You may be able to run a large company with skill and judgment, but be immature, ultra-sensitive, and needy at home. Civilized rules of conduct often get suspended. Intimacy is both unnerving and baffling.

HEALTHY RETREATS

Once our fears are aroused in the context of intimacy, we tend to go about calming them in unproductive ways. We make excessive demands of our partner, for affection, for unconditional regard. The trouble is, when people feel demands are being made of them, they tend to retreat and hide in ways that hurt their partner. They certainly do not listen.

Fears of intimacy typically limit our vulnerability by calling defensive strategies into play. Without a doubt, the defense of choice against the dangers of intimacy is withdrawal. Partners tune out. One may retreat into work. One walks out of the house, slamming the door. Another doesn't call for days. Whatever the way, we spend a great deal of time avoiding intimacy.

When one partner unilaterally backs off, it tends to be done in a hurtful manner. The other partner feels rejected, uncared about, and unloved. Typically, absolutely nothing gets worked out.

However, avoidance is not necessarily unhealthy. Partners can pursue a time out, where one or both

After many years of working with all kinds of couples, I have come to believe that human nature dictates that intimate relationships have to be cyclical.

work through their conflict in a solitary way that is ultimately renewing. What usually happens, however, is that when partners avoid each other, they are avoiding open warfare but doing nothing to resolve the underlying conflicts.

Fears of intimacy can actually be pretty healthy, when they're realistic and protective of the self. And they appear even in good relationships. Take the fears of commitment that are apt to surface in couples just before the wedding. If they can get together and talk through their fears, then they will not scare one another or themselves into backing off permanently.

After many years of working with all kinds of couples, I have come to believe that human nature dictates that intimate relationships have to be cyclical. There are limitations to intimacy and I think it is wise to respect the dangers. Periods of closeness have to be balanced with periods of distance. For every two steps forward, we often need to take one step back.

An occasional retreat from intimacy gives individuals time to recharge. It offers time to strengthen your sense of who you are. Think of it as constructive avoidance. We need to take some emphasis off what partners can do for us and put it on what we can do for ourselves and what we can do with other relationships. Developing and strengthening same-sex friendships, even opposite-sex friendships, has its own rewards and aids the couple by reducing the demands and emotional expectations we place on partners.

In our culture, our obsession with romantic love relationships has led us to confuse all emotional bonds with sexual bonds, just as we confuse infatuation with emotional intimacy. As a result, we seem to avoid strong but deeply rewarding emotional attachments with others of our own sex. But having recently lost a dear friend of several decades, I am personally sensitive to the need for emotionally deep, same-sex relationships. They can be shared as a way of strengthening gender identity and enjoying rewarding companionship. We need to put more energy into nonromantic relationships as well as other activities.

One of the best ways of recharging oneself is to take pleasure in learning and spiritual development. And there's a great deal to be said for spending time solving political, educational, or social ills of the world.

Distance and closeness boundaries need to be calibrated and constantly readjusted in every intimate relationship. Such boundaries not only vary with each couple, they change as the relationship progresses. One couple may maintain their emotional connection by spending one evening together a week, while another couple needs daily coming together of some sort. Problems arise in relationships when partners cannot agree on the boundaries. These boundaries must be jointly negotiated or the ongoing conflict will rob the relationship of its vitality.

S.O.S. SIGNALS

When you're feeling agitated or upset that your partner is not spending enough time with you, consider it a signal to step back and sort out internally what is going on. Whether you feel anxiety or anger, the emotional arousal should serve as a cue to back off and think through where the upset is coming from, and to consider whether it is realistic.

That requires at least a modest retreat from a partner. It could be a half hour, or two hours. Or two days—whenever internal clarity comes. In the grip of emotion, it is often difficult to discriminate exactly which emotion it is and what its source is. "What is it I am concerned about? Is this fear realistic considering Patrick's behavior in the present? He's never done this to me before, and he's been demonstrating his trustworthiness all over the place, so what am I afraid of? Is it coming from my early years of neglect with two distant parents who never had time for me? Or from my experiences with Steve, who dumped me two years ago?"

Introspective and self-aware people already spend their time thinking about how they work, their motives, what their feelings mean. Impulsive people will have a harder time with the sorting-out process. The best way to sort things out is to pay attention to the nature of the upset. Exactly what you are upset about suggests what your unmet need is, whether it's for love, understanding, nurturance, protection, or special status. And once you identify the need, you can figure out its antecedents.

The kinds of things we get upset about in intimacy tend to follow certain themes. Basically, we become hurt or resentful because we're getting "too much" or "too little" of something. Too many demands, too much criticism, too much domination. Or the converse, too little affectional, conversational, or sexual attention (which translates into "you don't feel I'm important" or "you don't love me"). Insufficient empathy is usually voiced as "you don't understand me," and too little responsibility translates into failure to take on one's share of household and/or financial tasks. All these complaints require some attention, action, or retreat.

SHIFTING GEARS

It's not enough to identify the source of personal concern. You have to present your concerns in a way your partner can hear. If I say directly to my partner, "I'm afraid you're going to leave me," he has the opportunity to respond, "Darling, that's not true. What gave you that idea?" I get the reassurance I need. But if I toss it out in an argument, in the form of "you don't care about me," then my partner's emotional arousal keeps him from hearing me. And he is likely to back away—just when I need reassurance most.

If people were aware that intimate relationships are by nature characterized by ambivalence, they would understand the need to negotiate occasional retreats. They wouldn't feel so threatened by the times when one partner says, "I have to be by myself because I need to think about my life and where I'm going." Or "I need to be with my friends and spend time playing." If people did more backing off into constructive activities, including time to meditate or to play, intimate relationships would be in much better shape today.

If couples could be direct about what they need, then the need for retreat would not be subject to the misrepresentation that now is rampant. The trouble is, we don't talk to each other that openly and honestly. What happens is, one partner backs off and doesn't call and the partner left behind doesn't know what the withdrawal means. But he or she draws on a personal history that provides room for all sorts of negative interpretations, the most common being "he doesn't care about me."

No matter how hard a partner tries to be all things to us, gratifying all of another's needs is a herculean task—beyond the human calling. Criticism, disappointment, and momentary rejection are intrinsic parts of intimate life; developing a thicker skin can be healthy. And maintaining a life apart from the relationship is necessary. Energy invested in other people and activities provides a welcome balance.

GOOD-ENOUGH INTIMACY

Since our intimate partner will never be perfect, what is reasonable to expect? The late British psychiatrist D.W. Winnicott put forth the idea of "good-enough mothering." He was convinced that mothering could never be perfect because of the mother's own emotional needs. "Good-enough mothering" refers to imperfect, though adequate provision of emotional care that is not damaging to the children.

In a similar vein, I believe there is a level of imperfect intimacy that is good enough to live and grow on. In good-enough intimacy, painful encounters occasionally occur, but they are balanced by the strength and pleasures of the relationship. There are enough positives to balance the negatives. People who do very well in intimate relationships don't have a perfect relationship, but it is good enough.

The standard of good-enough intimacy is essentially subjective, but there are some objective criteria. A relationship must have enough companionship, affection, autonomy, connectedness, and separateness, along with some activities that partners engage in together and that they both enjoy. The relationship meets the needs of both partners reasonably well enough, both feel reasonably good about the relationship. If one person is unhappy in the relationship, then by definition it is not good enough for them.

People looking for good enough intimacy are bound to be happier than those seeking perfect intimacy. Their expectations are lower and more realistic. Time and time again, those who examine the intricacies of happiness have found the same thing—realistic expectations are among the prime contributors to happiness.

"Love" and the Mental Health Professions: Toward Understanding Adult Love

By Stephen B. Levine, M.D.

This essay explores three aspects of the normal processes of adult-adult love: falling in love, being in love, and staying in love. It describes the emotions, defenses, and challenges inherent in each phase. Love is an ordinary but immensely powerful adult aspiration. As a term it is impossible to define in any singular sense. The attainment of its lofty purposes requires profound intrapsychic adjustments involving creative acts of imagination, the integration of ideals with reality, evolving adaptations to the partner, the maintenance of a positive internal image of the partner, and ongoing struggles to overcome self-interest. These adjustments have not been well characterized by the mental health professions. This is ironic since a large portion of our work involves caring for love's casualties—that is, people whose miseries relate to their inability to successfully negotiate the phases of love or whose happiness is limited by their partners who cannot. Six arguments for ending professional avoidance of the topic are offered, the most compelling of which are love's relevance to both the pathogenesis of mental suffering and to the art of psychotherapeutic healing.

The good life is one inspired by love and guided by knowledge.

Bertrand Russell[1]

The time-honored role of the mental health professions is clear: to take clinical responsibility for problematic emotional states. The distinct focus of our obligation is the relief of psychopathology. To the extent that our work is scientific, it is based on studies of the biological, social and psychological variables that create, maintain, or relieve these problems. The profound seriousness of the field has not wavered much during this century, but the psychopathologies that are of greatest interest, ideas about their etiology, and how mental health professionals actually function have evolved.

How best to prepare mental health professionals for their responsibilities is not as clear. I consider an understanding about the nature of love to be vitally important. But three obstacles keep this subject far from our sensibilities. The first is that health does not directly drive the engine of psychiatry's educational and research efforts. Concepts of normality are not the focus at governmental, pharmaceutical, clinical training, or service delivery levels. The second is that love has ubiquitous representations in our culture, from rock and roll to soap operas, from low-brow to high-brow art forms. The recurrent message of many of these activities is akin to "All we need is love," a phrase that may work in the theater, the pulpit, or songwriting, but not in the rooms where complex clinical realities are routinely confronted. The third is that love is beyond the tools of science, even the looser processes that we call clinical science and psychoanalysis.[2] Science rests on its power to predict outcome. The course of love is unpredictable, its shaping forces interact within the privacy of individual subjectivity, where science has never established a firm

From *Journal of Sex & Marital Therapy* (Fall 1996, Vol. 22, No. 3), pp. 191–199, Stephen B. Levine, M.D. Reprinted with permission from Taylor & Francis, Inc., Washington, D.C. © 1996. All rights reserved.

foothold.[3] So when we want to learn about love, we do not so much review scientific literature[4] as we read literature.[5]

These obstacles no longer deter me from the subject. In 25 years as a psychiatrist, I have learned that clinical work always pushes me beyond the reach of science into the realm of the patient's subjectivity. Science is not the only legitimate means of increasing our fund of knowledge or improving our clinical work, even though it is the most respected.[6]

Essayists on love, whether they be philosophers, theologians, literary critics, social scientists, or psychoanalysts, typically prepare their readers for the limitations of their work by commenting on how broad and deep the topic is. They point out that adult love is only one of many types of love that shape and color our lives. They emphasize that multiple view points on love are forever required since no one field, perspective, or person can have the last word on its evolving nature. I echo this standard prelude.

WHAT IS LOVE?

Is love a feeling, a force, a figment of imagination, a fixture of culture, or a genetic imperative? Although it is useless to aspire to one definition of love, compelling ideas about its nature do exist. For instance, the philosophy professor Irving Singer writes that "the meaning of love is to be found in our propensity to create ideals that liberate us from reality."[7]

I begin more prosaically, by considering adult love to be a powerful ambition—one that is synthesized by the combination of long existent cultural ideals[8] and unseen residues of relationships that begin in childhood.

Adult Love Is Largely an Ideal. Individuals long to live close to their personal ideal form of love. We expend much energy striving to attain harmony in our relationships. Conventionally, this involves mutual respect, behavioral reliability, enjoyment of one another, sexual fidelity, psychological intimacy, sexual pleasure, and a comfortable balance of individuality and couplehood. The latter is a balance between oneness and twoness which creates a sense of sameness out of difference.

Such harmony or the state of ideal love is attainable on earth, but evanescent. Usually, a gap exists between our private sense of ideal love and our actual experience of ourselves and partner in a relationship. The gap is a source of existential distress and, like all distress, is buffered by an array of competing life demands, defense mechanisms, and self-management techniques. When the buffering system works, one's love, while not continuously or completely harmonious, may be felt as good-enough.

FALLING IN LOVE

The Defenses. Falling in love is charming, but denial, idealization, and naïveté are more or less required. In the relatively brief process of falling in love, many of those around us feel that we have exaggerated the capacities and minimized the limitations of the newly loved. They often privately say skeptical things to one another about our psychological state: we are in denial about the obvious capacities and traits of the person; we are idealizing the new person; we do not appreciate the implications for the future of what we do see.

New love has the reputation for being transforming all over the ancient and modern world.[9] People who fall in love are often keenly aware of the need for something different in their lives. Some think that we fall in love out of this need for change. Denial and idealization enable us to break down the boundaries between ourself and the other to create a new personal identity as a couple. These defenses often convey the deep private hope of personal improvement. "I will be a better person and my life will be better with this person." The skepticism of others also has a voice within us, but it is often quelled by the new psychological intimacy with the partner. Although we may be denying, idealizing, and naive about some aspects of the person, we have a view of the partner that the external skeptics do not have. Some of the perceptions that derive from this knowledge may be more correct and trustworthy than the observations of our friends and family. We hope.

The Central Issue. A central issue faces everyone in a new love: Which is correct, my hope-generated judgment or my skepticism?

The Emotions. The trepidation that a person feels upon entering a new state of love is explained by this central issue, not merely by experience with past relationships. Calmly dealing with this question over time is made difficult by the excitement generated by our experiencing the new person as a means of easing some of our important social and psychological burdens. This excitement is variously described as: earth-shaking, trance-like, beguiling, or as an amazement, exhilaration, exultation, rapture. Falling in love is often sudden in onset, volcanic in intensity, and sensed as occurring from outside the self, for example, "I was struck by Cupid's arrow." Plato mythically explained the array of sensations when he had Socrates say that we have found our long-missing other half.[10]

Maturation,[11] character style, and gender may modify the process of falling in love somewhat, but the haunting question embedded in this emotional upheaval remains the same: "Am I wise or foolish in pursuing this new relationship?" While lovers assume that their new happiness predicts a good future relationship, skeptics, such as Freud, may diagnose a nonpsychotic delusion. Samuel Johnson once quipped that this mental state was a disease best cured by marriage.[12]

An Act of Imagination. If we say that falling in love requires an act of imagination, we may better understand that terms such as fantasy-driven, illusion, defenses, and affectual stimulation are the ordinary accompaniments or consequences of this momentous mental event. Imagination creates the images of a highly desirable life with a particular person. Attainment of that life then becomes the organizing force for much of the person's behavior. Imagination also creates the idealized internal image of the partner that will play a subtle role throughout the life of the relationship (and beyond). In order to survive, fresh love must be more than creative imagination, but it may not be less.

BEING IN LOVE

Reciprocity between two people is required to create the full intensity of falling in love. A crescendo is reached when we are reassured that something comparable to our internal upheaval over the newly loved is occurring within the other, that is, that we are becoming our beloved's beloved. "Pinch me, am I dreaming?" "I can't believe it!" A marvelous phase of happiness ensues, which we label "being in love." If falling in love requires a personal act of imagination, being in love requires the accurate perception of the other's creative burst. Being in love typically lasts much longer than falling in love, but it, too, is not forever. The initial intensity of being in love gradually diminishes and is replaced by a calmer, far less tumultuous period of happiness during which life is increasingly dominated by realistic concerns. Even so, the new partner is experienced as idealized, not merely in the sense that traits are overestimated or failings are not perceived, but in the sense that the person is finally on the way to realizing the grand ambition to love and be loved, and will do everything possible to stay on this high road.

The Beginnings of Love Involve More Than the Couple. Falling in love and its happy consequence, being in love, are more than processes occurring between two people. Their power, sentimentality, and allure stem from the profound, incompletely knowable hopes that are embedded in them, not only for the lovers, but also for family and friends observing them. Successfully falling in love restructures life*— both psychologically and socially—for all concerned.

Acting the Role of Being in Love. Western cultures now assume that the emotional excitement of new love is the proper beginning of a relationship. New love is celebrated in songs, movies, and fiction. These model for us what we should feel when we finally find our partner. When people allow the social processes of love to begin even though they are not privately profoundly moved, they may question whether they are "really" in love. "Are my motives for selecting this partner improper?" "Is this relationship a mistake?" "Am I just uncomfortable allowing myself to be emotionally swept away by anything?" While this private dialogue is occurring, many people must act the role of being in love while waiting until they grow to love their partner, just as is said to occur when marriages are arranged. When a relationship fails, our Western assumption about how love ought to begin creates the lamentation: "What a fool I was to be involved without love!" However, the intensity of the initial feelings does not protect one from future relationship misery. There is hope for those who managed to marry without the benefit of exultation and who did a little acting. No matter if love begins with beguiling charm or diffident practicality, the most enduring challenge is staying in love.

STAYING IN LOVE

The Lofty Purposes. Adult love relationships have a complex implicit purpose: Partners are chosen in the tacit hope that they will accompany, assist, emotionally stabilize, and enrich us as we evolve, mature, and cope with life's other demands. To put this another way, adult love is expected to combine three elements for each partner as the couple moves through the life cycle: sexual pleasure, cherishing of the person of the partner, behavioral caring for the partner.

Defenses Are Still Required. To realize this lofty purpose, each of us must rely at times on mechanisms of defense, including idealization, denial, and rationalization. Idealization enables us to hover closer to our ideal of loving and being loved. We idealize our partners in return for their devotion to us; it is an unconscious bargain we make with them: I will continue to bestow love onto you and you will continue to bestow love onto me.

We also need illusions about our partner's capacities, attributes, and attitudes toward us to minimize our disappointment with them. Chief among our

---

*"First love is exactly like a revolution: the regular and established order of life is in an instant smashed to fragments; youth stands at the barricade, its bright banner raised high in the air, and sends its ecstatic greetings to the future, whatever it may hold—death or a new life, no matter." — Turgenev.[13]

illusions is that our partner simply loves us without struggle. We assume this, despite our awareness that it is a recurrent struggle to love our partner. We also routinely rationalize away some of our disappointment by telling ourselves to be *realistic* about what can be expected from any partner. If the reality of our relationships is not close to our ideal, we try to move toward the ideal in the privacy of our minds. And there we may repeatedly emphasize what is close to the ideal (she is a good cook; he is a good father) rather than focus on what is not (I wish she could enjoy sports with me; I wish he were not so asocial). There are good reasons to be so *unrealistic* about our partners; after all, they have been chosen to accompany, assist, stabilize, and enrich us as we grow. Interfering with the long-term processes of love is done at great peril. We should take some hope that some people happily negotiate the years of marriage and attain its final accomplishment—the struggle to love and to be loved is ended. They surrender to the knowledge that they do love in their idiosyncratic ways and so do their imperfect partners. On the way to this distant goal, the internal sense of the partner changes focus many times.

Other Requirements for Managing the Gap. The distress created by the gap between our ideal and the real is far from constant. It ranges from high to low in response to many major and minor external events. Maintaining high quality psychological and sexual intimacy requires more than defense mechanisms. These dual challenges require good judgment about when to speak and what to say, a commitment to work with good humor toward realizing ideal love, the discipline to allow our loftiest values to govern our lives during the inevitable times of doubt, and the ability to apologize. As we settle into a long-term relationship, we inevitably see our partners more clearly. We see their recurring patterns of behavior, we better realize their strengths and their limitations, and we pass personal judgment on their integrity and trustworthiness. A large part of the private work of being in a relationship is dealing with the disappointment about our partner's styles, capacities, and treatment of us. This work is *not* ordinarily done with the partner; it is done within the self, alone in ongoing dialogues that we have with our disappointed conflicted selves.

Appraisal and Bestowal. Staying in love is the product of two ongoing hidden mental activities: the assessment of the partner's character (appraisal) and the granting of cooperation (bestowal).[14] People often erroneously assume that their partners simply and constantly love them. But a partner notices the other's behavior, interprets it, and decides whether or not to love. When love can be genuinely bestowed, it is

typically immediately reflected in cooperation, affection, and enjoyment of the partner. Another important consequence is typically not seen—the shoring up of the idealized internal image of the beloved.

Although we don't love our partners constantly, we allow them to think that we do. They make erroneous assumptions because we do genuinely feel love for them sometimes. And when we do not, our commitment to behave in a kind, helpful fashion may carry the moment. Our idealized image of our partner enables us to act loving because we do feel loving toward the partner's image—if not to the actual partner sulking upstairs. Continuing negative appraisals, however, interfere with sensations we called love, the commitment to love, and the internal image of the partner as lovable. We then find it difficult to bestow affection and cooperation and we cease to enjoy our partners.

Many people seem to expect to be loved regardless of their behavior or capacities. Young children are (ideally) loved unconditionally, older children and siblings are to some extent as well, but it is unlikely that most adults can continue to bestow love without some degree of positive appraisal. For unconditional love, adults usually turn to God.

The Intrapsychic Mental Buffering of Distress. Theoretically, distress about the inescapable gap must be buffered in some way. There must be an adaptive mental balance mechanism in operation under ordinary conditions because the fluctuations of distress can be sudden and dramatic.[15] When some new negative appraisal—such as realizing the social limitations of the spouse—destabilizes the balance, the resulting shift may be manifested by a sudden new pessimistic view of the partner. The person may think: "I am no longer in love. I am no longer willing to work privately to remain in this relationship. I have been kidding myself for too long." The person begins to appraise with a new harsher standard and to rewrite the history of the relationship. Bestowal ceases. Even apparently good relationships prove to be precariously balanced intrapsychically.

When such private destabilization occurs, the person may develop considerable anxiety, panic, guilt, or depression. Many of these intrapsychic dramas pass unnoticed by the spouse and family, or if their effects are noted, their source is not perceived.

Love Exists in Privacy. We know about the precarious balance of relationships because relationships exist in the deepest privacy of our individual psyches. Dependably affectionate, faithful, well-behaved people frequently express anger, disappointment, and outrage to themselves and imagine leaving their spouses for an improved version—all in this privacy, the same privacy in which idealization used to occur.

However, the culture is more familiar with the idea that love and loving relationships are both internal and external to each person. We emphasize that love is something that exists between two parties. When we observe couples being affectionate—that is, when the love that privately exists spills over the boundaries of self and social situations—we conclude that they really love each other. It is safer for mental health professionals to assume that love resides in two person's psyches—hopefully simultaneously. What they exchange publicly or privately may reflect their continuing ability to enjoy and idealize one another or may conceal their acting the part of love because of private disappointment or resentment. Therapists hear sentences like this from abandoned persons: "We made love just two days before and told each other how much we loved one another." Couples seeking marital therapy frequently comment on the irony that "everyone thinks we are the best, most loving couple." And, therapists repeatedly encounter an inexpressive spouse who deeply loves a partner, but is not able to openly express it.

What is said and done in a relationship is not as crucial as the partner's interpretation of what is said and done. Behavior works if the partner interprets it as meaning "I am loved; this is simply my partner's way." Of course, this conclusion sometimes is an illusion. The illusion of being loved buffers both the fluctuation of distress between the ideal and the real and the other distresses of everyday life.

Privacy is an arena where many relevant dramas routinely occur. These include the balancing acts between appraisal and bestowal, feelings thought of as love and those thought of as aggression, attractions to others and moral constraints, and alternative meanings considered for the same spousal behaviors.

As the perception "I am not loved" or the conclusion "I do not love this person" emerges in consciousness and gradually thunders its way into the couple's dialogue, abandonment becomes a distinct possibility. Both partners, their children, and their extended family may then readily earn a DSM-IV label, if a mental health professional is anywhere near them.

How We Use the Word "Love." The same word is used to describe our pleasure in wearing a favorite sweater and our complex synthesis of experience with a spouse of 50 years: we say we love a particular musical group and we label the rush of emotions at our child's wedding ceremony with the same word. It is useless to try to delineate a singular meaning for "love" in our language.

Love Is Not Simply a Feeling. Many writers refer to love as an emotion. Tomkins[16] and Nathanson[17] have taken great pains to delineate the nine basic affects. They consider *affects* to be hard-wired neural capacities with which all humans respond in gradient fashion to the environment. Love, per se, is not one of them. They distinguish the conscious experience of stimulated neural capacity, which they label *feelings*, from *emotions* which are feelings after they have acquired a personal and cultural context. For example, a child's *feeling* of envy is made into a guilt-tinged *emotion* by learning that in his family envy is a sin. Using the Tomkins/Nathanson scheme, I want to suggest that love is not a single feeling; it probably is a series of emotions, that is, feelings colored by past experience and associations with that feeling. The emotions that we call love are highly individually defined points on two of Tomkin's affective gradient: interest-excitement and enjoyment-joy.

Gandhi also thinks that love is not simply a feeling. He thinks of it far more complexly. He says that love is a force in nature—the essence of life—because it brings two separate people together into a new entity. He calls love an ontological force.[18]

Loving the Partner. The natural history of adult love begins with the anxious excitement of falling in love. It soon gives way to a more tranquil pervasive happiness of being in love and eventually evolves into loving the partner. We do not remain in love forever in the being in love sense. But we do say to ourselves and to others that we love our partners. The quality, intensity, and frequency of our enjoyment of our partner evolves. Our love, once fresh and filled with possibility, soon becomes the new structure of our lives. As this further unfolds, the sensations that we once interpreted as love may be less obvious to ourselves and others.

Loving the partner, which originally began as an ambition, is now closer to an attitude forged by commitment to values and personal discipline than to mere emotion. When love begins, emotions dominate; their subtle meanings relate to the possibilities of significantly changed structures of our lives. By the time we are in the loving-the-partner phase, the new structures of our lives predominate; emotions become subtle. Loving the partner rests upon our appraisal of the degree to which mutual respect, behavioral reliability, enjoyment of one another, sexual fidelity, psychological intimacy, sexual pleasure, and the balance of individuality and couplehood exist in our relationship. Loving the partner also rests upon the strength of the internal idealized image of the partner. Of course, our appraisals and our internal image are related. The emotions of love during this long phase do not usually ascend to predominance unless there is a threat of or actual loss, although we are expected to symbolically acknowledge our love through gift giving.

Long-Term Love Is a Battle for Many. Adult love is a lofty human potential that often has a disappointing outcome. Casualties are everywhere. Erich Fromm suggested that long-term love requires the remeeting of two people at their emotional genuineness.[19] This idea of genuineness recurs in various literatures. Some psychoanalysts, for example, understand that over decades, adult love reflects what we face in life, how well we face it, and the degree to which our partners can actually be with us in genuineness. Love is about the battles we fight within ourselves to simply be genuine and how their outcome may change subtly with each engagement.

SUGGESTIONS FOR STAYING IN LOVE

Because failures of adult love are major public health problems, it is important to conceptualize how to love. My suggestions rest upon the ideas that staying in love requires overcoming one's narcissism and increasing one's devotion to the partner and the couple. This in turn increases the ease with which a partner can bestow love. This is not *the* formula for happiness because it leaves out the individual art of balancing the needs of the self and the needs of the couple and all the complexity created by our individual past experiences.

1. Develop your capacity to simply listen to your partner speak.
2. Make clear to your partner what you like to do in life without demanding anything.
3. Err on the side of putting the good of the couple and the good of the partner ahead of your interests.
4. Give your partner the benefit of the doubt when you feel that you have been mistreated.
5. Speak frequently from the heart about subjects other than personal unhappiness with your partner.
6. Smile about your personal ambitions, knowing that most people do not achieve them.
7. Value sexual behaviors highly, even the inevitable disappointing ones.
8. Be aware that your partner's perception that you are generally interested in satisfying your partner's sexual needs is vital to the growth of love.
9. Love your body and its pleasures; stop taking your bodily imperfections so seriously.
10. Consider that integrity, honesty, and respect breed love, love breeds good sex, and good sex breeds love. It is a feedback loop.
11. Own and express your emotions, but don't always assume that they are the most important aspects of any interpersonal situation.
12. Do not abandon your ideal of love just because your partner is currently falling short of meeting its requirements.
13. Tell your partner how much you value loving and having sex, and don't be embarrassed to admit that although you are satiable when it comes to sex, you are insatiable when it comes to being loved.

The Metaphor of the Roadmap. Hopefully, these observations about the phases and complexities of adult love will prove useful to clinicians. I offer them as a sort of roadmap for the intrapsychic and interpersonal journeys of adult development. It is apparent to me that much of the usual journey of love has not yet been adequately charted. The ambition of love is often to maintain its lofty purposes until death. Unlike travel where we are typically most interested in the destination, in love we are preoccupied with the journey. In offering help to those who are experiencing the dangers inherent in love's journey, mental health professionals and patients may acquire a new appreciation of the journey itself.

WHAT IS THE SIGNIFICANCE OF LOVE TO PSYCHIATRY?

Today, two powerful forces continue to keep love on the extreme periphery of psychiatric consciousness. The first is economic. All the confusing demands of the emerging funding systems are currently driving services in the direction of diagnosis, pharmacotherapy, and brief psychotherapy by our least educated colleagues. The second is ideological, that is, the shift of psychiatry's interest to the biology of our brains from the meaning-making function of our minds.

Love is one important door to understanding both humanity and healing. In case the foregoing has not persuaded you that concepts of love may assist our work with various psychopathologies, I end by offering you six reasons to keep these concepts in our professional dialogue.

1. *Because problems of love are often related to psychiatric diagnoses.* One of our central tasks in life is to "keep it together."[20] Among the high prevalence, emotionally evocative existential dilemmas that we are required to "keep together" are those that derive from our love lives. When we fail, and lose our capacity to contain and well-manage ourselves, we often qualify for a diagnosis. Our emotional decompensations can be more fully understood and often better treated if clinicians grasp the thwarted ambitions that trigger symptoms. Much of the anguish of ordinary adult lives involves personal and interpersonal impediments

to loving. Psychiatrists can become so preoccupied with properly identifying and medically treating anguish that we lose sight of the possibility that the symptoms may have arisen in response to actual or threatened failures in love. The idea that failure in the sphere of love may lead to profound and lingering states of anguish should be considered by us, however, because helping people often requires making sense of their emotional states and restoring dignity to them about their ambitions.

2. *Because love is what patients talk about.* The absence of love, the fear of love, the mishandling of falling in love, threat of losing love, and coping with the loss of love are the major themes that are discussed in the doctor-patient dialogue when the doctor allows it to move beyond diagnosis and medication prescription. Other issues are also discussed. But what gets more air time? Work or love? Siblings or lovers? The aspiration to be rich or the aspiration to be loved?

3. *Because love is an important factor in emotional and physical health.* Love is widely conceptualized, based on various data sets, to promote stability, positive self-regard, emotional growth or maturation, physical health, and longer life. Love is good for the immune system.

4. *Because love is often the subtle ingredient in therapeutic improvement.* In therapies that tolerate discussion of what the patients feel about the therapist, therapists soon learn that affection for, excitement over, and sexual desire for the therapists are routine. Therapists often have to deal with their own affection, excitement over, and sexual desire for the patient. These emotional phenomena even happen in those therapies without an ideologic support for them because the trusting intimacy of therapy routinely provokes love and eroticization of the therapist.[21]

5. *Because not understanding love may predispose psychiatrists to ethical violations.* Some of the most egregious ethical violations during the life cycle of mental health professionals involve the lack of understanding of and poor capacities to deal with the emotional arousal stimulated within the psychological intimacy of patient care.[22]

6. *Because love is necessary to understand sexual health and dysfunction.* One needs a concept of love to understand the vagaries of sexual desire and sexual function in all persons, even those people for whom love is unattainable and those for whom it is antithetical to sexual pleasure.[23]

REFERENCES

1. Kuntz PG: *Bertrand Russell.* Boston, Twayne, 1986, p. 107.
2. Kernberg O: *Love relations: Normal and pathological.* New York, Yale University Press, 1995.
3. Rosenthal L: Introduction. *The world treasury of love stories.* New York, Oxford University Press, 1995, p. xiv.
4. Liebowitz MR: *Chemistry of love.* Boston, Little, Brown, 1983.
5. Gaylin W. *Rediscovering love.* New York, Viking, 1986.
6. Lear J: *Love and its place in nature: A philosophical interpretation of Freudian psychoanalysis.* New York, Farrar, Straus, & Giroux, 1990.
7. Singer I: *The nature of love, vol. 3. The modern world.* Chicago, University of Chicago Press, 1987.
8. Singer I: *The nature of love, vol. 1. Plato to Luther.* Chicago, University of Chicago Press, 1965.
9. Ackerman D: *The natural history of love.* New York: Random House, 1994.
10. Plato: *The symposium* (B Jowett, ed). New York, Tudor, 1956, pp 315–318.
11. Emerson RW: *Essays: First and second series, Love.* New York, Vintage, 1990, pp 97–107.
12. Glass C: *Speaking of marriage.* New York, Ten Speed Press, 1992, p. 34.
13. Turgenev I: *Spring torrents.* New York, Penguin, 1980, p 100.
14. Singer I: *The nature of love, vol. 2. Courtly and romantic.* Chicago, University of Chicago Press, 1984.
15. deRougemont D: *Love declared: Essays on the myths of love.* New York, Pantheon, 1963.
16. Tomkins S: *Affect/imagery/consciousness, vol. 4. Cognition, duplication and transformation of information.* New York: Springer, 1992.
17. Nathanson D: *Shame and pride.* New York, Norton, 1992.
18. Walsh A: *The science of love: Understanding love and its effects on mind and body.* Buffalo, Prometheus, 1991.
19. Fromm E: *The art of loving. An inquiry into the nature of love.* New York, Harper & Row, 1956.
20. Havens L: Lecture, American Psychiatric Association Meeting, Miami, 1995.
21. Levine SB: *Sexual life: A clinician's guide.* New York, Plenum, 1992.
22. Lazarus J: Ethical issues in doctor-patient sexual relationships. *Psychiat Clin N Am 18, 1:55–70, 1995.*
23. Levine SB. *On love. J Sex Marital Ther 21:183–191, 1995.*

Stephen B. Levine, M.D., is Co-Director of the Center for Marital and Sexual Health, 23200 Chagrin Boulevard #350, Beachwood, OH 44122, and Clinical Professor of Psychiatry at Case Western Reserve University School of Medicine.

A Reading for Critical Thinking

Celibate Passion

The hidden rewards of quitting sex

By Kathleen Norris

Celibacy is a field day for ideologues. Conservative Catholics tend to speak of celibacy as if it were an idealized, angelic state, while feminist theologians such as Uta Ranke-Heinemann say, angrily, that celibate hatred of sex is hatred of women. That celibacy constitutes the hatred of sex seems to be a given in popular mythology, and we need only look at newspaper accounts of sex abuse by priests to see evidence of celibacy that isn't working. One could well assume that this is celibacy, impure and simple. And this is unfortunate, because celibacy practiced rightly is not at all a hatred of sex; in fact it has the potential to address the troubling sexual idolatry of our culture.

One benefit of the nearly ten years that I've been affiliated with the Benedictines as an oblate, or associate, has been the development of deep friendships with celibate men and women. This has led me to ponder celibacy that works, practiced by people who are fully aware of themselves as sexual beings but who express their sexuality in a celibate way. That is, they manage to sublimate their sexual energies toward another purpose than sexual intercourse and procreation. Are they perverse, their lives necessarily stunted? Cultural prejudice would say yes, but I have my doubts. I've seen too many wise old monks and nuns whose celibate practice has allowed them to incarnate hospitality in the deepest sense. In them, the constraints of celibacy have somehow been transformed into an openness. They exude a sense of freedom.

The younger celibates are more edgy. Still contending mightily with what one friend calls "the raging orchestra of my hormones," they are more obviously struggling to contain their desire for intimacy and physical touch within the bounds of celibacy. Often they find their loneliness intensified by the incomprehension of others. In a culture that denies the value of their striving, they are made to feel like fools, or worse.

Americans are remarkably tone-deaf when it comes to the expression of sexuality. The sexual formation that many of us receive is like the refrain of an old Fugs song: "Why do ya like boobs a lot—ya gotta like boobs a lot." The jiggle of tits and ass, penis and pectorals assaults us everywhere—billboards, magazines, television, movies. Orgasm becomes just another goal; we undress for success. It's no wonder that in all this powerful noise, the quiet tones of celibacy are lost.

But celibate people have taught me that celibacy, practiced rightly, does indeed have something valuable to say to the rest of us. Specifically, they have helped me better appreciate both the nature of friendship and what it means to be married. They have also helped me recognize that celibacy, like monogamy, is not a matter of the will disdaining and conquering the desires of the flesh, but a discipline requiring what many people think of as undesirable, if not impossible—a conscious form of sublimation. Like many people who came into adulthood during the sexually permissive 1960s, I've tended to equate sublimation with repression. But my celibate friends have made me see the light; accepting sublimation as a normal part of adulthood makes me more realistic about human sexual capacities and expression. It helps me better respect the bonds and boundaries of marriage.

Any marriage has times of separation, ill health, or just plain crankiness in which sexual intercourse is ill advised. And it is precisely the skills of celibate friendship—fostering intimacy through letters, conversation, performing mundane tasks together (thus rendering them pleasurable), savoring the holy simplicity of a shared meal or a walk together at dusk—that help a marriage survive the rough spots. When you can't make love physically, you figure out other ways to do it.

The celibate impulse in monasticism runs deep and has an interfaith dimension. It is the Dalai Lama who has said. "If you're a monk, you're celibate. If you're not celibate, you're not a monk." Monastic people are celibate for a very practical reason: The kind of community life to which they aspire can't be sustained if people are pairing off. Even in churches in which the clergy are often married—Episcopal and Russian Orthodox, for example—their monks and nuns are celibate. And while monastic novices may be carried along for a time on the swells of communal spirit, when that blissful period inevitably comes to an end the loneliness is profound. One gregarious monk in his early 30s told me that just as he thought he'd settled into the monastery, he woke up in a panic one morning, wondering if he'd wake up lonely for the rest of his life.

Another monk I know regards celibacy as the expression of an essential human loneliness, a perspective that helps him as a hospital chaplain when he is called upon to minister to the dying. I knew him when he was still resisting his celibate call. The resistance usually came out as anger directed toward his abbot and community, more rarely as misogyny. I was fascinated to observe the process by which he came to accept the sacrifices that a celibate, monastic life requires. He's easier to be with now, he's a better friend.

This is not irony so much as grace: In learning to be faithful to his vow of celibacy, the monk developed his talent for relationship. It's a common story. I've seen the demands of Benedictine hospitality—the requirement that all visitors be received as Christ—convert shy young men who fear women into monks who can enjoy their company.

Celibates tend to value friendship very highly. And my friendships with celibate men, both gay and straight, give me some hope that men and women don't live in alternate universes. In 1990s America, this sometimes feels like a countercultural perspective. Male celibacy, in particular, can become radically countercultural insofar as it rejects the consumerist model of sexuality that reduces a woman to the sum of her parts. I have never had a monk friend make an insinuating remark along the lines of "You have beautiful eyes" (or legs, breasts, knees, elbows, nostrils), the kind of remark women grow accustomed to deflecting. A monk is supposed to give up the idea of possessing anything, including women.

Ideally, in giving up the sexual pursuit of women (whether as demons or as idealized vessels of purity) the male celibate learns to relate to them as human beings. That many fail to do so, that the power structures of the Catholic Church all but dictate failure in this regard, comes as no surprise. What is a surprise is what happens when it works. For when men have truly given up the idea of possessing women, a healing thing occurs. I once met a women in a monastery guest house who had come there because she was pulling herself together after being raped, and she needed to feel safe around men again. I've seen young monks astonish an obese and homely college student by listening to her with as much interest and respect as to her conventionally pretty roommate. On my 40th birthday, as I happily blew out four candles on a cupcake ("one for each decade," a monk in his 20s cheerfully proclaimed), I realized that I could enjoy growing old with these guys.

As celibacy takes hold in a person, as monastic values supersede the values of the culture outside the monastery, celibates become people who can radically affect those of us out "in the world," if only because they've learned how to listen without possessiveness, without imposing themselves. In talking to someone who is practicing celibacy well, we may sense that we're being listened to in a refreshingly deep way. And this is the purpose of celibacy, not to attain some impossibly cerebral goal mistakenly conceived as "holiness," but to make oneself available to others, body and soul. Celibacy, simply put, is a form of ministry—not an achievement one can put on a résumé but a subtle form of service. In theological terms, one dedicates one's sexuality to God through Jesus Christ, a concept and a terminology I find extremely hard to grasp. All I can do is catch a glimpse of people who are doing it, incarnating celibacy in a mysterious, pleasing, and gracious way.

The attractiveness of the celibate is that he or she can make us feel appreciated, enlarged, no matter who we are. I have two nun friends who invariably have this effect on me, no matter what the circumstances of our lives on those occasions when we meet. The thoughtful way in which they converse, listening and responding with complete attention, is a marvel. And when I first met a man I'll call Tom, I wrote in my notebook, "Such tenderness in a man . . . and a surprising, gentle, kindly grasp of who I am."

I realized that I had found a remarkable friend. I was also aware that Tom and I were fast approaching the rocky shoals of infatuation—a man and a woman, both decidedly heterosexual, responding to each other in unmistakably sexual ways. We laughed a lot; we had playful conversations as well as serious ones; we took delight in each other. At times we were alarmingly responsive to one another, and it was all too easy to fantasize about expressing that responsiveness in physical ways.

The danger was real but not insurmountable; I sensed that if our infatuation were to develop into love, that is, to ground itself in grace rather than utility, our respect for each other's commitments—his to celibacy, mine to monogamy—would make the boundaries of behavior very clear. We had few regrets, and yet for both of us there was an underlying sadness, the pain of something incomplete. Suddenly, the difference between celibate friendship and celibate passion had become a reality; at times the pain was excruciating.

Tom and I each faced a crisis the year we met—his mother died, I suffered a disastrous betrayal—and it was the intensity of those unexpected, unwelcome experiences that helped me to understand that in the realm of the sacred, what seems incomplete or unattainable may be abundance after all. Human relationships are by their nature incomplete—after 21 years my husband remains a mystery to me, and I to him, and that is as it should be. Only hope allows us to know and enjoy the depth of our intimacy.

Appreciating Tom's presence in my life as a miraculous unmerited gift helped me to place our relationship in its proper, religious context, and also to understand why it was that when I'd seek him out to pray with me, I'd always leave feeling so much better than when I came. This was celibacy at its best—a man's sexual energies so devoted to the care of others that a few words could lift me out of despair, give me the strength to reclaim my life. Celibate love was at the heart of it, although I can't fully comprehend the mystery of why this should be so. Celibate passion—elusive, tensile, holy.

Kathleen Norris is the author of Dakota *(Ticknor & Fields, 1993).*

Joy . . .

What Is Most Human About Human Sexuality Is Our Unique Capacity for Intimacy

It takes guts as well as gusto to get any of the glory.

By David Schnarch, Ph.D.

One of the great myths of American culture is the belief that we achieved sexual liberation in the 1960s. That was the era we convinced ourselves that sex is a natural function and gave ourselves permission to like sex. The squeaky clean effectiveness of "the new sex therapy" encouraged our technocratic society to believe we could break sex down into its component parts with the right technology, study it, and subdue it. We were about to discover the secrets of eroticism the same way we had cracked the atom.

Many people think it has already happened—that it happened way back then. Just 20 short years ago, clinicians thought that sexual happiness was inherent in sexual functions and successful completion of the sexual response cycle created as much pleasure as any sane person could want. There are many today who still believe this.

The notion that sex is a natural function was actually a giant step forward from the moral degeneracy view of sex that prevailed until that time. It was so widely believed that masturbation led to moral and mental decay that Kellogg's Corn Flakes was originally marketed as a cure.

The trouble is, the belief that sex is a natural function reinforced another widely held idea: the notion that good sex just happens. We expect good sex to happen naturally, especially if we love our partner.

"Society has never promulgated views about sexuality and intimacy to help people get the best of what human sexuality can be."

The idea that good sex just happens, like that of sex being a natural function, is predicated on the notion that sexual response is biologically programmed for all species.

But when good sex or good sexual function doesn't happen, some couples conclude they must not love each other enough. Or they wonder if there's something really screwed up because good sex supposedly happens naturally in the absence of pathology. When the expected genital response does not materialize, you're unwittingly predisposed to jump to conclude that there *is* something wrong with you.

In my 16 years as a sex therapist I have found that the "naturalized" view of sex is not so liberating as it once appeared. It pressures people to have sexual desire and genital response while it makes worrying about sexual performance seem inappropriate. And it obscures what is quintessentially human about human sexuality: our capacity for intimacy. The sex that comes naturally is reproductive sex. Intimate sex, however, is a learned ability and an acquired taste.

I was trained in the conventional beliefs. Blinded by the still-popular rationale that "natural" is naturally good, I never asked myself whether the people I treated for sexual dysfunctions were actually sexually happy. They got happier when their genitals worked. Then problems of sexual desire came into focus.

From *Psychology Today* (July/August 1994), pp. 38–43, 70, 74, 76, 78. Reprinted with permission from *Psychology Today* Magazine. © 1995 (Sussex Publishers, Inc.).

The fact that some people whose genitals worked and who had orgasms could have little desire for sex upset the entire field of sexual therapy in the late 70s. Problems of sexual desire violated basic assumptions about the way sex worked. But rather than change directions, sex therapists made sexual desire "natural" too, comparing it to the desire for food. Low sexual desire was thought of as "sexual anorexia," a kind of illness.

Three decades ago, approaching sex through a medical model legitimized it for scientific study. But the price has been a limited focus on anything more than just functional sex. The shining promise of the sex therapy of the 1960s and 70s never materialized. We must now face the difficult notion that what many of us regard as our "most meaningful sexual experiences" are only a pale version of what we are really capable of—profoundly transcendent communion with another human being.

We are likely to respond to such an assertion by defending our personal experience of sex as reflecting all there is to it, and that's understandable. Nobody gets a yardstick that measures "good sex," and no one gets a manual outlining the limits of human sexual potential.

Society has never promulgated views about sexuality and intimacy to help people get the best of what human sexuality can be. It has always been a palliative for the masses, and as long as it works somewhat okay, that is enough. As a result, we lack a language and concepts to guide us through the long traverse to sexual bliss. For example, we use the words intimacy and sex interchangeably, but they really do not mean the same thing. In fact, we use one to avoid the other.

What our confusion of terms does, however, is make us think they often occur together for most people. Actually, being profoundly intimate during sex is one of the pinnacles of personal development, and a stunning step for our species. Intimacy during sex is, as I shall later discuss, the cutting edge of human evolution.

INTIMACY

Sex can express the best that humans can be and also be a powerful vehicle for getting to that point of personal development. Sex can be ecstatic, self-realizing, and self-transcendent all at once. The great feelings of self-affirmation and declaration of our personhood can make our most powerful genital sensations seem like mere trifles. Experienced together, the physiological and the psychological make a very interesting concoction.

Sex can be more than just a euphemism for "making love." It can be the actual process of increasing love, of sharing it, of whetting your appetite for it, and of celebrating life on its own terms. This process, as I will show, is actually built into the nature of committed relationships. It happens almost spontaneously; the hard part is going through it.

The most important part of "making love" does not involve "skill"; it has more to do with personal development. That link is partly obscured by our attempt to reduce sex to a set of behaviors, and partly by the way we view intimacy. We think of intimacy as involving reciprocity, the expectation that your partner is supposed to understand, validate, and "be there for you" when you disclose your deepest secrets. In practice, intimacy commonly becomes, "I reveal something about myself and you tell me I'm okay. If you accept me, maybe I'm not as bad as I thought I was."

However, our common misconception destroys intimacy in long-term relationships and stops sexual novelty. It blocks people from moving forward sexually because it prevents the introduction of anything new. When we are young—or perpetually immature—our sexual preferences are more determined by avoiding what makes us too nervous, rather than by doing what we really like. The typical sexual relationship develops by each person ruling out what he or she won't do, and then doing whatever options are left. That means a couple is already doing everything consensual. To do something new, one has to suggest something the other has more or less ruled "off limits."

De facto, expanding a sexual relationship involves doing things that one partner doesn't want to do. And if you are dependent on your partner validating your sexual preference, you're stuck. You can't expand your shared sexual repertoire because your partner is not likely to stroke you for suggesting new things. And while I'm in no way encouraging marital rape, the path to expanding how we feel good sexually is paradoxically often through things that don't make us feel good at first.

The fact that most people without sexual dysfunction still have utilitarian mediocre sex reflects how few of us are willing to make the journey. Better sex is not a matter of technique or dexterity. To get it, you've got to hold onto yourself. That is the paradox: You have to learn to hold onto yourself emotionally while holding onto your partner physically.

While *other-validated intimacy* has its time and place, marriage is not often one of them. What is more often necessary and important in long-term committed relationships is a nonreciprocal intimacy I call *self-validated intimacy*. It involves self-confrontation and self-disclosure in the presence of a partner. Period. It doesn't say what your partner does.

It feels good when our partners agree with and validate us, but you can't count on it. If you demand it, you can land in the crazy conundrum that creates eternal insecurity: We put a spin on what we reveal about ourselves in order to get the response we want. Then we can never feel secure with those who accept us because we know they don't really know us. When you are willing to validate yourself, you can afford to let your partner know you as you are. You stop presenting yourself the way you want to be seen, and you just disclose with no other goal than being truly known.

Self-validated intimacy sounds like: "I want you to know me before I die. I want to share with you my days, which would otherwise be less meaningful. It would be nice if you agreed with me, wonderful if you liked me. But most of all I want to know that somebody really knew who and what I am. More than I fear your rejection I fear never reaching across my mortality, which separates me from you and others. I will care for my own feelings. Just know me—including my sexuality."

Intimacy, it should now be clear, is not always soothing and doesn't always "feel good." It is, however, how we forge ourselves into the people we would like to be.

Our culture is replete with misinformation about sexual intimacy—meaning intimacy during sex. Women's magazines, for example, regularly advise readers to dress themselves in Saran Wrap or do something else new. Everybody knows it is necessary to introduce novelty. Why don't we? Because it's a function of personal development, not knowledge.

It could be very exciting to do something novel like greet your sweetie at the door stark naked. The problem is the next step: What happens if he or she walks right by and asks what you fixed for dinner? Most of us would take our partner's response personally and feel devastated. We won't risk that because we lack the inner strength to handle this possibility. When you're so exposed, it's a test of personal integrity to remember your partner might be so frightened the only way he or she can handle it is to focus on pot roast. But don't make the common assumption that you "failed to communicate" just because your partner didn't handle your "question" well and you didn't like the "answer."

It's unrealistic (but common) to expect a partner to make the work of life easier—or to make sex easier, for that matter. For ease and efficiency, masturbation wins out. But sex with a partner can be a great teacher about life and relationships—and about oneself. A monogamous long-term relationship is a powerful way to explore the mysteries and paradoxes of human connection. Fundamentally, we are social animals. Deprived of feel-good human contact comfort, infants fail to thrive.

FEELING GOOD

Feeling good drives human evolution and our capacity for sexual experience. Sociobiologists like Helen Fisher, Ph.D., author of *The Sex Contract* and *The Anatomy of Love*, report that our ability to feel good with other people has literally driven the shape of human evolution—and prompted us to further evolve our capacity for feeling good. This is the force behind human females' evolutionary shift from estrus-related sexual receptivity to nonseasonal sexual desire; the development of a forward-tilting uterus permitting face-to-face intercourse; the natural selection of men for their capacity to pair bond; and our complex sexual-emotional interpersonal signaling system.

Bonded together by the ability to make each other feel good, our ancestors began staying together year round and paved the way for language, and with it, our capacity for self-reflection, our ability to bring high meaning to sex. All of these abilities came into being through our neocortex, the latest part of our brain to evolve. And with them came the ability to raise the "I/Thou" distinction, fundamental to intimacy, into an art form and to a spiritual plane. Perhaps if we were more open to the integration of sexuality and spirituality, we would not be so surprised to see sex, intimacy, and Martin Buber as bedfellows.

What we in Western society have previously considered human sexual response is more accurately a model of mammalian sexual response: it is purely physiological. True intimacy, however, is a self-reflective process, and the concept of self is rooted in the neocortex. This is what is most human about human sexuality.

Our neocortex increases our ability to give meaning to life. No other species has the capacity to bring to life and sex the meanings that we can, because of the subtleties we can make in meanings. Through intimacy we participate in evolution.

In contrast to a physiological model of human sexuality, I have developed a model of *human* sexuality, called The Quantum Model, that takes into account our neocortex and the impact of meanings and meaningfulness. We are meaning-making animals; the more meanings we bring to sex, the more richness our life has—and the greater our ability to feel good.

Several hundred thousand years ago, our species traded programmed sexual regularity for the ability to bring meaning to sex. The involvement of our neocortex in sex, however, not only paves the way for satisfaction—it's what causes most sexual dysfunctions.

The receiver's mental and emotional processes, how we feel about what we're doing during the time we're doing it, is a bigger determinant of the overall level of stimulation we experience than the tactile maneuvers. How we perceive physical contact can either potentiate, mitigate, or debilitate the sensate dimension, and plays a large role in whether our bodies function the way we think they're supposed to. It plays an even bigger role than orgasms do in determining whether or not we're "satisfied."

SEX AND SPIRITUALITY

The point of all this talk about brain function and intimacy is to help us recognize the significance of common experience. Our involvement in sex can vary from absolutely superficial—where two people are just triggering reflexes in each other's bodies—to the point of profound meaning. When we are profoundly involved in sex, it taps the core of who we are. In other words, we often have untapped sexual potential for feeling good.

Having sex at the limits of one's potential involves profound connection that takes place on multiple levels. The obvious one is profound connection with your partner—but there is also something higher. There's the experience of the oceanic, doing something that every generation around the world has done from time immemorial. You join the passing generations, part of the flow of life.

Strange things happen when we have sex at the limits of our potential. That we hear so little about this spiritual side of sex reflects how few people ever reach their sexual potential.

- There is time stoppage. It is a consequence of profound involvement.

- There's also a lack of awareness of pain. I work with people who have arthritis. I advise them to have sex in the morning, so they will have less pain—but to have less pain they have to be involved.

- There is a laserlike focusing of consciousness. Deeply engrossed, you become oblivious to extraneous noise, day-to-day reality fades, and your world ends at the edges of your bed. There is often a vacationlike sense of transportation.

- Age shifting is another phenomenon. You may be holding your partner's face in your hands and suddenly see, in a very loving way, what he or she will look like older, or exactly what he looked

like when he was eight years old. It is very moving.

In the timeless connection of profound sex—if we have the strength, and that is an important caveat—we have the opportunity to drop our mask, to drop our character armor, and to let ourselves be seen behind the eyeballs, metaphorically and literally. It's where we see ourselves and our partners against the backdrop of the mystery (and absurdity) of life. For this reason, I note how many people insist on having sex with their eyes closed or in the dark, and help my clients learn to have sex with their eyes open.

Another facet of the spirituality of sex reveals itself when people approach their sexual potential. There is a spontaneous shift in the nature of desire, from desire out of emptiness to desire out of fullness. The "blue-balls" or "horniness" biological model of desire that currently pervades both professional practice and society, is desire out of emptiness. It presumes that once you reach orgasm, you aren't interested in your partner anymore.

"For ease and efficiency, masturbation wins out. But sex with a partner can be a great teacher about life, relationships—and oneself."

People who desire out of fullness find they're already emotionally satisfied. They seek out their partner not for purposes of reassurance or validation but to celebrate what they *already* feel. Orgasm doesn't diminish desire for their partner, or for sex either. Afterwards, they don't roll over and go to sleep. They want to keep going until their soul, not just their body, is done.

Desire out of fullness carries with it a wonderful feeling of finally feeling clean about your sexuality. Your sexuality actually enhances your personhood rather than diminishes it. You feel desirous and desirable in and of yourself and clean about desiring others. If the Garden of Eden were recreated on earth, I think it would take form in our bedrooms through our capacity for sex and intimacy.

Slowly a different conceptualization of sex, a spiritual sexuality, is starting to evolve. There's a lot more to it than just shouting "Oh God" in mid-orgasm. Part of that great feeling lies in realizing you've reached a level of sexual development beyond what occurs between adolescents in the back seat of a '57 Chevy.

Western culture, however, has been highly sex negative (and continues to be in subtle ways). This is a result of the mind-body duality that has dominated Western thinking for centuries. For too long society has preached that liberation of the soul involves rejecting the pleasures of the flesh. In reality it occurs through sexual development and feeling good, rather than self-abnegation. Even the secular world has almost no culture of happy romantic love, and certainly not within marriage. There is little foundation to support modern expectations for feeling good in long-term relationships, which is one reason why so many feel so bad about trying to feel better about sex.

SEXUAL STYLES

Although most people think of sex as something that they *do*, we are here redefining sex as an expression of who and what you *are*. Eroticism determines who you copulate with and which behaviors you like. Eroticism is what turns you on. It's the style and manner in which you want to engage your partner sexually. It is the way you want to have sex. Eroticism is not the same thing as behavior, but is expressed in the nuances of behavior. It determines not just whether or not you like oral sex but the style of that oral sex.

Eroticism shows up in your sexual style, and people who give play to their eroticism often find style is more important than technical skill. Technical skill is just a tool. You need enough technical skill to express a variety of intents. The most important part of eroticism is a function of personal development—the breadth of meanings you can bring to sex.

"The most important part of eroticism is a function of personal development; it's the breadth of meanings you can bring to sex."

Meanings are conveyed in the minute nuances of sexual style. The more meanings you can bring to sex, the broader the possibilities for engaging your partner. The more subtleties you can have, the more novelty you can have—because there are limits to the ways to juxtapose two sets of orifices.

Sex is like a language. Some of us can converse just enough to get along, like travelers in a foreign land, limited to merely making love and/or the exaltation of body sensations. Some of us, however, are poets; we bring a large vocabulary of meanings to sex. As a wordsmith recognizes fine distinctions among words, the sexual poet can bring so much meaning to sex it takes all we can muster to figure out the meaning, even if we can't author the message the same way.

It is the meanings in sex that drive us crazy. Think, for instance, about one partner performing oral sex on the other. What about the issue of gusto? If your partner really doesn't like it (or you), you can tell him or her how to move their hand or mouth till their fingers fall off—you're not going to get what you're looking for. Your partner may be stimulating your genitals to exact technical specifications and you'll still be frustrated because you know something is missing.

You can bring another to orgasm and withhold from them at the same moment. We do that all the time. I call it *normal marital sadism* because it is so common in long-term relationships.

Eroticism is not for the weak because recognizing there is more to get involves realizing that you're not getting it. The question is, why? Am I not up to it? Is my partner not up to it? Is my partner up to it but withholding from me? And how am I going to get it out of him or her?

SEXUAL PRIME VS. GENITAL PRIME

In the process of teaching medical students and physicians at Louisiana State University School of Medicine in New Orleans, I've learned that reading textbooks can be a liability. Textbooks teach us that men reach their sexual peak in adolescence; women supposedly reach theirs shortly thereafter. This is untrue—but people live down to it just the same. The textbooks are actually focusing on genital responsiveness, the quickness with which a man will have an erection, his speed in getting a second erection and the strength of his ejaculations.

It *is* true that men reach their genital prime in adolescence. And it *is* downhill from there for everyone—if sexual prime is only measured by how quickly your body responds. But if you want intimacy with your sexuality—which has a huge psychophysiologic impact—then there isn't a 17-year-old alive who can keep up with a healthy 50-year-old. Intimacy has to do with what's inside you; there just isn't that much inside a 17-year-old.

As people get older, their capacity for self-validated intimacy—and intimate sex—increases. At age 16, a girl might let the guy "do it to her." When she's older, she'll "do" her partner. This ability arises from acceptance of herself in general and of her eroticism in particular. That usually doesn't happen until she's got a few stretch marks and cellulite. Maybe we've "had sex" or "made love" with one or more partners, but many of us have yet to "do" somebody or allow ourselves to be "done." In terms of sex at profound intensity or emotional depth, most of us are virgins.

Our mistaken emphasis on genital prime gives rise to what I call the "piece-of-meat model of sex." One consequence is that what you do sexually is a consequence of what your body looks like. Women often don't do behaviors they might otherwise like because of the way they think their body might appear to their partner. It makes people self-apologetic and not expect much as they get older. When you don't expect too much, and feel you don't deserve too much, you don't go looking for much.

Confusing genital prime with sexual prime also creates a power struggle inside the typical American family. Most families with an adolescent have a topsy-turvy power hierarchy. Everyone at home believes the teen has more sexual potential than do the adults (who are supposedly past their prime), with negative impact all around. The unstated assumption that parents are over the hill fosters defiance and the belief that parents are advising teens against sex only because they want their offspring to be as sexually frustrated as they are. There are not many parents who want to tell their kids: "Look, your Dad (Mom) and I have been banging away for 30 years and we're just getting to the point we're getting good at it."

If we teach teens that they won't reach their sexual potential for another 30 years or so, they can relax (and parents can too). It suggests teens may have a reason to listen to parents about sex. It means less pressure to be sexually active now, and less disappointment with the experience if they are.

No other culture expects young kids to do what older adults can. Only in our youth-dominated society do we end up with the perverted view that adolescence is the epitome of sexuality. It fits our model of romantic love: two strangers who really don't know each other.

DOWNHILL PHALLACY

Most people never reach their sexual potential. Those who do so are often well into the fourth, fifth, and sixth decade of life. Yet, for most people sex *does* run downhill with age, although it doesn't have to. The problem is not age, but expectation. Conventional beliefs and rules result in mediocre, downhill sex. We never realize our experience is a function of how we approach it—we think it reflects irreversible physiological processes.

As long as couples take a phallocentric approach to sex—as our society teaches—sex indeed is going to run downhill, because men's genital response slows with age. And if women always "stay in place"—which means one step behind the men sexually—then couples will often stop having sex when they get older.

The research is clear. Studies of geriatric couples in good physical health who stopped having sex found husbands and wives in agreement: it was the *man* who called the halt. In sex, the lowest common

denominator always runs the show. Early in relationships it's often the woman's reluctance that controls sex; in later life, it's the man's real or anticipated difficulty getting an erection that prevails.

It's not hard to understand how this happens: We believe that men in heterosexual relationships are supposed to be the sex experts and initiators. As the relationship starts out he is happy because he feels competent. She likes it because she doesn't have to demonstrate that she knows more about sex than he does; she feels taken care of. The two grease each other's identities and egos. He stimulates her and turns her on, and when she's (half) ready to be penetrated, he does. This works for 17-year-old boys because they have an instant erection, but the erection has nothing to do with their partner—seeing a brassiere on a clothesline has the same effect.

Over time in a relationship, more stimulation of every kind is needed. Sex gets boring because the couple is doing "the usual." In addition, the man now requires direct stimulation of the penis to have an erection. The woman needs comparable stimulation to become fully lubricated. The problem is, everybody believes the way you had sex at 17 is the way you're supposed to do it forever.

"Women often don't do behaviors they might otherwise like because of the way their body might appear to their partner."

Until there's a problem, nothing in their experience suggests to the woman that she is supposed to stimulate his penis, or to the man that it is okay for her to do that. He feels inadequate because he "shouldn't need it." She feels awkward doing it, and possibly thinks he finds her attractiveness fading. She doesn't want to start something he may not want to finish and she'd unfortunately probably take it as personal rejection. The result is two people believing they are not desirable to each other on account of their misbeliefs. They are less likely to get started, and more likely to interpret anything that happens negatively—in line with their misconceptions.

Indeed, men who focus on the sensation in their loins report a roll-off in sexual intensity as they get older. (Women often report the opposite, because they finally allow themselves to revel in their experience.) But couples who learn to integrate their increasing capacity for intimacy in their sex often report the most intense encounters of their lives. Intimacy acts as another kind of stimulation; it has a whopping psychophysiological impact.

Profound intimate connection, often experienced for the first time when spouses are well over 45, can do more than compensate for the role-off in physiological responsiveness. Many of the people who come for therapy or who attend intensive couples retreats connect with their partner at levels some people don't even know exists. The result is often stronger erections in men, and more intense orgasms for both partners, than they've had in years—or ever. But the process isn't "easy."

Achieving sexual potential requires the strength to change the rules in your relationship, usually with a reluctant partner. It's hard to do this as time goes on in a committed relationship because your partner becomes increasingly important to you (even if you don't like them). We get less willing to risk our partner's rejection, and less willing to show them a part of ourselves they have not yet seen. People often have to get to the point of desperation.

You also have to stand apart from almost everything you've ever been taught about sex, and use your own sexuality as a compass to explore what human sexuality can be. You have to follow what actually works, instead of a preconceived notion of what works. You have to become your own sexual scientist. In a sense, we are all pilgrims: Our capacity for intimacy has been around for a fraction of geologic time, and we don't yet have the owner's manual.

Long-term sexual partners can give up on themselves, or shed preconceived notions that worked (partially) only when they were younger. You have to claim your own life and your own bed, muster the courage to accept yourself, throw away the rule book, and see what works for you. It takes a tremendous amount of integrity and self-respect—often much more than people have. And yet, the challenge furthers the process of self-development.

THE SEXUAL CRUCIBLE

Very often, the reason we go on this ultimately liberating exploration is because our relationship is sinking. If you're able to float along with "adequate" genital functioning, you figure the old way is the right way. We want those sexual rules clear; they are our sole extant yardstick of adequacy. The difficult and frightening alternative is to believe in yourself. It usually takes sexual difficulty, sexual boredom, or the possibility of divorce to open us to a different course.

This is what I call the sexual crucible: When couples think they are falling apart, they are often on the verge of having the best sex of their lives. The fact that the relationship gets sexually boring eventually makes you push and shove in your relationship to create something new. It produces the stimulus for people to grow. It increases your level of personal development, forcing you to stand on your own two feet —or get divorced.

Sexual boredom is a dynamic part of committed relationships: It is often the catalyst in the sexual crucible, stimulating us to become people capable of having the sex we want. And in the midst of this anxious process, we stop being afraid of being anxious. Life rarely offers us the choice of being anxious or not. Adults realize that the choice is about which anxiety you're going to have. Ironically, the path to feeling good often involves recognizing things that don't feel good at all.

This just hints at the elegance of committed relationships. They are people-growing machines. What we think are "problems" are often the process of pushing ourselves (and each other) to become people capable of having the marriage we're angry we don't have.

The marital bed is where we play out our rituals of development. The Quantum Model offers a challenging solution: If you want better sex, you have to mature.

EYES-OPEN SEX

Normal sexual styles are designed to *limit* intimacy to tolerable levels, while getting one or both people to orgasm. Intense intimacy makes people nervous, particularly during sex. Therapists (who often have no greater capacity for intimacy than anyone else) have created a technology that can jumpstart your body and bring you to orgasm while it destroys intimacy.

Take the sex therapy approach of "by-passing," which teaches that you should fantasize about somebody or something else during sex if you're angry at your partner. This is the style many of us actually use without lessons from a therapist. Therapists have trained people, and couples have trained themselves, to have sex in a nonintimate fashion, to focus on your body, not on your partner.

Consider my favorite example: people commonly have sex with their eyes closed. We like to think it's really a preference, or it's more "romantic." I believe it's one reason we think love is blind. We would seemingly rather have sex with the fantasy in our head than the partner in our bed. Then we turn around 10 years later and complain, "You're not the person I thought you were." If you want intimacy, open your eyes during sex and look *inside* your partner, behind the eyeballs, while your partner looks inside you.

Having an eyes-open orgasm is the epitome of intimacy, and relatively few people get there. To do it, you have to integrate your partner into your mental sexual pattern to such an extent that your awareness of him or her *enhances* (rather than distracts) your sensory awareness of your own arousal. When you get down to it, awareness of our partner during sex is often a "distraction." It's an elegant demonstration that most of us are not profoundly intimate during sex.

THE COURAGE TO FEEL GOOD

Feeling good takes courage. Contrary to conventional wisdom, feeling bad is easier than feeling good. If feeling good were easy, there'd be more happy people. Being unhappy requires much less of you than does being happy. Feeling good involves the courage not to fold in the face of life's disappointments and frustrations. As it happens, the invitation to develop that courage comes in the visage of a partner who refuses to do something new sexually.

Loving, it turns out, is not for kids. It is not for the weak. The end result of every good relationship is that one partner buries the other. That's what it means to love on life's own terms. How many of us have the strength to love our partner, embracing what the character of C.S. Lewis says in the movie: *Shadowlands*: "The pain then is part of the pleasure now"?

SEX AND THE ART OF ARCHERY

Sex is a lot like Zen archery. The preparation to shoot the arrow is arduous. Shooting the arrow is easy. Once you do the hard work of personal development, all you do is let the arrow go. The arrow shoots itself. Sex flows.

Throwing away the rule book and holding onto yourself can be framed as believing in the God within, believing that there is a good part of you inside. The bedroom, then, becomes a place for spirituality to emerge. Spirituality is the application of faith to everyday life, including when you have your underwear down.

David Schnarch, Ph.D. is Clinical Associate Professor of Psychiatry and Urology at Louisiana State University School of Medicine in New Orleans, where he also conducts a private practice. He is the author of an acclaimed tome for professionals, Constructing the Sexual Crucible: an Integration of Sexual and Marital Therapy, *published by W. W. Norton (1991).*

PART 4

Controlling Fertility

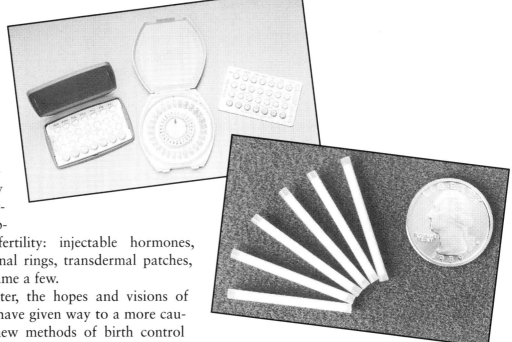

The 1960s ushered in the era of the birth control pill and the hope and promise of more diverse and effective methods of fertility control. Researchers thought they would soon bring to market a wide variety of options for controlling fertility: injectable hormones, hormonal implants, vaginal rings, transdermal patches, and a male pill, just to name a few.

Now, thirty years later, the hopes and visions of those earlier researchers have given way to a more cautious approach. Many new methods of birth control have become embroiled in lawsuits or endlessly delayed in the process of obtaining Food and Drug Administration (FDA) approval. The 1990s has seen the emergence of only three new methods: the female condom, the hormonal implant, and a new injectable form of contraception.

In this part, several of the readings examine the underlying reasons for the failure of the 1960s contraceptive revolution to come to fruition. Other readings discuss some of the newer methods for birth control and reexamine the tried and true methods that have been with us for a while.

A Reading for Critical Thinking

SILENT SPERM

How serious are the reports of the increase in male infertility?
And if the environment is the problem, are any men anywhere safe?
The author consults international experts on a growing scientific controversy.

By Lawrence Wright

A test tube of human ejaculate is a modest sight. The normal fertile male's contribution to the human-reproduction process is about three millilitres of semen—less than a teaspoonful—which may contain between twenty million and three hundred million sperm per millilitre. Semen, the milky-yellowish matrix that sperm swim in, is a rich tonic of Vitamin C, sugar, and certain proteins, enzymes, and alkaline substances, which protect the sperm against the acid environment of the vagina. To estimate the number of sperm in a millilitre of semen, a technician puts a drop of semen on a slide and, looking through his microscope, counts the sperm within a representative sector. The procedure is similar to the way the National Parks Service uses aerial photographs to approximate the size of crowds. Recently, both the quantity and the quality of the human sperm population have come into question. Although a decline in the sperm count has been noted before, in one part of the world or another—and generally dismissed—several new studies report a high proportion of damaged or misshapen sperm and depressed sperm counts in many countries. The apparent drop in the sperm count is so sudden and steep that it has caused some scientists to wonder whether the human species is approaching a fertility crisis. Their views have been amplified in a number of alarming articles in the press, and have set off a fierce debate that rages in scientific journals and conferences around the world. Some scientists are calling for bans on chemicals that may inhibit sperm production; others claim that there is not yet enough evidence even to know whether the sperm count is actually declining, much less that the human race is edging toward extinction.

The current concern is complicated by the fact that in the past the preponderance of research on human reproduction has focussed on the female, for the obvious reason that women bear the children, and also because it was thought that men are not usually the source of infertility in a relationship. Andrology, which is the study of male reproductive disorders, is a new and still small field. It is largely populated by doctors who were trained as gynecologists, for whom men are simply an adjunct to their main interest, or by pediatricians who became interested in males because they treat various problems of infant boys.

A woman produces a single egg every month, whereas a healthy young man produces more than a thousand sperm per second. This superabundance of sperm might seem to be one of nature's extravaganzas, because, in theory, only one sperm is required to fertilize an egg. In practice, however, men whose sperm count falls below twenty million per millilitre have reduced fertility, and those whose count drops below five million are often sterile.

One might imagine a hundred million sperm let loose in a single ejaculation as a sort of tadpole stampede, but a stampede is more orderly than the actual process of fertilization, which could perhaps be better understood as a hundred million tails looking for a hidden donkey. Sperm appear to move about entirely at random and that presumably accounts for the need to have such a vast invasion. Out of those hundred million sperm, only about a hundred thousand stumble through the vaginal canal into the oviduct, despite urging by orgasmic contractions, which nature seems to have intended to help shepherd the sperm into the proper chute. A few dozen may finally reach the egg,

From *The New Yorker* (January 15, 1996), pp. 42–55. Reprinted by permission of The Wendy Weil Agency, Inc. First published in *The New Yorker*.

but there must be one with enough vitality to bore a hole in the zona pellucida, a membrane that helps keep the egg intact. Obviously, then, the odds against any one sperm's reaching its goal are so overwhelming that casualties or greatly reduced numbers imperil the process. It takes a healthy army to achieve conception.

In 1990, a Danish pediatric endocrinologist named Niels E. Skakkebæk set up a department at the National University Hospital in Copenhagen to study the poorly understood phenomenon of male infertility and children's growth disorders. A quiet, physically fit man with skeptical hazel eyes, Skakkebæk, who is fifty-nine, gained a wide reputation for his brilliant studies of testicular cancer in the nineteen-seventies. In the last fifty years, there has been a startling rise in this formerly rare disease—which is particularly common in Denmark, where nearly one out of a hundred men are afflicted with it. Skakkebæk demonstrated that cells similar to precursor testicular-cancer cells can be found even in germ cells of aborted fetuses, indicating that the cancer might be caused by some pre-natal event, although the disease doesn't ripen into its pathological state until after puberty. In his pediatric practice, Skakkebæk was seeing many boys with mal-formations of their genitals, and other boys whose testicles had not descended; in fact, a 1984 study of two thousand Danish schoolboys found that seven per cent of them had one or both testicles lodged inside their bodies—a condition that may lead to sterility and a higher risk of testicular cancer. "They were small pieces of evidence that suggested that there was a problem," Skakkebæk recalls. "We had also been wondering why it was so difficult for sperm banks to establish a core of donors. In some areas of Denmark, they were having to recruit ten potential donors to find one with good semen quality."

Skakkebæk and his colleagues decided to study the sperm of Danish men. They looked first at men who were working in nonhazardous office jobs and at laborers who did not work directly with industrial chemicals or pesticides. Such men, Skakkebæk thought, would provide a healthy baseline against which more risky populations of men could be mea-sured. But these supposedly healthy men proved to have surprisingly low-quality sperm. For decades, it had been believed that the average man produced about a hundred million sperm per millilitre, and of that about twenty per cent was expected to be immo-bile. Roughly forty per cent was abnormal—having two heads or no tail, for instance, or being shaped like a cigar or an overinflated balloon. The only other mammals with similar high rates of mutated sperm are some endangered felines, like the cheetah. Skakke-bæk's study, however, revealed a situation that was far worse than what he had anticipated—that eighty-four per cent of the men had sperm quality below the already dismal standards set by the World Health Or-ganization. The men themselves seemed normal in every other respect.

Skakkebæk was not the first to discover that there was something wrong with the sperm population. In 1974, a provocative study had been done by C. M. Kinloch Nelson and Raymond G. Bunge at the Uni-versity of Iowa. The two physicians had become con-cerned about the number of patients coming to them for infertility evaluations. In the past, sperm counts had generally been conducted among men who were in infertile relationships—in other words, men who were more likely to have low sperm counts than the average man. Nelson and Bunge decided to look at the semen quality of men who were about to undergo vasectomies, and were presumably above average in fertility, since most of those who had been accepted for vasectomies at the clinic had fathered two or more children.

The Nelson and Bunge study reads like a casualty report from some devastating battlefront. In the three hundred and eighty-six fertile men they examined, the average sperm concentration was only forty-eight mil-lion per millilitre, and a scant seven per cent of the men had concentrations above a hundred million—the figure that the previous generation had declared to be average among fertile men. When Nelson and Bunge looked back at the records of men who had come to the hospital twenty years before for infertility evaluations, they found that a large proportion of these supposedly infertile men in the nineteen-fifties had higher sperm counts than the fertile men seeking vasectomies in the seventies. "Something has altered the fertile male population to depress the semen analysis remarkably," the two physicians warned in their final report. "This is obviously speculative, but the overall decrease in the sperm concentration and the semen volumes would tend to incriminate an envi-ronmental factor to which the entire population has been exposed."

After the publication of this report, other studies, in Philadelphia and Houston, also found low sperm counts and poor semen quality. These reports awak-ened the interest of John MacLeod, an eminent anatomist who had retired from the Cornell Univer-sity Medical College in 1972. Although semen analy-sis had been used to evaluate male fertility since the late twenties, it was MacLeod's work in the fifties that set the modern standards for fertility and semen qual-ity. Nelson and Bunge were suggesting that those stan-dards could no longer be met. This was a daring challenge to the medical orthodoxy of the time, since the elderly MacLeod was an august figure in the field: "the king of spermatology" is how Niels Skakkebæk remembers him. In 1979, MacLeod and his colleague Ying Wang published a lengthy critique of the work of Nelson and Bunge. While observing that the sperm counts of fertile males had shown a general decline since the thirties, when the average count in one New York study was a hundred and thirty-seven million per millilitre, MacLeod and Wang argued that there was no reason to accept the notion of a larger, over-all decline. They reported that their own studies showed no corresponding drop among men in childless relationships. Therefore, they reasoned, the apparent decline among fertile men was due to analytical error on the part of the investigators.

Like most people in the field, Niels Skakkebæk regarded MacLeod's conclusions as definitive, and so the subject of declining sperm counts disappeared from mainstream scientific discussion for more than a decade—until 1992, when Skakkebæk and his Danish colleagues decided to review all published studies of sperm counts around the world. Sixty-one studies were included in their survey—which was published in the *British Medical Journal*—going back as far as 1938 and involving a total of about fifteen thousand men with no history of infertility. Although the average sperm count varied from country to country, the clear trend was toward lower sperm counts in the present. The three Danish studies represented in the survey traced a decline in the average sperm count from eighty-six million per millilitre in 1944 to fifty-nine million in 1990. The United States, which provided most of the data, had a similar over-all decline.

On the basis of the findings of the world literature, Skakkebæk computed that the average sperm count in 1940 was about a hundred and thirteen million per millilitre, and that fifty years later it had fallen to sixty-six million. Moreover, the quantity of semen produced in the average ejaculation had also dropped significantly, and thus the total sperm count was even lower than the drop in concentration had indicated. Still more serious was a three-fold increase in men whose sperm count was below twenty million— the point at which their fertility would be jeopardized. "Sperm density has declined appreciably during 1938–1990, although we cannot conclude whether this decline is continuing," Skakkebæk and his colleagues wrote in their report. The Danish researchers linked the falling sperm count to the rise in testicular cancers and other abnormalities that had been found in the male reproductive organs, and they speculated that the results might reflect a widespread reduction in male fertility. Something that was not mentioned in their report—but could scarcely go unremarked upon

by anyone reading it—was what would inevitably happen if the sperm count declined further.

Are young men really less fertile than their elders were? Unfortunately, Skakkebæk's survey is not able to answer this question definitively, since most of the studies in question recorded only the year of ejaculation, not the age of the individual men at the time that the samples were taken. A study conducted in 1962, for instance, might have included men who were born over a period of four, or even five, decades, and thus twenty-year-olds and sixty-year-olds might well have been lumped in the same pile of data.

Skakkebæk and his colleagues represented their findings in the form of a graph that showed the worldwide sperm count over the past fifty years in a straight-line decline—like a ski slope. Their methodology, however, quickly came under fire from scientists, some of whom argued that another way of visualizing the sperm count was as a "Niagara Falls" graph—one that manifested a single, sudden drop in the nineteen-sixties and a levelling off thereafter. If that picture was accurate, then whatever event had caused the decline was probably over, and now the sperm count might actually be making a recovery. Other scientists argued that the counts in the past were artificially high. In any case, though, the fact was that the number of morphologically normal sperm produced by the average man had dropped below the level of those of a hamster, which has testicles a fraction the size of a man's.

Another criticism, which will be advanced in a spring issue of the medical journal *Fertility and Sterility*, argues that the high sperm counts reported in the United States in the past come from regions where the counts are still quite high. Harry Fisch, the director of the Male Reproductive Center at Columbia Presbyterian Medical Center, looked at three areas, including New York City, Los Angeles, and Roseville, Minnesota. He found that there had been an actual increase in the sperm counts in the last twenty-five years, but there were significant differences in the count among the three locations. The count in New York was 131.5 million, in Minnesota 100.8 million, but in California only 72.7 million. Fisch claims that his work refutes the whole notion of a decline in the world's sperm count, but he says that he is prevented from discussing the data prior to publication. Although it is true that a few studies have shown no decline over time in some areas, or even increases, a number of other studies document sharp drops in the sperm counts within particular populations in Belgium, Scotland, and London. The majority of the evidence points to a widespread decline in the sperm count, with significant regional differences that no one can explain.

If there is such a genuine decline, there should be a corresponding decrease in fertility. In the United States, according to the National Center for Health Statistics, the percentage of infertile couples has risen from 14.4 in 1965 to 18.5 in 1995. (In forty to fifty per cent of the cases, the male partners have been the source of the infertility.) But all measurements of fertility in human beings are unreliable, because it is difficult to judge the importance of life-style choices, such as waiting until relatively late in life to try to begin a family. It is clear that more and more couples are seeking infertility treatments or in-vitro fertilization using the semen of anonymous donors. But in the United States, just as in Denmark, the number of donors with good-quality sperm has become distressingly low. As early as 1981, researchers at the Washington Fertility Study Center reported that the sperm count of their donors, who were largely medical students, had suffered a steady decline over the previous eight years. The researchers worried that, if the decline continued at the same rate, there would be within the next decade no potential donors who could meet the approved or recommended standards.

After the Skakkebæk findings came out, various other researchers around the world began to publish new data about sperm counts. There has been little published research comparing racial and ethnic sperm counts, particularly in Africa and many Third World countries. But the studies that we do have show low counts nearly everywhere: the latest count in Nigeria is sixty-four million per millilitre; in Pakistan, seventy-nine and a half million; in Germany, seventy-eight million; in Hong Kong, sixty-two million. In Belgium, scientists note not only a substantial drop in the average count but also a far more disturbing fall in the percentage of healthy, motile sperm.

One of the scientific detractors who saw significant flaws in the Skakkebæk survey was Pierre Jouannet, a reproductive biologist, who is the director of the Centre d'Etude et de Conservation des Oeufs et du Sperme, at the Hôpital Cochin, in Paris. "In my lab, we always had the idea that there was no decline of sperm characteristics," he recently told me. Jouannet's sperm bank had several features that made it ideal for a controlled study. In contrast to the Skakkebæk survey, which had looked at different populations all over the world (reported on by scientists whose methodology had varied from one study to another) and had included both fertile and unfertile men, Jouannet and his coworkers at the Paris sperm bank had been using exactly the same procedures for twenty years; moreover, they had been testing a constant, homogeneous population—healthy, unpaid volunteers, who contributed their semen anonymously for the purposes of artificial insemination. Thirteen hundred and fifty-one men were included in the study, and each of them had previously fathered at least one child; in other words, they were men of proved fertility. Thanks to the French penchant for bureaucratic record-keeping, an impressive store of information had accumulated, and Jouannet and his colleagues believed that it would effectively overturn the hypothesis of a general decline in the quality and quantity of sperm—at least, in Paris. He was confident that the flag of French manhood was still flying high.

And so, in 1993, when the French researchers analyzed their data they were astonished to discover that the concentration of sperm had actually declined on average more than two per cent a year—from eighty-nine million in 1973 to sixty million in 1992. The quality of the sperm had also deteriorated, they found. It was possible, of course, that this drop might have been simply a consequence of life-style changes. For example, wasn't it likely that young French men were having sex more often than their fathers had? In that event, their sperm counts could register at somewhat lower levels, because they hadn't had enough time to recharge. But in fact the average number of sex acts per month—about 9.3 for a twenty-five-year-old French man—had not changed during that time. Jouannet and his colleagues created a subset of men who were in the same age range at the time of their donation and who had been abstinent for three or four days. Among this group, he discovered that the drop in the sperm count was even greater—3.7 per cent a year. The expected sperm count for a Parisian man born in 1945 was a hundred and two million, whereas the count of a man born in 1962 was exactly half that number. The lower sperm counts of Parisian men may be caused by environmental conditions or events of decades ago, so that boys born now could mature with higher sperm counts than their fathers. On the other hand, if the decline were to continue at the same rate, Jouannet says gravely, "it will take seventy or eighty years before it goes to zero."

"The sample comes in in the morning, and the first thing we do is establish the conventional criteria—measurements of ejaculate volume, sperm count, and motility," Stewart Irvine, a gynecologist at the Medical Research Council's Reproductive Biology Unit in Edinburgh, said as he took me through his reproductive-biology lab. "The next thing we do is process the sample in such a way as to separate the sperm from the stuff that it's ejaculated in." After stripping away the cloudy seminal matrix, Irvine's technicians are left with a pale-gray spot at the bottom of the test tube—a pure suspension of human sperm, like an effervescent drop of 7UP.

Irvine put a slide of purified sperm into the maw of a contraption called a Computer-Assisted Sperm Analyzer, or CASA. "This box contains a microscope, an image framestorer, and a microcomputer," Irvine said. The machine made a shuddering noise as it loaded the slide, and then there appeared on the computer monitor an image that looked like a pond of jostling catfish. Active sperm left a green wake on the screen, but there were also numerous red dots where the computer had identified immobile sperm. "By measuring the length of the track, you can tell how fast a sperm is swimming, and by measuring its wobble from side to side you can tell how much propulsive force it generates," Irvine said. "A sperm is like a boat with one oar. Let's see if I can catch that one."

He clicked on a wildly thrashing specimen, which to my eye was shimmying aimlessly across the screen. "This demonstrates quite clearly the sort of patterns that you see—this beautiful oscillatory movement," he said. "From previous work that we've done, we know that these sperm tend to do quite well in achieving pregnancies, because they've got good propulsive force. They penetrate barriers, and so on, whereas these sperm"—Irvine pointed to a sperm that was moving in a more ploddingly straightforward manner—"don't have much force behind them when it comes to knocking the door down, so to speak. Damn, look at that other one! A hundred and ninety microns a second! If you put your ear to the dish, you can hear the crack as he breaks the sound barrier."

Sperm are difficult to study, because they are so dynamic and are hypersensitive to change. The nurseries where the sperm are hatched are called Sertoli cells. The more Sertoli cells a man has, the larger his testicles, and the more sperm he can produce. It takes seventy-two days for the germ cells to mature into streamlined adult sperm, complete with head, midpiece, and whiplike tail. The head carries the payload —a compressed molecular dollop of DNA—surrounded by a helmet of enzymes that will help it break down the wall of the egg. The midpiece of the sperm appears to be little more than a helix of mitochondria—a cell's power stations—wrapped around the axial filaments like a ribbon around a Maypole. In January of last year, researchers at Johns Hopkins discovered receptors on the sperm midpiece which resembled the receptors our cells use to detect certain smells. Apparently, the egg emits a weak bouquet, which lures the nosy sperm into the oviduct. The tail is one long, snapping filament. Altogether, the sperm is an elegant testament to form following function. It is pure purposefulness—the male animal refined into a single-celled, highly perishable posterity-seeking rocket.

Like many scientists, Irvine had his doubts about the Skakkebæk survey when it was first published, but he happened to be conducting a study of Scottish males, and in the course of it he found that men born in the forties had an average sperm count of a hundred and twenty-eight million, whereas those born in the second half of the nineteen-sixties averaged only seventy-five million—a decline of more than forty per cent in a single generation. "In our population, we see an absolutely straight slope down," Irvine said. "I had a colleague visiting from Australia, and he had with him a laptop computer with lots of data from infertile Australian couples. He said, 'I'm sure these sperm-count drops are rubbish. I'm sure there are other explanations for it.' And I said, 'Well, just take your data and plot it by year of birth and see what you get.' He got the same result."

Irvine argues that in achieving pregnancy the quality of the sperm is more important than the quantity. But, according to most recent reports, the ranks of the average army of sperm are increasingly filled with damaged and unmotivated individuals. It's especially shocking when one compares the sperm of humans with that of other mammals. A bull with a five-per cent abnormality rate in its sperm would be shunned for breeding and turned into hamburger, but a man with those numbers could boast of being a splendid rarity.

Apart from his other failings, the human male is one of the least efficient of all sperm producing mammals. A rabbit produces twenty-five million sperm per gram of its testicle weight every day, whereas a man produces little more than four million. Other primates, like the rhesus monkey, which is less than half the size of man but has testicles fifty per cent larger, generate sperm nearly six times as efficiently—more than a billion sperm a day, compared with a hundred and thirty million for the average man. One shouldn't even discuss the boar and the ram.

If the human sperm count is declining, what could cause such a phenomenon? There is no one widely accepted theory. Instead, there is a bewildering array of hypothetical culprits, which range from the residues of birth-control pills in drinking water to the stress of urban living. From the sperm's perspective, modern life abounds with perils. Common antibiotics like penicillin and tetracycline can wipe out a sperm harvest. Tobacco, marijuana, and alcohol can affect spermatogenesis. The effects of these chemicals are usually limited to a brief period following a man's exposure to them; a man who stops smoking marijuana will probably see an improvement in the quality of his sperm within a few months. The testes are acutely sensitive to X rays; even a modest exposure can dampen sperm production for months. Chlamydia is a fertility-impairing venereal disease, and viruses like mumps and chicken pox can also devastate sperm counts. Men who work in in-door car-parking facilities, or spend a lot of time driving in tunnels, where they inhale lead-laden gasoline fumes, risk lower counts, as do agricultural workers who handle certain pesticides. One chemical in particular, dibromochloropropane, or DBCP, causes sterility, and has been banned in the United States. But it continued to be used as a pesticide in a number of other countries. DBCP has allegedly caused epidemics of childlessness among plantation workers.

In 1987, before the current discussion about declining sperm counts began, a group of scientists led by Ralph C. Dougherty, a professor of chemistry at Florida State University, attempted to correlate the drop in sperm counts with a number of variables. There seemed to be no link with such things as mean annual temperature, altitude, population density, or atmospheric radiation. The researchers did find that lower sperm counts were strongly correlated with an area's production of synthetic chemicals, number of automobile registrations, and consumption of meat, fat, and alcohol. More recently, scientists in Finland have found that men with high sperm counts tend to be better educated and to have more money than men with lower counts.

Urban living seems to lead to lower sperm counts. In part, it has been suggested, that may be because men who sit for long periods of time at a desk or behind a steering wheel tend to overheat their testicles, and that lowers their sperm count—just as a hot bath or a high fever will do. "One or two studies looked into underwear styles, and another implicated bicycle riding," Skakkebæk recalls disparagingly. "It was completely ridiculous. Danes have been riding bicycles for years. You don't get undescended testicles from riding bicycles. Tight underwear could never cause the increased problem of testicular cancer."

Stress may adversely affect sperm production. John MacLeod, in his many studies of semen among various populations, found one group with "phenomenally high" sperm counts: long-term prisoners. "One can only speculate why this should be so," MacLeod wrote in 1973. He pointed out that despite the violence that one associates with imprisonment, the life of long-term prisoners is well regulated and relatively stress-free. "They tend to be sequestered from many infectious agents as well as from the pressure to accomplish and to make daily decisions," he wrote. "They are reasonably active physically and keep regular hours." MacLeod theorized that this kind of highly regimented life had a beneficial effect on spermatogenesis. One of

the prisoners whom MacLeod examined produced as many as two and a half billion sperm per ejaculation.

Skakkebæk believes that the real source of the problem is much more ominous than the stresses of modern life. He sees the decline in the sperm count as only one part of a larger assault on the male reproductive organs, which is characterized by high rates of testicular cancer, undescended testicles, and hypospadias, a condition in which the urethral opening is on the underside of the penis, not on the tip. Whatever is happening to men, he believes, some part of it must take place during the early stages of human development—in the womb or else shortly after birth—because damage to the male urogenital system is evident even in certain very young patients. Changes in lifestyle won't help men whose sperm-producing capacity has been crippled at birth.

In Skakkebæk's opinion, the most likely villains are chemicals in the environment which masquerade as estrogen, the female hormone. These chemicals, which can have a temporary effect on adults, can cause permanent damage in boys whose sexual organs are not yet fully developed. There is a provocative model for this theory in the children of mothers who had taken diethylstilbestrol (DES), a synthetic estrogen that from the nineteen-forties to the early seventies was widely prescribed in the United States because it was thought to prevent miscarriage. A small number of the daughters of these women developed an extremely rare form of vaginal cancer at a surprisingly early age. By the time doctors stopped prescribing it, two to three million American women were estimated to have received the drug, even though there was never any evidence that it prevented miscarriage. Some of the estimated one million sons of these DES mothers also developed alarming problems, including not only low sperm counts but also undescended testicles and deformations of the penis—many of the same problems that were later found in Danish males.

DES has now been banned in most countries. "What we didn't know historically is what the level of exposure was in the rest of the world," Richard M. Sharpe, who is a research physiologist with the Medical Research Council in Edinburgh, told me. "There were many in the United States but relatively few in Britain."

Sharpe had known Niels Skakkebæk since 1975, when the Danish scientist was conducting a study in the onset of spermatogenesis in Scottish boys. In 1991, Skakkebæk revealed to Sharpe his findings about the dramatic worldwide drop in the sperm count. "Had it been anyone but Niels, I would have discounted it," Sharpe said. "But Niels is so careful, I knew he must be on to something."

Sharpe began to search for sources of estrogens in the environment that might disrupt the body's hormonal balance in the ways Skakkebæk had been observing. He learned that many different synthetic estrogens are still commonly used as growth promoters for livestock. These also produce meat that is as much as twenty per cent lower in fat. "And this is why there is an enormous industry out there for using estrogens as growth promoters in domestic animals," Sharpe said. "There's hardly an animal alive that's not treated in that way."

Late one Friday afternoon, a colleague suggested to Sharpe that an obvious source of estrogen in infants was powdered milk. Mothers around the world were increasingly using formulas instead of breast milk to feed their babies. In addition to the synthetic hormones that might be present in livestock, cows were more likely than in the past to be milked while they were still in calf—that is, when the levels of their natural hormones were extremely high. Sharpe spent the entire weekend fretting over the awesome responsibility of condemning cow's milk and possibly setting off a worldwide panic. On Monday morning, he telephoned a professor at Cambridge who had done experiments on milk, and learned that the higher levels of estrogen simply weren't present once the milk had been powdered before being blended into baby formula. Sharpe was terrifically relieved, but it left open the mysterious question of where all the estrogen had gone.

Like Skakkebæk, Sharpe thinks that the decline in sperm is linked to some event that affects the endocrine system, which governs the body's hormones. This must happen, he believes, either in the womb or shortly after birth. "I have absolutely no doubt this is the most important time in your life, certainly if you're a male," Sharpe said. "This is when your sperm-producing capacity as an adult is settled once and for all." Sharpe believes that if even a small amount of an extraneous synthetic estrogen slips across the mother's placental boundary at a critical moment and invades the body of a developing fetus, it can have a devastating impact on male sexual development.

Sharpe tested this assumption by introducing minute quantities of DES and several other synthetic estrogens into the drinking water of pregnant rats. "We were looking for small effects," Sharpe said. "What we found is that rats exposed during gestation and lactation via the pregnant mother reveal when they grow up that their sperm production is reduced by anything from five to fifteen per cent."

Sharpe and Skakkebæk reported these findings in an article in the May 29, 1993, issue of *The Lancet*, in which they also advanced the theory that various industrial chemicals were behaving like synthetic estrogens, and that these chemicals might be responsible for the falling sperm count and the rise of disorders in the male reproductive tract. "Of all the hormones we know, the estrogens are the most potent," Sharpe told me. "You can get biological effects from estrogen at levels so low you cannot measure them by any analytical method."

As Sharpe and Skakkebæk were wondering about other sources of estrogen exposure, Sharpe received a call from John Sumpter, a fish biologist at Brunel University, in Uxbridge, England. Sumpter reported that a number of fish in British rivers and streams had been turning up with odd-looking genitalia. They were suffering from a condition called intersex; that is, they contained genitals of both sexes. Male fish were actually producing a female protein, vitellogenin, which is used to make egg yolks. Below sewage outfalls in Northern England, investigators had found that one out of twenty fish were hermaphrodites. Beginning in 1986, Sumpter and his colleagues at Brunel had begun placing cages of male rainbow trout in the rivers below the sewage-treatment lagoons. They found massive responses, indicating that there were some compounds emanating from sewage-treatment works which demonstrate estrogen-like effects in nature.

At first, Sumpter and his colleagues suspected ethynyl estradiol, which is the main form of estrogen found in the contraceptive pill. Ethynyl estradiol is an extremely potent estrogen: the feminizing effect on male trout is evident at doses that are too small to be measured at all. The Pill is so pervasively used in Western cultures that its residue can be found in treated sewage. But it has not been ascertained whether it is also present in drinking water, and Sumpter decided to test other compounds that are readily found in the environment and many household products.

In addition to synthesized estrogens, there are more than a hundred thousand widely used industrial chemicals in the environment, and about a thousand new ones are introduced each year. Until now, these chemicals and their by-products have been tested only for their potential to cause cancer or birth defects—not for their ability to mimic human hormones. Chemicals are classified as estrogenic solely by their effect on living organisms. Cells have receptors that await particular hormones; in boys, for instance, cells with androgen receptors will be activated during puberty and stimulated to grow beards or produce sperm. It is disturbing to realize that these estrogen-like chemicals can pass undetected through a mother's body, creating havoc in the developing fetus.

Estrogens are good for the skin, and for that reason dermatologists prescribe birth control pills for women who may not be sexually active. Estrogens are often found in the more de-luxe shampoos, skin creams, and vaginal creams. Pregnant women rub estrogen lotions on their bellies to avoid stretch marks. Post-menopausal women who take estrogens for hormone-replacement therapy have far lower rates of Alzheimer's disease, osteoporosis, heart attacks, and arteriosclerosis than such women who don't. On the other hand, estrogen has been linked to higher rates of breast cancer, which in the United States has been rocketing upward since the nineteen-forties. One in nine American women will get the disease in her lifetime. Breast cancer in men—a phenomenon that was almost unseen until recently—is becoming increasingly common.

There may be other effects on the population, which haven't been understood. For instance, some girls who use certain estrogenized shampoos have been found to develop breasts prematurely. Also, girls throughout the world are now reaching puberty at an earlier age than ever before in history. Could this be connected to environmental estrogens? And if estrogens are increasingly used as growth promoters in the food we eat what will happen to us as a result? "You ask yourself why people are bigger and taller now," Sharpe told me. "And people say that's due to better nutrition. It probably is. You just wonder at the same time if there might be other factors at work."

If estrogen can cause physiological changes, it might be able to bring about behavioral changes as well. Patricia L. Whitten, a biological anthropologist at Emory University, has begun to explore the provocative idea that changes in sexual behavior, such as the declining age of first intercourse, may be tied to changes in the diet as well as biological differences in the human body which are caused by the increased burden of organic chemicals in the environment. We are only beginning to understand how human beings and other animals adjust to the panoply of chemicals that we continually introduce into the environment, and thus into ourselves.

There are isolated examples of other animals in nature that are experiencing reproductive problems quite similar to man's, including decreased fertility and sex reversals. As a result of the dumping of DDT into the Los Angeles sewer system over more than two decades, female Western Gulls—they have come to be called "lesbian gulls"—took to nesting together, because the males had apparently lost interest. In the early nineteen-eighties, the alligator population of Lake Apopka, Florida, crashed after a chemical-mixing plant spilled into the lake a large amount of a

pesticide called dicofol, which contains DDT. Researchers have found estrogen levels in female hatchling alligators that are nearly twice what they should have been, and juveniles' ovaries appear burned out—as if menopausal. The males register practically no testosterone. Penis sizes are smaller—three-quarters to two-thirds of what they used to be. Also in Florida, only about thirty-five panthers survive, and of those many of the males have undescended testicles. Until recently, this situation was attributed to inbreeding, but when scientists looked at the panthers' hormone levels they found that the males had twice as much estrogen as they had testosterone. The quality of the sperm was wretched: seventy-five per cent were deformed—almost as bad as the situation Skakkebæk found in the average Danish man.

Of course, natural estrogens have always been present in many plants, among them alfalfa, cabbage, spinach, and rye. One thinks of these phytoestrogens as harmless, even beneficial, but some of them have demonstrably powerful effects on animals. Some species of clover can lower sperm counts in rams and cause aberrant sexual behavior in ewes. Alfalfa can cause nymphomania in cattle, and sorghum can induce abortions. Certain phytoestrogens are particularly abundant in soya, which is an ingredient of many baby foods and is increasingly being used as a meat substitute. But it is not yet known whether the levels of phytoestrogens in soy products would be sufficient to have developmental effects on humans.

Although the impact of this highly estrogenized environment on humans is uncertain, it is well known that men who work directly with estrogen tend to become feminized. In 1989, there was a curious article in *Acta Cytologica* about a male mortician who visited a clinic in Philadelphia complaining of a mass in his breast. A mammogram and tissue examination revealed that he was indeed developing a bosom. For the past four or five years, he had been applying an embalming cream to the faces of the corpses that he prepared. Embalming cream is rich in estrogens, and when the mortician took to wearing rubber gloves his problem abated. Men who have worked in plants that manufactured DES or birth-control pills have also experienced enlarged breasts. A recent study in London of a thousand men who suffered from "male menopause"—a syndrome with symptoms that include a drop in libido and potency, accompanied by fatigue and depression—found a subgroup of men who had worked on farms where chickens and turkeys were raised. It was a common practice for domestic fowl to be implanted with estrogen pellets. These caponized birds are plump and tender, with the great swollen breasts that are so highly favored by chefs and consumers. Unfortunately, the farmers became partly caponized themselves. Caponizing birds by this method was outlawed after it was discovered that men who frequently ate estrogenized fowl—particularly waiters in chicken restaurants—exhibited low fertility and developed breasts.

In 1993, Sharpe and Sumpter decided to test various common chemicals to determine whether they had an estrogen effect—Sharpe with his pregnant rats and Sumpter with his male trout. Among the compounds that they tested were octylphenol and butyl benzyl phthalate—both exceedingly common. Octylphenol belongs to a class of sturdy compounds called alkylphenol ethoxylates (APEs), which have been found in river water at rather high levels. They are often used as emulsifiers and are found in detergents, paints, herbicides and pesticides, plastic wraps, textiles, spermicides and condom lubricants, cosmetics and hair colorings. APEs are very resistant to breaking down, and for that reason they have been banned in home detergents in the United Kingdom (though not in the United States). Phthalates, which make plastic flexible, are the most abundant man-made chemicals in the environment, and they are present in the human diet. When Sharpe and Sumpter tested these chemicals in animals at levels approximating average human exposure, they found effects similar to those of DES: male trout produced female proteins, and the male rat pups matured with smaller-than-average testes and lower sperm production.

The environmental-estrogen hypothesis opened up fascinating but disturbing possibilities. "The evidence we have from people like Niels Skakkebæk and his colleagues is very suggestive," Philippe Grandjean, a professor of environmental medicine at Odense University, in Denmark, told me. "We thought in the past that these toxic substances would act on a target—an enzyme or DNA or the cell membrane, or something like that. But what these endocrinologists have suggested to us is that industrial chemicals can actually mimic hormones. It looks as if the receptors aren't very good at recognizing what is a hormone and what's not a hormone—perhaps because they were never previously challenged. These receptors have been kept almost unchanged in the mammalian world, because they worked. They functioned very well. But in this century we have generated all these new chemicals and injected them into the environment, and suddenly the body is exposed to new substances that in some cases can interact with that receptor. The human species is totally unprepared for this, because it has never happened before. I think the perspective is both very exciting and very, very frightening."

For some scientists, however, there are too many things about the estrogen hypothesis that don't add up. "The estrogen link is total bunk," Stephen Safe, a professor of toxicology at Texas A. & M., told me. According to Safe's calculations, the amount of estrogenic industrial compounds that we consume is an inconsequential fraction of the natural estrogenic flavinoids we get from fruits and vegetables in our diet, and the hormonal effects of most of these industrial chemicals are puny in comparison with those produced by the body's far more robust forms of estrogen. In some Eastern countries, like Japan, the amount of estrogen in the diet is many times as high as it is in the West, mainly because of the high consumption of soy-based products, but there is no corresponding rise in breast cancer. On the other hand, the men in Asian countries, and particularly in Japan and Hong Kong, have comparatively small testicles and commensurately low sperm counts.

Safe admitted that he didn't have a clue to what could be causing lower sperm counts and other male reproductive problems. "Lord only knows," he said. "It may be a very regional thing. But just because Denmark has a problem and a few alligators in a swamp below a Superfund site develop small penises doesn't mean our sperm counts are going down or our reproductive success has declined. I just don't think we should extrapolate."

In 1993, as the debate about environmental estrogens was raging in the scientific journals, a very tall man appeared in the office of an orthopedic surgeon in Cincinnati, complaining of knock-knee. The man, who was twenty-eight, told the surgeon that he had been of average stature until the end of puberty, when his peers naturally settled into their mature adult height, but he had kept growing—far beyond the size of his parents. When he talked to the surgeon, he was six feet eight and wore a size-18 shoe. The surgeon took an X-ray, and it showed that the tips of the man's long bones, which are supposed to fuse together and signal the end of growth, were still separated. The tall man was otherwise perfectly ordinary-looking, but he had the skeleton of an enormous teen-ager. He was also, apparently, unique in medical history. No one else had ever simply not stopped growing.

It is generally believed that growth in males is arrested by male hormones called androgens, which are produced in both males and females. This assumption is based on the fact that the bones fuse at a time when testosterone, a male's most abundant androgen, is at a high level. One might conclude, then, that there was some deficiency in the male hormone that caused this young man to be trapped on an adolescent escalator. But men who lack an adequate amount of androgens or are insensitive to them also share a highly distinctive feature: they look like women, even to the point of having breasts and a vagina. Usually, they don't learn that they're men until the onset of puberty, when they fail to menstruate. This man looked like a man.

The tall man was eventually sent to see Eric P. Smith, an associate professor of pediatrics in the division of endocrinology at the University of Cincinnati College of Medicine. Smith noticed that the man had high levels of estrogen in his blood. "That was quite curious," Smith told me. "It was unusual to see in a man who appeared so normal. With estrogen at that level, one would expect to see breast enlargement." Instead, the patient had ordinary beard growth, a deep voice, morning erections, and normal heterosexual arousal to women.

Another possible explanation of the man's condition was that he lacked the ability to receive estrogen in his cells. But if that was the case, the tall man should never have been born, because without estrogen an embryo supposedly cannot implant itself in the uterine wall. But Smith had just learned of a strain of mice that had been created, in a National Institute of Environmental Health Sciences lab, with defective estrogen receptors. "That flew in the face of the dogma that such an animal would not survive," Smith said. He decided to test this hypothesis by administering to his overgrown patient massive doses of estrogen through skin patches, similar to the therapy given to men with prostate cancer or to transsexuals undergoing a sex change. After six months, however, the tall man showed none of the usual effects of estrogen therapy—weight gain, breast growth, headaches, mood alterations—nor had his bones fused. Smith concluded that his patient was resistant to estrogen and hypothesized that his estrogen receptors were defective. This finding was later confirmed by DNA analysis.

Until the estrogen-receptor mutant stepped into the discussions, the accepted wisdom had been that estrogen had only a very small role to play in male biological processes: it was considered to be a kind of androgynous artifact, like nipples on men. The tall man had demonstrated that our understanding of the role of hormones in human development was shockingly primitive and, in many cases, simply wrong. The typical male brain, for example, has estrogen receptors in certain regions, and it was thought that one of the few functions that this hormone might have in males was to "masculinize" the brain. But the tall man's brain was apparently already fully masculinized, and this left the function of those receptors still unknown.

More to the point, the tall man's sperm count was found to be low—twenty-five million per millilitre—and only eighteen per cent of his sperm was alive. "I must say I was surprised," Smith told me. "Intuitively, you would think that spermatogenesis would not be affected if your estrogen receptor was not functional—that, if anything, you might have more robust spermatogenesis."

Of course, it is dangerous to generalize widely on the basis of the case of a man who is in so many ways unique. But it turned out that the mice who were without estrogen receptors also had very low sperm counts. The case of the tall man, whose sperm-producing cells seemed unaffected by the presence of estrogen in his body, illustrates that something other than estrogen can be responsible for low sperm counts. In this scenario, other chemicals in the environment may affect the hormonal balance by blocking either the estrogen receptors or the androgen receptors, or both. It is possible that those chemicals are even more potent in their effect than environmental estrogens. Dioxin, which is a by-product of chemical manufacturing and of the pulp-and-paper industry, is present at low levels nearly everywhere in the environment, and it can cause an astonishing amount of damage. "Our studies [in rats] show that a single dose of dioxin administered during pregnancy permanently reduces sperm counts in the males by about sixty per cent," Earl Gray, who is a research biologist at the Environmental Protection Agency, told a House of Representatives subcommittee in 1993. Gray's lab has also been examining a widely used pesticide called vinclozolin. It is an antiandrogen, which is to say that it blocks the receptors of the male hormone. Vinclozolin administered to a pregnant rat emasculates the male pups to the point that they are indistinguishable from the females. But it has little effect on the females. It is clear that there are a number of other chemicals that have the ability to imitate or block human hormones, and scientists like Gray are only beginning to take an inventory of such compounds. "With sperm counts, I've been more impressed by the dioxins and PCBs than by the estrogens and anti-androgens," Gray said. "We get surprising effects at relatively low doses."

Even Richard Sharpe, whose research did so much to advance the environmental-estrogen hypothesis, admits that it remains unproved. "The remarkable thing about the whole DES episode in human beings is that, for something that was conducted on such a large scale, using colossal amounts of such a potent hormone, the effects on both the male and the female offspring were of such low incidence," Sharpe says. For Sharpe and many other scientists, the hunt for the cause of declining sperm counts is far from over.

Lately, he has actually begun to wonder if humanity has undergone an evolutionary mutation that may have seriously jeopardized its ability to produce sperm.

Whatever combination of factors is causing the sperm counts to fall, the answer seems to lie in the differences between the Danes and the Finns. A 1993 survey of six studies of Finnish men found that their average sperm count was a hundred and fourteen million per millilitre—nearly double the worldwide average and two and a half times that of Denmark. (Sweden and Norway have sperm counts slightly above Denmark's.) As Skakkebæk would have predicted, on the basis of the high Finnish sperm counts, the rate of testicular cancer in Finland is a fourth that of Denmark, and the prevalence of malformed penises is approximately a third. Yet these countries are near neighbors, with much in common in their diets, their cultures, and their environments. How could the men in these countries vary so widely in their sperm counts?

Several prominent scientists are investigating what is informally called the Mystery of the Finnish Testicles. Some of the explanations seem counterintuitive, if not comical. For instance, there is the well-known Finnish fondness for saunas. A hot sauna should temporarily flatten a man's sperm count. Spermatogenesis is extremely sensitive to heat—that's why a man's gonads are outside his body, and why the scrotum expands and contracts. Sperm like to be about two degrees cooler than the temperature of the body. But few scientists accept the notion that saunas somehow acclimate the testicles to higher temperatures than those which are thought to be caused by central heating and the modern sedentary life style.

Jyrki Suominen, who is an andrologist at the University of Turku, in Finland, and his colleague Matti Vierula, who is a lecturer at the university's Institute of Biomedicine, have a theory that could provide a novel solution to the Finnish-testicle mystery. "Studies show that man is a seasonal breeder," Vierula told me in Suominen's office, and he pointed to a graph that correlated the variations in the average Finnish sperm count with the months of the year. "Sperm counts are highest in the winter." Perhaps the summer heat depletes the sperm and Finland is less likely to suffer such losses because it has a cooler climate. Some researchers have theorized more broadly that global warming has thrown a blanket over sperm production. A study in New Orleans, however, compared sperm concentrations of men who worked in air-conditioned buildings with those of men who worked outdoors, and, surprisingly, both groups showed a twenty-per-cent decline in their sperm count during the summer months. This suggested that temperature was not a factor, though some other seasonal difference might be at work. Suominen and Vierula think that what distinguishes low summer sperm counts from high winter counts is the relative absence of light. If this is true, then one might speculate that the Finns have an advantage over the Danes in the form of longer nights. Vierula hypothesizes that people today live in a perpetual artificial summer. "When we use artificial light, we lengthen our days," he explains. "Some studies suggest that women's menstrual cycles react to the amount of light, and I think our testicles react as well."

Another plausible explanation is that significant genetic differences may predispose Finnish men toward larger testicles and therefore higher sperm counts. Most Finns come from different ethnic stock than the Danes do—they are related to the Hungarians—but there has been little scientific research into the comparative testes sizes of ethnic groups. Testes are measured with an orchidometer, which is a sort of necklace of beads of various sizes a doctor wears around his neck. With one hand, he gauges the size of a man's testicle, and with the other he tries to determine the bead of equivalent size, among beads ranging in size from a pea to a plum. Until a definitive study is done on the basis of this procedure, however, one can't say that the Finns are mostly plums and the Danes are mostly peas. One Finnish scientist, Risto Santti, a reproductive biologist at the University of Turku, downplays any notion of Finnish supremacy. "We're ordinary guys," he said. "We like to love. We like to work. There's nothing special with Finnish men."

Other theories examine life-style differences. Smoking is far more common among Danes than among Finns, and this could be a factor, since nicotine can damage a fetus in many ways. In addition, Finland is less densely populated than Denmark, so the level of stress may be correspondingly lower. Both populations eat lots of ham and dairy products, and also fish from the polluted Baltic Sea. Stephen Safe has studied the organochlorine levels in the blood of Danes, Finns, and other Scandinavians. "There's no difference," Safe told me. "It's probably something else."

But Santti is troubled by the increasing pollution of Finnish waters, which in some lakes and rivers is even worse than in Denmark. "In Finland, the otters are gone from some areas, the gulls are becoming less common, our seals are not normal," Santii said. "The paper-and-pulp industry has polluted our waters. The fish living downstream from pulp mills have reproductive problems." Logically, of course, this should mean that Finnish sperm counts will fall below those of the Danes, and not the opposite. "My educated guess is that the differences we see now reflect the life style and the environment of our countries thirty or more years ago," I was told by Jorma Toppari, who is a pediatrician with an interest in male reproductive problems. At that time, Denmark was already an industrial country, while Finland was comparatively more rural and less populated. Now the countries are far more alike. Toppari, who practices at the Turku University Central Hospital, points out that there are currently differences in the average sperm count even within Finland: the cities have far lower counts than the countryside. Men in Kuopio, which is in the lake district of southern central Finland, have an average sperm density of a hundred and thirty-three million nine hundred thousand per millilitre—the highest concentration recorded in the world in the last half century. Meanwhile, the count in Turku, Finland's second-largest city, averaged ninety million. These differences suggest to Toppari that as the Fins modernize they will have less to brag about. "I'm afraid Finland will follow the other countries later," he says with resignation.

By remarkable coincidence, Skakkebæk's 1992 report in the *British Medical Journal* coincided with the publication of an extraordinary science-fiction novel by the popular British author P.D. James, who is otherwise known for her detective novels. The premise of James's book, which is entitled "The Children of Men" and is set in the year 2021, is that males have lost the ability to produce fertile sperm. The novel's narrator writes, twenty-five years after the last human baby has been born:

> We should have been warned in the early 1990's. As early as 1991, a European Community Report showed a slump in the number of children born in Europe—8.2 million in 1990, with particular drops in the Roman Catholic countries. We thought that we knew the reasons, that the fall was deliberate, a result of more liberal attitudes to birth control and abortion, the postponement of pregnancy by professional women pursuing their

careers, the wish of families for a higher standard of living . . . Some European countries began to pursue a vigorous campaign to encourage the birth of children, but most of us thought the fall was desirable, even necessary . . . . As I remember it, no one suggested that the fertility of the human race was dramatically changing. When Omega came, it came with dramatic suddenness and was received with incredulity. Overnight, it seemed, the human race had lost its power to breed.

Although we are not at a point where our survival as a species is threatened, the fecundity of our children and grandchildren is certainly in question. Myriad chemicals in the environment may affect our hormonal balance, in ways that are still poorly understood. Stress and lifestyle choices also jeopardize the production of health and abundant sperm. The result, of course, is an increase in infertility, the gravity of which can only accelerate if sperm counts fall in succeeding generations.

Clearly, more research is needed to determine the scope of the problem. The most important unanswered question among the many theories that purport to explain the falling sperm count is whether the decline is permanent and irreparable. The hope, of course, is that some modern condition or habit has somehow waylaid the production of sperm, and that the cause needs only to be discovered and removed for the count to rebound. Unfortunately, the truth about the sperm count is that it is under attack from many different sources. "We are outraged and demoralized less by the impending end of our species, less even by our inability to prevent it, than by our failure to discover the cause," the narrator of "The Children of Men" complains. "Western science and Western medicine haven't prepared us for the magnitude and humiliation of this ultimate failure." So far, at least, this prophecy has been dismayingly accurate. It is as if manhood itself were waging a losing campaign against forces as yet unknown but frighteningly overwhelming.

Still Waiting
for the
Contraceptive Revolution

By Michael Klitsch

In the mid-1960s, when the oral contraceptive and the newly introduced IUD began to transform contraceptive practice around the world, hopes were high that even more effective methods would soon follow. Researchers' imaginations produced visions of hormonal injectables, implants, vaginal rings and transdermal patches, methods of nonsurgical sterilization, improved IUDs, menses inducers—even systemic methods that could be used by men. As recently as 1982, a U.S. government report contended that 10 new methods were likely to reach the market during the 1980s, and another 20 by the year 2000![1]

Thirty years later, much of the enthusiasm about contraceptive advances has waned. Only three new contraceptive methods received Food and Drug Administration (FDA) approval in the 1990s, none as soon as hopeful advocates had expected: the hormonal implant (now enveloped in lawsuits), an injectable hormonal method that took more than 20 years between its first FDA submission and its approval, and the female condom. The only other important changes were the gradual adjustment of pill formulations to expose users to a smaller total dosage of hormones and the introduction of new hormones already widely used in Europe.

The lack of decisive advances is not the result of a paucity of candidate methods. In 1993, an estimated 100 experimental contraceptive methods were being studied around the world.[2] Yet many of those methods had been in the works for years, and others were only slight modifications of products already on the market.

The slowing of the "contraceptive revolution" has not gone unremarked. In the late 1980s, the National Academy of Sciences (NAS) sponsored a series of meetings on the problems inhibiting contraceptive research and in 1990 published a book summarizing the conclusions.[3] The 1990s brought even more expressions of concern. Many have asked why, after years of intensive research activity, the appearance of new methods with the revolutionary impact of the pill and IUD remains far away.

WHAT ARE THE PROBLEMS?

A core set of factors has been identified as key to why contraceptive reality has failed to match 1960s expectations. The three main obstacles noted in recent evaluations were identified 10 or more years ago.

Regulatory and Legal Issues

Over the course of the 1970s and 1980s, many pharmaceutical companies in the United States gradually cut back or eliminated their contraceptive research efforts. This flight from research has usually been attributed to, among other factors, liability problems brought about by sizable legal judgments against some contraceptive manufacturers and corporate frustration with federal product safety regulation.

• *Product liability costs.* Manufacturers of IUDs, pills and spermicides have all paid sizable damage claims in the past several decades as a result of death or injury arising from contraceptive use. Not only have a few of these judgments been quite large, but the costs of defending against such lawsuits are high as well. Even noncommercial research organizations have been affected: According to the 1990 NAS report, liability costs for two not-for-profit groups active in contraceptive research, Family Health International and The Population Council, more than doubled over a two-year period during the 1980s.[4]

From *Family Planning Perspectives* (November/December 1995, Vol. 27, No. 6), pp. 246–253. Reproduced with the permission of The Alan Guttmacher Institute from Michael Klitsch. © 1995.

Although the report concluded that product liability litigation had "contributed significantly to the climate of disincentives for the development of contraceptive products,"[5] an analysis prepared by the Program for Appropriate Technology in Health (PATH) for a 1993 meeting on reproductive research reported otherwise. Some pharmaceutical executives downplayed the impact of liability concerns,[6] it said, noting the liability issues are simply a recognized cost of doing business in the United States.

Recent developments involving the hormonal implant (Norplant) dramatize how high the "cost of doing business" can sometimes climb, however. Nearly 200 lawsuits were filed against the implant's manufacturer, Wyeth-Ayerst, in 1994, 46 of them class-action suits.[7] These lawsuits alleged a variety of problems caused by the implant, ranging from scarring and emotional distress attributed to removal difficulties to claims of autoimmune disorders resulting from exposure to the silicone in the implant's shell.

Concurrently, implant sales fell from a rate of 600 per day in the early days following the method's introduction to only about 60 per day by early in 1995 (although some of that decline probably occurred because the initial demand for the implant had been satisfied). Felicia Stewart, deputy assistant secretary of health for population affairs, has said that "it's clear watching what's happening with Norplant why a company thinking about marketing a new contraceptive product might say it isn't worth making an investment."[8]

• *Government scrutiny of contraceptive products.* After serious problems arose during the 1960s and early 1970s among users of high-dosage oral contraceptives and the Dalkon Shield IUD (as well as among users of many noncontraceptive products), the FDA required pharmaceutical companies to meet higher standards of safety before they could market a new drug. The demands for additional animal and human trials, as well as more exacting FDA evaluation of the results, added years—and millions of dollars in additional costs—to the drug development process.

In recent years, concerned about the effects of overregulating the pharmaceutical industry, the FDA began to streamline the process of drug evaluation and approval.[9] In particular, the agency relaxed requirements for contraceptive methods that also protect against the acquisition of sexually transmitted diseases (STDs), and opened the way for the easier acceptance of data collected in foreign studies.

On the other hand, recent FDA plans to revise the approval process for compounds such as spermicides have renewed regulatory anxieties in the family planning community. For years, manufacturers of vaginal contraceptives have not had to receive formal FDA approval for their products as long as they were formulated following guidelines published by the agency in 1980. Early in 1995, though, the FDA proposed that each over-the-counter vaginal contraceptive be "tested in appropriate clinical trials under actual conditions of use" to establish its efficacy.[10] This change would require new tests for some products that have been on the market for decades. Rather than perform expensive tests for products that yield only a small profit, some manufacturers could stop selling spermicides altogether.[11]

Public Opinion and Politics

• *Changes in attitudes toward contraceptives.* In terms of their effectiveness and ease of use, the pill and IUD represented such a drastic improvement over barrier methods that they were adopted with great enthusiasm. In the years since then, however, popular concern over the side effects of the methods grew, and researchers soon saw how media reports of complications (or potential complications) affected contraceptive use.[12]

The coinciding growth in influence of the consumer movement and the women's movement produced more critical analyses of contraceptive side effects, and fed rising public perceptions that since contraceptives routinely are used by healthy women, their potential for complications and side effects should be as small as possible. Such expectations added an extra layer of difficulty to the development of any totally new approach to contraception, and probably also contributed to the pharmaceutical industry's hesitance to do much more than tinker with existing methods.

The explosion in STDs during the 1980s, and particularly the emergence of the human immunodeficiency virus (HIV) and AIDS, further complicated public attitudes. Only "low tech" barrier methods like the condom and spermicides offer protection against STD infection; the newer, more "high tech" methods, from the pill to the implant, offer little or no such security. In recent years, pressure has risen for a wider selection of methods that can prevent the transmission of pathogens—and against methods that cannot.

• *The abortion debate.* Almost since the earliest days of the battle over the legal status of abortion in the United States, contraceptives have been caught in the crossfire. For years, some antiabortion activists denounced contraceptive methods such as the pill and the IUD, charging that if they disrupt implantation rather than prevent fertilization, they are in fact abortifacients.

Such arguments, in turn, have had an effect on contraceptive research. For example, among a number of types of contraceptive vaccines now under development, the most advanced is a vaccine to prevent or interrupt implantation. Critics, however, condemn it as an abortifacient. Similar concerns have slowed development work on a monthly menses inducer.

Financial Issues

• *Profitability.* According to the 1993 PATH report, many companies view the limited potential of new contraceptives to attract additional customers in the United States to be the greatest deterrent to contraceptive research.[13] According to this argument, contraceptive markets in developed countries are mature and have little additional profit potential; in the absence of a revolutionary new method that could force its way into a crowded market, most companies prefer to continue selling their existing product line rather than to invest large sums in research on methods that might not produce any greater profits. In addition, some companies probably fear that instead of attracting new customers, a new product would simply be substituted for the company's other methods, adversely affecting the market share of existing, highly profitable products.

• *Research funding.* Although contraceptive research becomes more expensive as ever more exotic approaches are explored, the funds available for such research have not kept up with demand. An evaluation of funding for contraceptive research conducted in the mid-1980s found that in 1983, about $57 million was being spent world-wide on contraceptive development, down nearly 25% from the high of $74 million (in constant 1983 dollars) spent in 1972.[14] Federal spending on such research, according to the 1990 NAS report, became increasingly dominant in the 1980s, in part because of the steady decline in both industry and foundation support for contraceptive research.[15]

WHO SPONSORS THE RESEARCH?

For reasons outlined earlier, a number of American pharmaceutical companies instrumental in developing or marketing the first generation of modern contraceptives gradually left the field of contraceptive research. By 1995, there were only four private companies in the world that were known to be conducting research on new contraceptive methods. Two of these —Ortho and Wyeth-Ayerst Laboratories—are American companies, and two others—Schering AG and Organon—are European concerns. All market a number of contraceptives and have conducted research on various methods. Beyond these four, most private entities that participate in contraceptive research are fairly small start-up companies pursuing one or two approaches.

As the research role of private pharmaceutical interests faded, a host of U.S. public-sector organizations either stepped up their contraceptive development activities or initiated contraceptive research. These include such nonprofit institutions as Family Health International and the Population Council, each of which has had a long involvement in basic biomedical research and the shepherding of new methods to the market.

In addition, the Contraceptive Research and Development Program (CONRAD), which is supported primarily by the U.S. Agency for International Development and is based at Eastern Virginia Medical School, funds research on a wide variety of contraceptive approaches at research institutes, universities and private companies around the world. It's primary aim is helping to advance promising methods through the initial stages of safety and efficacy testing.

The U.S. government also directly supports U.S. contraceptive research through the Contraceptive Development Branch of the National Institutes of Child Health and Human Development (NICHD). In particular, the Contraceptive Development Branch often provides grants to fund clinical trials of new fertility regulation methods.

Internationally, the most important supporter of contraceptive research is probably the World Health Organization (WHO). Its Special Programme of Research Development and Research Training in Human Reproduction helps to coordinate international research efforts through task forces devoted to such areas as long-acting systemic methods, male fertility-regulating methods and vaccines.

In addition, there are several research programs established in developing countries, the most notable of which is the Indian Council of Medical Research, which has spearheaded important contraceptive vaccine studies. Another is the Programme of South-to-South Cooperation in Reproductive Health, which encourages a network of developing-country researchers to follow up on leads ignored or passed over by large pharmaceutical companies or developed-country research programs.

Finally, several private foundations, such as The Rockefeller Foundation, the Ford Foundation and the Andrew W. Mellon Foundation, contribute varying amounts of funds in support of programs or particular projects, both in the United States and overseas.

WHAT'S IN THE WORKS?
Spermicides and Barrier Methods

Arguing that vaginal methods are ignored in favor of systemic hormonal methods, women's health activists have persistently pressed for increased research on barriers and spermicides. In the early 1980s, only a strong campaign by feminist groups kept the cervical cap from being removed from the U.S. market after the FDA questioned its efficacy. Their efforts led to clinical trials that eventually brought FDA approval of the cap.[16] A few years later, the rising prevalence of STDs and HIV infection among women of reproductive age finally led to a reevaluation of the worth of barrier methods.

A few new barrier methods have debuted recently. The female condom, approved in 1993, was heralded as the first method to allow a woman to protect herself against infection; it remains unclear, however, how many women will use it.

In addition, a polyurethane condom for men was introduced in the western United States in 1994; before it could be marketed elsewhere, however, the FDA asked for a halt in distribution until reports of high breakage rates could be investigated.[17] Finally, a spermicidal gel containing nonoxynol-9 that is claimed to be effective for up to 24 hours has been marketed,[18] although no data on the method have yet been published or furnished to the FDA.

At the same time as these barrier methods were entering the market, another departed. Early in 1995, the manufacturer of the contraceptive sponge halted production of the method because of a dispute with the FDA over the manufacturing process at the company's plant.[19] The manufacturer's decision to stop producing the sponge arose from the costs it would have incurred in making the needed changes at its factory: The safety and efficacy of the sponge were not at issue in the dispute.

Several female barrier methods under development for years may appear on the U.S. market before the end of the decade. Femcap, a variation on the cervical cap, is shaped like a sailor's hat, fits snugly over the cervix and must be used with spermicide.[20] Another, called Lea's Shield, is an oval silicone rubber barrier resembling a diaphragm, but with a one-way valve that permits passage of cervical secretions.[21] Both are now in clinical trials: Femcap has begun small-scale safety studies, while Lea's Shield has entered a comparative trial (with the diaphragm) intended to test the device's safety and efficacy.

In addition, a new vaginal sponge made of polyurethane foam is under development; it contains low levels of three different agents—nonoxynol-9, benzalkonium chloride and sodium cholate—that are meant to serve as a combined spermicide and microbicide.[22]

The new sponge is just one illustration of the proliferation of research on spermicides, virucides and microbicides. Early in 1995, NICHD announced the funding of three large projects on microbicides to be used prior to intercourse.[23] One scientific group will be studying chemicals that coat the surfaces of mucosal cells and may be able to block herpes virus and HIV. Another group will examine a series of spermicidal compounds, as well as at least one nonspermicidal compound that could allow pregnancy while protecting women from infection. Finally, a third group will examine the microbicidal potential of naturally occurring peptide antibiotics.

At the same time, investigators are exploring the development of long-acting spermicidal suppositories, the addition of new chemicals to existing spermicides, and even entirely new products. (Neem oil, which is extracted from a tree native to India, is an example of the latter: When combined with two other natural compounds, neem extract has proven a potent spermicide in in vitro and animal studies.[24])

One highly promising, but long-range, approach is the use of recombinant DNA technologies to create monoclonal antibodies to combat microbes.[25] Combining these antibodies and dispensing them either topically (as with a traditional spermicide) or via a vaginal ring might offer the user highly specific protection against sexually transmitted infections.

Injectables

Injectable progestins were developed in the late 1950s, and Schering AG marketed the first injectable, norethisterone enanthate (known as NET EN), in Peru in 1967.[26] At about that time, Upjohn applied to the FDA for approval to sell depot medroxyprogesterone acetate (DMPA, also known as Depo-Provera) in the United States. However, early animal studies suggested that DMPA use might lead to an elevated risk of cancer; after nearly 25 years of controversy, expert panels, rejection and reapplication, the FDA finally approved DMPA in 1992,[27] on the basis of reassuring data from WHO multicenter studies.[28] In the intervening years, DMPA and NET EN became widely used around the world.

In addition, several combined injectables active for about one month per injection have also become available in Europe and a number of developing countries. Combined injectables were developed because of the tendency of progestin-only methods to disrupt usual menstrual bleeding patterns: By adding estrogens to the long-acting progestins, researchers hoped to create a method that would give women better cycle control. In 1964, Upjohn conducted clinical trials of a combination of DMPA and an estrogen, estradiol cypionate, but the company terminated its contraceptive research in the mid-1980s. WHO continued work on the injectable, however, and by 1994 the preparation (known as Cyclofem) had been registered in six developing countries (Bolivia, Guatemala, Indonesia, Mexico, Peru and Thailand), with preliminary steps toward marketing under way in another six.[29] In 1995, Upjohn exercised an option on U.S. rights to the injectable and announced that it would soon seek FDA approval for Cyclofem (to be marketed as Cyclo-Provera in the United States).[30]

Of the three other combined injectables, one consisting of NET EN and estradiol valerate was created by WHO and licensed to Schering AG, which has registered it in several Latin American countries.[31] Schering has not indicated whether it plans to market the injectable (called Mesigyna) in the United States, however. In addition, two other combined injectables are very unlikely ever to be used in the United States. One, marketed widely in Latin America, contains relatively large doses of estrogen and progestin; the other, known as Injectable No. 1, is not used outside of China.

Vaginal Rings

Research on vaginal rings—small silicone rubber devices that release a contraceptive hormone—also began in the 1960s. As the years passed, the number of vaginal rings under development proliferated, without any of them reaching the point of FDA consideration and approval. Two types of rings are currently being studied: one that releases only a progestin, and another that releases both a progestin and an estrogen. The biggest advantage of the progestin-only rings is that they can be used by women who are breastfeeding; their chief disadvantage is one shared by other progestin-only contraceptives—irregular menstrual bleeding.

A few years ago, among four progestin-releasing rings at various stages of development, a levonorgestrel-releasing ring developed by WHO was closest to going into general use. This device had a projected lifespan of three months, had undergone extensive testing in Great Britain and was about to enter large-scale production there.[32] However, its introduction was postponed at a very late stage when vaginal irritation was detected in a small number of users.

A vaginal ring with a projected lifespan of one year or more has been developed by The Population Council; this ring steadily releases a very low dose of a progestin called Nestorone. Efficacy trails are expected to begin in late 1995.[33] The method's developers anticipate that both breastfeeding women and normally ovulating women will be able to use this ring. Finally, Population Council researchers have also developed a ring that releases progesterone, a natural progestin, and will be used exclusively by breastfeeding women. This ring has been licensed in Chile and is expected to make its debut there shortly.[34]

The Population Council is also responsible for two vaginal rings that release a combination of progestin and estrogen: The first releases norethindrone acetate and ethinyl estradiol and can be used for up to one year; the second contains Nestorone and ethinyl estradiol, and is expected to be effective for 6–12 months. Both are in early phases of human trials; the Council is expecting to wait until full data have been collected on both versions of the combined ring, and then proceed to market with the better design.[35]

Although small-scale clinical studies of various vaginal rings have produced generally positive results, none of these devices have been marketed in the more than 25 years that they have been under development. Research efforts were slowed by two serious problems. In 1987, Dow Corning stopped producing a chemical crucial to the fabrication of one of the materials used in many of the vaginal rings. As a result, most had to be redesigned, with concomitant delays in testing and development.

Then came the discovery in 1992 of vaginal lesions in some women using the WHO ring. Most work on vaginal rings was halted while special studies of the vaginal effects of ring use were conducted. Preliminary results indicated that such lesions also occurred among nonusers and did not appear to be associated with the ring itself.[36] Nevertheless, the WHO ring was redesigned to be more flexible, and studies of the new ring design have been undertaken.[37]

A vaginal ring may yet become available for consumer use, but whether this method is marketed in the United States will depend in part on the developers' success in finding a commercial partner willing to sell the device. Other complications may still occur, however. For example, some chemical companies that produce medical-grade silicone rubber materials (such as those used in the ring) are considering withdrawing their products from the U.S. market because the manufacturers have repeatedly been included as plaintiffs in liability lawsuits over medical devices that use their materials.[38]

Implants

Although the introduction of the six-capsule contraceptive implant to the U.S. market has been problematic, its developers, The Population Council and Wyeth-Ayerst, are moving ahead with a second-generation implant, a two-rod system known as Norplant II; a new drug application for this method was officially submitted to the FDA in mid-1995.[39] The two rods, which release small amounts of levonorgestrel (the same hormone used in the six-capsule version), are expected to have an effective lifespan of at least three years. The use of two rods rather than six capsules will probably ease both insertion and removal difficulties.

Other hormonal implants are in much earlier stages of development, and may debut outside of the United States well before they are marketed here. For example, Organon is conducting large-scale human trials of a single-rod desogestrel-releasing implant (known as Implanon) that will be effective for at least two years.[40] In addition, the nonprofit consortium known as South-to-South Cooperation in Reproductive Health has begun early human studies of Uniplant, a single implant that releases the progestin nomegestrol acetate and will be effective for about one year.[41] Finally, The Population Council is working on a rod-like implant that will release Nestorone.[42]

A drawback common to all of these implants is that they need to be removed surgically. Thus, researchers are working to create biodegradable implants. One such implant, known as Capronor, is a capsule that releases levonorgestrel and is expected to provide one year of contraceptive protection before the capsule biodegrades.[43] Another approach being studied involves the injection of 4–6 small pellets consisting of norethindrone and cholesterol; this method is also expected to be effective for about one year.[44] Although both of these implants have been studied in women, at least several more years of human research may be needed before they can be referred to the FDA for approval.

Intrauterine Devices

The IUD is one of the oldest and one of the most effective of modern contraceptive methods, but currently has low prevalence and limited availability in the United States. Two IUDs are currently sold domestically: a Copper-T IUD also widely used around the world (the 380A) and a hormonal IUD with a useful life of only one year.

Although the introduction of new IUDs in the United States might raise the method's prevalence, there is little reason to anticipate new arrivals anytime soon. A hormonal IUD with a lifespan of three years, the LNg 20, is already approved for use in Finland and in Sweden.[45] However, its Finnish manufacturer, Leiras Oy, has not yet sought FDA approval for the device.

WHO has been conducting trials on a new frameless IUD (called CuFix 330) that lacks the IUD's usual stiff plastic skeleton; instead, the CuFix consists of a string of six copper beads suspended from the upper portion of the uterus by a nylon thread. The design is expected to produce less pain and bleeding than other types of IUDs, although early research has produced mixed results.[46]

Methods for Men

For most of the history of contraceptive research, scientists have focused on female methods. A consensus is forming, though, that systemic male methods should also be developed and promoted. An international symposium involving contraceptive researchers and women's activists that was held in 1990, for example, concluded that there was a clear need to increase the investment in research on male methods (as well as to convince men to become more personally involved in fertility regulation and reproductive health).[47] Even the 1994 International Conference on Population and Development included in its final document a statement that "high priority should also be given to the development of new methods for regulation of fertility for men."[48]

Moving beyond condoms to systemic methods for men may prove difficult, however. For example, although WHO has studied hormonal approaches to male contraception for more than two decades, no usable method has yet been produced. Recent WHO research has shown that weekly injections of the androgen testosterone enanthate will suppress sperm counts so that annual pregnancy rates are only about one per 100 person-years of use.[49] However, weekly injections would not be commercially viable, and developing acceptable dosages and injection schedules remains a stumbling block. WHO hopes eventually to develop a treatment that is either oral or can be administered by means of an implant.

Combining testosterone enanthate with a progestin (such a DMPA) or with another androgen may lead to a long-term injectable method for men. WHO and CONRAD have tested such approaches in only a handful of men, however.[50]

A dual-implant system for men is being examined by The Population Council. One implant releases a luteinizing hormone-releasing hormone analog that halts sperm production; the other releases a male hormone to prevent loss of potency and libido.[51] These implants are only now entering the first stages of human trials, however, and are a number of years away from general use.

Several other concepts for male systemic methods are even farther back in the development process. Mifepristone is believed to interfere with sperm motility,[52] but the use of this drug as a male method still must be tested in animals before human trials can begin. The serendipitous discovery by infertility researchers in New York that a hypertension drug, nifedipine, had produced infertility in a group of men has led to hope that it may serve as a reversible male method.[53] Although animal tests will not be needed for the drug, which is already FDA-approved, dose-finding

PART 4 – CONTROLLING FERTILITY

research must be conducted before efficacy trials can begin.

Along with such new possibilities, researchers are also reexamining an old lead—gossypol. Derived from cottonseed oil, gossypol stops sperm production but does not effect androgen levels. Studies published in the early 1980s revealed that the drug also reduced body levels of potassium, leaving users prone to temporary paralysis and irregular heartbeat.[54] In addition, infertility proved irreversible among some of the users. However, subsequent research has suggested that reduced doses of gossypol may avoid these problems but still maintain the antifertility effect. Over the next few years, South-to-South will be conducting a multicountry international trial of gossypol.[55]

Vaccines

Nearly 100 years ago, scientists learned that spermatozoa could provoke an immune reaction if they were injected into the body. Efforts at translating this information into a contraceptive vaccine began in the mid-1960s and focused on inducing an immune reaction to sperm.

In the mid-1970s, researchers realized that human chorionic gonadotropin (hCG) would also be a good candidate for a contraceptive vaccine, since this hormone is produced only during early pregnancy. After 20 years of research, though, the first small-scale human trial of an anti-hCG vaccine showed that nearly 20% of the women who received injections failed to develop an effective immune reaction.[56] Research continues on two anti-hCG vaccines, one created by India's National Institute of Immunology and one produced by WHO.

Meanwhile, other researchers continue to explore the feasibility of developing vaccines targeting a variety of proteins on the surface of the egg or on the surface of the sperm, in the belief that if either gamete could be coated with antibodies, fertilization would not take place. Another potential vaccine is aimed at disrupting a chemical that assists in the fusion of the sperm and egg. Scientists have found it harder than expected to identify molecules peculiar to the gametes or to the fertilization process, however, a necessary step so as not to provoke an autoimmune reaction among similar molecules elsewhere in the body.

Moreover, research into immunologic contraception is expensive, and only limited funding for such research has been available. Adding to the complexity of the situation is that contraceptive vaccine research has come under heavy criticism from both antiabortion and women's health activists. Those opposed to abortion object to the anti-hCG vaccines as being a form of abortion. For that reason, no U.S. government

research money has gone to study these vaccines[57] even though they are closer to actual large-scale human trials than an antisperm vaccine.

Meanwhile, in 1993, a network of women's health activists, the Women's Global Network for Reproductive Rights, began a drive to halt all contraceptive vaccine research around the world.[58] The group's objections range from worries that a successful vaccine could be administered to women against their will and that manipulating the human immune system may prove unnecessarily dangerous to concerns over the ethics of conducting such experiments and the "population control" perspective from which they believe the concept of contraceptive vaccines is derived.

Some of this opposition arises from a misapprehension that at one time was shared by the research community: that a contraceptive vaccine would prevent pregnancy permanently, much like vaccines against certain diseases. Most studies of candidate immunologic contraceptives have suggested, however, that the immunity wears out fairly soon, and that for extended contraception a number of booster injections would probably be needed. Thus, a contraceptive vaccine may prove to resemble current injectables more than it will disease vaccines.

Menses Induction

A reliable menses inducer would have several distinct advantages over other methods: the need to administer just one pill per month, rather than one per day; a smaller likelihood of long-term side effects; and the user's lack of awareness about whether fertilization had in fact occurred that month. Yet two decades of searching for a usable menses inducer, by WHO and by other institutions, has not been successful. Throughout the 1970s, researchers studied the use of prostaglandins to induce menses on a regular basis. The drugs proved fairly reliable, with efficacy rates approaching 90%. However, they also caused women much nausea and diarrhea. As a result, research on them gradually weaned.

In the 1980s, investigators turned their attention to antiprogestins as another means of interrupting implantation. WHO studies and research performed by Roussel-UCLAF demonstrated that the antiprogestin mifepristone, when combined with a mild prostaglandin, was a very effective early abortifacient.[59] However, mifepristone has less promise as a monthly menses inducer, in part because it can delay the start of the next menstrual cycle, making it difficult for a user to determine when to take subsequent doses.[60]

The development of a menses inducer is another area of research that has been slowed by abortion politics. First, because of differences in the wording of abortion laws around the world, menses inducers that interfere with implantation might be legal in some places but illegal in others. Similarly, a drug used after a woman knew that her period was late might be classified as an abortifacient, while the same drug used at—or just before—the time the woman expected her menses to occur might not be.

WILL RESEARCH AWAKEN?

Continuing high levels of abortion and of unintended pregnancy suggest that many couples are in need of a new approach to contraception. The reanimation of contraceptive research in the United States would help meet these needs and eventually could reduce the level of unintended pregnancy.

A concerted effort is now being made to accelerate research on contraception so as to recover some of the momentum lost in the 1970s and 1980s. In May 1995, the Institute of Medicine convened a workshop to discuss ways in which to promote public-private collaboration in contraceptive research. One month before, the Rockefeller Foundation sponsored a conference in Bellagio, Italy, on public- and private-sector collaboration in contraceptive research and development. The conference brought together, for the first time, senior representatives of the pharmaceutical industry and of public-sector programs to discuss how the process of contraceptive development could be reinvigorated by means of public-private collaboration. And in late 1994, the Institute of Medicine held a workshop on how contraceptive research efforts can take advantage of novel leads growing out of research into molecular biology.

These conferences were part of a larger Rockefeller Foundation-funded initiative entitled "Contraception-21," intended to "launch a second contraceptive technology revolution" for the 21st century.[61] Contraception-21 entails a five-component plan to mobilize new resources for contraceptive research: focusing research on methods that women feel a need for; reengaging the pharmaceutical industry in contraceptive research: applying new findings in molecular biology to the problem of preventing fertilization and pregnancy; accessing the technical and human resources of developing countries; and increasing the commitment of international donors.

How to reestablish the pharmaceutical industry's interest in contraceptive research is the principal focus of one area of the initiative. PATH, in particular, has analyzed why the public-sector organizations have experienced difficulties in "handing off" newly developed products to private-sector manufacturers.[62]

Among the reasons is an important difference in the process by which public-sector and private-sector organizations develop products: While public-sector agencies often choose an approach based simply on what will work, pharmaceutical companies usually use market research to determine customers' preferences regarding the ideal and the minimum acceptable combinations of characteristics for a particular product. The findings of such research then may be used to guide product research, permitting the developer either to refine a drug that is under development or to halt work on one that will never satisfy users' minimum criteria of acceptability.

The authors of the PATH report observe that in particular, public-sector organizations often lack a mechanism for terminating work on leads that may ultimately prove unpromising. The end result can be an inefficient use of the limited funding available for contraceptive research, very slow progress for all methods under development and the creation of a drug or device with limited commercial appeal.

Although in the past, public-sector research organizations have often worked together with private-sector companies to market new methods (such as the Population Council's licensing Wyeth-Ayerst to market the hormonal implant in the United States), such collaboration has usually occurred late in a product's development cycle. In an emerging alternative model for private-public collaboration in contraceptive research, a public-sector organization seeks to involve a private company at an earlier stage of product development than is currently typical, perhaps by using market research to demonstrate the commercial potential of a method well before it is actually ready to be marketed. (Both CONRAD and FHI have successfully used this approach in recent years.) Alternatively, a public-sector agent works with a private company to supply the expertise needed to move the private company's product toward FDA approval, with a quid pro quo of a low public-sector price or a share of royalties.

One recent example of public-private collaboration concerned efforts to bring the combined injectable Cyclofem to market. WHO took on the research responsibility for Cyclofem after Upjohn halted their contraceptive development work, and sponsored a series of studies evaluating the method's effectiveness and side effects. In the late 1980s, WHO awarded rights to the drug to the Program for the Introduction and Adaptation of Contraceptive Technology, which then licensed Cyclofem to the Concept Foundation, a nonprofit foundation in Thailand. This foundation, in turn, sought manufacturers for the drug and obtained approval for the drug in a number of developing countries. Subsequently, Upjohn exercised an option to pick up Cyclofem's U.S. rights from the Concept

Foundation, and may soon be selling Cyclofem in the United States.

The PATH report also suggests that the pharmaceutical industry is in the midst of a massive transition that will probably reduce the likelihood that drug companies will conduct all of the development work for a product in-house. As a result, it could become common for pharmaceutical companies to collaborate with small outside public or private organizations, especially on exotic or unusual drugs and devices. Such collaborative efforts will probably become particularly important as contraceptive research embraces new developments in molecular biology and biotechnology.

IS THE CONCERN MISPLACED?

In 1995, an American woman seeking a reversible method could choose from among oral contraceptives (more than 30 formulations), IUDs (two types), an injectable, an implant and a variety of barrier methods. Do such methods represent enough of a choice, or is a wider variety of methods needed? Although Americans are believed to be discontented with their current array of contraceptive choices, no good data currently exist to confirm individuals' opinions about the need for new methods or what contraceptive research priorities should be. (A poll conducted in 1988 suggested only that 82% of American adults favored continued government funding of contraceptive research.[63])

Several factors suggest that the current mix of reversible methods is inadequate, however. One is that approximately 1.5 million abortions are performed annually in the United States; likewise, there are about two million births each year that are considered either mistimed or unwanted. Surely many of these abortions and births could be avoided if more acceptable methods of contraception were available. Yet what hope is there that more contraceptive choices will become available at any time soon?

Liability reform (which was urged in the 1990 NAS report) may bring the pharmaceutical industry back into contraceptive research. The tort reform measures under consideration in Congress could change liability issues facing contraceptive manufacturers. For example, the broad product liability bill passed by the House of Representatives in March 1995 included language known as the "FDA defense"—that manufacturers cannot be liable for punitive damages if their product was approved by the FDA (so long as the information that they provided to the FDA was honest and complete). The Senate version of the bill, which as of October 1995 had not been voted on, does not contain such language.[64] Thus, even if the latter were passed, it would take a House-Senate conference to decide the provisions of a final bill.

However, with the pharmaceutical industry in the midst of important change, legislative actions such as tort reform may not be sufficient—or even necessary—to provoke movement on contraceptive research. Companies are now merging and rethinking their research and development strategies.* Some may choose to reenter the business if they are better insulated from lawsuits; others might decide that even favorable changes in the liability laws will not be worth the expense of reinitiating a contraceptive research effort, especially if new methods might endanger steady profits from established contraceptives.

Without reform, though, major change in the current situation seems unlikely, given the near impossibility of obtaining insurance against liability claims. In the past, some companies have "self-insured" methods by building a premium into the price of the method and then diverting a portion of the income to an insurance fund. However, self-insuring the pill was simple, because sales were high and expenses low. Self-insurance for the IUD and the implant, on the other hand, led to high initial prices for these devices. If a similar strategy is used with other novel methods needing infrequent resupply, the resulting high initial charges for them may blunt their potential.

Even in the event of tort reform sought by the pharmaceutical industry, however, the role of large companies will probably remain limited. Indeed, in the early days of the "contraceptive revolution," many of the most important developments were spearheaded by individuals or small companies that later grew into large manufacturers. Similarly, many new methods either marketed in the last few years or in advanced trials (such as the female condom, the polyurethane condom, new caps and diaphragms, and new sponges) were developed by small, single product companies (often with substantial assistance from public-sector entities such as CONRAD and NICHD).

Such firms will likely continue to be the engine for contraceptive development in the United States. First, they often are willing to take research risks that larger enterprises will not. In addition, although a shortage of capital can sometimes slow their research efforts, they are less attractive targets for liability suits because they lack "deep pockets."

On the other hand, small firms may be more suited to marketing niche products than to developing major new methods. Even the larger, better funded nonprofit organizations (such as The Population

*For example, Johnson and Johnson, the parent company of Ortho, recently acquired the smaller, more specialized Gynopharma, which produces the only copper IUD on the U.S. market. In addition; in July 1995, Searle a subsidiary of Monsanto acquired Syntex (and its women's health care products) from its corporate parent, Roche Holding Ltd.

Council) have experienced problems in completing their research in a timely manner when a new method presents technical problems. Such situations may require closer collaboration between small entities (either for-profit or nonprofit) and major manufacturers, and at an earlier stage than is presently the case.

Regardless of the results of liability and regulatory change, funding remains a key problem in contraceptive research. Worldwide, pharmaceutical companies are estimated to take in as much as $2.9 billion on contraception, but probably spend only about $22 million on contraceptive research.[65] Likewise, in 1992, the U.S. Center for Population Research targeted only about $14 million of its $140 million reproductive research budget at contraceptive development.[66] A recent attempt at estimating current spending on contraceptive research produced a figure of only $57 million for 1993, substantially less than the $69 million estimated for 1983.[67] Both of these figures are lower than previous estimates;[68] either estimate indicates little real growth or actual reductions in constant-dollar spending for contraceptive research.

The future of contraceptive research may lie in greater private-public collaboration in the funding and conduct of research. However, such coordination may require public-sector organizations to reconsider the appropriateness of some of the methods they have focused on, as pressure grows to justify expenditures to a for-profit partner with an emphasis on developing a marketable product. Furthermore, seeking the closer involvement of private pharmaceutical companies may increase the difficulty of proceeding with potential controversial methods, such as menses inducers or certain kinds of vaccines.

Overall, rather than being revolutionary, any new methods that reach the U.S. market before the end of the century probably represent the kind of steady evolutionary change that has characterized contraceptive development over the past decade or more. If methods that would transform contraceptive practice (as the pill and IUD did in the early 1960s) are to appear in the longer run, increased public support, a mobilization of ever-scarcer resources and closer cooperation between public-sector and private-sector entities will be needed.

REFERENCES

1. "Contraceptive Technologies in Development: Many Leads, Progress Slow," *Outlook*, Vol. 11, No. 2, June 1993.
2. M. F. Fathalla, "Mobilization of Resources for a Second Contraceptive Technology Revolution," in P. F. A. Van Look and G. Pérez-Palacios, eds., *Contraceptive Research and Development, 1984 to 1994: The Road to Mexico City and Beyond*, Oxford University Press, Oxford, U.K., 1994.
3. L. Mastroianni, Jr., P. J. Donaldson and T. T. Kane, eds., *Developing New Contraceptives: Obstacles and Opportunities,* National Academy Press, Washington, D.C., 1990.
4. Ibid., p. 137.
5. Ibid., p. 141.
6. Program for Appropriate Technology in Health (PATH), "Enhancing the Private Sector's Role in Contraceptive Research and Development." in P. F. A. Van Look and G. Pérez-Palacios, 1994, op. cit. (see reference 2).
7. G. Kolata, "Will the Lawyers Kill Off Norplant?" *New York Times*, May 28, 1995, Section 3, pp. 1 & 5.
8. Ibid., p. 1.
9. J. L. Fox. "For AIDS, the FDA May Be Reforming Itself," *Biotechnology*, 13:314–315, 1995.
10. "FDA Seeks Comments on Proposed Spermicide Rule," *Contraceptive Technology Update*, 16:48, 1995.
11. "Studies Found Plastic Condom Unsafe, Yet FDA Cleared It for Market," *AIDS Alert*, 10:61–64, 1995.
12. E. F. Jones, J. R. Beniger and C. F. Westoff, "Pill and IUD Discontinuation in the United States, 1970–1975: The Influence of the Media," *Family Planning Perspectives*, 12:293–300, 1980.
13. PATH, 1994, op. cit. (see reference 6).
14. R. Lincoln and L. Kaeser, "Whatever Happened to the Contraceptive Revolution?" *Family Planning Perspectives*, 20:20–24, 1988.
15. L. Mastroianni, Jr., P. J. Donaldson and T. T. Kane, 1990, op. cit. (see reference 3).
16. M. Klitsch, "FDA Approval Ends Cervical Cap's Marathon," *Family Planning Perspectives*, 20:137–138, 1988.
17. "Studies Found Plastic Condom Unsafe . . .," 1995, op. cit. (see reference 11).
18. "New Advantage 24 Contraceptive Gel Claims 24-Hour Effectiveness," *Contraceptive Technology Update*, 16:45–49, 1995.
19. "Only Manufacturer Discontinues Sponge Used for Contraception," *New York Times*, Jan. 11, 1995.
20. A. A. Shihata and J. Trussell, "New Female Intravaginal Barrier Contraceptive Device: Preliminary Clinical Trial," *Contraception*, 44:11–19, 1991; A. A. Shihata and E. Golub, "Acceptability of a New Intravaginal Barrier Contraceptive Device (Femcap)," *Contraception*, 46:511–519, 1992.
21. "New Device, 'Lea's Shield,' Being Evaluated in Studies," *Contraceptive Technology Update*. 12:110–111, 1991; W. L. Hunt, L. Gabbay and M. Potts, "Lea's Shield®, a New Barrier Contraceptive Preliminary Clinical Evaluations Three-Day Tolerance Study," Contraception, 50:551–561, 1994; and D. F. Archer et al., "Lea's Shield®: A Phase I Postcoital Study of a New Contraceptive Barrier Device," *Contraception*. 52:167–173, 1995.
22. A. Psychoyos, "PROTECTAID, a New Vaginal Contraceptive Sponge with Anti-STD Properties," in C. K. Mauck et al., *Barrier Contraceptives: Current Status and Future Prospects*. Wiley-Liss, New York, 1994, pp. 265–270.
23. P. M. Rowe, "Research into Topical Microbicides Against STDs," *Lancet*, 345:1231, 1995.
24. S. Garg et al., "Synergistic Spermicidal Activity of Neem Seed Extract, Reetha Saponins and Quinine Hydrochloride," *Contraception*, 50:185–190, 1994.
25. "Vaginal Devices May Provide Contraception, Prevent STDs," *Contraceptive Technology Update*, 12:129–130, 1991.
26. L. S. Liskin, "Long-Acting Progestins—Promise and Prospects," *Population Reports*, Series K, No. 2, 1983, p. K-19.
27. M. Klitsch, "Injectable Hormones and Regulatory Controversy: An End to the Long-Running Controversy?" *Family Planning Perspectives*, 25:37–40, 1993.
28. D. C. G. Skegg et al., "Depot Medroxprogesterone Acetate and Breast Cancer; A Pooled Analysis of the World Health Organization and New Zealand Studies," *Journal of the American Medical Association*, 273:799–804, 1995; and D. B. Thomas et al., "Cervical Carcinoma in Situ and Use

of Depot-Medroxyprogesterone Acetate (DMPA)," *Contraception*, 51:25–31, 1995.

29. C. d'Arcangues, "Long-Acting Systemic Agents for Fertility Regulation," in World Health Organization (WHO) Special Programme of Research, Development and Research Training in Human Reproduction, *Annual Technical Report 1994*, Geneva, 1995, pp. 19–27.

30. "Upjohn Buys New Contraceptive Compound," United Press International, Jan. 26, 1995.

31. L. J. Dorflinger, "Medical Contraindications and Issues for Consideration in the Use of Once-A-Month Injectable Contraceptives," *Contraception*, 49:455–468, 1994; and R. Lande, "New Era for Injectables," *Population Reports*, Series K, No. 5, 1995.

32. WHO, *Research in Human Reproduction: Biennial Report 1988–1989*, Geneva, 1990.

33. The Population Council, "Contraceptives and Other Reproductive Health Products Under Development by The Population Council," New York, Jan. 1995.

34. R. Thau, The Population Council, personal communication, June 19, 1995.

35. The Population Council, 1995, op. cit. (see reference 33), p. 2.

36. R. Thau, The Population Council, personal communication, June 19, 1995.

37. C. d'Arcangues, 1995, op. cit. (see reference 29), pp. 24–25.

38. B. J. Feder, "Implant Industry Is Facing Cutback by Top Suppliers," *New York Times*, Apr. 25, 1994, p. D1; and "Silicone Litigation May Force Out Major Supplier," *Contraceptive Technology Update*, 16:126–128, 1995.

39. R. Thau, The Population Council, personal communication, June 19, 1995.

40. G. C. Davies et al., "Release Characteristics, Ovarian Activity and Menstrual Bleeding Pattern with a Single Contraceptive Implant Releasing 3-Ketodesogestrel," *Contraception*, 47:251–261, 1993.

41. E. M. Coutinho, "One Year Contraception with a Single Subdermal Implant Containing Nomegestrol Acetate (Uniplant)," *Contraception*, 47:97–105, 1993.

42. S. Diaz et al., "Clinical Trial with Nestorone Subdermal Contraceptive Implants," *Contraception*, 51:33–38, 1995.

43. P. D. Darney et al., "Evaluation of a 1-Year Levonorgestrel-Releasing Contraceptive Implant: Side Effects, Release Rates and Biodegradability," *Fertility and Sterility*, 58:137–144, 1992.

44. C. L. Blaney, "New Approaches Seek Greater Safety, Appeal," *Network*, Vol. 15, No. 4, June 1995, p. 28.

45. The population Council, 1995, op. cit. (see reference 33), p. 2.

46. UNDP, UNFPA and WHO Special Programme of Research, Development and Research Training in Human Reproduction, World Bank: IUD Research Group, "The TCu 380A IUD and the Frameless IUD 'the Flexigard': Interim Three-Year Data from an International Multicenter Trial," *Contraception*, 52:77–83, 1995.

47. WHO and International Women's Health Coalition, *Creating Common Ground: Report of a Meeting Between Women's Health Advocates and Scientists*, WHO, Geneva, 1991.

48. United Nations, *Report of the International Conference on Population and Development*, A/CONF.171/13, New York, 1994, p. 89.

49. P. D. Griffin and G. M. H. Waites, "Methods for the Regulation of Male Fertility," in WHO, 1995, op. cit. (see reference 29), pp. 57–71.

50. Ibid.

51. The Population Council, "From Mice to Men: Creating a Male Hormonal Contraceptive," *Population Briefs*, Vol. 1, No. 3, New York, Sept. 1995.

52. "Mifepristone as Male Contraceptive?" *Scrip*, No. 1890, Jan. 21, 1994, p. 22; and W. R. Finger, "Future Male Methods May include Injectables," *Network*, Mar. 1995, p. 12.

53. "Nifedipine—a Male Contraceptive?" *Scrip*, No. 1894, Feb. 4, 1994, p. 27; and W. R. Finger, 1995, op. cit. (see reference 52), p. 12.

54. "Low Potassium Levels from Use of Gossypol Linked to Paralysis," *International Family Planning Perspectives*, 7:24–25, 1981.

55. W. R. Finger, 1995, op. cit. (see reference 52), p. 13.

56. P. Aldhous, "A Booster for Contraceptive Vaccines," *Science*, 266:1484–1486, 1994; and G. P. Talwar et al., "A Vaccine That Prevents Pregnancy in Women (Human Chorionic Gonadotropin/Birth Control Vaccine)," *Proceedings of the National Academy of Sciences*, 91:8532–8536, 1994.

57. P. Aldhous, 1994, op. cit. (see reference 56).

58. "Call for a Stop of Research on Antifertility 'Vaccines' (Immunological Contraceptives): A Petition Circulated by the World Global Network for Reproductive Rights," In/Fire Ethics: Newsletter of the International Network of Feminists Interested in Reproductive Health, Vol. 4, No. 1, 1995, pp. 1–3.

59. R. Peyron et al., "Early Termination of Pregnancy with Mifepristone (RU 486) and the Orally Active Prostaglandin Misoprostol," *New England Journal of Medicine*, 328:1509–1513, 1993.

60. WHO Task Force on Postovulatory Methods of Fertility Regulation, "Menstrual Regulation by Mifepristone plus Prostaglandin: Results from a Multicentre Trial," *Human Reproduction*, 10:308–314, 1995.

61. M. F. Fathalla, 1994, op. cit. (see reference 2), p. 532.

62. PATH, "Market-Related Issues Affecting the Participation of the Private Sector in Contraceptive Development," final report to The Rockefeller Foundation, Seattle, Nov. 30, 1994.

63. L. Harris and Associates, "America Speaks: Americans' Opinions on Teenage Pregnancy, Sex Education and Birth Control," report of survey conducted for Planned Parenthood Federation of America, New York, 1988.

64. A. Freedman, "Product Liability: Narrow Bill Crafted to Avoid Bogging Down in Senate," *Congressional Quarterly*, 51:1020–1021, 1995.

65. The Rockefeller Foundation, "International Research in Reproductive Health: A Guide to Agencies/Organizations," draft paper prepared for the WHO Special Programme for Research, Development and Research Training in Human Reproduction, New York, 1995, p. 12.

66. Ibid., p.26.

67. PATH, 1994, op. cit. (see reference 6).

68. R. Lincoln and L. Kaeser, 1988, op. cit. (see reference 14).

Michael Klitsch is editor of Family Planning Perspectives. *The author would like to thank Jacqueline Darroch Forrest and Lisa Kaeser of The Alan Guttmacher Institute for their assistance in the preparation of this article and for their comments on earlier versions of the manuscript; the author also appreciates the helpful comments of Mahmoud F. Fathalla, Henry L. Gabelnick, Gordon W. Perkins, James Shelton, Jacqueline Sherris, Rosemarie B. Thau and Paul F. A. Van Look.*

A Reading for Critical Thinking

On the Needless Hounding of a Safe Contraceptive

Norplant litigation

Abstract: *Since mid-1994, Norplant maker Wyeth-Ayerst Labs has been hit with more than ten times more lawsuits, 235, than in the first 3 years of US approval of the contraceptive. Part of blame goes to poor insertions of the device, but most is due to unfounded litigation, which discourages research.*

"Worse than a car crash." "Paralysed from the neck down." Mutilation, stroke, blindness, auto-immune disease. Norplant, the only radically new contraceptive device to become available in the past 25 years, is accused of terrible things. The stories are worrying. But are they true? And if not, why have they started to appear in the newspapers with increasing frequency in the past year?

Norplant was approved first for use in Finland in 1983 and has now been introduced in more than 40 other countries. America's Food and Drug Administration (FDA) gave its approval in 1990, since when about a million American women have used it. The device consists of six silicone tubes, each the size of a matchstick, that are implanted under the skin of the upper arm. The tubes contain a synthetic hormone that diffuses slowly into the bloodstream, protecting against pregnancy for five years.

In the first three years during which it was available in America, fewer than 20 lawsuits were filed against Norplant's American makers, Wyeth-Ayerst Laboratories. Yet the past 12 months have seen the filing of 235 lawsuits, including 50 class-action suits, causing a dramatic slump in sales. If the complaints are valid, fair enough. But what if they are not? The effect on the development of other contraceptives could be devastating.

THREE PIECE SUITS

The case against Norplant has three components: problems with positioning, with the hormone, or with the tubes. The first lawsuits and most of the horror stories about Norplant stem from faulty insertion. If the tubes are too near the surface of the skin, they may be spontaneously expelled—though this is rare. On the other hand, if the tubes have been put in too deeply, doctors may be unable to find them. Digging around and then removing them may be difficult for the doctor and painful for the woman. Once a removal has been botched, a second attempt may be even harder. For the woman concerned, it can be traumatic and sometimes disfiguring.

These problems, however, have little to do with the device and much to do with doctors and nurses. Wyeth-Ayerst offers courses in how to insert and remove Norplant, but some doctors seem to think that they do not need training. Even for those who have been trained, removing a badly inserted device can be difficult. But as doctors become proficient at insertion and removal, the problems should dwindle. More worrying are allegations against the device itself.

Hormonal contraceptives such as Norplant consist of synthetic versions of the hormones that regulate the menstrual cycle. Combined oral contraceptives (the pill) contain a mixture of oestrogen and progestogen. Other hormonal contraceptives (Norplant, an injectable contraceptive called Depo-provera, and an oral contraceptive called the "mini-pill") contain only progestogen. The particular synthetic hormone in Norplant, levonorgestrel has been used in formulations of the pill for many years. The new part is how it is delivered.

When the pill was introduced, the doses of both hormones in it were much higher than in today's pills. The early pills carried an increased risk of stroke; today's pills, if they are used by women who have no other risk factors such as smoking or high blood pressure, carry no increased risk. In some women, the pill may give rise to inconvenient side-effects such as acne, weight-gain and headaches. But the pill is also associated with benefits such as protection from cancer of the ovary and the womb. For progestogen-only contraceptives, the story is similar, although menstrual periods can become irregular and heavy.

Depo-provera—which has been in use in many countries for more than 25 years—is the contraceptive most similar to Norplant, although they contain different progestogens. But because Depo is injected, it produces an extremely high initial concentration of the hormone in the blood; Norplant releases its hormone continuously, and therefore more evenly. This is likely to lead to fewer side-effects, not more. Nor should the overall dose in Norplant be a problem: over five years it is lower than it would be from the pill over the same time.

Post-marketing surveillance in America by the FDA, and studies by the World Health Organisation in eight non-western countries, have found no serious problems associated with using Norplant. Indeed, the FDA has recently reiterated its support for the device. The chance that either the hormone itself or its slow release causes severe problems is tiny. That leaves the tubes.

The tubes have been implicated as a potential source of problems because they, like breast implants, contain silicone. But so do almost all prosthetic medical devices, from heart valves and pace-makers to testicular and penile implants. Silicone is the safest and most versatile biomedical material known. Besides, compared to most such implants, the tubes in Norplant are tiny—they contain 100 times less silicone than do breast implants—and rather than being made of gel, they are hard and therefore less likely to be absorbed into surrounding flesh.

But even for large, squishy implants there is no evidence so far that silicone causes auto-immune disorders. A report published recently by the British government's Medical Devices Agency evaluated 250

epidemiological studies and found no effect from silicone. Recent, large-scale epidemiological studies in America, including one published in the New England Journal of Medicine in June, have also not found that silicone increases the risk of these diseases.

Yet in 1994 a class-action lawsuit on behalf of women who claimed that silicone breast implants had injured them was settled with a payment of $4.25 billion—the largest ever. Dow Corning, maker of many of the breast implants and, before it curtailed its activities, a big supplier of silicone to other manufacturers of medical devices, contributed $2 billion. (However, as this article went to press, the settlement was in danger of collapsing.) So what is going on? If it is a mistake, it is an expensive one, and not just for Dow Corning.

The explanation comes in three parts. When the settlement was made, no good epidemiological studies existed. Now they do, and they exonerate silicone. Second, lawyers have a tasty incentive to drum up cases against silicone: $1 billion of the class-action settlement went straight to the plaintiffs' lawyers. Last, it is difficult to deal with claims so vague as to be unfalsifiable. Now that the epidemiological evidence indicates that silicone is in the clear, its critics no longer say that it causes specific disorders; instead they speak of a huge cluster of problems ranging from aches and pains to obstructive lung disease.

Lawyers across America are now trawling for silicone business, advertising for clients who have ever had a medical device containing the stuff. A class-action suit has been filed on behalf of men with penile implants. Lawyers advise clients who are happy with Norplant to have it removed. Like horoscopes, advertisements cover enough symptoms vaguely enough that many people are bound to think "that's me". Seminars with titles like "1995 Norplant litigation: The Growing Debate" and "Preparing the Medical-Devices Case" have sprung up around the country. Attending one costs $550 or more. Legal publishing houses have recently started up journals to record the litigation specifically on Norplant. Eyes light up with dollar signs.

This could be a disaster in the making. In poor countries, pregnancy is the leading cause of mortality for women of child-bearing age. Even in rich countries childbearing contains risks. Abortion can be emotionally traumatic, and where it is illegal, it can be incredibly dangerous. No contraceptive is perfect: condoms break, the pill gives some women headaches, diaphragms are messy and inconvenient, sterilisation is forever. Because Norplant reduces human error it is more effective than the pill at preventing pregnancy. If it is hounded out of use by relentless, unfounded and expensive litigation, who will risk the next attempt to make a better contraceptive?

Birth Control Failure

By Rita Rubin

Abstract: *A large majority of the six million unplanned pregnancies in the US each year could be prevented if doctors would recommend to women some highly safe and effective contraceptives that are seldom used. These include Norplant, Depo-Provera and the new types of IUDs.*

More than 90 percent of American women who want to avoid pregnancy report using a birth control method. Still, the reality is that nearly 6 in 10 U.S. pregnancies are unplanned. As a result, a quarter of the 6 million pregnancies in the United States each year are terminated.

The U.S. market for a new abortion method is huge, and one probably will be available by year's end. After years of controversy, the abortion pill RU-486 moved closer to final approval with the settlement last month of a lawsuit involving its former distributor. "I am convinced that this product will have a substantial impact," says Jack Van Hulst, chief executive officer of Advances for Choice, the new RU-486 distributor. The drug is likely to make pregnancy termination more accessible in areas lacking surgical-abortion providers. And it could supplant at least a third of surgical abortions.

But if the Population Council, a nonprofit international research organization and U.S. sponsor of RU-486, had its way, the demand for abortions would drop precipitously. Virtually everyone in the reproductive health field would rather see American women prevent unwanted pregnancies in the first place. As things now stand, the United States tops many industrialized countries in unplanned pregnancies and abortions.

And since 60 percent of women who terminate pregnancies say their contraceptives failed, better birth control could dramatically reduce U.S. abortions. But American women—and their doctors—are giving short shrift to some very effective methods that merit a second look.

Not only are some quite effective, but they'll probably remain American women's only choices for quite some time. Fear of costly litigation from dissatisfied users has deterred pharmaceutical companies from pursuing new methods.

Nearly half the couples with an unintended pregnancy were using birth control that failed, often because of misuse. Pills are forgotten. Diaphragms dislodge. Condoms slip off. The remaining couples were not using contraception because they thought it inconvenient or they worried about side effects or cost. People yearn for a contraceptive that is not just highly effective but perfectly safe, cheap, easy to use and protective against sexually transmitted diseases. Unfortunately, nothing like that exists.

Among the most effective methods in the United States, the most widely used remain three that have been available for decades: sterilization—either vasectomy or tubal ligation—and birth control pills. But three other equally effective methods are hardly used at all. Intrauterine devices, Norplant implants, and Depo-Provera injections each are used by only about 1 percent of American women who practice birth control.

Doctors don't know. Part of the blame for those methods' low rates of use rests with physicians, says

Daniel Mishell, chairman of obstetrics and gynecology at the University of Southern California School of Medicine. "It's a constant struggle to teach clinicians about birth control," says Mishell. Norplant and the contraceptive version of Depo-Provera weren't available in the United States until this decade, so many doctors never learned about them during their residencies. And most physicians trained since the infamous Dalkon Shield came on the market in the early 1970s wrongly regard all such IUDs as dangerous, Mishell says.

Shortly after the Dalkon Shield became available, users began reporting complications such as pelvic inflammatory disease. Apparently, the string attached to the IUD that enabled doctors to check its placement and remove it acted as a conduit for bacteria. The first lawsuits involving the device were filed in early 1972, and ultimately 195,000 people filed claims against its manufacturer. Legal action spread to makers of other IUDs and the physicians who inserted them.

Today, only two types of IUDs are sold in the United States, and they have made barely a dent in the contraceptive market. By comparison, IUDs are one of the most popular contraceptive methods in Europe—in some countries the choice of more than a quarter of women using birth control. IUDs used today have a simpler tail that is much less likely to harbor bacteria. And further analyses of epidemiologic studies found that the increased risk of pelvic inflammatory disease linked to IUDs actually stemmed from other factors: users who had multiple sex partners or harbored harmful bacteria in the lower part of their uterus when the device was inserted.

A serious drive to encourage IUD use in the United States is underway. Last year, concern over unintended pregnancies led to a government conference to dispel myths about the devices. And in 1995, Ortho-McNeil Pharmaceutical, a leader in the contraceptive field, acquired the small company that had marketed the copper-T IUD, sold as ParaGard in the United States. Only an inch-and-a-half long, ParaGard can be inserted in a doctor's office and left alone for up to 10 years. (Progestasert, the other IUD on the U.S. market, must be replaced annually.) It releases small amounts of copper that help prevent conception. The pregnancy rate during the first year of use is less than 1 percent if the device remains in place; in a small proportion of cases, it is expelled. And if left in the uterus for two years, it's the cheapest form of reversible birth control.

ParaGard may not be for everyone, though. IUDs offer no protection against sexually transmitted diseases. (Nor do any of the other most effective contraceptives, so experts advise using condoms with them.)

They can cause heavy or irregular bleeding. Ortho recommends that ParaGard users be in a monogamous relationship and have no history of pelvic inflammatory disease. And women who have had at least one child are less likely to expel the IUD from their uterus.

But Mishell says that women who don't meet these criteria might be IUD candidates. If no harmful bacteria are found in a woman's cervix, many experts say she can use an IUD with little risk of complications, even if she has multiple sex partners.

Next to IUDs, Norplant and Depo-Provera shots are the longest-lasting contraceptives. Like the pill, both suppress ovulation; Depo-Provera through an injection once every three months, Norplant via six matchstick-size implants inserted in the upper arm. Also like the pill, both can have such side effects as irregular bleeding, weight gain, and headaches.

Lawsuit heaven. But resistance to their use is largely due to other factors. American women have not clamored for Depo-Provera, says Mishell, because its contraceptive and adverse effects can last seven or eight months after the last shot. And Norplant, like the Dalkon Shield, has become a lucrative target for plaintiffs' attorneys. Norplant was introduced with great promise in 1991; the implants, which release a continuous low dose of hormones, provide effective contraception for five years. While Norplant has been used by more than 1 million U.S. women, its popularity has dropped significantly since 1994, when well-publicized lawsuits started being filed against its maker, Wyeth-Ayerst Laboratories.

The suits have blamed Norplant for a variety of ills, many of which are common to all hormonal contraceptives and are even listed as potential side effects in Wyeth's patient and physician information literature. Plaintiffs also have charged that Norplant is difficult to remove. But many family-planning experts blame that on doctors who never learned how to insert or remove it properly, not the method itself. "Together, the lawyers and the media have just about killed off Norplant," says James Trussell, director of the Office of Population Research at Princeton University.

At a Food and Drug Administration hearing last summer, a senior attorney for Wyeth reported that more than 650 lawsuits involving 13,000 plaintiffs had been filed against Norplant. Now under a court gag order, the company cannot talk about the lawsuits. Some birth control experts speculate that the litigation has discouraged Wyeth from introducing a second-generation implantable contraceptive, even though the device won FDA approval last August. The new implant consists of only two capsules, which would facilitate insertion and removal, that provide contraception for three years. A Wyeth spokeswoman would say only that the company is still working to improve the instrument used to insert the new implant.

Women who find themselves unexpectedly pregnant do have a backup method, although manufacturers' concerns about litigation have helped keep its profile low. Commonly called the "morning-after pill," emergency contraception actually entails taking two combined estrogen/progestin birth control pills within 72 hours of intercourse and two more 12 hours later. Studies have shown that emergency contraception pills can reduce the risk of pregnancy by more than 75 percent.

Neither Wyeth nor Berlex Laboratories, the two companies that now make pills that could serve as emergency contraceptives, has expressed a desire to promote this new use for its products. The FDA, interested in expanding birth control options, is trying to encourage drug companies to get into the emergency contraception business. So the agency is expected any day to take the unusual step of announcing that the method is safe and effective, even though no manufacturer has asked for such a ruling. The FDA's endorsement should make it more difficult to win a suit against a morning-after pill, says Trussell. And perhaps American women will gain wider access to one more weapon against unintended pregnancies.

Contraception Choices

The following are birth control methods and their failure rates in one year of average use:

Method	Unintended pregnancy rate*
No Method (Chance)	85.0
Spermicides	30.0
Withdrawal	24.0
Periodic Abstinence	19.0
Cervical Cap	18.0
Diaphragm	18.0
Condom	16.0
Pill	6.0
IUD	4.0
Tubal Ligation	0.5
Depo-Provera	0.4
Vasectomy	0.2
Norplant	0.05

*Figures are based on women of reproductive age, 15–44. Rates vary with age. Failure rates with perfect use are lower, but people rarely use methods perfectly.

Source: The Alan Guttmacher Institute

How Reliable Are Condoms?

They're the best protection against sexually transmitted diseases.
But several popular varieties failed our tests.

Everyday some 6000 people around the world become infected with HIV, most of them through sex. In the U.S., more than a million people carry the virus that causes AIDS, and the count rises by one every 13 minutes. Nearly everyone knows how AIDS is spread—and how to stop it. Three out of four Americans now know that latex condoms, used correctly and consistently, will block AIDS and other sexually transmitted diseases, says Melissa Shepherd, who heads AIDS education efforts at the Federal Centers for Disease Control and Prevention.

Condom sales, driven by the fear of AIDS, have climbed to 450 million a year in the U.S. Once only whispered about, condoms are now routinely advertised on cable TV and in magazines, are sold in supermarkets, and come in a dizzying variety of styles. (One brand alone promotes nine variations: lubricated, mint-scented, spermicidal, studded, sensitive, ribbed, colored, black, and snug.)

Yet many people who should use condoms still don't, apparently put off by the inconvenience or the feel. A recent survey of people with multiple sex partners, for instance, found that those who never use condoms, or use them inconsistently, outnumbered those who always use them by 11 to 1.

Now there's more bad news: Couples who do use condoms may not be getting all the protection they think they are. How well a condom works is in good part up to the users—some people are more likely than others to break condoms through misuse. But some breakage may be due to real differences among the brands and varieties.

To assess their reliability, we bought and tested 6500 latex condoms—37 different kinds. Among our findings:

- A half-dozen types of *Trojans*, the best-selling brand, too often flunked an air-inflation test.

Long part of many other countries' condom standards, that test was adopted by U.S. inspectors last year after we bought our condoms. Had such guidelines been in place when these condoms were made, and had Government inspectors checked production lots as we did, some lots of those *Trojans* probably would not have made it out the factory door. (One variety of *LifeStyles* condoms failed the same test.)

- Several condoms promoted as "stronger" did not do as well as others in our inflation tests. Inflating condoms checks their elasticity, which experts say is the quality that tends to keep a condom intact during intercourse.

- Several condoms promoted as "thin" are not especially so, according to our measurements. And the condoms that really are thinnest, although they passed the basic inflation test, tended to break more easily than did the other condoms we tested. They may not provide as much protection as their thicker counterparts.

For Prevention of Disease

Condoms are considered crucial for slowing the spread of sexually transmitted diseases, because the odds of transmission are cut nearly to zero if condoms are used consistently and correctly. If they're not used, here is the estimated chance that microbes will be transmitted from one infected partner to the other during a single act of intercourse.

Microbe for:	male-to-female	female-to-male
Gonorrhea	50 to 90%	20%
Genital herpes	0.2	0.05
AIDS	0.1 to 20	0.01 to 10

Source: K.M. Stone, HIV, STDs, and Other Barriers. In Barrier Contraceptives, Current Status and Future Prospects, 1994.

A PROTECTIVE BARRIER

It may not be obvious from the packaging, but all condoms are pretty much the same. They're nearly all made of latex, in the same basic shape, according to industry standards for size and thickness.

Latex condoms are produced by dipping a cylindrical form in liquid latex and heating it. Machines shape and trim the condom's ring; then the new condoms are washed and aged for a number of days, a "curing" that lets the rubber complete the chemical reactions that strengthen the latex. The final steps: rolling and wrapping individual condoms. The basic process hasn't changed much in 50 years.

The industry standards say a condom's width should be no greater than 54 millimeters—about 2⅛ inches—to prevent slippage; "snugger" condoms are about 10 percent narrower. The minimum length is 160 millimeters, roughly 6⅓ inches, but some products are up to 2 inches longer.

CONDOMS FOR CONTRACEPTION

As a contraceptive, condoms are cheap and easy to obtain, and usually cause no side effects. (A very small number of people are allergic to latex—see box "Two ways to Avoid Latex.")

For Birth Control

As a contraceptive, condoms are more effective than the diaphragm, less so than the Pill. Below are percentages of women relying on each method who nonetheless become pregnant over a year's time. If birth control is used perfectly—consistently and correctly—failures can be cut dramatically. If no birth control method is used, 85 percent become pregnant.

Method	Percentage Who Become Accidentally Pregnant in a Year
Spermicide	
Rhythm (calendar)	
Withdrawal	
Diaphragm and spermicide	
Condom	
Condom and spermicide	Not available
Pill	
Male sterilization Female sterilization	

■ Typical use
▨ Perfect Use*

0 5 10 15 20 25

Source: "Contraceptive Technology," Irvington Press; and "Family Planning Perspectives" journal.

*Estimated

They are not, however, perfect. The condom's reliability in preventing pregnancies depends on how it's measured. Researchers don't count the number of individual condoms that fail; instead they define contraceptive failure as the percentage of women who use a given method but nonetheless become pregnant over a year's time. For condoms, the typical rate is about 12 percent, somewhat worse than birth-control pills but better than the diaphragm (see graph). But researchers know that, as with other methods, the failure figures include many couples who don't use contraception every time.

If couples used condoms consistently and correctly, researchers estimate, the condom's failure rate would plummet to 2 or 3 percent, or perhaps even less. One way some couples might further reduce the failure rate—to an estimated one tenth of a percent, if used consistently—is to use condoms in combination with a vaginal spermicide.

STOPPING GERMS

As a means of preventing the transfer of disease causing microbes between sex partners, condoms have no equal. The condom shields the penis from cervical, vaginal, oral, or rectal secretions. At the same time, the partner is protected from potentially infectious semen and any lesions on the penis.

The need for such protection is apparently greater than many people realize: Every year, 12 million Americans—one-fourth of them teenagers—come down with sexually transmitted diseases. Chlamydia, the most common such disease but often unrecognized, can lead to tubal scarring that experts believe is a key factor in the quadrupling of ectopic pregnancies in the last 10 years. And AIDS is still increasing in the U.S., particularly among women. (Gay men still account for the largest number of AIDS cases; there's concern that condom use is falling among younger gay men.)

Chlamydia, gonorrhea, and AIDS—as well as other sexually transmitted diseases—are virtually 100 percent preventable with proper condom use. So well do latex condoms block germs that, since 1987, the U.S. Food and Drug Administration has allowed condom boxes to list all the diseases condoms help avert. More recently, the FDA told companies that the disease-prevention message was so crucial, they should also print it on the wrappers of individual condoms. Condom boxes warn that the product is intended for vaginal sex, but health officials say it's crucial to use condoms in anal and oral sex, too.

Preventing sexually transmitted disease is in some ways a more rigorous test of condoms than is preventing pregnancy. While conception is a concern only a

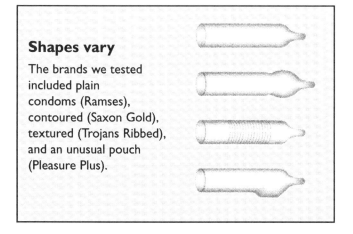

Shapes vary

The brands we tested included plain condoms (Ramses), contoured (Saxon Gold), textured (Trojans Ribbed), and an unusual pouch (Pleasure Plus).

few days a month, diseases can be caught all the time. Over the decades since the latex condom's introduction, epidemiologists have amassed considerable evidence that it does cut disease rates, but not quite to zero. A 1992 review in the American Journal of Public Health, summing up the results of many varied studies, found that condoms on average cut the risk of infection in half. But the authors said the studies included many couples who failed to use condoms properly or consistently.

When couples are strongly motivated to use condoms every single time, the score greatly improves. Herbert Peterson, chief of the CDC's women's health and fertility branch, cited two recent "blockbuster" studies on condoms' use against HIV. Both focused on heterosexual couples, with one partner carrying HIV at the start of the study, who continued to have sex regularly for two years or more.

In the first study, Italian researchers followed more than 300 healthy women in stable, monogamous

relationships with HIV-positive men, questioning the women closely about condom use and testing them periodically for HIV. Among women whose partners never or inconsistently used condoms, 12 percent eventually were infected with HIV. By contrast, fewer than 2 percent of the women whose partners always used condoms became infected.

The second report, from the European Study Group, showed even better results for some 250 uninfected men and women with HIV-positive partners. Among the half who used condoms inconsistently, 10 percent of the previously uninfected partners acquired HIV. When condoms were used all the time, however, HIV was never passed on to the healthy partner—even though the average couple had sex about 120 times over the course of the study.

"If everyone used condoms correctly and consistently, we could break the back of the AIDS epidemic," Peterson told us.

WHEN THEY FAIL

An estimated 2 to 5 percent of condoms tear during use. Most of those failures are thought to stem from misuse, not inherent product flaws. (And misuse is common: When the British Consumers' Association asked some 300 Englishmen to demonstrate putting a condom on a model penis, nearly one in five got it wrong—they tried to unroll the condom from the inside out.) Bruce Burlington, who heads the FDA's Center for Devices and Radiological Health, which is responsible for condoms, told a CU reporter that the difference in quality between the best and worst condoms on the market is "tiny compared with the problems that users introduce."

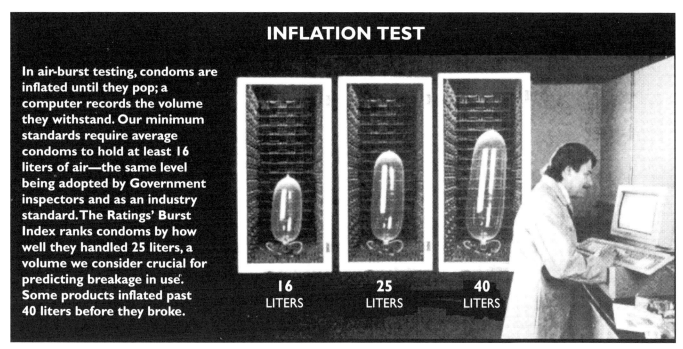

INFLATION TEST

In air-burst testing, condoms are inflated until they pop; a computer records the volume they withstand. Our minimum standards require average condoms to hold at least 16 liters of air—the same level being adopted by Government inspectors and as an industry standard. The Ratings' Burst Index ranks condoms by how well they handled 25 liters, a volume we consider crucial for predicting breakage in use. Some products inflated past 40 liters before they broke.

16 LITERS   25 LITERS   40 LITERS

When condoms do break despite being used correctly, it's probably caused by hidden weaknesses in the rubber. Both manufacturers and the Government take steps to catch flawed condoms before they can leave the factory.

Manufacturers test each lot of condoms for leaks and for strength, according to voluntary guidelines set by the American Society for Testing and Materials, the major U.S. standards-setting organization. Those tests, however, which destroy the condoms being

---

Other Condom Options

Two Ways to Avoid Latex

If latex condoms irritate your skin, the culprit may be the lubricant, the spermicide, or the materials used in processing; try switching brands. If that doesn't work, you may be among the small percentage of people whose skin is sensitive to latex itself. You have two other choices in condoms, each with pluses and minuses.

'Skin' condoms

Made from a natural pouch in lambs' intestines, these condoms cost several times as much as latex ones. The membrane is especially strong and may enhance sensitivity. The downside: they have small holes.

The microscopic pores can be up to 1.5 microns across. Since sperm cells are twice as wide as that, skin condoms still make an effective contraceptive. But viruses and some bacteria are far smaller than these pores (see diagram). Lab work has shown that HIV and the herpes and hepatitis-B viruses can pass through skin condoms. So these condoms must bear a warning that they are not intended for disease prevention.

We examined *Fourex* and *Kling-Tite Naturalamb* brands. *Fourex* condoms come folded, not rolled, inside plastic capsules (the condom is pulled

on, like a glove). We found the capsules surprisingly hard to open. *Kling-Tite* may be easier to don because it's rolled, like a latex condom. Skin condoms might slip off some men during intercourse because both *Fourex* and *Kling-Tite* are significantly wider than the latex condoms we tested: 78 and 68 millimeters, respectively (latex condoms average 52 millimeters). The *Fourex* has a rubber band rolled onto the base of the condom to prevent slippage. The *Kling-Tite*'s elastic band is sewn on more securely.

Polyurethane condoms

Last year, on the basis of limited testing, the FDA gave Schmid Laboratories approval to sell its new *Avanti* brand, a clear condom made of polyurethane. The agency justified approving the product because it felt a pressing public-health need to offer latex-sensitive people an alternative that could prevent disease as well as pregnancy. The *Avanti* condoms first appeared in Western states and should be available elsewhere by summer. But it's unclear just how much protection they offer. A label on the foil packet declares it "effective" against pregnancy and sexually transmitted diseases, while the label on the box warns that "the risks of pregnancy and STDs . . . are not known for this condom." The FDA says it has noted the discrepancy; the packet label will be changed to match the box.

The manufacturer says it has demonstrated to the FDA

that *Avanti* does block viruses and neither slips nor breaks more often than latex. Studies of its contraceptive value are under way.

We bought *Avanti* and *Avanti Super Thin*, which cost us $1.75 each, more than the most expensive latex condoms. Both products are in fact the same condom; the *Super Thins* come with more lubricant.

In the lab, we found the condoms thinner than any conventional condoms tested — roughly 0.04 millimeters. They are also among the shortest of condoms but wider than even larger-size latex brands (60 millimeters versus 55 or 56). That's probably because polyurethane doesn't stretch as much as latex. Despite the company's statements to the contrary, we suspect some men might have slippage problems. When we placed the *Avanti* on a model of an average-sized penis, we found we could pull the condom off quite easily.

Since *Avanti* isn't latex, the label claims that any lubricant may be used safely. We cannot comment on the *Avanti*'s strength. Because synthetic condoms are so new, researchers don't know how to compare their performance in standard tests against that of latex condoms.

Mixed messages

The box and packets of this new polyurethane condom bear conflicting messages about users' risks of disease or pregnancy. The correct answer, the FDA says: The risks are unknown.

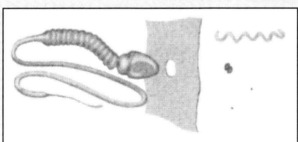

Partial Protection Condoms made from lamb membrane (A) block sperm (B), but have natural pores that may be large enough to let through the syphilis (C) and gonorrhea (D) bacteria, and the herpes (E) and AIDS (F) viruses.

Highly ranked condoms
Products that did especially well in our air-burst test were Excita Extra Ultra Ribbed, the domestic version of Sheik Elite, and Ramses Extra Ribbed. We judged Touch from Protex, which costs less than 35 cents each, A Best Buy.

examined, can be used only to spot-check a batch of condoms, not to check individual condoms before packaging and sale.

Companies can test every condom for leaks, with a gentler but telling electrical procedure. In one variant of the test, each condom is placed on a charged metal form and swept over by a soft, conductive brush. Minute holes in the condoms trip circuitry that shunts many "leakers" aside. Sometimes this test finds thin spots as well.

The FDA, which regulates condoms as medical devices, sends inspectors to factories unannounced. They review production records and examine stock at random, checking for cracked, moldy, dry, or sticky rubber. The inspectors also test the condoms—until now primarily with a water-leakage test. In this protocol, they pour 10 ounces of water into a condom, then press and roll it along blotter paper. Should leaks turn up in the equivalent of more than 4 per 1000 condoms in a run, the manufacturer must scrap the entire lot, perhaps tens of thousands of condoms.

In 1993, the latest year for which we could obtain data, the FDA rejected 2 of the 44 lots of domestic condoms it checked for leakage. The FDA tests every batch of imported condoms as well, though imports account for very few condoms used in this country.

Although the smallest hole the water test can find is 100 times bigger than the HIV virus, officials believe the test is sufficient. The laboratory and clinical studies of HIV persuade them that smaller holes are rare or possibly even nonexistent. Such minute holes are a problem for "skin" condoms, however (see box on Other Condom Options).

HOW WE TESTED CONDOMS

When we last tested condoms, in 1989, none of the brands we checked failed the water test. This time, we concentrated on air-burst testing, which we think better predicts breakage in use. Condoms are locked onto an apparatus that slowly inflates them until they're bigger than a watermelon and finally burst with the bang of a gunshot. Meters record the volume of air and amount of pressure the condom withstand.

Unlike tests of tensile strength—done by stretching a band cut from the condom—air-burst testing stresses the entire condom. Last year, the FDA added the air-burst test to its inspectors' repertoire, and asked the companies to include it in their internal quality-control regimens. The testing guidelines are expected to be adopted shortly as the industry standard.

Published research has linked a condom's air-burst volume to its resistance to breakage during use. Scientists believe that a condom's "extensibility"—its stretchiness—is what helps keep it whole during intercourse. The air-burst test assesses that vital quality.

We tested about 120 individual condoms for each of the 37 styles we bought. To see as many lots as possible for each product, we generally combined samples from five different lots, identifiable by date codes on boxes.

As the Ratings show, our tests were designed to answer two questions: whether a condom passes a minimal standard and, if so, how well it performs on a tougher test, a measure of a product's tendency to break in use. To make the first cut, our combined lots of each product had to pass the new Government air-burst requirement. That rule allows no more than 1½ percent of condoms in a lot to fall short of the required pressure and volume limits. Average-sized condoms, for instance, are supposed to inflate to at least about 16 liters (it varies with condom width) before breaking. Using statistical techniques, inspectors can sample a production run and project a failure rate for the entire lot.

Seven products we tested did not meet that minimal requirement. In each case, at least 4 out of 120 condoms broke too soon during inflation. Based on statistical projections, we believe that more than 1½ percent of condoms in at least some of those products' manufacturing lots would not have inflated to the required minimum volume of air. The products include six styles of *Trojans*—including, ironically, *Trojans Extra Strength*—and *LifeStyles Ultra Sensitive*. We downrated all seven in the Ratings.

For the 30 products that passed that initial screening, we then ranked condoms by a "burst index—the percentage of samples that withstood at least 25 liters of air. This volume is much greater than the standards specify, but we consider it a crucial measure. In a key study in the journal Contraception—which relied on 260 couples who used 4600 condoms—breakage was more likely among products from manufacturing lots whose condoms typically could not hold 25 liters of air before rupturing.

Condoms with higher scores on this index should offer greater protection. Three products turned in perfect scores in our tests: *Excita Extra Ultra-Ribbed Spermicidally Lubricated*, *Ramses Extra Ribbed Spermicidally Lubricated*, and the U.S.-made version of *Sheik Elite Lubricated* (distinguished from the Japanese-made version by a label on the box). The other high-scoring condoms include a mix of *LifeStyles*, *Ramses*, *Sheik*, and *Trojans* brands with varied lubricants, both straight and contoured.

RECOMMENDATIONS

Latex condoms work well—both to prevent pregnancy and to avoid sexually transmitted diseases. Unless you know your partner is uninfected, the CDC recommends—for disease prevention—that you use condoms, start to finish, for all sex—vaginal, anal, and oral.

Here are important factors to consider when selecting a condom:

Strength. Among the 30 products that passed our initial screening, those with a higher Burst Index should minimize the possibility of breakage during sex. Our findings don't match the claims on several packages, however. Five condoms we tested claim to be strong (or stronger than some other brand), but only one of those products—*Ramses Extra Ribbed Spermicidally Lubricated*—earned a top score on our Burst Index.

Sensitivity. When researchers asked a national sample of men in their 20s and 30s about condoms, the biggest gripe concerned sensitivity: Three out of four complained that condoms reduce sensation.

Some brands claim to enhance sensitivity, but it's not clear how they do. Some makers say a snug condom helps, but others say it's a looser fit (*Pleasure Plus* has a floppy pouch near the head, for instance). As a group, condoms promising sensitivity aren't especially thin, by our measurements.

What's more, even if a thin condom does heighten sensitivity, thin is not necessarily desirable. The thinnest products—*Beyond Seven*, a Japanese import; and *Sheik Super Thin* and *Ramses Ultra Thin*, both American—had some of the lowest burst scores; they passed our minimum standards, but may not always hold up as well as higher-ranked condoms. When inflated, one-fourth to one-third of those thinner condoms did not reach the crucial 25-liter mark before bursting.

If sensitivity is an issue for you, be aware that this is a poorly defined term. If you want to try some "sensitive" products, it's safest to start with the higher-scoring condoms that make this claim—such as

Using Condoms Wisely

Most of the products we tested provide adequate instructions, often including pictures. But some print the information on the inside surface of the box, which must be torn apart before the instructions can be read. That's unfortunate—good instructions are key for people unaccustomed to using condoms.

Here are the most important points to remember:

● Open an individual packet only when ready to use the condom—and open it gently, to avoid tearing the contents. If the rubber feels brittle or sticky or looks discolored, discard the condom—it's spoiled.

● Don the condom when the penis is erect but before sexual contact. Place the tip of the rolled-up condom over the penis. If there is a reservoir tip, first squeeze out the air. It there is no tip, leave a half-inch space at the end for semen, and squeeze the air out.

● Unroll the condom down the entire length of the penis (uncircumcised men should first pull back the foreskin).

● Right after ejaculation, grasp the condom firmly at the ring and withdraw before losing the erection, to prevent spillage.

● Use a new condom for each act of intercourse—never reuse condoms.

● Store condoms in a cool, dry place. Heat, light, and air pollution can all hasten deterioration.

● If you want additional lubrication, use only water-based lubricants, such as surgical jelly. Petroleum jelly and mineral-oil products (baby oil, cold cream, many hand lotions) all rapidly weaken latex. Even some lotions that easily wash off with water may contain oils; check the label.

● If a condom does fail, both partners should wash their genitals with soap and water. Urinating may also help to avoid infections. If the breakage is discovered after ejaculation, having a separate spermicide handy to apply quickly may help. Or a doctor can prescribe an intense dose of birth-control pills, which will block most pregnancies if used within 72 hours of intercourse.

Listed in order of air-burst performance [5]

Product	Cost PER CONDOM	Burst Index	Lubricant feel	Spermicide	Size (LENGTH x WIDTH)	Thickness	Comments
Excita Extra Ultra-Ribbed, spermicide	$1.00		glycerine	8%	193 x 53 mm	0.07 mm	Textured. Product renamed Sheik Excita Extra Ribbed.
Ramses Extra Ribbed, spermicide	0.99		glycerine	5	187 x 52	0.07	Textured.
Sheik Elite [1]	0.53		oily	—	187 x 52	0.07	Renamed Sheik Classic.
LifeStyles Vibra-Ribbed	0.44		glycerine	—	188 x 54	0.08	Wider than most. Textured.
Ramses Extra, spermicide	0.75		glycerine	15	200 x 51	0.07	Spermicide now 5%.
Ramses Sensitol	0.83		oily	—	192 x 52	0.07	—
Sheik Elite Ribbed, spermicide	0.68		oily	8	190 x 51	0.07	Textured. Renamed Sheik Classic.
Sheik Elite, spermicide	0.59		oily	8	190 x 51	0.07	Renamed Sheik Classic.
Trojan-Enz Large	0.75		jelly	—	214 x 56	0.07	Wider, longer than most.
Trojan-Enz Nonlubricated	0.47		—	—	191 x 53	0.07	—
LifeStyles	0.46		glycerine	—	186 x 54	0.07	Wider than most.
Touch from Protex, **A BEST BUY**	0.31[2]		oily	—	193 x 52	0.07	—
Trojan-Enz, spermicide	0.64		jelly	5	202 x 51	0.07	Heavier lubrication than most.
Saxon Gold Ultra Lube	0.43		jelly	—	191 x 51	0.08	Contoured.
Trojan Magnum	0.69		oily	—	205 x 55	0.07	Wider, longer than most. Heavier lubrication than most.
Trojan Very Sensitive	0.62		oily	—	206 x 50	0.07	Longer but narrower than most.
LifeStyles, spermicide	0.45		glycerine	7	189 x 54	0.06	Wider than most. Heavier lubrication than most.
Trojan Ribbed	0.64		oily	—	199 x 53	0.07	Textured.
Rough Rider Studded	1.04[3]		glycerine	—	186 x 53	0.10	Textured. Heavier lubrication than most.
LifeStyles Extra Strength, spermicide	0.65		oily	7	191 x 53	0.09	—
Gold Circle Coin Nonlubricated	0.60[4]		—	—	184 x 52	0.09	Shorter than most.
Sheik Elite [1]	0.53		oily	—	188 x 51	0.06	Discontinued.
Trojan Naturalube Ribbed	0.66		jelly	—	205 x 53	0.07	Longer than most. Textured.
Class Act Ultra Thin & Sensitive	0.33[2]		oily	—	193 x 53	0.06	Wider than most.
Kimono	0.39		glycerine	—	193 x 52	0.07	Contoured. Lighter lubrication.
Pleasure Plus	0.98		glycerine	—	197 x 51	0.09	Textured, with floppy pouch.
Beyond Seven	0.50		oily	—	194 x 50	0.05	Narrower than most. Lighter lubrication than most
Gold Circle Rainbow Coin Nonlubricated	0.67[4]		—	—	180 x 51	0.08	Various colors, contoured.
Sheik Super Thin	0.62		glycerine	—	193 x 51	0.05	—
Ramses Ultra Thin	0.88		glycerine	—	190 x 51	0.05	—
The following products, listed alphabetically, had an overall burst volume defect rate that exceeded 1.5%.							
LifeStyles Ultra Sensitive	0.46	—	glycerine	—	187 x 53	0.06	—
Trojan Extra Strength	0.78	—	oily	—	198 x 53	0.07	—
Trojan Mentor	*1.08 [4]	—	glycerine	—	181 x 52	0.07	Contoured. Has applicator and adhesive band.
Trojan Plus	0.66	—	oily	—	196 x 52	0.07	Contoured.
Trojan Very Thin	0.64	—	oily	—	195 x 53	0.06	Lighter lubrication than most.
Trojan-Enz	0.58	—	jelly	—	201 x 54	0.07	Wider than most.
Trojans Nonlubricated	0.49	—	—	—	200 x 53	0.06	No reservoir tip.

[1] Higher-rated product made in U.S.; lower-rated, in Japan (box flaps are marked).
[2] Purchased in boxes of 13.   [3] Purchased in boxes of three.   [4] Purchased in boxes of six.

[5] *Products tested were manufactured prior to the FDA's air-burst test requirements, which should reduce the defect rate.*

Notes on the table

Cost is the estimated average, based on a national survey. An * indicates the price we paid. Except where noted, we purchased boxes of 12.
Burst Index is the percentage of condoms that inflated to at least 25 liters in air-burst testing. Products with higher scores should offer greater assurance against breakage in use.

Lubricant feel indicates which substances feel like oil, glycerine, or surgical jelly.
Spermicide in the lubricant may offer some extra safety against disease and pregnancy if a condom breaks; the extent of this protection is unknown. Figure given is the concentration of nonoxynol-9.
Size was measured on unrolled, flattened condoms and are averages of several samples. Proper fit

affects comfort and may help avoid breakage or slippage.
Thickness is the average of three measurements along the length of the condom. The typical condom we tested is about 0.07 millimeters thick.
Comments identify textured condoms—which have raised bumps or rings—and contoured condoms—which generally flare out near the head of the condom.

the top-rated *Excita Extra Ultra Ribbed*—before trying thinner ones.

Size. Size does matter. If a condom is too tight, it can be both uncomfortable and more likely to break; too loose, and it is more likely to slip off. We measured the condoms: Width varied by 12 percent, product to product; length, by almost 20 percent. (The two types we tested that claim to be larger than average—*Trojan-Enz Large* and *Trojan Magnum*—were in fact longer and wider.) The Ratings give the details.

Lubricant. Many condoms come coated with various preparations that feel like oil, glycerine, or surgical jelly. Using a lubricated condom is largely a matter of preference. If couples wish to add their own lubricant, they should be certain not to use petroleum- or mineral-oil-based products, which rapidly weaken latex. (See "Using Condoms Wisely.")

Spermicide. Many condoms' lubricants include a small amount of nonoxynol-9, a spermicide that promises extra protection. It's a promise without much proof behind it. In the test tube, the chemical does kill sperm and inactivate a range of microbes, including HIV. But no one knows if it works as well in real use and if there's enough of it to make a difference if the condom breaks. (The CDC says it's optional, that the latex barrier alone should offer sufficient protection.)

Age. As condoms age, the rubber in them may weaken, so it's a good idea to avoid packages that are more than a few years old. (We found no sign of aging among the condoms we tested, which were all less than three years old.) Unfortunately, different brands date products differently. Bear this in mind when you're checking the label: Products containing spermicide are given a shelf life of roughly two or three years (to assure that the spermicide still works), while other condoms are allowed as many as five years on the shelf.

PART 5

Sexual Health and STDs

Healthy sexuality means confronting issues related to good physical health and the prevention of sexually transmitted diseases. So it is important that you know that sexually transmitted diseases (STDs) continue to exist in epidemic proportions. The Institute of Medicine's recently released Report on Sexually Transmitted Diseases estimates that every year 12 million Americans acquire a sexually transmitted disease. Over 25 different diseases are capable of being transmitted through sexual intercourse or other intimate sexual contact. Most people are frighteningly ignorant about STDs, including AIDS. AIDS, or **A**cquired **I**mmune **D**eficiency **S**yndrome, is the severe immunological disorder caused by HIV (the Human Immunodificiency Virus). Although much of the recent news concerning treatments for HIV/AIDS is encouraging, AIDS remains a fatal illness, and one of the modes of transmission for HIV is sexual contact.

In this section, the readings examine the current status of the HIV/AIDS epidemic as well as the "hidden epidemic" of sexually transmitted diseases. Also discussed in this section are prevention methods and the particular nature of STDs in women.

An often overlooked part of safer sex education is the impact of gender on behavior. Readings in this part examine this issue and look at important gender-related recommendations for proving the effectiveness of prevention programs. Part 5 ends with a look at the safest sex of all, fantasy sex. Often mentioned in safer-sex literature but seldom described in great detail, fantasy offers a viable option for exploring sexual desire in a safe way.

Bringing the Fundamentals of Gender Studies into Safer-Sex Education

By Janet Lever

A Reading for Critical Thinking

Condom advertisements and public service announcements to stop the spread of the human immunodeficiency virus (HIV) seem to be disproportionately aimed at women. Their content reveals two underlying assumptions—namely, that women are likely to encounter male partners who resist using condoms, and that women have enough power in their sexual relationships to overcome that resistance. These messages fail to take into account persisting gender roles that constrain the types of power that men and women can exert in different types of sexual relationships.*

The basic premise of 25 years of gender research—that men desire control and women are willing or forced to relinquish control—casts doubt on the prospect that many women, especially young women, can follow the recommendations of the safer-sex messages aimed at them. Strategies that depend on female assertiveness will work for some but are doomed to fail for many others. Campaigns that target men as the ones perceived by both partners to be "in charge" of sexual interaction might be more effective, since this message agrees more with real, rather than ideal, gender roles.

Not only do gender roles and stereotypes play a role in constraining styles of interaction between potential sexual partners, they also shape the assumptions of sex educators and the designers of advertising campaigns. Targeting women may reflect the common cultural belief, developed with the advent of the pill, that contraception is the woman's responsibility.[1] Targeting women, however, may also be based on the unquestioned gender stereotype of women as "gatekeepers" of sexual activity, and on the stereotype that

women have greater control over sexual impulses than men. However, gender research challenges the veracity of these old stereotypes, too.[2] The assumption that women hold more favorable attitudes toward condoms than do men and are therefore less likely to object to their use is also at odds with survey data.[3]

We have only to look at issues of *Family Planning Perspectives* for examples of advertisers' pitch to women. A recent ad for the female condom sends the following message, aimed at health educators and practitioners—when a woman's partner is unwilling to wear a prophylactic, advise her to wear one and protect herself.

The headline on another ad reads "*Why every woman should use a condom,*" even though the ad is for a male condom. The accompanying text starts with "We don't need a condom because he says he loves me," but continues with statistics showing that condom use rates among men are low, whereas the proportion who have lied about their sexual past is high. There is also a reminder that women pay a higher price for an unwanted pregnancy, followed by data on women's increasing risk of infection with a sexually transmitted disease (STD), including AIDS.

The ad ends with the phrase "every woman must be convinced that 'I love you' should mean 'I'll use condom.'" The message: his love and his words

*In a classic examination of sex and gender roles within the context of power, Lipman-Blumen defined power as "the process whereby individuals or groups gain or maintain the capacity to impose their will upon others, to have their way recurrently, despite implicit or explicit opposition, through invoking or threatening punishment, as well as offering or withholding rewards." (See: J. Lipman-Blumen, *Gender Roles and Power*. Prentice-Hall, Englewood Cliffs, N.J., 1984, p. 6.)

From *Family Planning Perspectives* (July/August 1995, Vol. 27, No. 4), pp. 172–174. Reproduced with the permission of the Alan Guttmacher Institute from Janet Lever. © 1995.

cannot protect you, only a condom can. In effect, the ad gives a woman the data and repartee with which to rebut a partner's claim that a condom is not needed.

Survey data on sexual practices tell us that health promotion ads and sex education curricula have not yet succeeded in persuading people to abstain completely or to use condoms at every sexual encounter. Condom use among adolescents and unmarried young adults is increasing, although recent data show that the practice is still far from universal.[4] Qualitative research methods are far better suited than surveys to providing additional insight into why couples resist using condoms. Focus groups, for example, which have long been respected for their utility in market research and political campaigns, are underutilized in health promotion planning.† They can be especially useful in shedding light on a problem because of the surprising directions conversations can take when a moderator probes for participants' opinions, experiences and problems with certain situations or products.

As an example, Landry and Camelo reported on focus-group encounters, held in Denver, in which young men and women spoke for themselves about obstacles to condom use.[5] When asked to reconstruct their contraceptive decisions, both male and female participants blamed their occasional failure to discuss or use condoms on embarrassment, alcohol or drug use, dissatisfaction with condoms for reducing physical sensation and disrupting sexual activity, and fear that they would slip or break. Among other reasons for nonuse were trust in their partner's assurance that they were not infected with an STD (despite the lack of medical confirmation) and, most simply, because a condom was not handily available.

However, an additional obstacle to condom use was not discussed in the Landry and Camelo groups, nor has it surfaced in any other report I have seen in over a decade of monitoring AIDS research. Namely, the maintenance of power over women, in and of itself, can lead to resistance to using condoms. This unacknowledged link between the assertion of power and some men's reluctance to comply with requests for the protection condoms provide was raised during a peer-led, all-male focus group conducted with five first-year and second-year students at an elite private

university in California. Here is the relevant portion of the tape recorded dialogue:

Leader: It's kind of uncomfortable when you're with a girl and someone has to pull out protection. One of you has to, but neither one wants to, so it's like, you're waiting for the other person to do it. How do you feel when a woman takes out a condom?

Bill: Well, I've never had it happen to me, so I can't tell you.

Len: Yeah, let's first say who has had a girl say that. See, I've gone out with girls who say (he lowers his voice in imitation of their whispers), "Uh-uh, unless you have protection," but I haven't had a girl say, "I've got some condoms in the glove compartment."

Bill: Well, I find it kind of common to be getting serious with a girl and she'll say, in a low whisper, "Do you have protection?" and if you say, "Yes," you get the picture that you have to stop, you have to do all the stuff. I mean, if it's the only way you're gonna get something, you might as well do it. Even though I *have* it on me, and I have it just for that use, it still kind of pisses me off. It's like, "Do you think I'm dirty, or what?"

Len: Yeah, it's like they're accusing you. I'd say, "Forget it." You get pissed off. (Background chorus of "Yeah's.")

Len: I'd be very uncomfortable, 'cause you'd feel like she's making you do something, 'cause girls aren't supposed to do that.

Leader: Ooh, don't let Janet [me, their professor] hear you say that.

Len: It's like, you're not used to girls telling you to do something.

Bill: But if it's a one-night stand, hey, what the hell, you gotta use it.

Len: Yeah, if it's the only way you're gonna get down her pants, you might as well use it.

How often does the battle for control motivate men to resist using a condom? From this very small group, it is hard to know how common the problem is. One methodological weakness of focus groups is that they are susceptible to group bias—that is, members sway each other. These southern California students, in all-male company, may have been displaying more agreement than they actually felt.

One of the method's strengths, on the other hand, is that subjects feel comfortable and encourage each other. In the presence of peers who expressed "socially undesirable" sentiments about male domination and aversion to safer-sex practices, some participants may have felt safe in agreeing with those sentiments, especially when no outside moderator or authority figure was present. Other same and mixed-sex focus groups that were not peer-led were held in Wisconsin

†A search of the AIDSLINE index produced only 23 titles from 1980 through 1994 for studies of adolescent sexuality education that included focus groups in the study design; of these, only two were conducted with nonminority U.S. teenagers. Three studies were done with special populations (minorities, prostitutes and drop-outs) and 18 were conducted outside the United States.

as well as California. Not surprisingly, the members of another male-only group in Wisconsin, for which I was the moderator, did not express similar sentiments, nor did any members of mixed-gender focus groups.

Whether the young men's dialogue was the product of group sway or group support, it yielded insight about an important gender issue that is totally missing in AIDS awareness campaigns—that young men are not accustomed to taking directives from young women. A young woman who halts the sexual action, even with a whispered plea for caution, may be seen by some as gaining control of a scenario that the young man thought he was directing.

It would be a mistake to generalize from focus groups to all young men, but focus groups are useful in generating hypotheses. The extent to which representative samples of young men would agree or disagree that female-initiated condom use challenges male authority becomes an empirical question for future systematic research. More to the point, we could test the hypothesis that the threat of female as-

"By reinforcing the notion that women should take the lead in initiating condom use, educators and advertisers may be putting into motion a power struggle that has little to do with safer sex . . ."

sertiveness triggers a reaction that makes some men resist condom use.

While the health education literature does not totally ignore the associations between condom resistance and concerns about masculinity, such associations are limited to particular subpopulations. The condom ad previously mentioned notes this when it states, ". . . many ethnic and minority cultures consider the use of condoms to be forbidden or unmanly."

But the focus-group dialogue suggests a more general gender dynamic. The woman's demand (more likely phrased as a request) rather than the condom per se may be what makes the young man feel less of a man; the issue of who is in control could be troublesome for many men, regardless of ethnicity or race. By reinforcing the notion that women should take the lead in initiating condom use, educators and advertisers may be putting into motion a power struggle that has little to do with safer sex, and one that makes protected sex less likely to occur.

Although men might like to feel they are in control during sexual encounters, they concede that women have the real power in their prerogative to refuse sexual overtures, especially in first encounters

and in the early stages of dating. According to Landry and Camelo, many focus-group participants reported that women demanded condom use, and some men acknowledged that they would not use a condom without the woman's initiative. As one Denver man honestly described his strategy of resistance ". . . if they are at the point where they are not going to have sex if you don't have a condom on, I try to talk them out of it."[6] The California men also conceded that they would use a condom if a woman insists, rather than miss a sexual opportunity.

In other words, young women do have some power in sexual situations and sex educators should reinforce their awareness of that power. The problem arises when we divert attention from the obvious source of that power by telling young women they have the power to display bold verbal initiative, a power some may, in fact, not have.

What proportion of young women are able to initiate a discussion about condoms or forcefully demand condom use as a condition for sex? We simply do not know. The men in the focus groups analyzed by Landry and Camelo said that they rarely discussed contraception with casual partners, but when they did, the women initiated the conversation. The participants' testimony indicates that some young women can initiate talk about condoms, but the fact that such conversations were rare suggests that many have difficulty raising the topic.

The concern about women's willingness and ability to take the lead in discussions about contraception was illustrated in my focus groups. The women, in demonstrating what they say to a partner, and the men, in imitating women's speech, were strikingly consistent in portraying women as speaking in a hushed tone. The most verbally aggressive participant in the Wisconsin women's group, Nicki, a 20-year-old junior from an affluent suburb, described her own past behavior in the following terms:

"After my boyfriend and I broke up, I felt if I go on the pill without a serious boyfriend, it's an excuse for me to have sex. But then every time I have ever had a one-night stand, I never had the nerve to come out and say, 'Do you have a condom or some form of protection?' But I'd always whisper something like 'Be careful' or 'I'm not on the pill' [she lowers her voice in demonstration]. I'd say that and that would cause him to withdraw. But that's still stupid thinking."

Was Nicki's whispering due to embarrassment (she certainly was not shy), or because she intuitively understood that her demure presentation would be less threatening to men's sense of control? Nicki admitted she did not have the nerve to use the word "condom," and the two male students confirmed that the women they know employ the euphemism "protection" when they mean "condom."

There is an important difference between Nicki's alternative statements, even if both are spoken in a lowered voice: "Be careful" is an order, whereas "I'm not on the pill" employs the "I" language strategy, which counselors recommend for stating one's needs or giving constructive criticism to a sexual partner.[7] "I cannot relax and enjoy this intimacy because I'm worried about pregnancy" has a very different impact from "You have to wear a condom if you want sex." "I" language emphasizes the initiator's feelings; "you" language is more likely to be perceived as an order or threat.

These whispered euphemisms illustrate what sex educators already know: Teenage and young adult women need more communication skills to help them raise sensitive, embarrassing subjects and discuss them comfortably. Contrary to stereotypes, there are also young men who want to use condoms who could benefit from guidance in condom negotiation dialogue. As one group participant in Wisconsin explained his failure to use a condom on a one-night stand, "I felt if I said that I wanted to use a condom after she said she was on the pill, she would've been offended."

Health educators and advertisers who believe in equality between the sexes face an ideological dilemma, however. If we continue to depend on female assertiveness in strategies to increase condom use, we then model gender roles as they ought to be, i.e., women should be able to make a straight-forward declaration of their intent to protect their bodies, but we place at risk those women who are unable to assert themselves and those who try but fail when faced with the protests of a dominant male partner.

Teaching young women a variety of less forceful, more ingratiating styles of communication (such as using a hushed tone of voice and various euphemisms) may be most effective for those who are somewhat submissive. However, such an accommodation of male dominance to expand safer-sex practices would be distasteful to many educators.

One part of the solution to the dilemma is to shift the focus and target men as the initiators of condom use. Urging men to initiate use would be more consistent with what actually occurs between casual partners. According to the male participants in the Denver focus groups, shortly before intercourse, most either produced a condom or asked their partner if she was using a birth control method.

Such reinforcement of male-initiated protection is also more consistent with gender roles that place the responsibility to "take charge" on men. Messages that appeal to the concept of the male as provider or

protector are similarly congruent with predominant gender roles.

Health curricula and advertising campaigns that stress a shared responsibility for contraception would be even better than those that simply shift the target from women to men: Targeting men and women alike is ideologically compatible with a belief in equality between the sexes, and it doubles the chance that at least one partner will act responsibly. When we do target women, we cannot afford to ignore gender realities we might find unsettling when we frame messages about sexual communication. But the recommendations need not be sexist. Learning to use "I" versus "you," for example, is a useful communication skill for both men and women, whether bold or shy. Learning how to articulate one's own needs while being sensitive to the other person is the most persuasive way to influence the other's behavior.

At a minimum, educators ought to acknowledge, rather than ignore, the gender role and relationship realities in condom negotiation. Ironically, a young woman may have more power to avoid risky sexual behavior during a one-night stand or in a casual dating relationship, when the man may place a higher value on getting sex than on being in control. Sexuality education may help women realize their power to be the one who says "yes" or "no" in such encounters. In a steady relationship, by contrast, the man may care more about being the dominant partner, and use the threat of a break-up to get what he wants. But women could do this also.

As relationships become established, many steady couples give up the protection of condoms and switch to pill use; messages to them should emphasize mutual monogamy and joint medical tests to rule out any infections from previous partners. Recognizing how gender roles and relationship status affect sexual behaviors and power dynamics will help us create better AIDS and STD prevention campaigns.

REFERENCES

1. K. Luker, *Taking Chances: Abortion and the Decision Not to Contracept*, University of California Press, Berkeley, Calif., 1975.
2. M. Fine, "Sexuality, Schooling, and Adolescent Females: The Missing Discourse of Desire," *Harvard Educational Review*, 58:29–53, 1988.
3. J.S. Brown, "Development of a Scale to Measure Attitudes Toward the Condom as a Method of Birth Control," *Journal of Sex Research*, 20:255–265, 1984; and S.M. Kegeles, N.E. Adler and C.E. Irwin, Jr., "Sexually Active Adolescents and Condoms: Changes Over One Year in Knowledge, Attitudes, and Use," *American Journal of Public Health*, 78:460–461, 1988.
4. U.S. Department of Health and Human Services, "Selected Behaviors that Increase Risk for HIV Infection, Other Sexually Transmitted Diseases, and Unintended Pregnancy Among High School Students—United States, 1991," *Morbidity and Mortality Weekly Report*, 41:945–50, 1992; K. Tanfer et al., "Condom Use Among U.S. Men, 1991," *Family Planning Perspectives*, 25:61–66, 1993; L. Ku et al., "Young Men's Risk Behaviors for HIV Infection and

Sexually Transmitted Diseases, 1988 Through 1991," *American Journal of Public Health*, 83:1609–1615, 1993; and The Alan Guttmacher Institute, *Sex and America's Teenagers*, New York, 1994, pp. 33 and 35.

5. D.J. Landry and T.M. Camelo, "Young Unmarried Men and Women Discuss Men's Role in Contraceptive Practice," *Family Planning Perspectives*, 26:222–227, 1994.
6. Ibid, p. 225.
7. R. Crooks and K. Baur, "Communication in Sexual Behavior," in *Our Sexuality*, fifth edition, Benjamin/Cummings Publishing, Redwood City, Calif., 1993, pp. 213–242.

Janet Lever is associate professor of sociology at California State University, Los Angeles; health policy consultant at The RAND Corporation, Santa Monica; and coauthor of the "Sex and Health" column for Glamour. The author gratefully acknowledges the comments of Lisa Bain, Sandra H. Berry, Susan H. Evans, Rosanna Hertz, David E. Kanouse, Kristin Luker, Fran Rosen, Pepper Schwartz and Gail Zellman.

Update on HIV Infection

By Peter J. Ungvarski, MS, RN, FAAN

Here's a global overview of the HIV pandemic, highlighting recent developments
you need to know about, from virus types to the latest treatments and diagnostic markers.
After each section, you'll find a list of references to further expand your knowledge
of the most intensely researched and controversial disease in the world.

Fifteen years after the first reports of gay men with unusual illnesses, the worldwide pandemic of HIV infection rages on. Yet much has changed. Researchers have charted the virus's molecular anatomy and gained an understanding of its protean genome. Both in the United States and elsewhere, HIV has reached more diverse populations. While prevention remains difficult, efforts to forestall transmission in certain groups have paid off. People with AIDS are living longer, and the emergence of new antiretroviral drugs and more sophisticated treatment regimens has raised hopes that HIV infection may soon be controlled like other chronic diseases, with dramatic gains in survival and quality of life.

From the start, nurses have played an important role in the response to the HIV pandemic. Whether you care for patients with HIV every day or only occasionally, you need to stay up-to-date on the latest developments in this field. Individuals with HIV infection are often quite knowledgeable about their disease—indeed, some feel they know more than their nurses do.

Here I'll look at what's new on a number of fronts in the worldwide effort against HIV disease, including virology, epidemiology, prevention, and treatment.

HIV's GENETIC DIVERSITY

An unusual feature of HIV is its genetic diversity, which complicates testing and vaccine development and, it's suspected, may have implications for therapy. Currently, we know of two major strains of HIV, both

of which cause AIDS: HIV-1, found worldwide but most prevalent in the Americas and Europe; and HIV-2, prevalent in West Africa but uncommon elsewhere. Blood screening by the Centers for Disease Control and Prevention has identified 62 people in the United States with HIV-2, 48 (77%) of whom were born in or had traveled to western Africa or had sex with someone from that region.

HIV-1 exists in types or *clades*, which have been designated group M or group O. Group M comprises 10 distinct genetic subtypes—types A, B, C, D, E, F, G, H, I, and J—which vary in geographic distribution. Although clade B predominates in North America and Europe, A, D, and E have been detected in American servicemen who acquired HIV-1 while on overseas duty. Clades A, B, C, and E and HIV-2 have been found in India.

Group O viruses (the O stands for "outlier") differ so much genetically from those in group M that they aren't detected by the enzyme immunoassay (EIA) tests available in the United States and Europe. Group O viruses have been detected in fewer than 100 people in western and central Africa (Cameroon, Gabon, Niger, Nigeria, Senegal, and Togo), in nationals of these countries living in Europe, and in one French national. In 1996, the first case of infection with HIV-1, clade O, in the United States was identified, in a woman who had immigrated from Africa. The CDC is currently working with the manufacturers of HIV test kits to ensure that the tests are reconfigured to detect all known HIV-1 variants, including type O.

From the *American Journal of Nursing* (January 1997, Vol. 97, No. 1), pp. 44–51. © 1997 by Lippincott-Raven Publishers, Philadelphia, PA. Used with permission.

To complicate matters, about 10% of viral isolates from HIV-1-infected people don't fall neatly into one subtype or another, but instead are hybrids. Indeed, researchers have found evidence of such recombinants as A/E and B/F in several countries.

Sources: Update: HIV-2 infection among blood and plasma donors: United States, June 1992–June 1995. *MMWR: Morbid.Mortal.Wkly. Rep.* 44:603–606, Aug. 18, 1995; Brodine, S. K., et al. Detection of diverse HIV-1 genetic subtypes in the USA. *Lancet* 346:1198–1199, Nov. 4, 1995; Quinn, T. C. Global burden of the HIV pandemic, *Lancet* 348:99–106, July 13, 1996; Identification of HIV-1 group O infection; Los Angeles County, California, 1996. *MMWR: Morbid.Mortal. Wkly.Rep.* 45:561–565, July 6, 1996; Ezzell, C. Recombination between HIV-1 clades not so rare. *J.NIH Research* 7(6):24–26, 1996.

FOUR PHASES OF THE HIV PANDEMIC

The HIV pandemic has evolved through four phases—*emergence, dissemination, escalation,* and *stabilization.* Emerging silently from rural areas, the virus came to cities through rural-urban migration of infected individuals and was disseminated worldwide through migration and travel. From there, the rate of infection escalated.

In the developed world, HIV was transmitted most frequently through anal intercourse between men and the use of contaminated syringes by IV drug users. In some countries, particularly those in sub-Saharan Africa, the most common route of transmission has been heterosexual intercourse. During the 1980s, the incidence of infection and AIDS rose quickly. Stabilization has been noted in Australia, North America, and western Europe. But this leveling off is yet to be seen in many developing regions, such as southeast Asia, where an estimated four million cases of HIV infection have emerged over the past five years.

According to the World Health Organization, 1.3 million cases of AIDS have been reported in 193 countries. Taking into account underdiagnosis, incomplete reporting, and reporting delays, estimates have reached six million cases in adults and children worldwide, with five million deaths. Current estimates hold that approximately 10,000 people become infected daily; infection rates are on the rise in sub-Saharan Africa and southeast Asia. At present, the worldwide total of infected individuals is estimated at 20 million, raising the specter of unprecedented AIDS morbidity and mortality statistics. (Worldwide epidemiological data are estimates because HIV testing isn't done in developing countries, due to lack of economic and clinical resources.)

Sources: Quinn, T. C. Global burden of the HIV pandemic. *Lancet* 348:99–106, July 13, 1996, Caldwell, J. C. and Caldwell P. The African AIDS epidemic. *Scientific American* 274(3):62–68, Mar. 1996. World Health Organization. AIDS: Global data. Weekly Epidemiology Record 70:353–355, 1995.

CHANGING FACE OF AIDS IN THE U.S.

According to the CDC, as of July 1996, 548,102 AIDS cases were reported in the United States: 540,806 in adults and adolescents, 7,296 in children under age 13. Of these individuals, 201,975 adults and 3,127 children were alive. Accurate statistics on the number of people who have HIV infection but haven't developed AIDS aren't available, since many states don't keep figures on asymptomatic infection and many individuals don't know they're infected. The most recent estimates range from 650,000 to 900,000 people in the United States who are infected with HIV but don't have diagnosed AIDS.

Important epidemiological trends have emerged in the 1990s. There's some good news: Over the past few years, the number of AIDS cases reported annually to the CDC has declined—from 106,618 in 1993, to 79,897 in 1994, to 74,180 in 1995.

But shifts in the demographics of AIDS have presented challenges to health care workers. For the first time, there are as many blacks as whites in the ranks of people with AIDS—in 1995 each group accounted for 40% of the AIDS population. Blacks and Hispanics represented the majority of cases among both men (54%) and women (76%). Perhaps more telling, the reported AIDS incidence rate per 100,000 among blacks was six times higher than that among whites and twice that among Hispanics. (The lowest rates were among Native Americans, Alaska Natives, and those classified as Asian or Pacific Islander.) Many researchers believe these data reflect differences in such socioeconomic factors as education and income rather than race. Information on education or income isn't collected in AIDS case reporting.

How people acquire HIV has also changed. In a CDC review of the first 500,000 AIDS cases in the United States, comparison of statistics from 1981 to 1987 with those from 1993 to 1995 found that the proportion of cases that involved IV drug users increased from 17% to 27%, and that in which transmission reportedly occurred through heterosexual intercourse rose from 3% to 10%. The percentage of AIDS cases in women increased from 8% to 18%. Especially significant was a decline in the proportion of AIDS cases that involved men who had sex with men, from 64% to 45%.

AIDS is on the rise in adolescents and young adults. Ages 13 to 29 now account for 18% of the nation's AIDS cases, with the highest increases noted in the South and Midwest. Between 1987 and 1993, the HIV-related death rate for ages 15 to 24 rose 38%. The need to focus on prevention of HIV infection in adolescents by promoting safer sex is clearly underscored by the pregnancy and birth rates among American teenagers: The rates are not only rising but exceed those of other developed countries.

Perhaps the most overlooked population of individuals with HIV is adults over the age of 50. In 1995, older adults accounted for 11% of the cumulative total of AIDS cases—up from 10% just one year earlier. Women over age 50 are acquiring HIV primarily through heterosexual contact. Researchers have found that older adults receive little, if any, education on condom use and are less likely to use condoms when having sex.

Finally, HIV has moved from the coasts to the heartland. Although the prevalence of AIDS remains highest in large cities of the Northeast, significant increases have been noted in small cities and rural areas, and the highest rates of increase in AIDS prevalence have been in the South and Midwest.

> *Several studies have found increased mortality among AIDS patients treated at hospitals with less experience with the disease.*

Sources: Centers for Disease Control and Prevention, *HIV/AIDS Surveillance Report* 8(1):3–33, 1996; Karon, J. M., et al. Prevalence of HIV infection in the United States, 1984–1992. *JAMA* 276:126–131, July 10, 1996; Holmberg, S. D. The estimated prevalence and incidence of HIV in 96 large US metropolitan areas. *Am.J.Public Health* 86:642–654, May 1996; Centers for Disease Control and Prevention. *HIV/AIDS Surveillance Report* 5(4):5–33, 1993; Centers for Disease Control and Prevention. *HIV/AIDS Surveillance Report* 6(2):5–39, 1994; *Centers for Disease Control and Prevention.* First 500,000 AIDS cases: United States, 1995. *MMWR: Morbid.Mortal.Wkly. Report* 44:850–853, Nov. 24, 1995; Singh, G. K., and Yu, S. M. Trends and differentials in adolescent and young adult mortality in the United States, 1950 through 1993. *Am.J.Public Health* 86:560–564, Apr. 1996; Spitz, A. M., et al. Pregnancy, abortion, and birth rates among US adolescents: 1980, 1985, and 1990. *JAMA* 275:989–994, Apr 3, 1996; Whipple, B., and Scura, K. W. The overlooked epidemic: HIV in older adults. *Am.J.Nurs.* 96(2):22–28, Feb. 1996; Murphree, D. D., and DeHaven, M J. Does grandma need condoms? Condom use among women in a family practice setting. *Arch.Fam.Med.* 4:233–238, Mar. 1995.

LIVING LONGER WITH AIDS

In the 1980s, the average survival time after AIDS diagnosis was reported to be 11 months. In the 1990s, it rose to 15 to 20 months. A large prospective study of gay men who were HIV positive but had no clinical manifestations on enrollment found that from 1985 to 1988, 83% of men with CD4 lymphocyte counts of 201 to 350 cells/mm^3, 53% of those with counts of 101 to 200, and 22% of those with counts of 0 to 100 survived 2.5 years. For 1989 to 1993, the percentages increased to 91%, 71%, and 54%, respectively. Most experts have attributed improved survival prospects to the introduction in the late 1980s of antiretroviral agents and prophylactic drug therapy to prevent opportunistic infections, particularly *Pneumocystis carinii* pneumonia.

Clinicians' experience in AIDS care also appears to influence survival. Several studies have found increased mortality among AIDS patients treated at hospitals with less experience with the disease. Other research has shown that survival time more than doubles when patients are treated by physicians who have extensive experience in HIV infection and AIDS. Primary care physicians may not be up to the task: One study of their ability to recognize signs of HIV infection found that only 26% were able to detect and diagnose Kaposi's sarcoma, 23% could identify oral hairy leukoplakia, and 17% could detect diffuse lymphadenopathy.

HIV-infected women have poorer survival rates than men, one study found, though no difference was seen in the rate of disease progression. Possible contributing factors cited by researchers include less access to or use of health care resources, lower socioeconomic status, homelessness, domestic violence, substance abuse, and lack of social support.

The contribution, if any, of race to survival prospects remains unclear. Careful analysis of available data seems to indicate that unequal socioeconomic status and access to care and appropriate drug treatment may underlie survival differences. One study found that blacks referred to an HIV clinic were less likely than whites to receive antiretroviral therapy and *P. carinii* prophylaxis. Other research has suggested that equal access to proper care may eliminate differences in survival that seem to be related to race, sex, and IV drug use.

Sources: Bacchetti P., et al., Survival patterns of the first 500 patients with AIDS in San Francisco. *J.Infectious Dis.* 157:1044–1047, May 1988; Osmond, D., et al. Changes in AIDS survival time in two San Francisco cohorts of homosexual men, 1983–1993. *JAMA* 271:1083–1087, Apr 13, 1994; Tu, X. M., et al. Survival differences and trends in patients with AIDS in the United States. *J.Acq.Immune Def.Syndr.* 6:1150–1156, Oct. 1993; Enger, C., et al. Survival from early intermediate and late stages of HIV infection. *JAMA* 275:1329–1334, May 1, 1996; Bennett. C. L., et al. Relation between hospital experience and in-hospital mortality for patients with AIDS-related *Pneumocystis carinii* pneumonia: Experience from 3,126 cases in New York City in 1987. *J.Acq.Immune Def.Syndr.* 5:856–864, Sept. 1992; Stone, V. E., et al. The relation between hospital experience and mortality for patients with AIDS. *JAMA* 268:2655–2661, Nov 18, 1992; Turner, B. J., and Ball, J. K. Variations in inpatient mortality for AIDS in a national sample of hospitals. *J.Acq.ImmuneDef.Syndr.* 5:978–987, Oct. 1992; Kitahata, M. M., et al. Physician's experience with the acquired immunodeficiency syndrome as a factor in patients' survival. *M.Engl.J.Med.* 334:701–706, Mar. 14, 1996; Paauw, D. S., et al. Ability of primary care physicians to recognize physical findings associated with HIV infection. *JAMA* 274:1380–1382, Nov. 1, 1995; Brown, L. S., et al. Natural history of HIV-1 infection and predictors of survival in a cohort of HIV-1 seropositive injecting drug users *J.Natl.Med.Assoc.* 88:37–42, Jan. 1996; Chaisson, R. E., et al. Race, sex, drug use and progression of human immunodeficiency virus disease. *N.Engl.J.Med.* 333:751–756, Sept. 21, 1995; Currier, J., and Piesler, N. Demographics of HIV survival revisited. *AIDS Clinical Care* 7(11):94, 1995; Moore, R. D., et al. Racial differences in the use of drug therapy for HIV disease in an urban community. *N.Engl.J.Med.* 330:763–768, Mar. 17, 1994; Laraque, F., et al. Effect of comprehensive intervention program on survival of patients with human immunodeficiency virus infection. *Arch.Intern.Med.* 156:169–176, Jan. 22, 1996; Melnick, S. L., et al. Survival and disease progression according to gender of patients with HIV-1 infection. The Terry Beirn Community Programs for Clinical Research in AIDS. *JAMA* 272:1915–1921, Jan. 22, 1994.

PREVENTING MOTHER-INFANT TRANSMISSION

A major development in the effort to prevent the spread of HIV was the finding, reported in 1994, that antiretroviral treatment could reduce the risk of perinatal transmission in pregnant HIV-positive women. A French and American clinical trial demonstrated that zidovudine (Retrovir), given during pregnancy and labor to women who hadn't previously taken antiretroviral agents and to newborns for the first six weeks of life, lowered the incidence of HIV infection in infants by about two-thirds—to 8.3% compared with 25.5% among infants in a placebo group.

While the benefits of prenatal antiretroviral treatment are clear, the risks aren't. Studies of birth defects attributed to zidovudine therapy during pregnancy haven't demonstrated that the drug in fact increases the incidence of congenital abnormalities. However, since the trials didn't include women in their first 14 weeks of pregnancy, it's currently recommended that zidovudine be administered only after the first trimester.

Preventing maternal transmission requires testing pregnant women for HIV, which has been controversial. Most clinicians agree that HIV infection should be discussed routinely with all pregnant women and with all women considering pregnancy, and that HIV antibody testing should be offered as well. But legislation has been proposed mandating HIV testing of all pregnant women. Proponents of such laws assert that identifying more infected pregnant women would help prevent HIV transmission to infants. Opponents point out that such laws might discourage women from seeking prenatal care, possibly resulting in harm to both the women and their babies.

Even if testing is encouraged rather than required, caregivers must consider women's psychosocial and mental health needs. A study by researchers at San Francisco General Hospital, who interviewed women identified as HIV-positive during pregnancy, has shed light on the distress these women experience. Among the findings:

- Women saw health care services as putting them at risk for public exposure and as sources of stress.

- They believed that their only means of obtaining care and social services was to enroll in research protocols.

- They felt they had to keep their HIV infection a secret as long as they were asymptomatic, out of fear of isolation, guilt over partner relationships, and concern for their children.

- They complained that they were often forced to educate not only themselves and their families about HIV disease, but their caregivers as well.

Having to weigh the benefits and risks of prenatal antiretroviral therapy only adds to the women's stress. In its guidelines on the use of zidovudine therapy during pregnancy, the CDC advises clinicians not to be coercive, to be linguistically and culturally sensitive, and to provide counseling appropriate for the patient's educational level.

Sources: Connor, E. M., et al. Reduction of maternal-infant transmission of human immunodeficiency virus type 1 with zidovudine treatment. *N.Engl.J.Med.* 331:1173–1180, Nov 3, 1994; Birth outcomes following zidovudine therapy in pregnant women. *MMWR: Morbid. Mortal.Wkly.Rep.* 43:409, 415–416, June 10, 1994: Recommendations of the U.S. Public Health Service Task Force on the use of zidovudine to reduce the perinatal transmission of human immunodeficiency virus MMWR: *Morbid.Mortal.Wkly.Rep.* 43(RR-11):1–20, June 10, 1994; Lester, P., et al. The consequences of a positive prenatal HIV antibody test for women. *J.Acq.Immune Def.Syndr.Hum.Retroviral.* 10:341–349, Nov 1, 1995.

VALUE OF NEEDLE EXCHANGE PROGRAMS

Needle exchange programs (NEPs), which have been tried in the United States, Canada, United Kingdom, the Netherlands, and Australia, have shown promise in helping stem the spread of HIV among IV drug users. Also referred to as syringe exchange programs, they not only provide injectable drug users with clean needles and syringes and alcohol swabs, but often also offer condoms, counseling, and access to social and health services.

A recent study by investigators in New York found evidence of reduced incidence of HIV infection among IV drug users. This follows research showing that NEPs can reduce the use of contaminated needles and is associated with lower risk of two other bloodborne infections, hepatitis B and C. No evidence has been found that NEPs increase the use of injected drugs.

Yet because of laws based on prevailing attitudes in the United States about IV drug use, NEPs have often operated as illegal-but-tolerated or illegal, underground programs. All but five states—Alaska, Connecticut, Iowa, North Dakota, and South Carolina —prohibit possession of drug paraphernalia. California, Delaware, Illinois, Massachusetts, New Hampshire, New Jersey, New York, Pennsylvania, and Rhode Island also have laws requiring a prescription to purchase needles and syringes. In Connecticut, where prescription and drug paraphernalia laws were partially repealed, the incidence of needle sharing among drug users has declined, as has the incidence of occupationally acquired needlestick injuries among law-enforcement officers.

In 1995, both the National Research Council and the Institute of Medicine concluded that NEPs can slow the spread of HIV and advocated removing federal and state restrictions against such programs. But no legislatures have yet taken any action.

Sources: Des Jarlais, D. C., et al. HIV incidence among injecting drug users in New York City syringe-exchange programs. *Lancet* 348: 987–991, Oct. 12, 1996; Syringe exchange programs: United States, 1994–1995. *MMWR: Morbid.Mortal.Wkly.Rep.* 44(37):684–685, 691, Sept. 22, 1995; U.S. General Accounting Office. *Needle Exchange Programs: Research Suggests Promise as an AIDS Prevention Strategy*, Report to the Chairman, Select Committee on Narcotics Abuse and Control. Washington, DC, The Accounting Office, 1993; Groseclose, S. L., et al. Impact of increased legal access to needles and syringes on practices of injecting drug users and police officers—Connecticut, 1992–1993. *J.Acq.Immune Def.Syndr.Hum.Retrovirol.* 10:82–89, Sept. 1, 1995.

ADVANCES IN ANTI-HIV TREATMENT

Until recently, the mainstays of drug treatment for HIV infection have been nucleoside analogs. These drugs inhibit the activity of reverse transcriptase, an enzyme HIV needs to transform its RNA genetic material into DNA, the first step in the replication process. They prevent the spread of HIV to new cells but don't interfere with viral replication in cells that are already infected. Since 1987, the Food and Drug Administration has approved five such drugs for sale in the United States: zidovudine, didanosine (Videx, formerly known as ddI), zalcitabine (Hivid, ddC), stavudine (Zerit, d4T), and lamivudine (Epivir, 3TC).

Clinicians and researchers discovered that the use of one nucleoside analog alone (monotherapy) induced viral resistance, the ability of the virus to replicate and infect cells in the presence of the drug. When they tried combining two nucleoside analogs, they found that such combination therapy promotes a more sustained antiviral effect, delays drug resistance, and has a greater effect on a wider range of cellular and tissue reservoirs of HIV.

In 1995, the FDA approved the first of a new group of antiretroviral drugs—protease inhibitors (see *New Drugs*, "A New Class of Anti-HIV Drugs Debuts," July 1996). These drugs act against an enzyme, HIV protease, that cleaves a larger viral precursor protein to produce three smaller proteins necessary for assembling infectious viral particles. When protease is inhibited in infected cells, a noninfectious virus results. Protease inhibitors are a major development in antiretroviral therapy because viral strains resistant to one drug may be susceptible to agents that focus on a different point in the virus's life cycle.

As of December 1996, three protease inhibitors had been approved by the FDA: saquinavir (Invirase), indinavir (Crixivan), and ritonavir (Norvir). These drugs work best in combination with nucleoside analogs. Short-term studies of such combination therapy have shown dramatic improvements in overall health and well-being and sharp reductions in levels of HIV in the blood. (We'll look at "viral load" measurement shortly.)

Resistance figures to be a problem with protease inhibitors as it is with nucleoside analogs. There are two types of resistance: *genotypic*, in which the viral genetic material mutates, and *phenotypic*, in which the virus becomes less sensitive to the drug. The possibility of resistance to each of the protease inhibitors has been demonstrated in laboratory studies. It's unclear how long resistance would take to develop in patients. As with nucleoside analogs, cross-resistance is another possibility: Viral strains resistant to one protease inhibitor may resist others, too. A new protease inhibitor, nelfiavir (Viracept), not yet FDA-approved, hasn't so far been found to cause cross-resistance. This means that should the virus eventually develop resistance to this new drug, the other protease inhibitors can still be prescribed.

Subtherapeutic levels of the drug can promote resistance and cross-resistance. To minimize this risk, advise patients to take the prescribed dose of the drug or drugs at the specified intervals, to follow dietary recommendations (saquinavir should be taken within two hours of a meal, ritonavir with food, and indinavir without food), and to avoid missing a dose and then taking a double dose. Dosages shouldn't be reduced in response to adverse effects. A better solution is a "drug holiday": stopping the drug for several weeks and then either reintroducing it or switching to another agent.

Numerous drugs may interact with protease inhibitors by either increasing or decreasing plasma levels. This isn't necessarily harmful. For example, ketoconazole (Nizoral) increases plasma levels of saquinavir. Since only about 4% of orally administered saquinavir is absorbed, adding ketoconazole to the drug regimen is considered beneficial. On the other hand, rifampin and rifabutin (Mycobutin) decrease plasma levels of all three protease inhibitors and so usually aren't coadministered with the drugs. To be

Among the many obstacles to vaccine development has been the genetic variability of the virus.

sure that no harmful interactions occur, drug screens for interactions should be performed for all patients. Most pharmacies do this when filling a prescription.

Although the available evidence clearly supports combination therapy, several issues remain unresolved: when to initiate therapy and when to switch drugs, which combinations are best, and in what sequence drugs should be prescribed given that development of resistance may necessitate switching drugs. These unanswered questions have left many clinicians viewing 1996's breakthroughs with guarded optimism.

In the current climate of cost containment, the price of drugs will also play a part in prescribing decisions. For example, saquinavir alone costs $5,800 per year and, combined with zidovudine and lamivudine, the cost of treatment climbs to $11,830 per year.

Another class of antiretroviral agents under study is non-nucleoside reverse transcriptase inhibitors. The FDA has approved one of these drugs, nevirapine (Viramune). Unrelated to nucleoside analogs, these agents, as their name suggests, also hinder the activity of reverse transcriptase, but apparently through different mechanisms. Trial results show that the drugs work best when taken in combination with nucleoside analogs by patients who have not previously taken a nucleoside analog. The use of nevirapine with protease inhibitors isn't currently recommended.

Recently, there was encouraging news on an experimental treatment that takes a new approach—rather than blocking replication of the virus, it seeks to bolster immune response. In a one-year trial of interleukin-2, a cytokine that regulates proliferation and differentiation of lymphocytes, 31 patients receiving the agent (administered through intermittent infusion in cycles of five days every two months) had increases in CD4 counts of a magnitude and duration not seen in previous studies of antiretroviral drugs. Associated increases in plasma levels of HIV—a possible risk of such treatment—weren't seen. The study wasn't designed to assess effects on clinical progression, but the use of such immunomodulator therapy in combination with antiretrovirals holds great promise.

Sources: Hirsch, M. S., and D'Aquila, R. T. Therapy for human immunodeficiency virus infection. *N.Engl.J.Med.* 328:1686–1695, June 10, 1993; Caliendo, A. M., and Hirsch, M. S. Combination therapy for infection due to human immunodeficiency virus type 1. *Clinical Infectious Diseases* 18:516–524, Apr. 1994; Bechtel-Boenning, C. State-of-the-art antiviral treatment of HIV infection. *Nurs.Clin.North Am.* 31(1):1–13, Mar. 1996; Mascolini, M. The roiling uncertainties of antiprotease prescribing. *J.Int.Assoc.Physicians* AIDS Care 2(2):6–10, 1996; Lipsy, J. J. Antiretroviral drugs for AIDS. *Lancet* 348:800–803, Sept. 21, 1996; Kovacs, J. A., et al. Controlled trial of interleukin-2 infusions in patients with the human immunodeficiency virus. *N.Engl. J.Med.* 335:1350–1356, Oct 31, 1996.

MONITORING DISEASE PROGRESSION

In part because clinical manifestations of HIV infection develop gradually and differ widely from person to person, clinicians and researchers have used certain laboratory test values, called surrogate markers, to monitor disease progression and to evaluate the efficacy of antiretroviral therapy. The number of markers used has grown in recent years.

Until 1990, the standard had been the absolute count of CD4 lymphocytes (also known as T4 helper cells), the immune cells that are progressively depleted in HIV infection. A CD4 count below 500 cells/mm^3 is considered abnormally low; a count below 200 is a criterion for diagnosing AIDS in an HIV-infected person, under the CDC's definition.

Absolute CD4 counts, however, may be influenced by variables among laboratories as well as concurrent illness or even the time of day. These factors may alter results by as much as 50 to 300 cells/mm^3. Clinicians soon learned that a more consistent surrogate marker is the percentage of lymphocytes that are CD4 cells. A value of 40% or greater is normal; 14% or below indicates severe immunosuppression. But both CD4 counts and percentages reflect immune status, not HIV activity.

A more direct measure of disease progression is viral load or burden—the amount of HIV RNA (genetic material) in plasma. Three tests are currently used to measure viral load: RT PCR (quantitative polymerase chain reaction), bDNA (branched-chain DNA), and NASBA (nucleic acid sequence-based amplification). In each, results are reported in copies per milliliter. Fewer than 10,000 copies/mL indicates a low risk for clinical progression; 10,000 to 100,000, a moderate risk; and more than 100,000, a high risk.

One of the primary objectives of antiretroviral therapy is to produce logarithmic declines in the patient's viral load. For example, a patient who starts on antiretroviral therapy with a viral load of 500,000 copies/mL, but has a viral load of 50,000 copies/mL (a one-log reduction) or 5,000 copies/mL (a two-log reduction) four weeks later, is having a favorable therapeutic response.

Viral load testing is usually performed as part of the initial work-up, when CD4 counts indicate immune system deterioration, and three to four weeks after starting or changing antiretroviral therapy. Illnesses such as influenza, herpes, and pneumonia can cause a temporary elevation in viral load, as can vaccines such as that for influenza, so testing is best delayed when the patient has an acute infection or has been recently vaccinated.

Although high viral loads generally correlate with a low CD4 cell count and low levels with a high CD4 count, the correlation is weak. Some patients with low CD4 counts have low viral loads, and vice versa. Therefore, CD4 count isn't a reliable substitute for viral load when evaluating disease progression or the effectiveness of treatment.

Sources: Sax, P. Viral load testing. *AIDS Clinical Care* 8(4):31–32, 1996; Mellors J. W., et al. Prognosis in HIV-1 infection predicted by the quantity of virus in plasma. *Science* 272:1167–1170, May 24, 1996.

RIDDLE OF LONG-TERM NONPROGRESSORS

From the very beginning of the HIV pandemic, clinicians and researchers suspected that they would eventually see HIV-infected individuals who never became ill. By 1993, they did, leading them to coin the phrase *long-term nonprogressors (LTNPs)* to refer to the estimated 5% of HIV-1-infected people who remain asymptomatic despite documented evidence of HIV infection for more than 10 years. These LTNPs have normal and stable immune profiles, and they haven't required antiretroviral therapy.

Although HIV continues to replicate in LTNPs, these individuals have vigorous serum antibody responses that result in an extremely low viral burden, while their lymph tissue and immune function remain intact. Researchers continue to study LTNPs with great interest, hoping to gain insights that could aid development of new treatments and vaccines. Recent findings have suggested resistance to infection may be conferred by a defect in a gene for a receptor on CD4 lymphocytes, to which both certain immune system molecules and HIV bind.

LTNPs, by the way, shouldn't be confused with long-term survivors—people who have lived eight years or more after a diagnosis of an AIDS-defining disease. Such individuals have all the clinical manifestations of

Health Care Workers and HIV: What Are The Risks?

To date, there are 51 documented cases of health care workers (HCWs) acquiring HIV through occupational exposure. There are another 108 reported cases of infection that may have occurred through occupational exposure; these HCWs, besides being exposed to HIV in the workplace, had other risk factors. Although most of the HCWs seroconverted after percutaneous exposure, some did so after exposure of broken skin or mucous membranes. The average risk to an HCW for infection from all types of reported percutaneous exposure to infected blood is 0.3%. That risk increases when the exposure involves a deep injury, visible blood on the injuring device, a device previously placed in the patient's vein or artery, or a patient who died of AIDS within 60 days of exposure (such patients are presumed to have high titers of HIV).

Prophylaxis with zidovudine alone has been shown to reduce the risk of seroconversion by 79%. Last year, the United States Public Health Service revised its recommendations for postexposure prophylaxis of HIV infection. The new recommendations include combination antiretroviral therapy after most types of exposure, with zidovudine and lamivudine, plus either indinavir or saquinavir for high-risk exposures. Under the recommendations, therapy should be started within one to two hours of exposure and continued for at least four weeks. Postexposure prophylaxis involves a complex drug regimen and doesn't always prevent infection, underscoring the importance of following precautions to prevent transmission of bloodborne pathogens.

The controversy over infected HCWs has resurfaced since recent reports of clinician-to-patient transmission of both hepatitis B virus (HBV) and hepatitis C virus (HCV). In one case, a thoracic surgeon transmitted HBV to at least 19 patients during surgery, without any evident breaches in infection control. In a second incident, a cardiac surgeon may have transmitted HCV to five patients during surgery, although investigators couldn't pinpoint the circumstances and mechanisms of transmission. Expert review of these cases has suggested that the current CDC guidelines for bloodborne pathogen transmission during invasive procedures may have been inadequate. The guidelines don't cover shear injuries to the fingers during suture tying (especially with surgical wire), punctures inflicted by bone edges during sternal closure, or occupational transmission of HCV.

It's noteworthy that, since the AIDS panedemic began, only one report of possible transmission of HIV from a HCW to a patient has been made.

Sources: Centers for Disease Control and Prevention. *HIV/AIDS Surveillance Report* 8(1):3–33, 1996; Tokars, J. I., et al. Surveillance of HIV infection and zidovudine use among health care workers after occupational exposure to HIV-infected blood. *Ann.Intern. Med.* 118:913–919, July 15, 1993; Centers for Disease Control and Prevention. Update: Provisional Public Health Service recommendations for chemoprophylaxis after occupational exposure to HIV. *MMWR: Morb.Mortal.Wkly.Rep.* 45:468–472, June 7, 1996; Harpaz, R, et al. Transmission of hepatitis B virus to multiple patients from a surgeon without evidence of inadequate infection control. *N.Engl.J.Med.* 334:549–554, Feb. 29, 1996; Esteban, J. J., et al. Transmission of hepatitis C virus by a cardiac surgeon. *N.Engl. J.Med.* 334:555–560. Feb 29, 1996.

HIV infection, and they require antiretroviral treatment as well as prophylaxis of and therapy for opportunistic infections.

Sources: Bartnof, H. S. Long-term non-progressors, survivors and HIV positives. *BETA* pp. 29–32. June 1995; Montefiori, D. C., et al. Neutralizing and infection-enhancing antibody responses to human immunodeficiency virus type 1 in long-term non-progressors. *J.Infectious Dis.* 173:60–67, Jan. 1996; Dean, M., et al. Genetic restriction of HIV-1 infection and progression to AIDS by a deletion allele of the *CKR5* structural gene. *Science* 273:1856–862, Sept. 27, 1996.

PROGRESS TOWARD AN AIDS VACCINE

Since 1987, some 15 experimental HIV-1 vaccines have been tested in the United States in 25 trials involving more than 1,900 healthy, noninfected adults. The trials, conducted by the AIDS Vaccine Evaluation Group in the National Institute of Allergy and Infectious Diseases of the National Institutes of Health, have sought to identify vaccines that can immunize uninfected persons or prevent those already infected from developing the disease.

Most of the vaccines developed so far are genetically engineered versions of proteins found in the virus's envelope or core, rather than whole killed or attenuated virus. Two important candidates have been the envelope glycoproteins gp160 and gp120; the latter contains a region of the envelope that attaches to CD4 lymphocytes. The trials have shown that gp120 vaccines induce more neutralizing antibodies than gp160 vaccines do. On the other hand, the gp160 vaccines induce more vigorous proliferation of lymphocytes. It's also been found that vaccines developed in mammalian cells perform better and that more antigen stimulates better immune responses than less antigen.

Among the many obstacles to vaccine development has been the genetic variability of the virus. Another has been the inability of antibodies raised by vaccines to consistently neutralize viral isolates in laboratory experiments.

Preparation is under way for phase III trials in the United States to study vaccine efficacy in preventing infection. Researchers are enrolling volunteers at high risk for HIV infection, monitoring risk behavior, engaging target communities in planning the trials, detecting early infection, evaluating strategies for informed consent, and considering behavioral interventions that could augment future trials. As of last month, 4,884 people have been recruited in Boston, Chicago, Denver, New York, Philadelphia, San Francisco, and Seattle.

Sources: NIAID; Doepel, L. K. Fauci presents NIAID strategy for HIV vaccine development. *NIAID AIDS Agenda* Mar. 1996, Haynes, B. F. HIV vaccines: Where we are and where we are going. *Lancet* 348: 933–937, Oct. 5, 1996.

CHALLENGES TO NURSING

As the HIV pandemic continues, so do the challenges to nursing. One challenge—a formidable one—is to keep up-to-date on what's known about HIV infection and how to prevent and treat it and illnesses related to it.

For those who want to advance their understanding of HIV infection, there's the Association of Nurses in AIDS Care (ANAC; 11250 Roger Bacon Drive, Suite 8, Reston, VA 20190-5202; 703-437-4377). ANAC has local chapters throughout the United States, holds an annual national conference, and produces a bimonthly peer-reviewed nursing journal and a quarterly newsletter. ANAC offers a recently introduced certification in HIV/AIDS nursing.

We are also challenged to expand our contribution to primary prevention, if the number of new infections is to continue to decline. The fact that HIV is not only reaching a more diverse population but is also spreading to small cities and rural areas makes it imperative to screen our patients for any behavior that might place them at risk for HIV infection. We must learn more about and become comfortable with caring for substance users, taking sexual histories, and offering sexual counseling. This is especially true for advanced practice nurses who provide primary care. It might help us to realize and communicate to each other that learning to respect other people's values and preferences in no way implies that we must surrender our own.

Nurses have always acted as patient advocates. The challenge that role presents has increased as public officials press for laws that would infringe on the rights of individuals with HIV, such as those mandating HIV testing for pregnant women. Since Lillian Wald, nurses have spoken out in support of the rights of the disenfranchised. More than ever, the HIV epidemic in the United States is reaching such disenfranchised groups as women, the poor, the homeless, immigrants, and people of color. People who refuse HIV testing usually have valid reasons—fear of rejection or discrimination, or lack of access to proper care.

Whether you practice in a hospital or home, in the inner city or in a rural community, you're on the front line in the fight against HIV infection. The more you know, the more you become involved, and the greater the difference you can make.

Peter J. Ungvarski is a clinical nurse specialist in HIV infection and clinical director of AIDS services for the Visiting Nurse Service of New York, NY.

Truth or Consequences: Dishonesty in Dating and HIV/AIDS-Related Issues in a College-Age Population

By Michael J. Stebleton, BA, and James H. Rothenberger, MPH

Abstract: *This article examines the issue of dishonesty in dating among college students as it relates to the HIV/AIDS epidemic in the United States. The authors surveyed 171 undergraduates at a large midwestern university in January 1991. They conducted an analysis by gender and found significant differences in responses of male and female students. Of those students involved in monogamous relationships, 36% of the men and 21% of the women reported being sexually unfaithful to their current partner or to any of their previous partners. A greater percentage of women than of men inquired about past sexual histories before engaging in sexual activity. In addition, men admitted they had lied to their sexual partner or partners more often than did women. Because a large portion of HIV/AIDS and STD education involves teaching students to inquire about previous sexual histories, the results of this study should influence the direction and content of behaviorally focused educational programs. The authors also address implications for health educators and clinicians.*

Key Words: *dishonesty in relationships, HIV/AIDS, monogamy, sexual activity, sexually unfaithful*

Although the exact number of HIV-infected university students in the United States is undetermined, recent research has attempted to estimate the magnitude of the HIV/AIDS epidemic on college campuses.[1,2] The results of these studies indicate that, at the beginning of the nineties, an average of 2 students in every 1,000 were infected with HIV (0.2%). The overall seroprevalence rate of 0.2% found on university campuses is lower than the rates found among other populations known to be at risk. The HIV/AIDS epidemic, however, is clearly a serious concern among the college-age population.

A major strategy in AIDS education has been to encourage sexual partners to inquire about each others' previous sexual histories. According to a study conducted at several colleges in southern California, however, 60% of the women and 47% of the men indicated that they believed they had been lied to for purposes of sex.[3] Additional results on the issue of dishonesty in dating appeared in data from a similar survey that found that more than half of the students who had sexually transmitted diseases (STDs) reported that they had unprotected sexual intercourse when infected. Furthermore, 22% of these students admitted that they did not inform their sexual partners at the time.[4]

Although some researchers contend that lying could be considered an act along the continuum of violence against women,[5] dishonesty within relationships has not been adequately addressed in terms of

From the *Journal of the American College Health Association* (September 1993, Vol. 42), pp. 51–54. Reprinted with permission of the Helen Dwight Reid Educational Foundation. Published by Heldref Publications, 1319 Eighteenth St., N. W., Washington, D.C. 20036-1802. Copyright © 1993.

its relationship to health. Work in the field of interpersonal violence[6] suggests that it is the damage to the victims' sense of trust and security—not the sheer physical damage of the acts—that yields traumatic consequences. Accordingly, dishonesty in a sexual relationship may not only place the victim at increased risk for STDs—including HIV infection—but also damage his or her future capacity for trust and intimacy.

The current study was designed to examine the issue of dishonesty in dating among college students, as well as to inquire about attitudes, behaviors, and sexual practices as they relate to the HIV/AIDS epidemic. We did not attempt to address the role of intoxication and its relationship to honesty in communication and sexual activity.[7]

METHOD

To ascertain the comparability of the data from the California study for a midwestern university, we conducted a similar study among students recruited from an undergraduate public health course at the University of Minnesota in January 1991. The survey was administered in an introductory alcohol and drug class. This minimized chances that students who responded to the survey would be more likely to describe health-protective behaviors than would students who were enrolled in a personal health or sexuality course. The study was approved by the university's Human Subjects Research Committee prior to implementation. Participation in the study was anonymous, and subjects were informed that only aggregate data would be used. We told subjects in both a consent form and in a cover letter that the survey contained questions that were personal and sexually explicit and that they could omit any question or discontinue their participation at any time.

RESULTS

In the Minnesota study, 171 students completed the survey (119 women and 52 men) out of 245 students registered for the course (175 women and 70 men). Two students did not respond to every question, so the final tabulation included 169 replies. The students in the sample were predominantly female, Caucasian, heterosexual, and unmarried; their mean age was approximately 22 years, and 61% of the respondents were sophomores or juniors at the university. Thirty-six percent of the subjects were education majors, and 28% were majoring in liberal arts. The class demographics by race were comparable to those shown in the University of Minnesota 1991 Minority Enrollment Report. According to this census, approximately 92% of the students enrolled at the University of Minneosta in 1991 were Caucasian.[8]

Of the students who completed the survey, 72% indicated that they were currently involved in a monogamous relationship (*monogomy* was defined as an exclusive relationship with a nonsexual or sexual partner). Of the students involved in monogamous relationships, approximately 91% were sexually active (*sexually active* was defined as oral, vaginal, or anal sexual behavior to the point of orgasm with another partner). Twenty-eight percent of the sample responded that they were not involved in a monogamous relationship, and approximately 64% of these students claimed they had been sexually active within the past year.

We found a clear gender difference in men's and women's responses to the statement "I believe that two partners should be in love before engaging in sexual intercourse." Approximately 7 out of every 10 women (68%) strongly or moderately agreed with this statement, and 43% of the men believed that two partners should be in love before engaging in sexual intercourse.

Most health education programs covering HIV and other STDs encourage nonmonogamous partners to inquire about each others' past sexual histories before engaging in sexual activity. Nonmonogamous respondents were asked, "Before engaging in sexual activity, did you ask your partners about their past sexual history?" The results showed that three quarters of the men and more than one third of the women "never did ask" partners about past sexual history, and none of the men asked every partner (see Table 1).

One of the primary objectives of this study was to examine the amount of dishonesty and lying that occurs in monogamous and nonmonogamous sexual relationships. Of those students involved in monogamous relationships, 36% of the men and 21% of the women had been sexually unfaithful to their current partner or to any of their previous partners. We defined *sexually unfaithful* as oral, vaginal, or anal sexual behavior with a different sexual partner outside of one's primary relationship.

Subsequent questions asked both monogamous and nonmonogamous respondents, "Have you told a lie in order to have sex?" and "Do you believe that

TABLE I
Responses of Nonmonogamous Students to the Question "Before Engaging in Sexual Activity, Did You Ask Your Partner(s) About Their Past Sexual History?"

Response	Women (%)	Men (%)
Yes; asked every partner	42.1	0
Yes; asked some partners	21.1	25
No; never did ask	36.8	75

TABLE 2
Students' Yes Responses to Questions About Lying to Have Sex

Question	Monogamous		Nonmonogamous	
	Women	Men	Women	Men
Have you ever told a lie in order to have sex?				
%	6.8	33.3	3.3	22.2
n	88	33	30	18
Do you believe that you have ever been lied to in order to have sex?				
%	43.2	36.4	56.7	22.2
n	88	33	30	18

you have ever been lied to in order to have sex?" The results, summarized in Table 2, showed that, among both monogamous and nonmonogamous individuals, a much higher percentage of men than of women had told lies to have sex and that a higher percentage of women than of men believed they had been lied to by a partner who wanted to have sex.

DISCUSSION

Several limitations must be kept in mind regarding the results of this survey. First, when compared with the total University of Minnesota undergraduate enrollment, the study population is biased in favor of upper division students in liberal arts and education majors. Second, we deliberately excluded ethnicity questions so that individual responses could not be identified. We made this decision primarily because of the low minority enrollment (approximately 8%) at the university. Although the sample was representative of the class, it was not large enough or representative enough to generalize to a total undergraduate population. One of the purposes of this study, however, was to provide general guidance to health education and AIDS-prevention programs, rather than to develop a research base on student sexual behaviors.

From our perspective, we can make several comments about the results. First, we did not expect that such a high percentage (72%) of undergraduate students would identify themselves as being in a monogamous relationship. Although we could not find comparable surveys that would indicate whether this figure was high or low, we believed it to be high. A possible explanation is that, in the qestionnaire, the term *monogamous* was not defined in terms of duration. Researchers may view monogamy as a long-term commitment, and students may have a different perception in terms of timespan. The concept of frequent "serial monogamy" with several partners in a timespan, but with only one partner at a time, may be more the norm on college campuses.

Second, the results we obtained about questioning of sexual partners regarding previous sexual histories were significant in terms of major gender differences. The authors' assumption that few men would ask about sexual histories was upheld, but the finding that more than 63% of the women asked about previous sexual histories was unexpected. This may add to the belief that men rarely think that female partners could have had previous sexual partners—perhaps, in part, a result of denial. The assumption that there is little dialogue regarding sexual histories is weakened by the finding that 42% of the women asked every partner about previous sexual activity and 21% asked some partners.

Third, it would appear that lying in order to have sex is more a male than a female behavior. Among both monogamous and nonmonogamous respondents, between five and seven times as many men as women admitted to lying for purposes of sex. We also uncovered a disturbing trend suggesting that more monogamous than nonmonogamous respondents (both men and women) lied. This could be the result of the small size of our sample or the issue of serial monogamy discussed above. It might also mean that, as monogamy becomes the only acceptable alternative in a "safe-sex" world, we will see an increase in lying behavior. Just as the Victorians claimed to have low rates of sexual activity but, in reality, rates of sexual activity remained constant, so today more people may identify themselves as monogamous when, in actuality, they may be sexually active outside of their primary relationship.

Fourth, the number of female respondents who felt that they had been lied to in order to have sex was far greater than the number who said they, themselves, had lied. Almost an equal number of men felt they had been lied to as the number who had lied. This could indicate a reinforcing belief of victimization on the part of women, who may view themselves as being personally honest, but who are partners of basically dishonest men. The male respondents, on the other hand, may simply not believe that a female partner would ever lie to them, and therefore "just do not get it." The results of this question may be a further indication of the vast differences in socialization between the genders.

IMPLICATIONS

This survey may have significant implications for the types of educational programs dealing with HIV and STD education in which health educators engage. There may also be significant implications for clinical interactions.

Health educators must first realize the significant gender differences in perceptions and behaviors between women and men. Several books have focused on the communication differences between genders that may be helpful to the programmer.[9,10]

Second, health educators need to question seriously the advisability of basing a major component of their HIV/STD campaigns on encouraging partners to inquire about previous sexual histories. If almost 50% of partners can be expected to give dishonest responses, the usefulness of this strategy may be limited.

Third, if programs include data on the frequency of lying behavior, the message of self-protection, with an emphasis on abstinence and consistent condom use, may be more viable.

Fourth, new directions in HIV/STD programming need to be explored. For example, we are in the process of designing programs that teach students to be more aware of lying behaviors. Using the work of Ekman, we expect to develop a series of workshops to increase awareness and detection of dishonesty in sexual situations.[11] Although Ekman teaches detection techniques to nurses, our workshops are not as intense as Ekman's but still leave the student with the impression they can be more aware of possible lying situations. One series of workshops will be led by a professional, the other series by peer educators. Six-month follow-ups may show that self-protective behaviors have increased, even though the participants actually retained no real skills for detecting lying. Furthermore, a difference may be found between messages provided by professionals and messages provided by peers. Other new directions that are behaviorally based would include negotiation skills and basic interpersonal communication techniques.

Clinicians, in addition to being aware of the implications for health educators, may have other concerns. First, the clinicians may be placed in a counseling role when they're confronted with a patient who first realizes a partner's dishonesty at the point of an STD diagnosis. Second, all patients should be encouraged to engage in self-protective behavior if they choose to be sexually active. Third, clinicians need to be aware that their definition and perception of monogamy and sexual activity may not be the same as their patients' perception of these concepts.

In an era when diseases surrounding sexual activity have profound implications, all of us need to be aware that neither love nor hormonal activity is a shield against dishonesty.

NOTE

Portions of this article were presented at the American College Health Association (ACHA) meeting on May 23, 1992, in San Francisco, California.

REFERENCES

1. Gayle HD, Keeling RP, Garcia-Tunon M., Kilbourne BW, Narkunas JP, Ingram FR. Prevalence of the human immunodeficiency virus among university students. *New Engl J Med.* 1990;323(22):1538–1541.
2. Biemiller L. An average of 2 students in 1,000 found infected with AIDS-linked virus. *Chron Higher Educ.* 1989; May 24:A30.
3. Cochran SD, Mays VM. Sex, lies, and HIV. *New Engl J Med.* 1990;322(11):774.
4. Centers for Disease Control. *CDC AIDS Weekly.* 1990; Dec 3:4.
5. Leidig MW. The continuum of violence against women: Psychological and physical consequences. *J Am Coll Health.* 1992;40(4):149–155.
6. McCann IL, Pearlman LA. Constructivist self-development theory: A theoretical framework for assessing and treating traumatized college students. *J Am Coll Health.* 1992; 40(4): 189–196.
7. Giarrusso R, Johnson P, Goodschilds J, Zellman G. Adolescents' cues and signals: Sex and assault. In: Johnson P, (chair), Acquaintance rape and adolescent sexuality. Symposium, Western Psychological Association; San Diego, CA, April 1979.
8. University of Minnesota 1991 Enrollment Report. Minneapolis: 1991.
9. Tannen D. *You Just Don't Understand.* New York: Ballantine Books; 1990.
10. Coates J. *Women, Men, and Language.* London: Longman; 1986.
11. Ekman P. *Telling Lies: Clues to Deceit in the Marketplace, Politics, and Marriage.* New York: Norton; 1985.

Michael J. Stebleton is a graduate student in public health at the University of Minnesota in Minneapolis, where James H. Rothenberger is an instructor in the School of Public Health.

Confronting a Hidden Epidemic: The Institute Of Medicine's Report on Sexually Transmitted Diseases

By Patricia Donovan

An estimated 17 million Americans acquire a sexually transmitted disease (STD) every year. More than 25 different infectious organisms can be transmitted sexually, and five STDs—chlamydia, gonorrhea, AIDS, syphilis and hepatitis B—are among the country's 10 most frequently reported infections. Infection rates for some STDs in the United States are the highest in the industrialized world; in some cases, they rival those reported in developing countries.

If detected and treated at an early stage, many STDs are curable. However, others are not. More than 55 million Americans are believed to be infected with an incurable viral disease such as genital herpes or human papillomavirus (HPV). Once infected, individuals are forever at risk of transmitting these diseases to their sexual partners.

Women are more likely than men to become infected with an STD, and because they are less likely to have symptoms, women typically suffer more severe health consequences than do men. Cervical cancer, for example, which is linked to some strains of HPV, kills more than 4,500 women each year. At least one million women per year experience an episode of pelvic inflammatory disease (PID), a complication of undetected chlamydia or gonorrhea that can give rise to infertility or a life-threatening ectopic pregnancy. In addition, many STDs can be transmitted to a child during pregnancy or birth, and can result in stillbirth, as well as other serious consequences. Moreover, STD infection can make both men and women more susceptible to infection with the human immunodeficiency virus (HIV).

Besides their enormous impact on individuals, these infections also create a huge financial burden for the country. While no comprehensive data on costs are available, expenditures on direct medical care and related services, as well as the indirect costs attributed to loss of productivity associated with the seven major STDs* and their related syndromes, totaled an estimated $10 billion in 1994. If the economic consequences of HIV and AIDS are included in the estimate, total costs associated with STD-related illnesses reached almost $17 billion.

A "HIDDEN EPIDEMIC"

The public is largely unaware of the serious health consequences and financial costs associated with the high prevalence of STDs in the United States. To call attention to this "hidden epidemic" and to study ways to address the problem, the Institute of Medicine (IOM) in 1994 convened a 15-member expert panel. Its mandate was to "(a) examine the epidemiological dimensions of STDs in the United States and factors that contribute to the epidemic; (b) assess the effectiveness of current public health strategies and programs to prevent and control STDs; and (c) provide direction for future public health programs, policy and research in STD prevention and control"[1] [p. 1-1]. The Institute directed the panel to focus its efforts on STDs other than HIV infection.

The panel's report, released in November 1996, concluded that the United States lacks "an effective national system for STD prevention" [p. 6-3]. According to the report, prevention is hampered by a variety of factors, including a reluctance to discuss sexual issues and the resultant lack of awareness about STDs, the media's irresponsible treatment of sex, the fragmentation of services, inadequate training of health professionals and insufficient resources.

---

*Chlamydia, gonorrhea, syphilis, chancroid, genital herpes, human papillomavirus and hepatitis.

From *Family Planning Perspectives*, (March/April 1997, Vol. 29, No. 2), pp. 87–89. Reproduced with the permission of The Alan Guttmacher Institute from Patricia Donovan. © 1997.

According to the IOM, bold leadership from policy-makers in both the public and the private sectors and at the local, state and national levels is needed in order to overcome these obstacles. The IOM recommends that strategies to enhance STD prevention efforts focus on promoting healthy sexual behavior, developing strong leadership, encouraging greater financial support for STD prevention, targeting services to adolescents and other hard-to-reach groups and ensuring universal access to high-quality services.

HEALTHIER SEXUAL BEHAVIOR

Numerous biological, social and behavioral factors contribute to the high rates of STDs in this country—among them the asymptomatic nature of many infections, delayed detection and treatment, poverty, substance abuse, and sexual risk behavior such as inconsistent condom use. Nonetheless, the report stresses that the first obstacle that must be overcome in order to effectively address STD prevention is the "secrecy" that surrounds sexuality and the stigma associated with STD infection.

According to the IOM's report, society's unwillingness to confront sexual issues undermines STD prevention in a variety of ways. It hinders the dissemination of accurate, straightforward information about STDs in education programs for adolescents and impedes communication between parents and children as well as between sex partners. Moreover, society's reluctance to address sexuality compromises the ability of doctors and other health care professionals to counsel their patients about prevention and impedes research on sexual behavior. Furthermore, the mass media contribute to societal ambivalence by presenting sexual messages and imagery in an unbalanced manner.

The lack of frank discussion about sex, the IOM panel points out, has contributed to a glaring lack of public awareness about STDs and to misperceptions about individual risk and the consequences of infection. The report notes a recent survey in which almost two-thirds of respondents knew little or nothing about STDs other than HIV, and it cites other research suggesting that most people seriously underestimate both their risk of acquiring an STD and the possible health consequences of STD infection. The report states that even clinicians are generally poorly informed about STDs. In sum, the panel warns that the lack of accurate information about the risks and consequences of STDs may actually encourage people to engage in behavior that increases their chances of becoming infected.

The IOM report proposes that an independent, long-term national campaign be established to address these problems and to promote "a new norm of healthy sexual behavior" [p. 6-13]. It should be led by nationally recognized leaders in entertainment, media, sports, business and labor, as well as by elected officials, and it should be funded largely by private foundations. Moreover, the report states, the campaign should mount a major initiative to promote public discussion and awareness of sexuality and STDs, and advocate increased public and private funding for STD prevention.

Noting that the media commonly depict premarital sex, cohabitation and non-marital relationships as normal behavior, yet are largely silent about contraceptives, STDs and "the harsh realities" of unplanned pregnancy and early childbearing, the report recommends that television, radio, print, music and other mass media accept ads and sponsor public service messages that promote condom use and other means of protection against STDs and unintended pregnancy, including postponing the initiation of sexual intercourse. The report adds that these messages must be aired at times when adolescents are likely to be watching or listening, and in publications that young people commonly read. In the past, the media have been generally unwilling to take such action.

To facilitate the development of effective prevention messages and interventions, the IOM report recommends that the federal government continue to support survey research on sexual behavior, which it calls "a crucial but underdeveloped tool for directing and targeting STD prevention programs" [p. 5-21]. The report urges that teenagers be included in these surveys, and that Congress reject any attempts to impose a parental consent requirement on minors' participation. Such restrictions would jeopardize efforts to obtain information from adolescents, such as those seeking confidential reproductive health care, who may be most in need of specific interventions.

STRONGER LEADERSHIP

Primary responsibility for tracking and preventing STDs currently rests with the federal Centers for Disease Control and Prevention (CDC) within the Department of Health and Human Services (DHHS), as well as with state and local health departments. In general, private health care providers have been reluctant to offer STD services, or have simply refused.

Developing effective STD prevention programs will require active participation and strong leadership by both the public and private sectors, the report declares. It urges the federal government to develop basic clinical standards for STD services, to coordinate a comprehensive national surveillance system that collects data on STDs from all providers* and to support state and local health departments in their efforts to provide universal access to services. The report also urges state health departments to implement comprehensive STD prevention programs, to support local health departments in their efforts to provide STD services and to collect information on reportable diseases from public and private providers. Local health departments are urged to assume similar responsibilities at the community level.

Even as its report stresses the need for the public sector to make STD prevention a higher priority, the panel acknowledges that these agencies lack the resources and the organizational capability to fully implement a national prevention system. The private sector must therefore assume greater responsibility for STD prevention, the report concludes, both in terms of providing services and of promoting public discussion and raising awareness.

The panel also believes that the public and private sectors must work together more closely. Accordingly, the panel proposes the establishment of a long-term independent roundtable to facilitate collaboration. The roundtable would serve as a neutral forum where representatives from all levels of government, the private health care sector, business, the mass media, schools and community-based groups could work together to develop and implement a comprehensive system of STD services. In light of the demonstrated synergy between STD infections and HIV susceptibility, the IOM also recommends that STD prevention be an integral component of a national strategy to prevent HIV infection. Furthermore, public and private agencies involved in cancer prevention should support STD prevention as a way to avert STD-related cancers, including cancers of the liver and cervix.

INCREASED FINANCIAL SUPPORT

In FY 1995, the public sector spent about $231 million on STD prevention and an additional $105 million on STD-related biomedical and clinical research. At these levels, the IOM estimates, the public sector spent only $1 on STD prevention for every $43 spent on treatment and other STD-related costs, while it invested only $1 in biomedical and clinical research for every $94 in disease-related expenditures.

However, the panel stresses, STD prevention is highly cost-effective. For example, every $1 spent on early detection and treatment of chlamydia and gonorrhea saves an estimated $12 in treatment costs and lost productivity. Accordingly, the IOM urges increases in funding for STD services by all levels of

government as well as by the private sector. It also recommends that the federal government continue to provide funding designated specifically for these services. Consolidating STD funding into a block grant that covers many public health programs, as several DHHS and Senate proposals have suggested, would have "a devastating impact on STD prevention," [p. 6-29], the report warns. Such changes would likely make state politics, rather than objective considerations of public health or social needs, the critical determinant of funding levels.

TARGETED SERVICES

Three million teenagers acquire an STD every year. Adolescents are at greater risk of STDs than adults for several reasons: They are more likely to have multiple sex partners, to have high-risk partners and to engage in unprotected intercourse. In addition, adolescent females are biologically more susceptible to cervical infections than are older women.

Most teenagers are sexually active by the time they finish high school and are therefore at risk of STD infection. Indeed, many of the serious health consequences of STDs that appear in adults, such as cancer and infertility, are the result of infections acquired or behavior begun during adolescence or young adulthood. Therefore, the report concludes, a national effort to prevent STDs must focus on teenagers. It recommends that adolescents be encouraged to delay intercourse "until they are emotionally mature enough to take responsibility for this activity" [p. 6-38]. Recognizing that many young people will not heed this advice, the panel also recommends that teenagers have access to information and instruction in how to prevent STDs and unintended pregnancy.

Along with endorsing mass media campaigns targeted at teenagers, the IOM calls upon school districts to ensure that schools provide age-appropriate STD-related health education, as well as access to condoms and confidential clinical services (including STD screening, diagnosis and treatment). The report recommends that information and services be made available to students before they become sexually active and stresses the need for access without parental consent. Access to school-based clinical services is important, the report explains, because teenagers tend to use regular health care facilities infrequently and have little ability to pay for services on their own.

In addition to targeting teenagers, the IOM calls for special efforts to bring services to substance abusers, commercial sex workers, prisoners, the homeless and other groups that have high rates of infection and are difficult to reach in traditional health care settings. The panel recommends that STD programs

---

* STD incidence is underestimated because many private health care providers do not report STD cases to their local health department.

collaborate with drug and alcohol treatment facilities, prisons, migrant health centers and programs in other settings that provide services to these high-risk populations. The report also urges the National Institutes of Health and other federal agencies and private companies to collaborate in the development of diagnostic tools, such as rapid saliva and urine tests, that would be especially useful in mobile clinics and other nontraditional settings.

UNIVERSAL ACCESS

STD services are provided in a variety of settings: Clinics operated by state and local health departments; community-based centers such as family planning and prenatal clinics; and doctors' offices and other private health care settings. According to the report, these services are typically fragmented, inadequate and sometimes of poor quality.

An important strategy for expanding access to care, the IOM argues, is to incorporate into primary and reproductive health care services the full range of STD services, including screening, diagnosis and treatment, partner notification and treatment, and health education and counseling. The IOM believes that this strategy will increase the likelihood of early detection of STD infection and will expand opportunities for prevention counseling, since primary care is apt to foster an ongoing relationship between the clinician and the patient.

The IOM report notes that private health plans, and especially managed care plans, have the potential to improve the quality of and access to STD services, although very few private health plans currently make the prevention and treatment of STDs a high priority. In part, the report explains, this is because most health plans do not perceive STDs to be a serious problem among their members, and, since many plans have typically relied on the availability of public STD services, they have not developed the capacity to provide STD-related care. The report calls upon health plans generally, and managed care plans in particular, to increase their involvement in STD prevention, not only among their members but in the larger community as well. It recommends that both private practitioners and managed care providers offer comprehensive STD services to their clients and to their clients' sex partners, regardless of the partners' insurance status.

Even with the expansion of STD-related services to other providers, the IOM says, public STD clinics must continue to function as a "safety net" for services to uninsured and underserved persons. But, the report notes, services in those clinics vary widely in quality, scope, accessibility and availability. Many clinics, particularly those in large cities, are overwhelmed with patients; as a result, recruitment of highly qualified professionals is difficult, and the care provided is often impersonal. To remedy these problems, the report urges local health departments to establish partnerships with medical, nursing and other professional schools to provide staffing and management of STD clinics.

It also recommends that health departments collaborate with other community-based providers, such as family planning clinics, school-based programs, university and hospital medical centers and private practitioners to improve access to care and enhance the quality of services. The report points out that in contrast to STD clinics (where clients are primarily males), family planning clinics serve large numbers of women. Moreover, CDC-supported demonstration projects to provide widespread screening and treatment of women and their partners in family planning clinics have resulted in significant reductions in the prevalence of chlamydia, the most common bacterial STD in the country.

Another key to improving the quality of STD services is better training of health care professionals. Training in STD prevention and management in U.S. medical schools is generally poor, the report points out, and many clinicians, particularly in the private sector, are unaware of both the prevalence of STDs among their patients and the potentially serious consequences of these diseases. As a result, the report says, clinical STD care is often inappropriate or inadequate.

"STDs are hidden epidemics of tremendous health and economic consequences in the United States," the report concludes. "An effective system of STD prevention will have to be developed at the local, state and national levels, with full participation of both the public and private sectors. The process of preventing STDs must be a collaborative one. No one agency, organization or sector can effectively do it alone; all members of the community must do their part. A successful national initiative to confront and prevent STDs requires widespread public awareness and participation and bold national leadership from the highest levels" [p. 6-69].

REFERENCE

1. T. R Eng and W. T. Butler, eds., *The Hidden Epidemic: Confronting Sexually Transmitted Diseases.* Institute of Medicine, Washington. D.C., 1996.

Patricia Donovan is a contributing editor for Family Planning Perspectives *and senior associate for law and public policy, The Alan Guttmacher Institute, Washington, D.C.*

STDs in Women:
What You Need to Know

*The incidence of STDs in women is growing at an alarming rate.
Here's an overview of the diseases that most often affect women,
the signs and symptoms to watch for, treatment guidelines,
and teaching strategies you can use.*

By Nancy C. Sharts-Hopko, PhD, RN, FAAN

The statistics are staggering: 13 million new cases of sexually transmitted diseases—not counting HIV and AIDS—are reported in the United States each year. And the brunt of the STD burden, both in risk and consequences, falls on women.

More than 350,000 cases of chlamydia and nearly 200,000 cases of gonorrhea in women were reported in 1995. The incidence of AIDS is rising fastest among women. Between 1981 and 1995, it was reported that 71,818 women had AIDS, but the number of cases has nearly doubled since 1993—10,000 were reported in 1995 alone.

Women are twice as likely as men to be infected by a partner with an STD (the warm, moist vaginal environment promotes growth of flora, and microscopic tears in the mucosa during intercourse provide portals for infection). Yet women are less likely to get health care when they're infected because they may not know they're infected—some STDs, such as chlamydia and gonorrhea, typically show no symptoms in women. An estimated 85% of women with chlamydial and gonococcal pelvic inflammatory disease (PID) don't seek treatment.

Apart from the risk of AIDS and death, the most serious complications of STDs are problems affecting women: PID and subsequent infertility, ectopic pregnancy, and chronic pelvic pain and cervical cancers associated with human papillomavirus and herpes simplex virus type II. Hospitalizations and initial office visits for PID have declined since the 1980s (perhaps because more women are being treated as outpatients), but in 1993, some 313,000 women were diagnosed with PID in emergency departments. In addition to the personal suffering, the financial costs are high. PID costs over $4.2 billion a year in treatment-related expenses, while infertility resulting from PID costs over $1 billion per year.

STDs cause one-third of all perinatal, neonatal, and maternal deaths. To take just a few examples of the risks: A mother who has *Candida albicans* may pass on neonatal oral thrush; chlamydia can lead to premature delivery or fetal death; the mother's gonorrhea can cause blindness in the infant; and herpes simplex virus type II can be passed to the infant, causing permanent disability or death. An HIV-infected infant is vulnerable to, among other things, recurrent infections and neurological deficits.

HOW BIG IS THE PROBLEM?

It's hard to grasp the true size of the STD problem. For one thing, STDs aren't always reportable. For every case of syphilis that is reported, it's estimated, three are not. Only 35 states mandate HIV reporting. Also, private physicians tend not to report STDs, and overwhelmed clinic staff simply may not have the time to do the paperwork.

Identifying the people with the diseases is obviously critical to reporting and thus to defining incidence. Increased screening is helping to clarify the incidence of chlamydia, which has been a nationally notifiable condition only since 1994. Similarly, putting women's signs and symptoms on the list of AIDS-defining criteria has been a big step forward. Many women have died of HIV-related complications without ever being identified as having HIV, simply because the criteria reflected the male experience.

Another reason for the difficulty in pinning numbers down is that women tend to be tested late in the HIV disease process, sometimes due to poverty and lack of access to health care (HIV tends to disproportionately affect low-income women), or to fear—of jeopardizing a relationship with a partner who provides financial support, of losing sex clients, of losing child custody. They may also delay seeking treatment because they don't know they have symptoms of HIV or because they're overwhelmed by the illness-related needs of others in the household.

Ironically, although the HIV/AIDS process is the most notorious of STDs, HIV/AIDS services are often conducted separately from other STD care, reflecting different funding sources and bureaucratic structures. This same division can be observed in textbooks and in the online cataloging of clinical and research literature. Such a distinction tempts health professionals to discount the seriousness of non-HIV STDs. This is a grave error because, aside from the risks associated with them, non-HIV STDs are both a marker for HIV in the population and a risk factor for contracting it. For example, recent research has shown that penile gonorrheal exudate contains a far greater concentration of HIV than is found in the semen of HIV-infected men who don't have gonorrhea. And the lesions associated with non-HIV STDs provide an easy portal for HIV.

WHY STDs FLOURISH

As a result of massive, vigorous public health efforts, infectious diseases in general were well controlled in the United States during the years following World War II. However, two trends contributed not only to a rise in both familiar and new STDs, but to the emergence of antibiotic-resistant strains. First, as antibiotics became more common, both health care providers and the general public developed a rather cavalier attitude toward contagion, and second, oral contraceptives, which were perceived to alleviate risks associated with sexual intercourse, became generally available in the 1960s.

Another trend that has had a drastic impact on prevalence of STDs is changing attitudes toward sex.

Until about 25 years ago, syphilis and gonorrhea were the most commonly recognized STDs. Today, well over 50 diseases are listed as sexually transmissible.

More people are sexually active, starting at younger ages, and—since we're living longer—for more years. University of Chicago researchers seeking to quantify the risk of HIV in American society compared a group of women born between 1953 and 1972 and a group born a generation earlier, between 1933 and 1952. They found that 57% of the younger generation had had sex before age 18, compared with 32% among the previous generation. What's more, 24% of the younger generation had had three or more sexual partners before the age of 18, versus just 4% among the older women.

In fact, STDs are largely a "young" problem, with 86% of cases occurring in adolescents and young adults aged 15 to 29. By age 21, approximately one in five people has been treated for an STD.

Adolescents and young adults are more at risk for STDs because they may be more likely to have multiple concurrent or sequential partners, to engage in unprotected sex, and to choose higher risk partners. Young women may be more susceptible to some STDs, such as *Chlamydia trachomatis*, due to cervical ectopy and lack of immunity. Young people also must cope with obstacles such as lack of insurance, lack of access to health care, and even confidentiality issues.

In 1990, the Department of Health and Human Services first released its national health objectives in *Healthy People 2000*. The goals included reducing gonorrhea to no more than 225 cases per 100,000 people and *Chlamydia trachomatis* infections to no more than 170/100,000; and confining annual incidence of HIV to no more than 800/100,000 and AIDS to no more than 98,000 cases.

Since then, DHHS has noted both losses and gains. By the mid-decade evaluation, a greater percentage of youngsters, especially girls, had engaged in sexual intercourse by age 15. The DHHS also cites a higher occurrence of nongonorrheal urethritis and first-time herpes simplex type II. On the brighter side, more high school students and older adolescents, particularly girls, are using condoms, are less often engaging in risky sexual behavior, and are more often getting tested for HIV. The survey also notes drops in the incidence of gonorrhea and recurring gonorrhea; primary, secondary, and congenital syphilis; genital warts; PID; and sexually transmitted hepatitis B.

AN EXPANDING LIST OF STDs

Until about 25 years ago, syphilis and gonorrhea were the most commonly recognized STDs. Today,

What Causes an STD?

Transmission	Mostly sexual	Sexual contact with oral-fecal exposure	Can be sexual
Viruses	Cytomegalovirus Hepatitis B HIV-1, HIV-2 HSV-II Human papillomavirus	Hepatitis A	Human T-cell lympho- tropic virus type I Hepatitis C, D HSV-I Epstein-Barr virus

Bacteria	*Calymmatobacterium*
	   granulomatis
	Chlamydia trachomatis
	Haemophilus ducreyi
	Neisseria gonorrhoeae
	Treponema pallidum
	Ureaplasma
	   urealyticum
		Shigella
		Campylobacter
			Escherichia coli
			Gardnerella vaginalis
			Mycoplasma hominis
			Group B
			   streptococcus
			Other vaginal bacteria

Fungi,
Protozoa,
Ectoparasites
	Phthirius pubis
	Sarcoptes scabiei
	Trichomonas vaginalis
		Giardia lamblia
		Entamoeba
		   histolytica
		Cryptosporidium
		   parvum
			Candida albicans
			Leishmania

well over 50 diseases are listed as sexually transmissible (that is, they may be, but aren't always, transmitted through sexual contact). Chlamydia and herpes simplex virus type II have been widely recognized as STDs in the United States only since the early 1970s. Hepatitis B is a late entry, now primarily transmitted via sexual contact, as opposed to 20 years ago when the oral-fecal or blood contact routes were far more prevalent. Nearly half of the adults in developed countries carry cytomegalovirus (which is why testing and treating CMV routinely would be prohibitively expensive).

The most common STDs affecting women are chlamydia, gonorrhea, syphilis, condyloma (human papilloma virus, or HPV), herpes simplex virus (HSV), and HIV.

Chlamydia, gonorrhea, and syphilis, which are bacterial infections, are transmitted sexually through contact with infectious exudate or seminal fluid. Chlamydia, true to its asymptomatic nature, has a poorly defined incubation period. It usually manifests as a cervicitis. Gonorrhea's incubation period is about a week; it may appear as a cervicitis or urethritis, or as a more invasive disease. Both, if untreated, are likely to ascend the reproductive tract and become a PID.

Syphilis can take as long as three months to manifest in symptoms. Left untreated, it progresses through three stages. In the primary stage a chancre appears at the point of contact with infectious exudate, followed by a rash on the palms or soles, which resolves within weeks to 12 months. A latent period

can last for years, during which time infectious lesions can appear in the skin and mucous membranes. Five to 20 years after the initial infection, the patient may develop central nervous system symptoms.

HPV, HSV, and HIV are viral infections transmitted through direct contact with infectious blood or other body fluids. In general, viral infections may enjoy lengthy incubation periods (one to 20 months for HPV, two to 12 days for HSV, up to 10 years for HIV), during which they can be transmitted.

HPV manifests as cauliflower-like lesions at the point of contact with the virus—cervix, vagina, vulva, perineum, anus, rectum, oral pharynx, or groin. While warts often regress spontaneously, they may recur. Some types of HPV are associated with cervical cancer. HSV may begin with flulike symptoms, followed by one or more painful sores at the point of contact, lasting about a week. Stress and the hormonal changes associated with menstrual periods may bring on a recurrence.

HIV too is associated with a flulike syndrome, appearing around six weeks after infection, followed by a long latent period during which the immune system is being attacked. The immune breakdown is behind the wide range of opportunistic infections that characterize HIV. In women, these infections include repeated episodes of vaginal candidiasis, PID, and an especially aggressive cervical dysplasia that proceeds rapidly to neoplasia.

The most common signs and symptoms of STDs in women are dysuria; sores and wartlike growths at any point of sexual contact, such as the cervix, vagina, labia, perineum, anus, and mouth; rash; vaginal discharge that is more copious, thicker, or thinner than usual, foul-smelling, or discolored; inguinal node swelling or pain; vaginal itching, burning, or irritation; painful bowel elimination; dyspareunia; bleeding or spotting after intercourse; or lower abdominal pain. (See *Common STDs: Symptoms and Treatment. . . .*).

In men, the most common signs and symptoms are dysuria; sores or wartlike growths on or around the penis, perineum, anus, and rectum, which may cause painful elimination; rash; penile discharge; and inguinal node swelling or pain. Particularly suspicious in women are recurrent vaginal yeast infections (*Candida*), protracted PID, and unusually aggressive cervical dysplasia, which are also the common signs of HIV/AIDS in women. Advise your female patients to be aware of sores or lesions in the mouth, genitalia, perineum, groin, rectum, and anus. To guard against the asymptomatic STDs, urge anyone at risk to be screened.

Because antiretroviral therapy in pregnancy, during labor and delivery, and for the first two months of life has been shown to reduce the risk of perinatal HIV transmission to just 8% of infants of infected mothers, many professional associations, including the American Nurses Association, now support offering HIV testing to all pregnant women. State health departments require testing for Medicaid recipients, who must sign a consent form before any pregnancy expenses are paid.

Some organizations, including the American Medical Association, now support mandatory testing in pregnancy; nursing organizations do not. Mandatory testing seems unduly punitive to women. No other group is forced to be tested, and there is no mandate to identify the men who infected them. It's considered by many to be a violation of the women's right to privacy, particularly when many states have HIV/AIDS confidentiality laws in place.

CURRENT TREATMENT

The 1993 CDC treatment guidelines for common STDs are being reviewed this year, and a revision will be published by the Massachusetts Medical Society.

Nonviral infections are generally eradicated with antibiotics or microbicides. Chlamydia responds to

Particularly suspicious in women are recurrent vaginal yeast infections, protracted PID, and unusually aggressive cervical dysplasia.

doxycycline, gonorrhea to ceftriaxone, and syphilis to penicillin. Women may develop vaginal candidiasis while on antibiotics; fortunately, alternative therapies are available.

So far, viral infections can be treated but not eradicated. Acyclovir can reduce the discomfort and duration of a herpes eruption (famciclovir, a new alternative, can be taken twice a day, rather than acyclovir's several times a day). Various treatments are used for HPV, including chemical cautery, cryotherapy, or interferon injections into the lesions, but none are definitive.

Research and development in antiretroviral treatment for HIV/AIDS is outpacing the dissemination of published information. Currently, HIV is controlled with various antivirals, usually in combinations ("cocktails") that are altered on the basis of frequent viral load testing. Drugs used to treat HIV are potent and are associated with numerous adverse effects, particularly nausea and loss of appetite.

Access to these therapies and care in general, however, remains a major problem for women, for several reasons: lack of risk identification and screening; lack of awareness of resources, such as public health departments; and lack of insurance to pay for services and medications.

ASKING THE RIGHT QUESTIONS

The chain of STD transmission can only be broken by reaching, teaching, and treating individuals, patient by patient. But too many health care providers don't integrate sexual-risk discussions into their first nonemergency contact with patients. Many nurses may not take complete sexual histories from patients because it's low on their list of priorities or because screening conditions aren't ideal. Or they may be reluctant to take sexual histories—uncomfortable with explicit sexual language, concerned about offending clients, misguided about patients' level of risk, or anxious about their own possible responses to information revealed by the client. Unfortunately, patients may be less likely to reveal their sexual health concerns if they perceive that nurses are reluctant to deal with them or don't share their values.

Taking a patient's sexual history requires a combination of tact and forthrightness. Perhaps the most critical skill you'll need is the ability to listen carefully and respectfully, paying attention to the patient's body language. Let her know that, because sexual health is an important aspect of total care, you'll need to ask direct questions about her risk for STDs. (Never

FOR MORE INFORMATION

American Social Health Association
P.O. Box 13827
Research Triangle Park, NC 27709
For personal health history forms or STD materials:
(800) 783-9877 (bulk orders)
(919) 361-8400 (individual orders)

CDC National HIV/AIDS Hotline
(800) 342-AIDS (English)
(800) 344-7432 (Spanish)
(800) 243-7889 (TTY Service for Deaf)

CDC National STD Hotline
(800) 227-8922

Massachusetts Medical Society
Revised CDC STD treatment guidelines
$4/copy
(800) 843-6356

COMMON STDs: PREVALENCE, SYMPTOMS, AND TREATMENT

DISEASE	PREVALENCE	SYMPTOMS	PRIMARY THERAPY
Acute urethral syndrome (*E. Coli*, others)	10%–25% of reproductive-age women/year	Painful, urgent or frequent urination, hematuria, dyspareunia. Pyelonephritis may follow if untreated.	Doxycycline 100 mg PO BID Sulfamethoxazole 1.6 g + trimethoprim 320 mg PO single dose
Chlamydia *Chlamydia trachomatis*	4 million cases/year; 270/100,000 women are infected; leading cause of preventable infertility, ectopic pregnancy	Mucopurulent cervicitis, cervical edema, erythema, and easily induced endocervical bleeding.	Doxycycline 100 mg PO BID x 7–10 days Azithromycin 1 g PO x 1 day
Cytomegalovirus	50% of adults	Infection usually not apparent, but syndrome similar to mononucleosis may occur. Recently linked to cardiovascular disease in men; unexamined in women to date.	None, except in AIDS patients
Gonorrhea *Neisseria gonorrhoeae*	Estimated 1.5 million cases/year; 200/100,000 women	Initial urethritis or cervicitis, often unnoticed; vulvovaginitis, pharyngeal, anorectal infection, abnormal menses, dysuria. Uterine invasion in 20% of cases.	Ceftriaxone 125 mg IM x 1 day; Ciprofloxacin 500 mg PO x 1 day; [Note: According to the CDC, a growing number of *N. gonorrhoeae* isolates have demonstrated reduced susceptibility to ciprofloxacin]; Cefixime 400 mg PO x 1 day; Ofloxacin 400 mg PO x 1 day
Hepatitis B	5%–20% of population; >150,000 new cases sexually transmitted/year; 4,000 infected infants/year	Insidious onset with anorexia, vague abdominal discomfort, nausea/vomiting, arthralgias, rash, hepatomegaly, jaundice. Fever absent or mild. Can result in chronic liver disease, hepatic cancers, hepatic failure, death. 1% fatality.	No specific therapy; HBV is the only STD for which vaccine exists; CDC recommends vaccination of all infants and adolescents. Advisory Committee on Immunization Practices recommends vaccination of all persons with recent STD and those with more than one partner in the last six months.
Herpes simplex virus type II	30 million adults	Painful or itchy vesicles on cervix, vulva, perineum, legs, buttocks, anus, mouth. Initial infection and recurrences may be accompanied by flulike syndrome and malaise. Can cause meningitis. May be associated with cervical neoplasia.	*1st episode, genital:* Acyclovir 200 mg PO 5x/day x 7–10 days; *Proctitis, 1st episode:* Acyclovir 400 mg PO 5x/day x 5 days; *Recurrent:* Acyclovir 200 mg PO 5x/day x 5 days; *Suppressive:* Acyclovir 400 mg PO BID; *Severe:* Acyclovir 5–10 mg/kg IV q8h x 5–7 days; *HIV-infected:* Acyclovir 400 mg PO x 3–5 days until resolution [Note: famciclovir (125 mg BID x 5 days) and valacyclovir (500 mg BID x 5 days) are new alternatives for recurrent genital herpes]
HIV/AIDS	Estimates vary: from 1 to 12 million infected	Flulike syndrome lasting one to two weeks within first three months; latent period of months to years; onset of opportunistic infections, constitutional and neurologic symptoms, increasing until death.	Combination antiretroviral therapy with AZT, DDC, DDI
Human papilloma virus	50% of sexually active women; 3 million new cases/year	Cauliflower-like fleshy growths in vagina, cervix, anus, rectum, larynx; may stimulate cervical cancer.	Cryotherapy or cryoprobe; Podofilox 0.5% solution BID x 3 days, then 4 days off; Podophyllin 10%–25% in compound tincture of benzoin 1x/week x 6 weeks

(Continued)

COMMON STDS: PREVALENCE, SYMPTOMS, AND TREATMENT (continued)

DISEASE	PREVALENCE	SYMPTOMS	PRIMARY THERAPY
Syphilis *Treponema pallidum*	12/100,000 women	Chancre at point of contact within four to six weeks, followed by maculopapular rash on palms and soles up to 12 months; after five to 20 years' latency, CNS and cardiovascular manifestations.	*Primary, secondary, or <1 year duration:* Benzathine penicillin G, 2.4 million units IM; *Unknown duration or >1 year:* Benzathine penicillin G, 7.2 million units divided in 2.4 million IM 1x/ week x 3 weeks; Doxycycline 100 mg BID x 14–28 days
Trichomonas	20% of women during reproductive years	Excessive frothy, green-yellow foul-smelling vaginal discharge; range from no symptoms to erythema, strawberry cervix, edema, pruritis, dysuria, dyspareunia.	Metronidazole 2 g PO x 1 day or 500 mg PO BID x 7 days

Source: CDC, 1993 sexually transmitted diseases treatment guidelines. *MMWR Morb.Mortal.Wkly. Rep.* 42 (RR-14): 1–73, Sept. 1993.

assume that a patient is not sexually active or at risk for an STD.) The woman can then accede to or decline this assessment. Interview the patient in a private location when she is fully clothed. Only document information that is critical for her health care.

Open-ended questions (such as "What role do drugs or alcohol play in your life?") are more revealing than fixed-response questions. Questions about sexual behaviors may be less emotionally charged than questions about lifestyle. For instance, rather than asking "Are you unfaithful?", ask "Do you ever have sex with people other than your partner?" Lifestyle questions ask the patient to label herself—and how people label themselves can be very different from their actual behavior. Start out with general questions first, then move on to more specific questions. Your patient may find it reassuring if you couch questions in terms of "normalcy"—that is, "many other people . . ." For example, "Many women engage in oral sex. Is that a practice that you and your partner[s] engage in?" Use language your patient can understand—even slang, not clinical jargon (for example, "had sex" versus "engaged in intercourse"). Also remember to clarify the discussion by asking your patient what she thinks you meant. For example, to some women, the term "sexually active" may mean vigorous sex or sex with many partners.

If there is time for just one question, it should be: "What do you do to protect yourself from AIDS?" If time permits, also ask:

- Have you had sex in the past year?
- If yes, with how many different people this year?
- In this year, have you had sex with men, with

Ask your patient what she thinks you meant. To some women, "sexually active" may mean vigorous sex or sex with many partners.

women, or with both?

- What can you tell me about your sexual experiences before this year?
- Have you ever had a sexually transmitted disease of any kind?
- Have you ever shared needles or injecting equipment with another person?
- Have you ever felt that a sexual partner put you at risk for disease?
- What do you do to protect yourself from unplanned pregnancy?
- How many times have you used an over-the-counter treatment for a vaginal infection in the last year?
- Does intercourse cause you pain or discomfort?
- Is there anything else about your sexual experiences that I need to know to ensure good health care for you?

You might also ask about blood transfusions before April 1985, workplace exposure to blood, and alcohol and drug use. Questions about specific sexual practices can reveal risk for trauma or infection.

SENSITIVE TEACHING STRATEGIES

Taking a sexual history gives you an opportunity to initiate or reinforce prior teaching about STD risk reduction. Discuss what, if anything, the woman and her partner use as contraceptives, and reinforce that abstinence, long-term mutual monogamy, and use of condoms protect best against STDs.

Other strategies that reduce the risk of STDs include the correct use of latex condoms with nonoxynol-9 every time there is sexual contact (oral, anal, or genital), or polyurethane condoms in cases of latex allergy. If condom use is out of the question, advise your patient to use a barrier contraceptive with a spermicidal jelly, cream, or foam.

There's some evidence that spermicides have germicidal properties, and that a diaphragm or cervical cap offers some protection against cervical or upper reproductive tract infection. However, the evidence has not been strong enough to persuade the FDA to label these products "protective against STDs."

Don't assume your patient knows how condoms are correctly used (model penises can be used for return demonstrations). Also, some women aren't aware that only water-based lubricants such as K-Y jelly or Surgilube should be used with latex condoms.

Some of your patients may not be aware of the female condom, which is intended to protect the entire vaginal region. With "perfect use," that is, correct insertion every time, the female condom has a failure rate (pregnancy or infection with an STD) of 5% in 12 months of use. "Typical use" is associated with a failure rate of 21%. The female condom has a three-year shelf life, and 36 states offer Medicaid reimbursement or its equivalent for this product. Many of the women who have tried it felt it was too unyieldy to be practical. However, it's a method of protection that is available without prescription and is within the woman's control.

In contrast, the male condom is better than 95% effective with perfect use and 88% effective with typical use. But there are many reasons why male condoms may not be the woman's best option. One disadvantage is that the man must be willing to use it. Prostitutes and women who have abusive partners may be physically or financially threatened if they suggest a condom. Poor self-esteem is another barrier to condom use—some women don't feel they can insist on it.

One of the biggest barriers is perception of need. In discussing contraceptives and STDs with these patients, you need to know when to stop. Beyond a certain point, the patient may tune you out anyway if condom use doesn't fit into her style of sexual activity.

Advise your women patients that sexual practices that result in physical trauma create portals for infections. Excessive drinking or drug-taking can impair judgment and increase sexual risk-taking. Caution patients against sex with partners who use IV drugs, are HIV-positive, are from areas with high prevalence of HIV, or have had sex with such individuals. Teach patients to avoid having sex with anyone who has visible oral, inguinal, genital, perineal, or anal lesions. Washing and urinating before and after intercourse can lessen the chance of infection. Patents should also be taught never to share hypodermic needles or razors.

Nurses often see women whose relationships suffer from an imbalance of power. When a patient doesn't have the power to enforce the behavioral changes that reduce risk, you'll need to help her identify the measures that are feasible, as well as refer to her for help on the basic relationship issues. In-depth discussion with both partners is the ideal scenario for teaching about STDs. Lacking that, including a detailed sexual history in the usual nursing history whenever possible is the next best option.

WHAT ELSE CAN BE DONE

The emergence of HIV/AIDS as a significant threat to the health of women and their children has refocused attention on infectious diseases in general and STDs in particular. Far from being benign, STDs lead to tremendous heartache and large health care expenditures. While the Department of Health and Human Services considers control of STDs a priority, government initiatives have yielded mixed results to date.

One of the greatest impediments to controlling STDs is clinicians' failure to recognize the risk, particularly among middle-class patients.

Devising effective educational strategies has been the focus of considerable funding and activity since the nature of the HIV epidemic was recognized in the mid-1980s. Programs to prevent syphilis and gonorrhea have helped reduce incidence, although certain groups remain at higher risk (such as blacks for syphilis and Hispanics for gonorrhea). More people have become aware of genital herpes over the last 30 years; consequently, more may have sought treatment. Similarly, with an $8.3-million national chlamydia prevention program in place since 1994, chlamydial infections may begin to decline as well.

Prevention and outreach programs are most successful if the developmental level and ethnic or cultural background of the target population are taken into consideration. Numerous projects have demonstrated that peer education is more effective than professional education. One successful federally funded community outreach program for HIV prevention pays low-income minority women in rural south-central New Jersey to be trained and to train others in their community (who also receive a small stipend for attending the program).

In other community outreach programs, community members are taught and certified in HIV education via, for example, the American Red Cross HIV education program. They then conduct small group or one-to-one sessions in their neighborhood. Attendees who realize that they're at risk for HIV or another STD are directed to testing sites or can contact their local health department for referral to an STD clinic if they don't have a health care provider. The CDC is now funding projects to make successful education and outreach program plans available to communities across the country.

Health care providers can help maximize the impact of these programs if they:

- educate all clients about the realities of STDs;
- incorporate risk assessment and STD screening into routine comprehensive health services;
- ensure prompt treatment for all patients diagnosed with STDs;
- offer HIV testing to all pregnant women;
- counsel patients with STDs about the need for simultaneous treatment of all sex partners; and
- educate all patients about STD risk reduction, including contraceptive choices.

One of the greatest impediments to controlling STDs and HIV/AIDS is clinicians' failure to recognize the risk, particularly among their middle-class patients. Public health initiatives targeting health care providers, such as the national AIDS Education and Training Center program, focus on making STD and HIV/AIDS prevention and case-finding part of every nonemergency patient contact, regardless of the setting.

Education needs to be a priority in patient care from puberty through old age. Some nursing homes, for instance, realizing that the threat of STDs doesn't disappear when someone turns 65, have established STD education programs for residents. With more resources available and with both clinicians and patients becoming more aware of the dangers of STDs, these scourges of women's and children's health may eventually become diseases of the past.

SELECTED REFERENCES

Abel, E., et al. Self-esteem, problem solving, and sexual risk behavior among women with and without Chlamydia. *Clin.Nurs.Res.* 3:353-370, Nov. 1994.

Benenson, A. S., ed. *Control of Communicable Diseases Manual: An Official Report of the American Public Health Association*, 16th ed. Washington, DC, The Association, 1995.

Blackwell, A. L., et al. Health gains from screening for infection of the lower genital tract in women attending for termination of pregnancy. *Lancet* 342:206-210, July 24, 1993.

Centers for Disease Control and Prevention, Division of STD Prevention. *Sexually Transmitted Disease Surveillance, 1995* [On-line data base]. The Center, 1996.

Centers for Disease Control and Prevention. *National HIV/AIDS Hotline* [Personal communication]. September 12, 1996.

Centers for Disease Control and Prevention. *National HIV/AIDS Hotline*. Feb. 16,1997.

Centers for Disease Control and Prevention. 1993 sexually transmitted diseases treatment guidelines. *MMWR Morb. Mortal.Wkly.Rep.* 42(RR-14):1-73, Sept. 1993.

Detzer, M. G., et al. Barriers to condom use among women attending planned parenthood clinics. *Women Health* 23(1): 91-102, 1995.

Fogel, C. I. Sexually transmitted diseases. In *Womens Health Care* edited by C. I. Fogel and N. F Woods. Thousand Oaks, CA, Sage Publications, 1995, pp. 571-609.

Garrett, L. *The Coming Plague: Newly Emerging Diseases in a World Out of Balance.* New York, Farrar, Straus and Giroux, 1994.

Janssen, R. S., et al. HIV infection among patients in U.S. acute care hospitals: Strategies for the counseling and testing of the hospital patients. The Hospital HIV Surveillance Group. *N.Engl.J.Med.* 327:445-452, Aug. 13, 1992.

Moss, G. B., et al. Human immunodeficiency virus DNA in urethral secretions in men: Association with gonococcal urethriris and CD4 cell depletion. *J.lnfect.Dis.* 172:1469-1474, Dec. 1995.

Provisional cases of selected notifiable diseases, United States, weeks ending January 18, 1997 and January 20, 1996 (3rd week) [Table]. *MMWR Morb.Mortal.Wkly.Rep.* 46:66-67, Jan. 24,1997.

Quinn, T. C., and Cates, W. Epidemiology of sexually transmitted diseases in the 1990s. In *Advances in Host Defense Mechanisms. Vol. 8: Sexually Transmitted Diseases* edited by T. C. Quinn et al. New York, Raven Press, 1992, pp. 1-37.

Rakel, R. E., ed. *Conns Current Therapy.* Philadelphia, Saunders, 1995.

Recommendations of the U.S. Public Health Service Task Force on the use of zidovudine to reduce perinatal transmission of human immunodeficiency virus. *MMWR Morb.Mortal. Wlky.Rep.* 43(RR-11):1-20, Aug. 1994.

Risen, C. B. A guide to taking a sexual history. *Psychiatr. Clin.North Am.* 18 :39-53, Mar 1995.

Sharts-Hopko, N. C., et al. Problem-focused coping in HIV-infected mothers in relation to self-efficacy, uncertainty, social support, and psychological distress. *Image J.Nurs. Sch.* 28:107-111, Summer 1996.

U.S. Department of Health and Human Services. *Healthy People 2000: A Midcourse Review and 1995 Revisions.* Boston, Jones & Bartlett, 1995.

U.S. Department of Health and Human Services. *Healthy People 2000: National Health Promotion and Prevention Objectives* (DHHS Pub. No. PHS 91-50212). Washington, DC, U.S. Government Printing Office, 1991.

Weis S. S., et al. The use of nonoxynol-9 for protection against cervical gonorrhea. *Am.J.Public Health* 84:910-914, June 1994.

Zhou, Y. F., et al. Association between prior cytomegalovirus infection and the risk of restenosis after coronary artherotomy. *N.Engl.J.Med.* 335:624-630, Aug. 29, 1996.

Nancy C. Sharts-Hopko is professor, College of Nursing, Villanova University, Villanova, PA.

The Safest Sex

It's now seen as **abnormal** **not** to have sexual **fantasies.** Their big **advantage**: You have **total control** over everything that happens. But **what** do your sexual fantasies **say** about **you?**

By Peter Doskoch

Ah, sexual fantasy. It has one big advantage over sexual reality: You have total control over everything that happens. You won't be humiliated or suffer at the hands of a brutish lover— unless, of course, that's what you want. Consider the possibilities. Your fantasy partner can be a celebrity, the guy who works down the hall, or your best friend's mate. You enjoy complete choice of venue; a tropical island, an elevator, a tree swing. And the activity in question can range from romantic, longing glances to sexual gymnastics that would strain a circus contortionist.

So perhaps the most surprising fact about our fantasies is this: The sexual scenario we most often imagine is . . . ordinary, non-kinky intercourse with a past or current lover. Despite the potential for limitless freedom, our fantasies generally stay firmly tethered to reality.

Don't worry if you assumed most fantasies were a bit more risqué. Even in today's tell-all culture, sexual fantasies remain one of our last taboos, something that people simply don't discuss.

"We tell each other almost everything—our sexual habits, who we lust for, how much money we make," notes Columbia University psychiatrist Ethel Person,

M.D., author of *By Force of Fantasy*. "But I do not know the sexual fantasies of my closest friends. We regard fantasies as too revealing. They're treasured possessions, yet we're ashamed of them."

Even psychologists long found sexual fantasy vaguely disreputable, ignoring the topic almost entirely for the first half of the century. But the last two decades have produced a flurry of new information, say University of Vermont psychologist Harold Leitenberg, Ph.D., and South Carolina's Kris Henning, Ph.D. And it turns out that a lot of what we thought we knew is wrong.

Women say the physical setting of a fantasy, and the associated smell, sounds, and textures, are more important than do men.

IMAGINARY LOVERS

The misconceptions about sexual fantasies began with Freud himself. In 1908 he declared that "a happy person never fantasizes, only a dissatisfied one." Later thinkers embroidered this theme, developing what has become known as the deficiency theory.

"People still believe that fantasies are compensation for lack of sexual opportunity," says Leitenberg. "That if your sex life was adequate, you wouldn't have to fantasize."

But the data show that, if anything, frequent fantasizers are having more than their share of fun in bed. They have sex more often, engage in a wider variety of erotic activities, have more partners, and masturbate more often than infrequent fantasizers, Leitenberg and Henning report in *Psychological Bulletin*.

The association between fantasies and a healthy sex life is so strong, in fact, that it's now considered pathological *not* to have sexual fantasies.

masochistic fantasies of being tied to a bed, and he might be perfectly comfortable because he sees that as respite from having to be in control; whereas some feminists are ashamed because they have masochistic fantasies and they feel that the fantasies are contrary to their political beliefs."

Such guilt exacts a heavy toll. Those who fret over their fantasies have sex less often and enjoy it less, even though the content of their fantasies is no different from those of the guilt-free.

Percentage of men who say they've fantasized about deflowering a young girl: 61

And no wonder. Researchers studying sexual fantasies confirm that everyone has them, from adolescence onward. Well, almost everyone: About five percent of men and women say they have never had a sexual fantasy (or won't admit to it). Person believes that these fantasy-free folks are getting a vicarious fix elsewhere—from movies, for example. Or else they simply aren't paying attention to their own thoughts.

Most adults say they first remember fantasizing between the ages of 11 and 13. From there they quickly pick up speed. Sexual fantasies and thoughts are most common in hormone-addled teens and young adults. In one study, researchers asked people at random times during the day whether sex had crossed their minds during the past five minutes. Among 14- and 15-year olds, 57 percent of boys and 42 percent of girls said *yes*. Affirmative responses were less common with increasing age: among 56-to 64-year-olds, 19 percent of men and 12 percent of women answered yes.

Once you get beyond age, though, it's hard to predict whether a given person has lots of fantasies. Attempts to identify a "fantasy-prone" type of individual have been woefully unsuccessful. Even religious and political views provide few clues. Conservatives have just as many fantasies as liberals—despite the fact that, according to one study, nearly half of conservative Christians feel sexual fantasies are "morally flawed or unacceptable."

The devout aren't the only ones who have mixed feelings. One in four people feel strong guilt about their fantasies, reports Leitenberg. Most of this hand-wringing "involves people who feel guilty about fantasizing while making love to their partners," he says. Even among sexually adventurous groups like college students, 22 percent of women and 8 percent of men said they usually try to repress the feelings associated with fantasy.

Guilt also strikes when fantasy and personal ideology collide. "There are people who feel that their sexual fantasies are not a part of them," Person says. "The CEO of a *Fortune* 500 company may have

But even unusual and "deviant" fantasies give little reason for concern in healthy individuals. It's true that we sometimes use fantasies as a springboard for later sexual hijinks. But the path from fantasy to deviance is anything but direct.

Rape fantasies, for instance, are far more common than rapes themselves. And as an extreme example, consider that only 22 percent of child molesters say they had sexual fantasies about kids *before* their first molestation. So unusual fantasies are a concern only when they become compulsive or exclusive, or for individuals "in whom the barrier between thought and behavior has been broken," say Leitenherg and Henning.

TONIGHT'S EPISODE . . .

Exactly why your fantasies differ from those of your friends is not well understood. But theories abound. Certainly personal experience and the things we see, hear, and read about enter the mix.

External stimuli like sexy advertisements or scantily clad passersby, in fact, may be responsible for the oft-noted observation that men fantasize more than women. In a sample of college students, researchers found that men fantasized or thought about sex 7.2 times a day, compared to 4.5 for women. For each sex, two of those fantasies were internally triggered. But men reported twice as many externally provoked thoughts.

Our favorite internally triggered fantasies probably attain preferred status through classical conditioning, the same process that had Pavlov's dogs drooling at the sound of a bell. Fantasies that accompany orgasm are particularly reinforced, for instance, making them more arousing next time around. From there "we embellish them, change them," says Person. "They're like an evolving series." Scenarios that don't accompany arousal are discarded.

While the most common fantasies involve routine sex with a past, present, or imaginary partner, that's not to say that we don't occasionally give our fantasy muscles a more strenuous workout. In addition to those decidedly "vanilla" scenarios, Leitenberg and Henning describe three other primary flavors of fantasy:

- **Novel or "forbidden" imagery.** This includes unconventional settings, questionable partners like strangers or relatives, and ligament-straining positions worthy of the *Kama Sutra*. Or as Dr. Seuss once asked (albeit in a somewhat different context): "Would you, could you, in a boat? Could you, would you, with a goat?"

Percentage of young marrieds who say their spouse knows their sexual fantasies: 1 in 4

- **Scenes of sexual irresistibility.** Here the emphasis is on seductive power: overcoming the reluctance of an initially indifferent man or woman through sheer animal magnetism. Or the irresistibility may take numerical form in fantasies involving multiple partners.

- **Dominance and submission fantasies.** In these, sexual power is expressed either ritualistically—in sado-masochistic activities—or through physical force, as in rape fantasies. Such fantasies are surprisingly common. Person reports that 44 percent of men have had fantasies of dominating a partner. Other studies found that 51 percent of women fantasized about being forced to have sex, while a third imagined: "I'm a slave who must obey a man's every wish."

None of this means, of course, that real-world rape victims "really want it." "Women who find submission fantasies sexually arousing are very clear that they have no wish to be raped in reality," say Leitenberg and Henning. In their fantasies, women control every aspect of what occurs. And their scenarios are far less brutal than real-life attacks. Typically the fantasy involves an attractive man whose restraint is simply overwhelmed by the woman's attractiveness. These fantasies serve the same psychological purpose as scenes of irresistibility. "It's different means to the same end," says Leitenberg. "We want to be desired."

Incidentally, researchers find little difference in the fantasies of hetero- and homosexuals—except in the gender of participants.

Women report less jealousy than men do if their partner's fantasies involve another person.

had, women were more likely to describe romance and commitment while men mentioned a greater number of sexual acts.

In another study of 300 college students, 41 percent of the women—but only 16 percent of the men—said that while fantasizing they focused on the "personal or emotional characteristics of the partner." Men, however, were four times as likely to focus on their fantasy partner's physical characteristics. Sociobiologists argue that these discrepancies represent evolved behavioral differences between men and women. But even if that's true, Leitenberg observes, there are certainly cultural pressures for women not to think about sex outside of a committed relationship, lest they be labeled a "slut."

The romance/genitalia dichotomy isn't the only major differences in male and female fantasies, report Leitenberg and Henning. Here are some others:

1. Men are more likely to imagine themselves doing something to a woman, and their fantasies focus on her body. Women, on the other hand, tend to envision something being done to them and to concentrate more on their partner's interest in her.

2. Male fantasies more often involve sex with two or more partners at one time. In one study, a third of men had fantasies about sex with multiple partners—twice the number of women. Guys are also

Percentage of gay men who report having a homosexual fantasy before age 13: 83

HARLEQUIN AND HEFNER

It doesn't take a Ph.D. to figure out that the fantasies of men and women differ. Just look at the fantasy scenarios that publishers push.

Men have *Playboy*: big-busted women exposing their attributes, in almost clinical detail, from a

variety of angles and positions. For women, on the other hand, there are tales like *The Bridges of Madison County* and cookie-cutter Harlequin romances. The covers may depict heaving bosoms and Fabio's muscular physique, but the sex always comes packaged within an emotional, passionate romance.

While all this may change as sexual roles and cultural attitudes change, fantasies still fall along those gender lines. When male and female college students were asked to write out in detail three fantasies they

more likely to switch partners in mid-fantasy.

3. Both sexes imagine overpowering a partner or being forced to submit to another's wishes. But men are more likely to have domination fantasies, while women tend to see themselves submitting to a partner's sexual wishes. One researcher reports

that 13 percent of women but only 4 percent of men said that their favorite fantasy was being forced to have sex.

4. Men have a greater variety of fantasies. Asked to check off all those they had experienced in the past three months (on a list of 55), male collegians indicated 26 of them. Women listed only 14.

DREAM ON

There's still a lot no one knows about sexual fantasies. Is the frequency and range of fantasies similar in other cultures? How does the content of fantasies change over one's lifetime? And what happens when we act on our fantasies? Does it spoil them—or make them more vivid? "We have no idea," admits Leitenberg.

But what we do know is proof enough that fantasies are an essential part of our sexual repertoire. Far from being a sign of sexual inadequacy or deprivation, fantasies are associated with a healthy, happy sex life. "The people who have the most sexual problems fantasize least," Leitenberg notes.

Indeed, fantasy's power to arouse us—some folks say they can achieve orgasm solely from sexual thoughts, or "thinking off"—proves that the brain is as potent a sexual organ as one's genitalia. And though most erotic thoughts are relatively ordinary, our more imaginative flights allow us to explore our sexuality without risk of physical harm or social rejection. Consider this finding: Imagining having sex with your current lover is a popular fantasy when you're not engaged in sexual activity—while imagining sex with a new partner is a popular fantasy during intercourse.

Most of us need no further justification for fantasy beyond the fun factor. "Sexual fantasy is a natural part of being human," says Leitenberg. "It's pleasurable. So why not fantasize?"

The Tattle of the Sexes

	Men	Women
Think about sex one or more times a day	54%	19%
Have had imaginary sexual encounters with 1000 or more partners	32%	8%
Have fantasized during masturbation	86%	69%
Focus on visual imagery during sexual fantasy	81%	43%
Focus on feelings or emotions	19%	57%
Began fantasizing during intercourse the first time I had sex	36%	18%
First fantasy inspired by a relationship	6%	31%
First fantasy inspired by sexy older person like a teacher	27%	7%

PART 6

Legal and Ethical Issues

Society has been transformed by a host of cultural changes and technological innovations. These have resulted in a number of legal and ethical issues related to human sexuality.

Sexual harassment, acquaintance rape, gay marriage, artificial insemination, and surrogate parenting are issues of the 1990s that are the result of the sociocultural and technological changes of the past 30 years.

The revolution in personal computing and the growth of the World Wide Web and the Internet have created the ability to move huge amounts of information from anywhere in the world in a nanosecond. No one can yet fully grasp the power of this transformation in information processing.

The Internet and high speed, powerful computers have created a variety of legal, ethical, and moral issues related to sexuality and obscenity. Although we still employ a definition of obscenity that embraces local community standards as its defining criteria, the Internet, in a manner of speaking, is capable of bringing the red-light districts of Amsterdam and Thailand into our family rooms. How can community standards of decency be applied to global phenomenon?

We will examine these and other issues related to the legal and ethical basis of sexuality in this section.

A Reading for Critical Thinking

Six cases to challenge your moral gyroscope

Is *This* Sexual Harassment?

By Robin Warshaw

Sexual harassment? Not you. You're the new breed of male, sensitive to the age-old gender stereotypes women have had to battle as they gain the equality and respect rightfully theirs in a male-dominated business world. As far as you're concerned, bartering promotions for sexual favors is inappropriate office conduct of the worst sort—the kind of behavior that not only demeans co-workers but also tarnishes your own character and diminishes managerial effectiveness.

No. In this matter your conscience is as shiny and clean as Sir Galahad's shield.

So throughout the long media blizzard precipitated by Anita Hill, Clarence Thomas and the Senate judiciary peanut gallery, you sat snug and cozy, hands warming by the fire of your own morally appropriate behavior. But when the storm subsided, you may have found a new America waiting to challenge your conduct.

It is an America in which women, overcoming their fear of reprisal and disbelief, are bringing their grievances to court in record numbers. In the first half of 1992 alone, reports of harassment made to the Equal Employment Opportunity Commission increased more than 50 percent over the previous year.

It is also an America that is finally ready to take these grievances seriously. And while you may applaud this trend that's finally packing muscle onto what was formerly a pleasant but ineffective civil rights sentiment, the bottom line is that you may get caught in the crossfire.

The problem faced by men in this new environment is twofold: First, while most media-worthy cases of sexual harassment involve spectacularly colorful

instances of inappropriate behavior, the majority of unheralded arguments currently being heard in the nation's courts don't fit so neatly into the public's perceptions of right and wrong. Harassment sometimes is in the eye of the beholder, and what may be one man's clumsy attempt at friendship or even honest romance may be one woman's sheer hell.

Complicating the whole matter are the hazy boundaries of the law. Except in cases of actual assault, there's still no steadfast uniformity regarding the type of behavior the courts and mediating agencies should judge to be harassing.

The following cases have all been culled from legal battles and disputes brought before public hearing examiners. Each has been chosen because it explores in some fashion the gray areas that lie just outside the realm of obviously inoffensive and threatening behavior. As you read them, ask yourself: Are the women involved simply too sensitive? Or are these in fact bona fide cases of harassment? Before you read the verdict, make your own judgment and see whether your behavioral gyroscope is guiding you straight and true—or wobbling dangerously.

★ ★ ★

Case #1

IS SEX BETWEEN CONSENTING ADULTS HARASSMENT?

The Securities and Exchange Commission office was a sociable place to work—sociable, that is, if you were one of several employees, including supervisors, having romantic affairs with each other, holding frequent parties and leaving the office during the day to go drinking.

From *Exec* (Summer 1993), pp 62–65. Reprinted with permission from Rodale Press, Inc. © 1993.

But one female attorney who did not participate in the carousing found her co-workers' behavior repulsive. She claimed she was harassed by the environment in which she had to work. Moreover, she said, women who had affairs with male supervisors were rewarded with bonuses and promotions. The woman conceded that no one had pressured her for sex or denied her any promotions because she wasn't one of the crowd.

Was she being too touchy?

THE DECISION: Although the woman wasn't harassed on a quid pro quo (give something to get something) basis, a judge ruled that the "pervasive" behavior in the SEC office had created an offensive work environment. She was awarded back pay, a promotion and her choice of two jobs. The SEC also agreed to an outside review of its personnel practices.

THE EXPERT ANALYSIS: "That's a hostile work environment—no question about it," says Thomas A. McGinn, a human-resources consultant in Charlottesville, Virginia, and co-author (with Nancy Dodd McCann) of *Harassed: 100 Women Define Inappropriate Behavior in the Workplace* (Business One Irwin).

Socializing at work has its limits, and those limits certainly were crossed in the Roman Empire-type revels at that SEC office. Federal guidelines warn specifically that an employer who gives benefits to anyone in exchange for sex may be held liable for discriminating against other workers. But any affairs within an office— even among peers—can raise the potential for unequal treatment of nonparticipants.

★ ★ ★
Case #2
THAT'S ENTERTAINMENT?

Few things are as boring as most corporate meetings. In an attempt to liven up the presentations, an oil company brought a barely clad woman on a motorcycle to a regional meeting, according to a sexual-harassment complaint filed by a female supervisor for the company.

Moreover, she charged, when the corporation held a sales meeting at a restaurant, the entertainment was provided by strippers. And at a slide show held for employees, one slide featured the female supervisor's clothed rear end.

Was the woman harassed?

THE DECISION: The federal judge presiding over this case noted that the incidents were without question inappropriate but weren't "sufficiently severe or pervasive to constitute a hostile environment." That noted, he found that no harassment had taken place.

THE EXPERT ANALYSIS: Surely there are other ways to entertain and inform employees, suggests

Anthony M. Micolo, a human-resources representative with Eastman Kodak in New York City. As for the incidents in the case: "I would probably feel myself, as a man, uncomfortable with this stuff," he says.

More to the point is that while a "hostile environment" charge often needs more than one or two incidents to substantiate it, other judges might find episodes such as the preceding sufficient to establish a pervasive climate of harassment. Micolo points out that corporations need to consider what conduct will be deemed acceptable. "Above and beyond sales goals and operational goals, there have to be people goals," he says. "You have to view the work environment as one that's productive to employees, not oppressive to them.

★ ★ ★
Case #3
JUST A FRIENDLY RIDE

A midwinter snowstorm hit so hard that one Virginia corporation sent its workers home early. A female word-processing technician needed a ride, which was readily offered by a male engineer for whom she had done some work. He assured her that his four-wheel drive vehicle would have no trouble navigating the storm.

Indeed, it didn't. When they arrived, he entered her apartment. He says he only kissed her. She says he tried to kiss and fondle her, despite her protestations. When she complained to their employer, the man was reprimanded and warned he would be fired if he committed another such act.

Was he simply a clumsy guy looking for companionship or a threatening menace?

WHAT HAPPENED: The woman's lawyers showed in court that the corporation had received previous complaints from other women about the man's behavior. After a ruling determined that the company had a legal responsibility to prevent the incident, the employer made an out-of-court settlement.

THE EXPERT ANALYSIS: According to Louise Fitzgerald, a psychologist and researcher on sexual harassment at the University of Illinois at Champaign, such a scenario is common but not innocuous. "This is unwanted sexual attention of a predatory nature and is a violation of someone's right to bodily integrity." In research Fitzgerald conducted among working women, 15 percent had been victims at work of undesired attempts at touching, fondling, grabbing or kissing.

★ ★ ★
Case #4
THE CHUMMY BOSS

The new secretary thought it strange that her boss walked her to her car every night, but she believed it was to offer security. She couldn't explain why he walked her to the bathroom, hovered over her desk, left her personal notes about her appearance or bought her gifts. She complained about this to her friends, but not to management.

She hoped that by letting her boss know she was happily married, the unwanted attention would stop. Instead, when she was hospitalized for back surgery, he called frequently, visited, sent notes and brought flowers. When she returned to work, he tried to give her back rubs whenever he noticed her stretching. She told him to stop. Finally, she spoke to a supervisor, who told her to talk to her boss again. Ultimately, she quit the job after her boss accused her of having an affair with a male co-worker and threatened to withhold a promised raise if it was true.

Was the boss anything more than an annoying pest?

WHAT HAPPENED: A local human-relations commission ruled in the woman's favor and the company offered a $6,700 settlement. She declined the settlement and went to court.

Then a federal judge asserted that no harassment had taken place. He ruled that the boss's conduct "would not have interfered with a reasonable person's work performance or created an intimidating, hostile or offensive working environment." He added that the woman's protests to her boss "were not delivered with any sense of urgency, sincerity or force." Legal experts say such cases will now more often be decided by juries, with verdicts increasingly likely to favor complainants.

THE EXPERT ANALYSIS: Some argue that in order to dispel any hint of sexual harassment in an office, all friendly interactions would have to stop. However, Jonathan A. Segal, a management attorney in Philadelphia who advises companies on sexual harassment issues, disputes that dour view. "An occasional compliment is not harassment," he says, "but an excessive interest in an employee's private life is."

Segal spends most of his time providing employers with preventive education on how to avoid situations such as the one above. "Any thorough training program would make clear that what this individual did was wrong," he says. Moreover, he adds, complaints should never be handled by the individuals charged with harassment.

★ ★ ★
Case #5
THE WRITING ON THE WALL

A woman learned that obscene cartoons about her had been posted in the men's room of her office

building. The graffiti sketches depicted various sex acts and mentioned her name.

The lewd illustrations remained on display in the public bathroom for a week, even after the company's chief executive had seen them. It was only after he learned the woman was upset about the cartoons that they were removed.

Was the office worker sexually harassed or was she just the target of crude, yet childish, pranksters?

WHAT HAPPENED: The court sided with the woman, determining that the cartoons were "highly offensive to a woman who seeks to deal with her fellow employees and clients with professional dignity." The employer agreed to pay her full salary and psychiatric bills until she found new employment.

In a similar case, a federal judge in Jacksonville, Florida, determined that pinup calendars and posters of women's genitals that were displayed at a shipyard were a "visual assault on the sensibilities of female workers," constituted sexual harassment and kept women out of jobs there.

THE EXPERT ANALYSIS: Where certain men might feel flattered or amused to have their names attached to sexually explicit cartoons, most women would likely feel shame and humiliation. Joan Lester, director of the Equity Institute, an Emeryville, California, consultancy in multicultural issues, points out that for a woman to be chosen for such treatment is "chilling and intimidating." It's also potentially dangerous: "The cartoons could be an incitement to sexual violence." For the targeted woman, that fear—coupled with the ridicule—could quickly destroy her work world.

It would have been far better if a male co-worker had taken the pictures down immediately, but such allies for women are often rare in work settings. "There's the fear (for a male co-worker) of breaking rank, that his masculinity will be questioned," says Lester. The situation was worsened by the company president's knowledge of the drawings. "It shows he didn't have an understanding of the human consequences and the legal issues," Lester adds.

★ ★ ★
Case #6
WHAT IS REASONABLE

Two office employees, female and male, worked at desks just a few yards away from each other. One day they went to lunch together.

When the man later asked the woman out for yet another lunch (and perhaps a drink), she turned him

> *What may be one man's clumsy attempt at friendship or even honest romance may be one woman's sheer hell.*

down. After that rebuff, he began sending her love letters, including one that was three pages long and single-spaced. The woman became increasingly frightened about the unwanted attention and filed a sexual harassment complaint.

Was the man just doing some harmless, old-fashioned courting?

WHAT HAPPENED: The woman's case was dismissed at first by a judge who called the man's behavior "trivial," but an appellate court, in a precedent-setting decision, found that sexual harassment should be viewed as a "reasonable woman" might experience it and remanded it back to the lower court. More and more future cases will be decided using this "reasonable woman" standard.

THE EXPERT ANALYSIS: In a society in which sexual assault is not uncommon, such persistent, unwelcome advances from a man are frightening.

"Physical size and physical well-being have a lot to do with it," says San Francisco labor attorney Cliff Palefsky, who represents plaintiffs in sexual harassment cases. That's why, Palefsky explains, if a man is subjected to excessive staring by a woman, he might think, "So what?" But when the situation is reversed, "it's enough to give a woman the creeps." Most men, he adds, have never experienced such scary intrusiveness.

Because of men's and women's disparate views, the evaluation of sexual harassment charges is now moving away from the legal tradition of using a "reasonable man's" (or "reasonable person's") interpretation of an incident to judgments based on how a "reasonable woman" might view an event. Palefsky says the concept has received quick acceptance. "This isn't paternalistic protection for women," he says. "It's a reality. There's such a huge difference in perspective."

The End of Obscenity

Jeffrey Rosen

On June 11, three judges in Philadelphia struck down parts of the Communications Decency Act. The decision, *ACLU* v. *Reno*, is being justly celebrated as the *New York Times* v. *Sullivan* of cyberspace, an occasion for dancing in the chat rooms. The three judges understood how the old First Amendment battles are being overtaken by new technologies; and in an endearingly self-dramatizing touch, they had their separate opinions distributed on floppy disks. But for all their sophistication about the technical difficulties of regulating free speech in cyberspace, the judges were forced by the Supreme Court's archaic obscenity doctrine to rely on an implausible premise: that it's possible to distinguish obscenity (which can be banned) from indecency (which must be protected) in an age when cyberspace has made the notion of local community standards increasingly untenable.

The best of the three *Reno* opinions was written by federal district judge Stewart Dalzell, who concluded that the Internet, like the printing press, should be entitled to the highest level of First Amendment protection. This represents a welcome break with the American judicial tradition of underestimating the social significance of new media. When the telegraph and telephone emerged in the nineteenth century, they were viewed as vehicles of transportation, like the railroads, rather than vehicles of expression, and were regulated without concern for the First Amendment. When radio and television began to flourish, judges allowed Congress to regulate them as public utilities, because of the limited spectrum of available channels. Judge Dalzell concluded that the Internet is entitled to at least as much protection as traditional print media, *if not more*, because it realizes the goals of the First

Amendment even more completely. The new cyberspace technologies are reducing the costs of entry for both speakers and listeners and creating relative equality among them. As a result, Dalzell noted, in cyberspace, even more than in newspapers and magazines, "astoundingly diverse content is available," fulfilling Justice Holmes's romantic metaphor of a perfectly deregulated marketplace of ideas.

Dalzell's greatest contribution was to recognize the decentralized chaos of the Internet as a central First Amendment value. Since the 1920s, leading free speech theorists, from Walter Lippmann to Robert Bork, have emphasized the communal value of civic debate about "matters of public importance" and have downplayed the competing libertarian value of individual self-expression. This communitarian tradition has been invoked to justify all sorts of censorship of purportedly "worthless" speech, from anarchist polemics during World War I to racial epithets today. Dalzell, by contrast, celebrated the fact that, in cyberspace, the lack of a centralized censoring authority means that decisions about what speech is valuable and what is worthless are left in the hands of individual speakers and listeners.

By purporting to regulate "indecent" speech, as measured by "contemporary community standards," Dalzell concluded, the Communications Decency Act threatens the very chaos that represents the Internet's greatest strength. Because there's no technologically feasible way to limit the geographic scope of every Internet "speaker," and no economically feasible way to screen the location and age of each potential "listener," everyone runs the risk that his speech will be found "indecent" or "patently offensive" in some community he had no intention of entering. Graphic

From *The New Republic* (July 15–22, 1996), pp. 6, 41. Reprinted by permission of *The New Republic*. © 1996 The New Republic, Inc.

language "routinely acceptable" in New York City, such as Tony Kushner's *Angels in America*, might be actionable if downloaded in Tennessee. All three judges concluded, therefore, that the "indecency" standard was too subjective to give citizens fair notice of what speech might be illegal.

But isn't the federal obscenity standard vulnerable to precisely the same objections? "The Government can continue to protect children from pornography on the Internet through vigorous enforcement of existing laws criminalizing obscenity and child pornography," Dalzell declared. But Dalzell's own reasoning calls the distinction between indecency and obscenity into question. If indecency can't be coherently defined, because of the elasticity of "community standards," defining obscenity is even harder. Dalzell points approvingly to the only federal Internet obscenity conviction, *United States* v. *Thomas*, affirmed by an appellate court last year. The images in question were uploaded by Robert and Carleen Thomas, the mom-and-pop proprietors of the Amateur Action Bulletin Board in Milpitas, California, and were downloaded in the heart of the Biblebelt in Memphis, Tennessee. The Thomases claimed they were entrapped by a governmental postal inspector, who intentionally chose to download the pictures in Memphis to take advantage of Tennessee's conservative community standards. But the *Thomas* case confirms Dalzell's most powerful insight: that in an age when cyberspace has broken down physical boundaries, it makes little sense to allow the morals of a geographic community to dictate what is acceptable for a virtual community of consenting adults.

Dalzell's Maginot line between indecency and obscenity is being threatened by cultural changes, too. In 1973, when the Supreme Court declared that obscenity should be judged by local rather than national community standards, there was an informal consensus that hard-core material could be banned, while soft-core material had to be protected. (Justice Potter Stewart was said to be guided by a droop test.) A decade later, however, this consensus broke down entirely when a federal court held that "detailed portrayals of genitalia, sexual intercourse, fellatio, and masturbation" are not obscene "in light of community standards prevailing in New York City."

Exactly a century ago, in upholding an obscenity conviction called *Rosen* v. *U.S.* (no relation), Justice John Harlan announced that "every user of the mail must take notice of what is meant by decency, purity, and chastity in social life and what is deemed obscene, lewd, and lascivious." (The defendant, Lew Rosen, mailed nude pictures tantalizingly covered with "lamp black" that readers could rub off with a piece of bread.) Today, by contrast, it's absurd to expect each of the millions of speakers on the Internet to try to predict the moral sensibilities of the thousands of geographic communities that their words and pictures may enter without their knowledge or consent. The Philadelphia judges deserve credit for enumerating the ways that the Emersonian individualism of cyberspace threatens the integrity of geographic communities. But they were too quick to deny the radical implication of their own insight: traditional definitions of obscenity will have to be reconsidered as well.

A Reading for Critical Thinking

Prostitution and the Case for Decriminalization

By Laurie Shrage

Responses to prostitution from the left have been radically contradictory. Marxist thinkers, for example, are committed to study social phenomena in terms of systems of production and their related labor forms. But they rarely treat prostitution as a kind of work; instead they treat it as a side effect of the moral decay, corruption, or cultural collapse that occurs under particular social conditions. Why? Leftists generally respect working-class people and their political and economic struggles. Yet they rarely exhibit respect toward prostitute organizations or their political activists and intellectuals. For the most part, such groups and individuals are ignored.[1] Again, why?

Many on the left want to believe that prostitution would not exist or would not be common or tolerated in a world free of economic, gender, and sexual exploitation. The problem of prostitution would solve itself once other problems are solved. Yet speculative judgments like this one are abstract and academic. Prostitution isn't any single thing—a unitary social phenomenon with a particular origin—and so it doesn't make sense to argue about whether it would or wouldn't be present in this or that type of society. Working from crosscultural and historical studies, I have examined institutionalized and commodified exchanges of sexual services between women providers and their male customers in many different social contexts.[2] I conclude that there are (or have been) places and times where exchanges of sexual service between women and men are (or were) relatively free of gender and class domination. How then should leftists respond to the varieties of prostitution in the contemporary United States, where the labor practices involved are shaped by pernicious class and gender asymmetries?

I want to argue that we should include in our political agendas the dismantling of the legal and social structures that criminalize prostitution and stigmatize prostitutes. In conjunction with this project, we will need to invent regulatory alternatives to the current punitive systems of control. These are the primary aims of numerous prostitute civil rights and labor groups, and I think both feminists and socialists should support them, though not for the libertarian reasons many representatives of these groups give. Arguments for decriminalizing prostitution can be made by appealing to notions of workers' rights and the dignity of low-status work; they need not appeal to the libertarian ideal of total freedom from governmental intrusion into the lives of presumably independent individuals. These arguments can also be strengthened by accepting a robust pluralism with regard to sexual customs and practices. I don't mean that we cannot criticize sexual practices, only that the criticism must take into account different cultural conceptions of human sexuality and not dismiss out of hand those that are unfamiliar. Again, this desire to understand alien customs should not be confused with a libertarian laissez-faire morality. The libertarian sees sexual desires as a natural force that society should respect; the pluralist understands that desire, including the desire for noncommodified sex, is shaped by cultural and social forces.

Feminist theorists have argued that prostitution involves the sexual and economic subordination, degradation, and exploitation of women and girls. Many forms of prostitution are indeed brutal and

From *Dissent* (Spring 1996), pp. 41–45. Reprinted by permission of *Dissent* Magazine from Laurie Shrage. © 1996.

oppressive: the near slave conditions that have been reported recently in brothels in Thailand, the use of "comfort women" by the Japanese during the Second World War, the prostitution that exists around U.S. military bases and in many contemporary urban spaces ("streetwalking," "massage parlors," "escort services," and so on). Women and girls have been tricked, or physically and economically coerced, into the prostitution business and then kept in it against their will. Women have contracted fatal diseases; they have been beaten and raped. These are common aspects of contemporary prostitution that anyone concerned with social justice must address. But we must also ask whether the legal structures that have been set up to control and discourage prostitution—including voluntary prostitution where it exists—also oppress women. Both women who work as prostitutes and women who are suspected of doing so (usually poor women of color) are frequently harassed, manipulated, and exploited by police officers and others who have power over them. Criminalization contributes to the stigma that prostitutes bear, making them more vulnerable to hate crimes, housing and employment discrimination, and other violations of their basic rights.

Because both the operation of prostitution businesses and their legal suppression typically sacrifice women's interests, feminists generally oppose both prostitution and its criminalization. Many feminists aim to devise nonpunitive, extralegal responses, such as providing other work opportunities. Yet there has been no concerted feminist attempt to undo the laws that define acts of prostitution as criminal offenses and impose penalties on participants—more often the female vendors than the male customers. Certainly feminist groups have not given the decriminalization of prostitution the same priority they have given to other issues, such as ensuring the legality of abortion, reforming rape and sexual harassment laws, and desegregating corporate management and the professions. Moreover, feminists have been more vocal in opposing sex businesses than the laws that criminalize the activities of commercial providers, and thus have contributed to creating a climate conducive to the continued degradation of prostitutes.

Feminists have not mobilized around the decriminalization of prostitution because of our lingering ambivalence about the subject. Some question whether commodified exchanges of sexual services are ever voluntary and regard prostitutes always as manipulated victims rather than autonomous agents —a view that requires us to second guess the motives, desires, and values of all prostitutes. Other feminists argue for decriminalizing only the prostitute's work

while maintaining the criminal status of pimping, pandering, and so on. But this requires the state to determine which of the prostitute's partners are exploiting her and which are not—unless we wish to punish all the prostitute's possible business partners, including her spouse, boyfriend or girlfriend, parents and siblings, and other comrades.

Although feminists are fully aware of the varieties of abuse prostitutes suffer, many of them fear that decriminalization will lead to more prostitution and thus more exploitation of women and children. So they are willing to tolerate the often brutal enforcement of laws against it. Yet realistically, we are more likely to discourage the exploitation of women and children by regulating the labor practices followed by sex businesses. If businesses that provide customers with personal sexual services could operate legally, then they would be subject to the same labor regulations that apply to other businesses (given the nature of the work, additional regulations might be necessary).[3] Such businesses would not be allowed to treat workers like slaves, hire underage workers, deprive them of compensation for which they contracted, or expose them to unnecessary risks. The businesses could be required to enforce health and safety codes, provide workers with a minimum income and health insurance, and allow them to form collectives to negotiate for improved working conditions, compensation, and benefits.

Many feminists find it frightening to imagine a society where sex can be purchased as easily as soap, where selling sex is an occupational option like selling shoes, and where businesses that profit from commercial sex are as legitimate as Ben and Jerry's. Such imaginings usually lead to the question, "What next?" This is the slippery-slope argument, which is elaborated as follows: "Are we now going to allow the sale of x?'—where x is your favorite tabooed object (babies, vital organs, bombs, and so on). The answer to this question is "No—not unless by tolerating the commercial distribution of x we can better protect the rights of particular people or better realize some moral ideal." By tolerating the commercial distribution of sexual services within certain limits, we can better protect the rights and interests of those who seek these services and, importantly, those who choose to earn income by providing them.

Though it is useful to ask what social forces lead some people to seek the relatively *impersonal* provision of *personal* sexual services, we should be equally critical of the cultural assumptions embedded in this question and in our various answers. At best, such excursions may help us understand how prostitution is shaped by large and small capital interests, as well as dominant gender, racial, and sexual ideologies, and thus how to devise regulatory instruments that discourage the recognizable forms of abuse, exploitation, and humiliation.

The argument I am making is simply this: that the forms of exploitation and abuse suffered by prostitutes are similar to those suffered by other workers (though they are often more intense because of the illegal status of this work). Therefore these abuses should be addressed by mechanisms that improve the condition of workers generally. Sweatshop conditions should not be tolerated, violations of workers' constitutionally protected rights should not be tolerated, customers should not be permitted to engage in behaviors that endanger the workers' health or well being, care should be taken to avoid harm to noninvolved third parties, contracts for compensation and services should be voluntary and take into account the interests of all affected, and when these conditions are met such contracts should be respected (though not necessarily enforced by outside authorities). If the sex trade were regulated like other businesses, we would not have a perfect world—labor would still be underpaid and exploited and needs would still go unmet—but the world would be modestly improved.

The prostitute has often served as a symbol for the degraded status of the worker in capitalist societies, and prostitution itself has been evoked as a metaphor for the general relationship between workers and owners under capitalism. It is also used to represent other often exploitative social relationships, between husbands and wives, for example. But the metaphor works only if we assume that prostitution is universally exploitative and degrading, so that activities likened to it are cast as illegitimate. Rather than make the Marxist point that exchanges of sex or labor for money in a capitalist market are necessarily exploitative, the point of the metaphor is that the exchange of labor for money under capitalism is like the exchange of sex for money in *any* circumstances. But the assumption that all sex commerce is inherently exploitative fails to take into account the diversity of actual and possible practices. The degradation of the worker under capitalism is more like the degradation of someone who is forced to sell his/her labor—sexual or nonsexual—but it seems redundant to point this out. By insisting on the inherent and unqualified degradation of sex commerce, those who use the metaphor only add to the degradation they presumably oppose.

Prostitutes—like gays, lesbians, and other sexual dissidents—are commonly viewed as threatening to families. But those who see them in this light often have a very narrow notion of what constitutes a

family. In her book *The Comforts of Home: Prostitution in Colonial Nairobi*, Luise White describes relationships between prostitutes and their customers that might be compared to informal polyandrous unions, where a variety of physical and social needs are met—needs that more conventional families also serve.[4] In the United States and elsewhere, many prostitutes have children, partners, and parents that they support through their work. Prostitutes and those with whom they are socially intimate and interdependent, and with whom they share households, are in fact families, and they deserve the same social supports as other families. Laws that criminalize prostitution tear families apart, separate parents and children, and render sex workers and their intimate partners criminals.

All this said, some may feel that there is still something immoral or objectionable about the prostitute's work, and that we would be better off suppressing the practice and finding other livelihoods for the people involved. At least three articles appearing in academic journals and books in recent years bear the title "What's Wrong With Prostitution?" Each attempts to locate just what it is that distinguishes prostitution from other human activities, although one concludes contrary to the others that nothing is deeply wrong with waged sex work.[5] Perhaps one way to approach the intuition that there *is* something inherently wrong is to compare commercial sex to other work that is very similar to it. For example, many prostitutes like to compare themselves to sex therapists, educators, and entertainers. Annie Sprinkle likens her work to both bodily and spiritual forms of guidance and help. Either we must show that there is something wrong with these activities or we must show that the analogy between prostitution and sex therapy/education/entertainment doesn't hold. Frankly, I can't see how to show either.

One fear that many feminists have about legalizing prostitution is that this should create just one more female job ghetto where women are coerced into stereotypical and subordinate roles, and low-paying, low-status, dead-end work. Furthermore, the industry's "products" would very likely reproduce status hierarchies among people based on age, race, class, gender, physical ability, and so on. Subordinate service roles would be filled—as they already are in the illegally run sex industry—by age, class, race, and gender subordinates, and their commercial sexual availability would perpetuate myths about the inferiority of persons from the subordinated groups. These are legitimate fears, and supporters of decriminalization have to consider how such outcomes might be avoided.

One of the first things to be said is that although the overwhelming majority of customers for prostitution are male, not all prostitutes are women. It's important to notice that some prostitutes serve customers of the same gender as themselves, the same economic class, and the same socially defined racial category. Though a great deal of contemporary prostitution involves heterosexual white, bourgeois males exploiting working-class or underclass women (especially women of color), keeping prostitution illegal will not affect this situation. Instead, by developing programs and policies that address poverty, racism, and sexism, and by regulating a legal sex industry, we can hope to make those who are socially oppressed less vulnerable to exploitation from those who aren't.

Anyone who advocates the legalization of prostitution needs to address the "But would you want your daughter . . . ?" argument. I suppose the only way to answer this question/objection is to take it personally—I happen to have a daughter who is now eight. This argument is meant to expose the hypocrisy of anyone who has made the assertions I've made. For, not surprisingly, my answer is "No, I wouldn't want my daughter to be a prostitute." So how can I accept this occupation for others? Well, first of all, this isn't all of my answer. The more nuanced answer is that, although I would prefer my daughter to be a mathematician, pianist, or labor organizer, were she to seek employment in the sex trade, I would still want the best for her. Her choice would be less heartbreaking to me if the work were legal, safe, reasonably well paid, and moderately respectable. In arguing for the decriminalization of prostitution, we need not go from the extreme of deploring it to the other extreme of romanticizing it. This objection works only if these are our only alternatives.

If prostitution remains criminalized, what can we expect? In Hollywood, some prostitutes will continue to profit from the instant celebrity status that being arrested at the right time and with the right customer can bring. But the average prostitute will continue to be abused by her (or his) clients and co-workers, exposed unnecessarily to disease, socially marginalized and demonized, harassed by public officials. and separated from her children and other family members; her children will suffer from neglect and poverty. And underage workers will continue to be used, with or without their or their family's consent. Perhaps, a large and coordinated effort to decriminalize prostitution for the sake of workers and their families is one more battle we need to wage with the radical religious right.

NOTES

1. One recent notable exception to this is Shannon Bell's *Reading, Writing, and Rewriting the Prostitute Body* (Bloomington: Indiana University Press, 1994).
2. *Moral Dilemmas of Feminism: Prostitution, Adultery, and Abortion* (New York Routledge, 1994).
3. Roger Matthews proposes some general guidelines for regulating prostitution informed by radical rather than liberal principles in "Beyond Wolfenden?: Prostitution, Politics and the Law," in R. Matthews and J. Young, eds., *Confronting Crime* (London: Sage, 1986). See also my discussion of his proposals in *Moral Dilemmas of Feminism*, pp. 83–87 and 158–161.
4. Luise White, *The Comforts of Home: Prostitution in Colonial Nairobi* (Chicago: University of Chicago Press, 1990).
5. See Christine Overall, "What's Wrong With Prostitution?: Evaluating Sex Work" in *Signs* 17 (Summer 1992), pp. 705–724; Carole Pateman, "What's Wrong With Prostitution?" in *The Sexual Contract* (Stanford: Stanford University Press, 1988), pp. 189–218; and Igor Primoratz, "What's Wrong With Prostitution?" in *Philosophy* 68 (1993). pp. 159–182.

A Reading for Critical Thinking

Female Circumcision Comes to America

Performed by new immigrants, veiled in deference to a cultural tradition of the developing world, female circumcision is becoming an American problem

By Linda Burstyn

It is a late-summer night, nearly midnight in Washington, D.C., when the taxicab comes for Mimi Ramsey. She steps into it with a worried look in her eyes and her mouth firmly set. She is on her way to yet another stranger's house, where she will again — for the umpteenth time in the past year — talk about the most personal and most secret of African customs, offering herself as a sort of human roadblock in the traffic of tradition.

At the house Ramsey is kissed on both of her cheeks by her hostess, an Ethiopian immigrant like herself, and ushered into a dimly lit living room decorated with rugs and cloths from their homeland. There she spends the next several hours huddled together with the young mother, Genat, talking in conspiratorial whispers.

"Mother says she will do it anyway, herself — when I'm out of the house — if I don't agree to get it done soon." Genat confides to the woman she hopes will help her. "She says she will take a razor blade and do it." Ramsey nods. She has heard this story many times before, and responds by reciting a long list of reasons why the older woman must be stopped, trying to give Genat the courage to buck tradition and disobey her mother. "You cannot let her do this to your child. Please. It is wrong. You know how painful it is. How damaging. Your daughter may hate you for life for what you allow to happen to her."

Genat shakes her head. She doesn't want her baby girl, just born in this country, to be circumcised, as is customary in her native land, but her mother is adamant.

"She believes in it so strongly," Genat says. "She said if I don't do these things, the girl will grow up horny. She'll be like American girls. And how will I be able to go back to work if my mother is not here to care for my child?"

It is not until many hours later, after a long, sleepless night and a fruitless morning discussion with the older woman, that Ramsey, discouraged, finally ends this peculiar house call. "Please send your mother home," she advises Genat. ' Go on welfare if you have to, but don't let your mother stay in the house and do this to your baby."

To Mimi Ramsey, a forty-three-year-old nurse who lives in San Jose, California, scenes like this one are increasingly familiar. An activist in a growing movement in this country to halt the practice of female circumcision — also called female genital mutilation, or FGM —she, among others, is trying not only to persuade her compatriots to end the practice but also to persuade America to address FGM as a serious health and human-rights issue. It is not an easy task. Even though the details of some of the extreme yet common forms of the practice are as horrifying to most Americans as Nazi human experimentation or brutal child abuse, documentation is hard to come by, and resistance to infringing upon the traditions and mores of another culture is difficult to overcome.

"We don't warn [immigrant] families that we consider this child abuse," says Catherine Hogan, the founder of the Washington Metropolitan Alliance Against Ritualistic FGM. "When you wrap this issue in the cloth of culture, you just can't see what's inside.

From *The Atlantic Monthly* (October 1995), pp. 28–35. Reprinted by permission of Linda Burstyn, a freelance writer based in Washington, D.C.

This is a clear case of child abuse. It's a form of reverse racism not to protect these girls from barbarous practices that rob them for a lifetime of their God-given right to an intact body."

Americans who are aware of the practice, which has been performed on some 100 million to 130 million women and girls worldwide, assume that it is a fact of life only for girls who live in faraway places — a form of barbarism that doesn't touch American homes, schools, or doctor's offices. This is simply not true. As more and more African immigrants move to this country, bringing with them their food, practices, and traditions, perhaps hundreds more daughters of African parents are circumcised in the United States every year.

Many of the immigrant mothers who are making these decisions about their daughters know little or nothing about their own anatomy. They are told that if the clitoris is left alone, it will grow and drag on the ground; that if their daughters are left uncircumcised, they will be wild, and will crave men; that no man from their home country will marry them uncircumcised (although many African men say that they prefer uncircumcised women for sex and marriage); that circumcision aids in menstruation and childbirth (although the opposite is true in both cases); and that it is a religious — usually Islamic — requirement (although none of the major Islamic texts calls directly for FGM). And so these women and their husbands come to the United States filled with misinformation, and remain blindly dedicated to continuing this torturous tradition.

Azza, an Egyptian immigrant who moved to the United States fifteen years ago and now lives in Louisiana, plans to take her ten-year-old American-born daughter back to Egypt in a few months to have her circumcised. "They say it helps us control our emotions," she says. The thirty-three-year-old mother is confused about whether or not she wants to put her daughter through the procedure, first saying that she and her husband are not sure what they are going to do, and finally saying that it is up to him and the Egyptian doctors to decide.

Frequently families will chip in to bring someone from the homeland to the United States to perform circumcisions, because it's cheaper to import a circumciser than it is to send several girls abroad. A taxi driver in Washington, D.C., who hotly defends the practice says that he recently had his daughters circumcised that way. "I stood over her to make sure she

cut enough," he says. "I wasn't going to let my daughters have those things!"

As more and more immigrants from countries that practice FGM come to make their homes in Western countries, these countries are facing the task of confronting a custom that is rigidly adhered to and yet taboo to discuss. The United States has not given FGM the attention or the illegal status that many other nations have given it. The United Kingdom has a full-fledged and longstanding anti-FGM movement that involves the country's social-service agencies. France, Canada, Denmark, Switzerland, Sweden, and Belgium all have outlawed the practice. The first attempt to prohibit FGM here died in the previous Congress. However, the legislation has been reintroduced by its original co-sponsors, Representatives Pat Schroeder, of Colorado, and Barbara-Rose Collins, of Michigan. Senator Harry Reid has proposed similar legislation in the Senate. Three states, New York, Minnesota, and North Dakota, have passed laws making the practice of FGM a felony unless it is medically necessary.

Knowing that federal legislation to deal with FGM is far from a certainty, a growing number of people are joining the battle to stop FGM in America. They want this country to start documenting the extent of the practice here and to use the courts and social services to put an end to it — an aim they're finding it difficult to achieve at a time when so many cities are struggling with other pressing issues.

"It's a serious problem in most urban centers in the United States," Hogan says. "There just hasn't been enough empirical documentation of it. But what we see when we see it, anecdotally or empirically, is just like incest was in its time — or child abuse. It's the tip of the iceberg."

Several recent events have helped to strengthen this movement. Probably the most high-profile of these were the publication of Alice Walker's novel on the subject, *Possessing the Secret of Joy*, and the production of Walker's documentary film, *Warrior Marks*, which was shown in cities throughout the United States. Also significant was the well-publicized court case of a Nigerian woman living in Oregon who won asylum in this country by pleading that her daughters would be in grave danger of being forcibly circumcised if they were sent back to their homeland.

Women's-rights groups such as Population Action International, Equality Now, RAINBOW, the Washington Metropolitan Alliance Against Ritualistic FGM,

Frequently families will chip in to bring someone from the homeland to the United States to perform circumcisions, because it's cheaper than sending several girls abroad.

and the Program for Appropriate Technology and Health (PATH) and other groups form a loose information-and-activist network on FGM. More important, immigrant women who were circumcised as children have joined forces to fight the tradition among compatriots in this country.

Soraya Mire, a thirty-four-year-old Somali film maker who lives in Los Angeles, has been touring the country with her film *Fire Eyes*, which shows African children being circumcised. Asha Mohamud, a Somali who has worked as a pediatrician and who lives in Alexandria, Virginia, now directs several FGM projects in Kenya and the United States for PATH. Mimi Ramsey has made it her avocation to visit African businesses and communities in this country and proselytize against FGM.

Ramsey typifies many who, after hearing about FGM in the media, have finally been able to talk about an experience long suppressed. For years, she had gone to doctors for help with the aftereffects of her radical circumcision. For years doctors, either because they were stunned by what they saw or because they were trying to be culturally sensitive, said nothing to Ramsey about what had been done to her and simply prescribed various topical creams and jellies to ease her pain. But in February of last year all that changed.

"I went to a doctor for the problem I have down there." Ramsey says. "He asked me, 'Why did they do this to you? Why did they remove all your genitalia?' He was in shock." After returning to her apartment, depressed and confused, Ramsey, a devout Christian, prayed for some answers. Later that night she saw a television program about FGM and the Nigerian woman's asylum case in Oregon. It answered many of her questions. "I was angry and still am. The morning after the show I got up and called all the African women from my address book who live in the United States. I asked them, 'Are you a victim too?' And they said yes. I said, 'Let's talk about it. I'm not going to shut up anymore.'"

Most of the talk about circumcision in this country has focused on male circumcision, as people have made the case that it causes physical and psychological pain to infant boys. When it comes to women, "circumcision" is at best a misnomer.

"Cutting off the clitoris is equivalent to cutting off much of the penis," Asha Mohamud says.

This is why opponents and medical leaders use the more descriptive and more accurate term "female genital mutilation." Although in a tiny percentage of cases FGM consists of a small cut to the hood of the clitoris, typically it is much more severe. It usually involves the complete removal of the clitoris, and often the removal of some of the inner and outer labia. In its most extreme form — infibulation— almost all the external genitalia are cut away, the remaining flesh from the outer labia is sewn together, or infibulated, and the girl's legs are bound from ankle to waist for several weeks while scar tissue closes up the vagina almost completely. A small hole, typically about the diameter of a pencil, is left for urination and menstruation. The cutting is usually done with a razor, a kitchen knife, or a pair of scissors. It is rare for any anesthesia to be used. The age at which FGM is performed varies among countries and communities. In some countries it is done on infants in the days or weeks after birth; in others, such as Senegal, it is part of an elaborate rite of passage that comes with puberty. In parts of Nigeria and Burkina Faso, FGM is practiced during the seventh month of a woman's first pregnancy, in the belief that if the baby at birth comes in contact with its mother's clitoris, it will die.

There is no doubt within the medical community that FGM is a brutal, harmful practice. A World Health Organization report on FGM says,

> The immediate physical effects — acute infection, tetanus, bleeding of adjacent organs, shock resulting from violent pain, and hemorrhage — can even cause death. In fact, many such deaths have occurred and continue to occur as a result of this traditional practice. The lifelong physical and psychological debilities resulting from female genital mutilations are manifold: chronic pelvic infections, keloids, vulval abscesses, sterility, incontinence, depression, anxiety and even psychosis, sexual dysfunction and marital disharmony, and obstetric complications with risk to both the infant or fetus and the mother.

The American and British medical professions have in the past practiced FGM to varying degrees. There are reports of clitoridectomies having been performed as recently as the 1950s, to cure nymphomania and melancholia in girls. In the nineteenth century both clitoridectomies and female castration (removal of the ovaries) were practiced by British and American physicians, as cures for melancholia, masturbation, nymphomania, hysteria, lesbianism, and epilepsy. The American medical profession stopped performing clitoridectomies decades ago, only to find itself today confronting the practice in patients from cultures that perform FGM.

The United States is at best ambivalent about its responsibility in preventing and punishing female circumcision. In fact, there is almost no legal protection against it.

It is far easier to convince Americans of the horrors of FGM than it is to persuade them that it is enough of a problem here to warrant action. Proving just how widespread the practice is in the United States is a critical step. The legislation proposed in both the House and the Senate calls for the Department of Health and Human Services to gather data on the number of females living in the United States who have been subjected to FGM. However, the current lack of such data means that opponents can only point to anecdotal evidence to estimate the extent of FGM.

"I think some people leave some traditions behind, but some traditions are stronger than others." Mohamud says. "This is one that is very strong. The community here sees explicit sex on television, they hear a lot of alien things, and so it becomes more urgent for mothers to do this to their daughters so the girls don't fall into loose groups. They think if they don't follow the tradition, they don't know what will happen."

It is estimated that at least 7,000 women and girls immigrate to the United States each year from countries where at least a majority of females, if not all of them, are circumcised. Most of these new immigrants live in California, New York, and the Washington, D.C., area. It is difficult to determine the true circumcision rates in their home countries, because in most the practice is not discussed publicly. Nevertheless, rough estimates of what is common in each country suggest that almost half the women of Africa have been circumcised. The rate of FGM in Somalia is nearly 100 percent, in Ethiopia over 90 percent, in Egypt 50 percent. The list of places where it is traditionally practiced includes twenty-six countries in Africa and various areas of the Middle East, Asia, and South America. Even if only a small percentage of newly arrived families from these countries maintain the tradition of FGM, these figures suggest that hundreds of young girls either brought here or born here are in danger each year.

Mimi Ramsey spent part of the past year trying to track down circumcisers rumored to be living in this country. But not all families depend on finding a circumciser. Last September, Ramsey heard about a man in San Jose who had just circumcised his daughter over the objections of his wife. He had waited until his wife left the house and then locked his three-year-old in the bedroom with him and performed the FGM. 'He said that she was too wild." Ramsey says. She liked to play outside too much. She had friends who were boys. He said this will tame her."

If a native-born American father had mutilated his daughter, the action would incontrovertibly constitute child abuse. But this country is at best ambivalent about its role and responsibility in preventing and punishing FGM. In fact, other than in the three states previously mentioned, there is almost no legal protection against FGM for girls in the United States, both because it's difficult to uncover and because, absent a specific law against the practice, courts are unsure about how to punish it. One effort at prosecuting a woman in Georgia who cut off her niece's clitoris failed in part because of the legal confusion surrounding the problem.

Legislating these issues is going to be really crucial." says Leah Sears, a justice on the Supreme Court of Georgia who has been doing research on FGM and legal questions pertaining to it. "Legal issues concerning FGM are complex. Can an adult woman do this to herself? We American women consent to have our breasts enlarged, which is another bizarre thing women do for the pleasure of men. Is that so different? I think we need comprehensive legislation in this area."

In England and Canada — places where people from FGM-practicing countries have immigrated — laws against FGM and against taking a child out of the country to circumcise her have been passed. France has also made FGM illegal, and in 1993 it sentenced a Gambian woman to five years in prison after she paid $70.00 to have her two daughters circumcised. The medical associations in most of the Canadian provinces have passed prohibitions with strict penalties against circumcision and reinfibulation (sewing the vagina nearly shut again after childbirth). They have also begun educational efforts in those communities where FGM is most likely, preferring to discourage the practice rather than punish a parent after a girl has been circumcised. Unlike the United States, these countries take it for granted that FGM is occurring. Even though most U.S. legal experts interpret child-abuse laws broadly to cover FGM, very few preventive measures, such as education and community outreach, have been implemented in this country.

In this legal vacuum doctors and others who provide social services that could educate and inform communities about FGM and protect uncircumcised girls are caught in the ethical bind of trying to show respect for another culture and at the same time guide people away from a harmful practice that is very much a part of that culture. For instance, in response to growing concern about FGM, the American College of Obstetricians and Gynecologist released a statement opposing all medically unnecessary surgical modification of female genitalia (although doctors here continue to perform cosmetic reduction surgery on both the clitoris and the labia), and declared that

FGM should be stopped; but its guidelines end there. Some hospitals and doctors continue to reinfibulate women and to say nothing against parents' plans to circumcise their daughters. An article published in 1993 in the *American Journal of Obstetrics and Gynecology* clinically details one obstetrician's efforts to deliver a child vaginally from an infibulated woman. The article, written as a guide for dealing with such a situation, ends with a recommendation on how to perform reinfibulation and concludes, "The issue of whether the woman will want her own infant daughter circumcised also needs to be discussed so that she can make an individual, culturally appropriate and educated choice."

"My patients say doctors are often shocked when they see them, and don't know how to help them," says Carol Horowitz, an internist who cares for East African immigrants in Seattle. "I try to deal with them with respect and dignity and try to help them with their problems, surgically or nonsurgically.' Horowitz says that she is mindful of the risk of offending her patients when she educates them about the harmful aspects of what was done to them or counsels them against circumcising their children — and that some doctors with whom she has worked will not broach the subject at all. "To many patients, a circumcised vagina is normal. Any change is going to have to come from within that community."

Teachers, nurses, and administrators in elementary schools located in areas with many African students are often ill equipped to detect and help a child at risk for mutilation, or to help a child following this potentially traumatizing experience. "There was a time I got a call from someone in northern Virginia," Asha Mohamud says. "They heard of a girl in a school who was at risk. The teacher was teaching about sex education, and the young girl pointed out the clitoris and said, 'That part is really bad, and my mother is taking me back in the summer to have that cut out.'" Mohamud tried to find the girl, but by the time the story had reached her, it was too late. The girl had already graduated and returned from her trip to Africa.

"If that family-life teacher was aware she could have done something immediately," Mohamud says. "It's something also that made the issue more urgent to us. Things are happening here right under our own noses. Girls are probably being taken back right now."

A desire to educate both the officials in her adopted country and immigrants from her native one drives Mimi Ramsey. The New York–based international women's-rights group Equality Now is raising money to fund Ramsey's efforts so that she will be able to spend more time doing what she does best: taking her message to the streets.

In a dark restaurant in Los Angeles paper placemats are decorated with maps of Ethiopia. Shiny red-vinyl booths are filled with brightly dressed residents of the local immigrant community. Original Ethiopian artwork and African posters cover the walls. The smell of cooked meat and the sound of quiet laughter surround the booth where Ramsey sits, with her just served lunch. Her own conservative dress is more likely to be found in Orange County than in Addis Ababa. She bows her head and prays aloud: "Please, God, save girls from being tortured. Please. God. Please. Thank you."

Just minutes after she begins her meal of traditional Ethiopian bread dipped in a stew of vegetables and meat, she gets up and approaches a table of four Ethiopian men. She exchanges pleasantries in their native language, Amharic, but quickly the conversation turns tense. A few English words are mixed with the foreign ones. A man says, Tradition." Ramsey replies, "Let's talk about it." and squeezes in next to the men.

"In this country you see a lot of young women unmarried, pregnant." Yashanu, an Ethiopian taxi driver in his mid-forties, says, leaning back in his chair. "Maybe if American girls were circumcised, this wouldn't happen. When I was growing up, a girl had to stay within the family. She could be home no later than five or six in the afternoon. But in this country there are no rules." He shakes his head. "When you circumcise a woman, they're less active sexually and more interested in their schoolwork."

Mimi describes the physical pain, the burning and irritation, she still feels from what was done to her when she was six years old. She takes a small tube of cream from her purse and shows it to them. The cream is supposed to soothe her damaged nerve endings. "I can't enjoy sex," she tells them. "I feel nothing. I will never forgive my mother for doing this to me. Will you join me in stopping people from doing this to little girls? We have to help them," she says, smiling, touching one of the young men on his arm.

By the time Mimi stands up, thirty minutes later, the three younger men, all of whom knew vaguely about FGM because they had had sex with women who were circumcised, are horrified. They each promise earnestly to call their families back in Ethiopia to talk with them about the practice. But the older man remains unconvinced.

Across the street, at another African-owned restaurant, Ramsey speaks to a table of very modern-looking young women. One of them, a beautiful twenty-five-year-old in jeans who works for a Hollywood studio, pulls Ramsey aside and hands her a piece of paper. On it is the name of one of her close friends, a Los Angeles resident, who is planning to take her baby daughter back to Ethiopia for a circumcision in a week's time.

In her own community Ramsey patrols the African shops and restaurants like a diligent security guard. Her golden-brown face lights up whenever she sees a person she recognizes as a fellow Ethiopian, and she immediately engages in traditional greetings before turning the subject to that which is taboo.

Was this done to you?" she asks the women. "It was done to me. I'm trying to stop this practice. Will you join me?" These encounters, usually the first time these women have ever discussed the issue, often end with tears, an embrace, and an exchange of phone numbers.

Beletu, a thirty-five-year-old Ethiopian immigrant, lives with her husband and their three daughters just outside Washington, D.C., in Maryland. She has had all three of her daughters circumcised — the youngest, two and a half, just last summer, durring a short trip back to Ethiopia. "People practice without knowing," Beletu says regretfully, now that she has learned about the harmful aspects of the procedure. "Even though I lived here years, I didn't know. Nobody told me. I wouldn't have put my daughters in this situation if I had known." Five months pregnant with another girl, she vows to leave this one uncircumcised.

"My mother told me it's protection for us — from boys," says Azza, the Egyptian immigrant in Louisiana. "It's very bad pain. I don't want my daughter to have it, but it depends on what the doctor tells us." When told that information exists about the medical effects of the procedure, she begs for it to be sent to her. "The more education the better," she says. "It's done from generation to generation by word of mouth. But why is it done?" I'm confused about it."

Soraya Mire, the Somali film maker, is one of a handful of women trying to find the finances and forums to educate an immigrant population that views FGM as a comforting tie to the morality and traditions of its homeland. She uses screenings of her documentary as opportunities to discuss the issue. Like others, Mire is motivated by her own experience as a mutilated woman.

They use vegetable thorns to sew because they are very strong," Mire says, describing the process of infibulation that she experienced. "The stitches stay in until marriage. Then three days before the wedding they ask the groom. Do you want to open her or do you want us to open her? A good man will say, You go ahead and do it. Others want to tear the woman open themselves.

"I get calls from people within the community asking me if I know someone who will circumcise their children. I of course say no, and try to talk them out of doing it. I got a call last year from a man in L.A. who said he had just performed a circumcision on a girl. He said, 'She had a problem with her clitoris and I corrected it. There's nothing you can do to stop it.'"

Last year Mire went into hiding after receiving death threats from Somalis who were angry about what they saw as her traitorous behavior. She is now cautious when she's out in public and is reluctant to divulge the whereabouts of her secluded Los Angeles-area home.

At the Raleigh Studios, in Los Angeles, she shows her film to an audience of thirty-two people. The viewers cringe as they watch. A young girl is shown being held down. The circumciser reaches for a razor blade. The audience recoils. Mimi Ramsey is part of that audience. She drops her head to her lap and sobs.

After the film is over, Ramsey is asked to speak. She walks to the front of the stage but is still overcome. She simply cries and gasps, unable to talk for several minutes. The theater is perfectly silent except for her crying. Finally she speaks.

"I was struggling and calling my mother," Ramsey says in a hushed and breathless voice, trying not to break down again. "Little did I know that my mother had set me up. She paid for it to be done to me. This is something we all have to struggle with. While we're watching this, more little girls are being cut. My best friend was cut. She was my friend. My buddy. They did her the same day they did me, only she bled to death. What I'm doing now, I'm doing for her. I'm doing it for my buddy. She died for no reason. Please, let's fight it together. Please. Please."

Ramsey is still shaking an hour after the screening. "I need to go home, to face my mother. I need her to say she's sorry. Then I want her to go through Ethiopia with me, talking to women — talking them out of doing this to their daughters. She needs to go ahead of me. I will stand back and let her take the lead. It's only through this that I will forgive her."

Back home in San Jose, sometime later, Ramsey hears again from Genat, in Washington. Genat has sent her mother back to Ethiopia. She happily reports that her daughter is safe. Crying, Ramsey thanks her, returns the phone to its cradle, and bows her head in prayer.

A Reading for Critical Thinking

Sexuality and Television Advertising: An Historical Perspective

Judy Kuriansky, Ph.D.

Click. A group of women taking a "Diet Coke break" gather to eye a bare-chested construction worker hunk.

Click again. A chimp chooses two female chimps and two Little Caesar's pizzas.

Click again. A young man hijacks his older female boss for a joyride in a Volkswagen Passat.

It's voyeurism, favorite fantasies, and beefcake—all using sex to sell: an appeal that started with the advent of television itself and continues today despite current conservatism and the fear of sexually transmitted diseases (STDs).

And it is not surprising. Sexual themes grab attention and increase ratings—from news to soap operas, from tabloids to dramas.

Beer is one category that led the way for using sexual themes to sell. A black-and-white spot in the 1950s showed a tired husband growing perky after drinking a Pabst beer, chasing his wife around the room, and disrobing. Color television ushered in many more scenes of booze-inspired partying with barely clothed women. Car spots also pioneered the sexy sell, with models like Catherine Deneuve and Farrah Fawcett draped over the hood or stroking the wheel and seat suggestively.

All-too-hot spots reached an all-time high in 1980 when then-15-year-old Brooke Shields panted that nothing came between her and her Calvins. Though some versions of the ad were banned from television, and the ad agency eventually resigned as a result of protests, jeans sales doubled and Klein's company growth skyrocketed from that point on.[1] Madison

" . . . to keep people from going to the refrigerator, you have to astound them. And sex does."

Avenue was sold on shock appeal and provocative poses.

The sexy sells also sparked outrage from consumer, religious, and special interest groups who complained to networks and advertisers about declining morality and children's exposure to sexual topics.[2] The controversy hit the courts when a group of female employees sued Stroh's brewery for sexual harassment and named the company's "Swedish Bikini Team" campaign (featuring buxom, blond, bikini-clad women) as contributing to a "hostile work environment." The spots were pulled, the "Bikini Team" was retired, and the case was settled for an undisclosed amount, although the judge ruled that the ad was not admissible evidence.[3]

Just last year, the Federal Bureau of Investigation (FBI) investigated a new Calvin Klein advertisement featuring an underage teen stripping for a photographer. Civil liberties lawyers argued that the situation did not constitute child sexual abuse. Meanwhile, the jeans once again flew off the racks to prove to advertisers that such controversy pays off.[4] The ploy also worked recently for Candies hiking boots. A furor erupted over the censorship of scenes of a nude couple straddling a chair, and the company received more free exposure than paid air time.[5]

Benetton is one company that distinctively eschews both censorship and commercialism, with photographer Oliviero Toscani's controversial and confrontational images of 56 penises, a hermaphrodite, and a person dying from AIDS.[6]

From *SIECUS Report* (Sexuality Information and Education Council of the United States) (June/July 1996), pp. 13.

What is acceptable on American television is often tame compared to other parts of the world where full frontal nudity sells everything from shock absorbers to sardines. In a Danish television spot, a newspaper is draped over a man's erect penis as he spies on ladies in the neighboring steam room. Skin is "in" in Brazil where one spot shows a woman wearing a wristwatch and nothing else. France's successful Perrier bottled water campaign (banned in the United States) shows a woman's hand suggestively caressing a bottle of the spring water as it uncorks and bursts.

Cloaking sexuality in romance is one way out of controversy. The Taster's Choice soap opera-like spots follow a handsome neighbor invited in for coffee, and whatever else. Humor also relieves the anxiety of sexual suggestion. In another ad, Annie Potts (of *Designing Women* fame) is lifted into a hunk's arms while extolling the virtues of large popcorn kernels.

Television advertising frequently results in confrontations among creative, social, and religious forces. But sex will always sell. As Candies' Chief Executive Officer Neil Cole says, "In 30 to 60 seconds, to keep people from going to the refrigerator, you have to astound them. And sex does."[7]

REFERENCES

1. "The Bum's Rush in Advertising: Some Turn-On Commercials Appear to Be Turn-Offs.' *Time Magazine,* December 1, 1980, p. 95.
2. Ibid.
3. Personal communication, 1993.
4. "Dateline," NBC-TV News, September 12, 1995.
5. "On Candies Hiking Boots," *Adweek,* June 21, 1993, p. 34.
6. Lecture at the New School for Social Research, New York, NY by Oliviero Toscani, November 14, 1995.
7. N. Cole, personal communication, 1995.

A Reading for Critical Thinking

Why Is Date Rape So Hard To Prove?

By Sheila Weller

With acquaintance rape cases now a TV spectator sport, lots of women I know are having some variation of this black-humored fantasy: You're on the witness stand, watching an expensively suited defense attorney pace around as he spits out accusations: What about those one-night stands six years ago? Your taste for double margaritas? Is it true that you met this man at a nightclub? And weren't you wearing a lace camisole under your blouse? That's the last straw. You stand up, rip the fuzzy blue dot off your face and say, "I give up! Let the bastard walk. It's not worth this trying to convict him."

After the past year's parade of well-publicized rape cases, such fantasy seems all too black and none too humorous. First there was the William Kennedy Smith case, during which the New York Times implied that rape complainant Patricia Bowman's speeding tickets bolstered a schoolmate's claim of her "little wild streak." More recently, when a young Manhattan architect accused three New York Mets of rape, her ex-boyfriend, Mets pitcher David Cone, reportedly told her that no one would believe her and her reputation would be ruined. He turned out to be right on both scores. The *New York Post* trumpeted the headline: "Mets accuser was 'No Vestal Virgin.'" And in early April, the Florida state attorney, pointing to a lack of physical evidence, decided to drop the case. The message to women has been clear: Many of us would not make believable accusers.

Not that a woman who says she's been raped shouldn't be scrutinized. After all, what about the reputation of the accused? There's no getting around the fact that acquaintance rape is a crime in which the victim and the sole eyewitness are often one and the

same. Both sides admit they had intercourse. The only issue is consent. When it's her word against his, it's only fair that her credibility and ulterior motives be questioned.

But that doesn't mean the woman is the one who should go on trial. All too often the legitimate question "Did this woman consent to intercourse?" leaps dangerously to "Was she leading him on?" In another recent case, a group of young men from prominent Tampa families admitted to drugging a woman and then raping her. The defense argued that by willingly accompanying the men after a night of drinking, she invited the ensuing events. The men were acquitted.

No wonder so few women actually report being raped. A new study by the National Victim Center estimates that one in eight women in the United States has been raped, in most cases by someone she knew, but that only about 16 percent of the rapes were reported. Of those cases that are reported, the majority are dropped by the prosecutor, according to Gary LaFree, a sociologist at the University of New Mexico and author of *Rape and Criminal Justice*. Only the rare resilient case, roughly one to 5 percent of all rapes, actually reaches the courtroom.

The road into and out of that court room can be so treacherous that even some rape counselors question whether it's worth it. "When I first started working here," says Colleen Leyrer of the Washington, D.C., Rape Crisis Center, "I was uncomfortable not encouraging a woman to prosecute. Now, after seeing victims go through a second trauma as a result of prosecuting, I urge the woman to decide for herself."

It's a tough decision — one that a woman should make with both eyes open. "If it's likely the case will end in acquittal, and if the woman's wavering, then I

From *Health* (July/August 1992), pp. 62–64. By Sheila Weller, reprinted with permission from *Health*. © 1992.

probably wouldn't recommend prosecution," says Andrea Parrot, a rape expert and psychologist at Cornell University.

But how does a woman know whether her case is likely to end in acquittal? How can she know if it will even make it to the courtroom? The people who deal with acquaintance rape cases daily — prosecutors, judges, defense attorneys — know firsthand why so few of them end in conviction. Here's what they say makes acquaintance rape so hard to prove.

Unless the woman is a girl scout or virgin, the jury will give more weight to her character than to the evidence.

Even the Mike Tyson conviction seemed to confirm this theory: Wasn't Desiree Washington a naive, churchgoing teenager? "A woman who has a good reputation, does not dress suggestively, has a nine-to-five job, and goes home after work will be looked on more favorably by a jury," says Brooks Leach, sex crimes prosecutor in Columbia, Alabama.

In a study of 880 rape cases, sociologist Gary LaFree found that a complainant's "questionable" character was the best predictor of a defendant's acquittal. "We found that juries were most swayed by things like whether she had been drinking or even if she had birth control pills in her pocket," says LaFree. Juries find it more important that a woman frequents bars than that the man had a gun; more important that she had sex outside of marriage than that she was physically injured in the rape; more important that she was a "party girl" than that her clothes were torn that evening.

But you don't have to be a wanton woman for your morality to be suspect. Anyone who's had multiple sexual partners or an abortion is vulnerable. Even though 40 states now have "rape shield" laws making details of an accuser's past sexual life inadmissible in trials, such legislation is hardly foolproof. "There's an insidious way to get around the law," says sociologist Susan Caringella-McDonald. "Defense attorneys question the woman about her past sexual activity; the prosecutor objects; the judge sustains the objection — but the jury's already heard it so the damage is done."

Many well-off defendants hire private investigators to scout for information on accusers that can either be "leaked" at the trial or used to derail a case before it reaches the courtroom. "We'll do a surveillance of a rape complainant to find out: Does she go to parties and bars? Leave with somebody? Come home drunk?" says attorney Marshall Stern of Bangor, Maine. "You can't use these findings on the stand, but it's a bargaining tool with the prosecutor. If

you say, 'See, she smoked dope here . . . ,' he may not think he has the winning case he once had."

Even a woman who's been sexually abused in the past might be considered less credible if that comes out in court, says Nancy Hollander, president of the National Association of Criminal Defense Attorneys: "If she has a history of abuse, we can use it to suggest that it's left her misunderstanding signals and thinking she was raped when she wasn't."

The more romantic contact the woman had with the man, the tougher her case is to win. "You can almost diagram it," says Nancy Diehl, assistant prosecuting attorney for Detroit's Wayne County. "Fair to good is: The woman was in her or his house with him voluntarily, but she didn't have a previous relationship with him, it wasn't late at night, and she didn't kiss him. The more of those conditions that change from negative to positive, the harder it gets to win the case."

Patricia Bowman's case, for instance, was crippled by the lateness and the kissing. "When a woman has been acting in a way that juries see as encouraging a sexual encounter, they tend to say, 'Lady, you can't act like that and then change your mind,'" says Rock Harmon, deputy district attorney in Oakland, California. One of the most outrageous examples of this kind of bias occurred in the Tampa case. A defendant (later acquitted) explained at the trial that the complainant used profanity, smoked cigarettes, and dressed in green stretch pants: "She was not commanding as much respect from the guys as we would normally give other, more ladylike females."

Women jurors can often be hardest on women, perhaps because they want to deny that they too could be victims. Larry Donoghue, head of one of the sex crimes units of the Los Angeles district attorney's office, finds that female jurors are especially biased against assertive, ambitious women. Men are often surprisingly empathetic. "Fathers and grandfathers

Juries don't have much sympathy for a woman who was a willing participant up to the time of the alleged rape.

seem to take a protective attitude toward the victim," says Des Moines–based trial consultant Hale Starr. "But religious home makers are the worst jurors for the victim. Their attitude is, 'I would never have gone to that room with that man . . .' They're unforgiving."

Still, there are some surprising exceptions. In a recent Detroit case, jurors convicted a man for the rape of a topless go-go dancer who had accepted a ride from him, changed into her street clothes in the back of his van, and driven with him in search of cocaine. Nancy Diehl says an eyewitness's testimony and strong physical evidence pushed the jurors past the tendency to believe that the woman "got what she deserved."

Rarely are there broken bones with acquaintance rape, but that doesn't mean there's no physical evidence. Even if a woman is uncertain whether she wants to pursue a complaint, she should go immediately to a doctor's office or the hospital for an examination. Forcible as opposed to consensual sex is often medically verifiable, even in long-sexually-active

Unless there's physical evidence, it's her word against his.

women. "When a woman is having consensual sex with a man, she needs to do what is referred to as a 'pelvic tilt' to accommodate his penis," says D.A. Donoghue. "In forcible sex, the last thing that she wants is to accommodate him. His force can lead to anything from reddening to bruises to lacerations. If it's just reddening, you've got to identify it fast, or it fades. It's not perfect evidence, but it can make the difference between winning and losing."

Immediate report of the assault also makes a rape victim appear more genuine. "Juries look for an immediate outcry. They want to see that she wasted no time telling the authorities," says Barry Levin, a defense attorney in the St. John's College case in which seven men were charged with gang-raping a black woman student. Levin, who plea-bargained his client down from a felony to a misdemeanor, says he got his biggest boost from the complainant, who waited a month before reporting the rape. The same holds true for the woman who accused the three Mets players a year after the rape. The prosecutor said her long delay and the resulting lack of physical evidence meant she didn't have a case.

"If you delay, the defense is going to say, 'See? She made it up to get back at the guy,' and the jury will believe it," says D.A. Nancy Diehl. "My advice always is: Report first, then decide. If you choose not to pursue the complaint, you can always back out of it."

The accuser should be calm but not robotic, testifying with feeling but not appearing overly emotional. Despite the harrowing experience she's endured, a victim who cries may be viewed as unstable. A calm but concerned woman, able to summon up the trauma without relapsing into it — like Desiree Washington — appeals more to juries.

Believability is crippled when the accuser tells a story that contains even a few loose threads, which defense attorneys use to unravel her entire story. Many prosecutors say that this is what most damaged Patricia Bowman's case: Her story was inconsistent and prosecutor Moira Lasch did her no favor by

letting those inconsistencies reach the court room. "I did not find Bowman's story credible, and Lasch did not confront this before trial," says Karvn Sinunu, head of the sexual assault division of the Santa Clara County, California, district attorney's office. "I listened to Bowman say that she kissed him 'but it wasn't sexual' and I thought, You can kiss a husband of twenty years good-bye in the morning and it isn't sexual, but you don't kiss someone you've just met and it isn't sexual.' When you try to make your story sound better, the jury ends up seeing through it."

Even when a prosecutor catches all evasions well before the trial, they can come back to haunt the complainant and end up destroying her case. D.A. Donoghue tried a case in which a very credible woman had initially told police she was forced into the rapist's car: "She was too embarrassed to admit she had misjudged the man's moves when he offered her a ride home and had gotten into the car voluntarily." Though she corrected her story by trial time, the original falsification was bandied about by the defense attorney: If she had lied about that, then she could have lied about the whole thing. The defendant walked.

A skilled prosecutor plays devil's advocate early on, gently pushing the woman past her urge to apply face-saving spin control to her memory of the ordeal. "The woman needs to convince me that she was raped," says D.A. Nancy Diehl. "I say, 'Look, I need the whole truth. No matter how bad you think it looks, if you tell me, I'll be able to explain it to the jury.'"

Emotional or conflicting testimony can destroy a woman's credibility.

These days, with Desiree Washington's success as inspiration, prosecutors say more women are deciding to press charges on a crime that has mostly been endured in silence and shame. But individual women can't be expected to live their day-in-and-day-out lives as political symbols, or as statistics in a war against apathy. In the end, the decision to pursue prosecution is deeply personal. "Victims and psychiatrists tell me it's therapeutic to prosecute," says Donoghue. Wanda Jones, who became a victims' service officer in Birmingham, Alabama, after she was raped by seven men, says the experience of seeing her rapists brought to justice was empowering. Says sociologist Andrea Parrot: "Some women, even understanding the likelihood of the man's acquittal, need to go through with prosecution to feel whole and vindicated. In those cases, I'd say go ahead."

Sheila Weller is the author of Marrying the Hangman, *recently published by Random House.*

Are You Ready for Virtual Love?

... a psychiatrist looks at cybersex

By Avodah Offit, M.D.

Jane, a twenty-eight-year-old dress designer, sits at her computer in Chicago and communicates with her friend Peter, a book illustrator in New York. They make contact two or three times a day and tell each other everything. Jane asks for advice about a fight she had with her mother; Peter describes a recently developed allergy to his leather watchband and asks for sympathy because soon he may not be able to wear leather shoes. They share an interest in skiing, in impressionist art, and in mystery stories. They compare recipes for Indian food.

Jane and Peter have a warm and close relationship, a love that travels in the virtual reality between their computers, a virtual love. Their degree of intimacy would not be unusual if they were old college friends, lovers, or longtime office buddies. But the two of them have never looked into each other's eyes, never laughed together, never even seen each other. Not only have they never met, but they see no reason to. They give each other all the love and support they need strictly on E-mail.

For many of us, the new world of electronic mail seems to come out of an episode in Star Trek. But to more than twelve million communicators in America and tens of millions more all over the planet, the future is now. From friendship to dating, from courtship to marriage, some people's lives channel almost entirely through computers.

How does E-mail work? Anyone can avail herself of it by paying a fee to a company like America Online or Compuserve. All you need is a modem to turn your computer into a telephone that transmits images instead of sound. Then you type a message onto your computer screen and send it instantaneously to the address of someone who reads it on his screen whenever he chooses. You can write to one person with reasonable confidentiality (though E-mail privacy laws are currently hazy), to a group, or to an even broader audience if you connect to the Internet. Most companies have their own groups, like private clubs. Certain groups specifically discuss love, sex, romance, and erotica.

Much may be said in praise of E-mail as Cupid, E-mail as Eros, E-mail as simple sexual stimulant. But how do I, a practicing psychiatrist and sex therapist, view this phenomenon? Is it psychologically healthy or some disease of technology? How is it that people can fall in love via machine, often without ever seeing each other? Should we take precautions before jumping into cyberspace? What are the benefits, and what are the quandaries and hazards to reckon with? Is the world headed for international pornography on the electronic network? Or could we be trending toward an intergalactic love-in?

Certainly, romance seems to blossom like jimsonweed in the vast and virtual plains of cyberspace, that intangible ether between one computer and another. It flowers for thousands of strangers and for people who write to me to tell me their stories as more and more lovers are finding their mental mates on E-mail.

From the Heart Corporation/Walraven/*Cosmopolitan* (January 1995), pp. 154–157. Reprinted by permission of Avodah Offit, M.D. © 1995. Dr. Offit, a psychiatrist in private practice in New York City, is the author of *Virtual Love, a Novel* and *Night Thoughts: Reflections of a Sex Therapist* published by Jason Aronson, Inc.

A young woman, marrying a man she met online, recently wrote to me that wherever she'd go in cyberspace, she would find him "across a crowded screen." Whether in a group discussing language, nature, photography, or—their final common interest—frogs, he'd be there with her. Another couple—one I've read about—had a mutual interest in E-mail itself, a consuming passion. They were married in an online ceremony.

As a psychiatrist, I think these attempts at sensible affiliation are brave and adventurous. The new connections encourage a life of the spirit to become a life of the heart. Before monogamy and commitment, however, perhaps E-mail most obviously invites people to flirt—and to do it in the safety of the home. Which is why E-mail has been said to be the most fun people can have with their pants on.

Cyberspace also allows a wide selection of "lovers"—or people with whom one is more intimate than simply friendly. There are no rules or contracts about fidelity, no embarrassing moments. You can have as many virtual lovers as you want, with no particular ethical consequences. On the other hand, the E-mail devotee may become addicted to the thrill of many "affairs" or suffer unrequited love. Invasion of privacy, frauds by people who assume multiple identities, jealousy, harassment and victimization, obscenity and sexual pathology are all out there in cyberspace— even as they are elsewhere. But perhaps the most intriguing danger of E-mail is its ability to foster relationships that are like the patient-to-therapist connection, with one person developing exaggerated erotic dependence on another. Women (and men too) often "fall in love" with their psychiatrists, people who they imagine will forever take care of them emotionally, physically, and financially. This same transference may occur on E-mail if the distant correspondent comes to be perceived as an imaginary parent or caretaker.

Recently, a patient spoke to me of "losing her mind" to a man on the other end of her computer connection. Intensely in love with a person whom she knew only as Polestar, this woman wrote to him two to five times a day—every time she had a moment of loneliness, an erotic feeling, or a sexual urge. She told him not only of how she wanted to be together with him, having dinner, going to the movies, taking a walk, but also of all the sexual activities she dreamed of—the kissing, caressing, and heated passion in the hotel room where she fantasized they would one day meet.

He became her mental companion, someone who was with her in her imagination at all times, because she could communicate with him whenever she wanted, without really disturbing him. She told him

all about her life too—her childhood, her hopes and how they were dashed or fulfilled. He became the ultimate obsession.

Then, unpredictably—and unhappily—the man simply stopped writing, stopped answering, stopped encouraging her fantasies. Deprived of her daily correspondence, she became depressed, anxious, fearful, and empty. Suicide crossed her mind. She was becoming paranoid too, worrying that in some obscure way, her E-mail lover would use everything she had written against her. He knew all about her; she had withheld nothing. She began to regret what she had revealed, constructing scenarios of how he would betray her.

While it's more than likely that this woman would have erected a similar set of expectations and betrayals in life-before-E-mail, it's worth knowing that the form and structure of this new communication lends itself to such an outcome. And it's the more vulnerable among us, those more likely to operate from the safety of their home than to go out into the world, who are affected most. The patient, a victim of some careless—or perhaps deliberate—Casanova, needed antidepressants and a course of tranquilizing medication until it became apparent that her invisible man would in all likelihood do her no harm and she could forget about him.

The investment of extensive emotional commitment in a figure—or figment—of one's imagination also becomes a threat in a variety of other ways peculiar to E-mail. The multiple identities people may assume in cyberspace allow for a variety of emotional frauds, typified by the following case of a young man who sat at his console regularly, weekends and every night after work. The beloved male in the lives of five women, he deliberately encouraged their passion for him, their confessions to him, their idealization of his warmth, empathy, and what they imagined to be his physical beauty. They fantasized about flying with him in the antique two-seater he pretended to own, or running along an ocean beach until, out of breath, they tumbled into lovemaking.

The young man transmitted the same lies to all his women. One of them, suspicious of the generalities in his notes, sent a few of his messages to her group to see if anyone else had received the same letters. The other four wrote to her that they had indeed been relating to the same man. Alas, the discovery meant true heartbreak for one of the respondents, who had arranged her life around leaving her job to travel with the epistolary lothario on their honeymoon.

Virtual love affairs can run into real trouble when the communicators, who obviously share great mental rapport, turn out to have little or no physical compatibility. One couple who came to me for sex therapy had met in cyberspace because of their mutual interest in reading mysteries. They even started to write a mystery novel of their own, with each suggesting chapters and plot twists. When their hero and heroine embarked on a fictional love affair, the correspondents began to meet off-line and to think seriously about their own lives together. Their problem was that the man related by writing E-mail because he had severe inhibitions about physical lovemaking. The disembodied format suited his needs perfectly. He had been brought up in a fundamentalist sect that abhorred all sexuality and deemed sexual pleasure a sin. He did not enjoy touching, having intercourse, or ejaculating. Although he had a great deal in common with his mystery-reading E-mail companion, it was clear that he would need years of psychotherapy, in addition to sex therapy, to be a conjugal husband.

All of which leads to one of the most surprising aspects of computer relationships that comes up in a psychiatrist's office, and that is how unaware people are of their own emotional habits. Love wants to overlook all, sometimes desperately. One young couple who met on the Internet and conducted long cross-country conversations about their work—they were both physicists interested in astronomy, he at Princeton and she at Berkeley—spent every night online, going over their theories, explaining complex ideas to each other. Occasionally, they'd get together, quite successfully, midway in Chicago, where the windy, cold climate did not discourage their torrid love affair. He then invited her east to live with him and do graduate study, an offer she readily accepted. Because they had little money, his parents agreed that she could live with the family.

As it happened, she could not have foreseen that he—by her standards—would be too meticulous, obsessive, exacting, and excessively clean in a household dominated by a compulsively orderly mother. He, for his part, could not have foreseen that she, by his standards, would be sloppy and disorganized. In addition, he was restrained emotionally while she was outspoken. Although their minds were perfectly in tune, their corporeal selves were disastrously mismatched. Ultimately, she continued on toward her graduate degree, but without him. Unless he underwent therapy, he would live forever—spotlessly and with his mother—at home.

A newer danger for those who dare the virtual space of cybersex is the extramarital E-mail correspondence. It needn't be hotly erotic to arouse jealousy, although sometimes—like telephone sex—it can be quite explicit. In the case of Phyllis and James, the correspondence is only indirectly sexual, yet the couple feels sufficiently guilty and sensitive to keep their electronic liaison a secret. Phyllis, after all, is married, and James lives with a long-term lover.

The couple was not prepared for how meaningful their online relationship would become and now are not content with its resolution as a secret, but they know there have been divorces because a neglected spouse has been jealous of the time spent online. Exactly how to prepare for the intensity is difficult to say. E-mail companionship can be a new kind of spectral friendship, even a spiritual companionship, unlike any in the accustomed world. It should be approached with sacredness and caution, a sense of wonder, and an acknowledgment that you are dealing with major emotional forces—the power of people's minds to reach directly to each other.

Of course, beyond the main emotional problem inherent in cyberspace (its tendency to enhance feelings of love) lie the quicksands created by a new breed of jokers, charlatans, and even deviants, who have as much right to respond to public communications as anyone else. People may present themselves as different from what they are, pretending to be gay, straight, lesbian, male, female, transsexual. They may assume multiple identities, pretend to be anything from a child/virgin to an experienced call girl, from a seductive sadist to a submissive masochist. Cyberspace enables them to enter secret worlds without having to go, say, to a gay bar and posture as a gay. They can learn the language, understand the loves and resentments, join the culture without ever having to buy a drink, talk to anyone, or engage in a homosexual act.

One man commented—online—that pretending to be a woman both educated and humiliated him. Whenever he spoke seriously, he complained, some male in his group would begin sexual repartee instead of offering a cogent argument. And this experience, he said, gained him new respect for the enormity of woman's burden.

Yet much as such pretense may be liberating, the schemers (and scammers) may involve innocents, even children, in their charades, which can lead to unfortunate meetings in real time and place. A person presenting an emotional problem or desire for communication may be harassed by individuals who sit at their computers all day looking for victims to torment. While there are many wonderful people inspired by love and world community in cyberspace, the numbers of the perverse are growing, and you should therefore enter the public groups with caution. The next person to attempt to dominate world thinking in a bloody, fascistic fashion could well start his or her message on the Internet.

On a less federal but equally insidious level, a major source of trouble stems, paradoxically, from an attempt to protect privacy by some services allowing their members to take on many code names, thus enabling them to assume multiple identities. While this can be an exciting extension and enlargement of the personality, there are those who use it to establish false relationships, to create scenarios of abuse and abandonment.

One woman I spoke to became a member of an online women's group to discuss problems with her body image. She confessed disliking her protruding stomach, her fat thighs, her heavy breasts. Another member of the group requested that they communicate privately, which she agreed to do. Her respondent complained of small breasts and wide hips. They discussed their most intimate histories, details of sex with men who did and did not enjoy their bodies. After several months of being drawn into descriptions of intensely explicit erotic detail, the "small" woman revealed herself to be a man. He expressed his desire to have sex with the larger one because the image of her abundant body turned him on. He exonerated himself on the grounds that it should be helpful to know that her body attracted him, but quite naturally, the self-conscious woman felt betrayed.

Contacting an abnormal person is one of the dangers of communicating online. Of course, it's a major difficulty in life too, and the computer protects only because the distance between two machines is far greater than the distance between two bodies. Yet a story appeared recently in the press about a man who lured a child online to an off-line assignation. Given that children are often more computer-literate than their parents, families would do well to monitor their kids' cyberspace habits, at least casually and with as much interest as they would give to their children's whereabouts in other situations. When it looks like Johnny is doing his homework, someone may be trying to get into Johnny's pants. Pederasts, as we've seen, have been known to make deliberate efforts to snare and addict youngsters to on-screen sex—and to take it offscreen as well.

The world of specifically sexual writing and graphics flourishes online too, just as it does in other media. But although it is no more or less reprehensible on computer than anywhere else, in one way cyberotica differs significantly from the other forms in that online, the creator of the sexual scenario has a heyday. People can self-publish their sexual tales, which may be as long and as deviant, if not actively perverse, as the teller wishes, provided an appropriate group is selected for their display. Some of the groups run stories that are amateurish, ghastly, violent, and boring. Not that you have to read them. I consider here the writer—the person whose need to write obscenely

may be a compulsion, whose life may be spent creating these monstrosities for the screen. Without E-mail, would that person be doing the same thing in some other form? Is cyberspace reducing the numbers of telephone callers or writers of dirty mail to innocent victims? Whatever, it's certainly bringing such people out in armies, which provide untold hours of stimulation for armchair masturbators.

Witness a man I heard about whose wife accidentally found his bills for telephone sex and gave him an ultimatum: Stop, or let's separate right now. He stopped. But he picked up computer sex, writing obscene stories, requesting that fellow writers out there deliver the sexual encouragement he required for fantasy stimulation. His wife thinks he's working late on his accounts. His phone bills bear no specifics about the time he uses.

Consider, too, the online bondage-and-discipline groups, which have recently created a major new psychological distress. People find their way into reading the material in these groups and then try it out, often becoming hooked. I know of one couple who, having met off-line, were having a perfectly pleasant sexual relationship until they started to explore the B & D groups online "just for fun." Pretty soon, the man began to tie up his partner for sex in the way online practitioners described. From there, it was only a small step to whipping her with a length of rope, after which he comforted her with gentle caresses and protective words. She allowed him to hurt her in order to merit the caressing, the comforting, the gentleness, but it troubled her severely that she submitted willingly to such physical abuse. Finally, when she felt herself becoming addicted to the pain in order to intensify the pleasure, she came to therapy. Not long afterward, she left the relationship—and not least of all because the act of whipping a woman had become, for her lover, an indelible part of his arousal.

On the positive side of online erotica, one woman advertised for the partner of her dreams in a romance group. She described herself and stated the type of man she wanted and what he would have to do to win her attention. Very explicitly, she described not only the new courtship—daily messages of attention and self-revelation on E-mail—but also the old seductions: flowers, small gifts, theater tickets, champagne and caviar in a cool restaurant on a warm summer evening. More to the point, she also described—in great detail—the kind of long and caring foreplay she would need before making love. A year later, she is considering marriage to the third man who presented himself. He seems ideal to her in his courtly approach to romance. They have some personality differences to work out, for which they are seeking help, but an excellent match may be in the making.

As a psychiatrist, I would hope that writing about sex in any fashion is basically healthy. In my new novel, Virtual Love, two psychiatrists who specialize in sex therapy fall in love in cyberspace. For them, E-mail is a powerful stimulus for erotic self-revelation and discovery, freeing them, as it does, to reveal their sexual histories without relating to each other too soon.

The stories in Virtual Love are not only about the erotic lives of these two psychiatrists but also about their fictional patients, whose sexual pasts are often tragic. I try to show that the quest for love is at the root of most sexual behavior, even the perverse and bizarre, and that the ability to love may survive sexual damage, even infidelity, incest, sadism, and other betrayals. Virtual Love, although extremely explicit in certain paragraphs, is intended to heal, not to titillate. But reading and writing erotic tales, whether or not intended to arouse, is merely another way of thinking about one's potential for love and pleasure. My bias is that writing about sex is fine—on the page or on the screen.

As a psychiatrist, of course, I'm also aware of the capacity of E-mail to feed into the desire to escape reality and live in the world of fantasy. But to view that as a potential danger is to fall in with the self-appointed moralists who have a long tradition of warning the world against the perils of reading, thinking, acting in new ways. Just as the world has come to terms with other pastimes once looked upon as subversive, we will all come to terms, eventually, with the problems and pleasures of cyberspace. Meanwhile, you could meet the love of your life through a steaming correspondence. Or the pathological sex criminal who lives next door could be watching through the window as you respond to his invitation to meet him later tonight!

PART 7

Working with the World Wide Web

In this part, you will find the following:

- WebLinks: A Directory of Annotated World Wide Web Sites
- Web Site Evaluation Form
- Web Journal

For each Web site listed in the directory, you have been provided with a site **name,** site **address** (or Universal Resource Locator), and a brief **description** of what can be found at each site. Each site has been numbered for easy reference and referral, and the sites are listed alphabetically by site name.

Before accessing these Web sites, you may want to review "Using the World Wide Web As a Resource: **Health Information On-Line**"at the front of the book. It contains useful background information on the technology of the Web and how to make the most of your time online. You may also want to review the **Quick Reference Guide to Topics/Readings/Web Sites,** which coordinates readings with Web sites.

The Web Site Evaluation Form can be used in any of a number of ways. Use the questions on the form to guide your work on a Web site. Or ask your professor if you can fill out the Web Site Evaluation Form and turn it in for extra credit in your course. The Web Journal can be used as your personal address book for making notes about sites you have visited. You can record your reactions to a site and briefly note what you find.

WebLinks:
A Directory of Annotated Web Sites

[For your convenience, the **Quick Reference Guide to Topics/Readings/World Wide Web Sites** at the front of the book correlates the readings in the book with Web sites from the directory that follows. Also, please review the description of *Updates to WebLinks (http://www.morton-pub.com/updates/updates.stml)* that appears in the front of the book in the section **A Note from the Publisher** for additional information about Web sites.]

A

AIDS Virtual Library   No. 1

❂ http://www.planetq.com/aidsvl/index.html

This frequently updated index site offers links to everything from information about safer sex to statistical and research databases on HIV/AIDS. Links only—highly selective, well organized, easy to navigate.

Alan Guttmacher Institute   No. 2

❂ http://www.agi-usa.org

This is the home page of the Alan Guttmacher Institute, a think tank that researches and reports on human reproductive health issues. Birth control, abortion, and other aspects of reproductive health are explored at length. Links to recent Institute articles and to external sites. Site posts and answers an interesting *Question of the Week*; for example, Who is eligible for publicly funded contraceptive care in the United States?

American Civil Liberties Union   No. 3

❂ http://www.aclu.org

The American Civil Liberties Union's home page presents information and provides links to a wide variety of topics. Included is coverage of reproductive rights and HIV/AIDS. Learn more about the ACLU and its network.

American Journal of Public Health   No. 4

❂ http://www.apha.org/

This site is a good source of information on sexually transmitted diseases, HIV/AIDS, and other health issues. Public health resources and legislative information are included. The American Public Health Association is the nation's oldest organization committed to serving the public's health.

American Psychological Association   No. 5

❂ http://www.apa.org

This thorough and authoritative site presents information resources in psychology. Click on *PsychNET* to access the APA's primary Web documents, including the APA newsletter and the APA's journals in all the specialty areas of psychology. There is a searchable database of abstracts on over 1,350 scholarly journals. There is also specific information for students who are considering careers in psychology.

American Social Health Association: Frequently Asked Questions   No. 6

❂ http://www.sunsite.unc.edu/ASHA/faq/faq.html

Useful information on sexually transmitted diseases and HIV/AIDS is presented. The questions most frequently answered by the American Social Health Association (ASHA) are answered here. No links from this page to external sites, just straightforward, to-the-point Q & As. This page is part of a Sun Microsystems site maintained at the University of North Carolina that includes the ASHA (http://sunsite.unc.edu/ASHA), whose mission statement is: "Stop sexually transmitted diseases (STDs) and their harmful consequences to individuals, families, and communities."

Ann Rose's Ultimate Birth Control Links   No. 7

❂ http://gynpages.com/ultimate

Specific details are presented by a birth control educator on birth control and childbearing. Lots of useful information and helpful links to related topics, including political and religious debates on contraception, are provided.

Army Times Online Home Page   No. 8

❂ http://www.armytimes.com/

The home page for *Army Times: The Independent Weekly* online. This site has links to the *Army Times*, *Navy Times*, and *Air Force Times*. These are excellent sources of information on current issues facing service men and women, including issues of women in the military and sexual harassment.

Assertive Communication   No. 9

❂ http://www.umr.edu/~counsel/assert.html

Text only page on assertive communication—what it is and how to practice the skills necessary to be assertive. Page links back to the home page for the Center for Personal and Professional Development (CPPD) at the University of Missouri-Rolla. Scroll to the end of the CPPD's home page for links to more online text pages on *Decisions About Sex* and *Long Distance Relationships,* among other topics.

Association for Couples in Marriage Enrichment(ACME) No. 10

⊕ http://members.aol.com/acmefla/mission.html

The Association for Couples in Marriage Enrichment is a non-profit organization with the goal of providing the tools and support to married couples who wish to actively strengthen their relationships. The site includes links to related resources, including books and educational materials, answers to FAQs, and details on conferences. Visitors can send messages via E-mail.

Association of Voluntary and Safe Contraception No. 11

⊕ http://www.avsc.org./avsc/

The Association of Voluntary and Safe Contraception brings this page to the Web. Solid facts are provided on contraceptive options, including temporary, permanent, and special needs (i.e., postpartum women, people with sexually transmitted diseases, and others). Good links lead visitors to recent publications, working papers, and issues in the news.

Avert AIDS No. 12

⊕ http://www.avert.org/

Facts and statistics on HIV/AIDS are presented by the AIDS Education and Research Trust, based in the United Kingdom. Many links lead to discussions on HIV/AIDS in adults, children, and pregnant women. Lots of detail and information on current issues are included.

B

Birth Control Pills No. 13

⊕ http://www.nau.edu/~fronske/bcp.html

Text provides details on birth control pills and how they work. Statistics are included. Limited links take visitors to sites on chlamydia and condoms.

Birth Control Trust No. 14

⊕ http://www.easynet.co.uk/bct/

The Birth Control Trust is a British-based organization that provides online information about contraception, abortion, and reproductive policy in the United Kingdom.

Bisexual Resource Center No. 15

⊕ http://norn.org/pub/other-orgs/brc/index.html

The Bisexual Resource Center presents a comprehensive site with a large number of links. Visitors can explore the myths versus facts about bisexuality and access the center's publications and bookstore.

Body Health: A Multimedia AIDS and HIV Information Resource No. 16

⊕ http://www.thebody.com

This easy-to-use site boasts a search engine and many links on HIV/AIDS. Safer sex fact sheets, health tips for people living with AIDS, and an "Ask the Expert" service are included. This is an award-winning site.

The Breast Cancer Roundtable No. 17

⊕ http://www.seas.gwu.edu/student/tlooms/MGT243/
breast_cancer_roundtable.html

This site focuses on the possible link between abortion and breast cancer. Visitors can find current information about breast cancer from online journals and research studies. Links are included to opinions and facts on each side of the debate.

C

CDC Division of STD Prevention No. 18

⊕ http://www.cdc.gov/nchstp/dstd/dstdp.html

This is the home page for the Centers for Disease Control's Division of STD Prevention. With up-to-the-minute news including the latest published articles from various news sources, STD prevention partnerships, publications and reports, links to other resources (STD prevention and treatment guidelines), STD prevention training, and hotlines.

CDC National AIDS Clearinghouse No. 19

⊕ http://www.cdcnac.org/

The CDC National AIDS Clearinghouse is a service of the Centers for Disease Control and Prevention. At this site you will find links to up-to-date information and resources on HIV/AIDS and sexually transmitted diseases. Order publication, search CDC online databases, take an interactive tour of the CDC National Aids Clearinghouse, view the Poster Gallery, or link to external, related sites.

Center for AIDS Prevention Studies No. 20

⊕ http://www.caps.ucsf.edu/capsweb

A search engine and fact sheets are featured at this home page of the Center for AIDS Prevention Studies. Details on HIV testing, research, and other AIDS-related information is provided. Links lead visitors to related, external sites.

Centers for Disease Control and Prevention (CDC) No. 21

⊕ http://www.cdc.gov

The U. S. Department of Health and Human Services' Centers for Disease Control and Prevention presents information, resources, and links dealing with HIV/AIDS and sexually transmitted diseases. Visitors can access an up-to-date source of morbidity data on sexually transmitted diseases and the CDC journal *Morbidity and Mortality Weekly*.

Circumcision No. 22

⊕ http://www.cirp.org/cirp/

This site from the Circumcision Information and Resources organization provides comprehensive data on circumcision. Visitors can search the Circumcision Reference Library or the Circumcision Information Pages. Many links lead to related information.

Circumcision Issues No. 23

⊕ http://www.eskimo.com/%7egburlin/circ.html

Useful details are provided on male and female circumcision. Fact sheets and many links provide further data.

Coalition for Positive Sexuality No. 24

⊕ http://www.positive.org/cps/Home/index.html

This is the home page for the Coalition for Positive Sexuality. The site features a search engine, a forum for teens to talk about sex, an opportunity for "sexperts" to answer FAQs, and links to related resources.

Collected Domestic Partners Information No. 25

⊕ http://www.cs.cmu.edu/afs/cs.cmu.edu/user/scotts/
domestic-partners/mainpage.html

Domestic partnerships and same-sex marriages are discussed at this site. Links lead to scientific articles, public broadcasts, and information on federal lawsuits and policies.

Condommania   No. 26

🌐 http://www.condommania.com/contents.html

This site is devoted exclusively to information and resources about condoms. Explores every facet of condoms.

Condoms   No. 27

🌐 http://www.coolware.com/health/joel/condom.html

Simple all-text page provides data on condom effectiveness. A condom's role in the prevention of AIDS is also explored.

Contraceptive Contemplation   No. 28

🌐 http://www.tripod.com/living/contraceptive/index.html

Thorough exploration of contraception is presented. A memory game is featured. Links are provided to sites offering general information and specific details on various forms of birth control, including condoms, diaphragms, morning-after pills, etc.

The Cyberporn Debate   No. 29

🌐 http://www2000.ogsm.vanderbilt.edu/ cyberporn.debate.cgi

This site, sponsored by Vanderbilt University, focuses on the debate over cyberporn. It provides full-text articles, references, and other resources about sex on the Internet. The national debate over First Amendment rights and restrictions on the Internet and other emerging media is ongoing, and you can start here for facts and informed opinion.

D

Defense News Online   No. 30

🌐 http://www.defensenews.com/

This is the home page of the international defense community's newsweekly, *Defense News*. This publication is devoted to issues related to the nation's defense and the men and women serving in the armed forces. A primary source for breaking news on issues in the military.

Depo-Provera   No. 31

🌐 http://users.vnet.net/shae/wissues/depo.html

The advantages and disadvantages of using Depo-Provera as a contraceptive are discussed. Links focus on current issues concerning this birth control method, including the risks, side effects, and more. Data are presented.

Divorce Online   No. 32

🌐 http://www.divorce~online.com/

This site serves as a complete resource on issues pertaining to divorce. Many links are provided to articles, FAQs, and information on the financial, legal, and psychological aspects of divorce. Visitors have the opportunity to send E-mail messages to others in similar situations or the page editors.

Divorce Source   No. 33

🌐 http://www.divorcesource.com/

Divorce Source is a network that provides details about counseling, the legal process, alimony, and other issues concerning divorce. Interactive forums cover a wide range of topics, from saving a marriage to child custody. Links are provided to publications, articles, and state-by-state information. Province-by-province data for Canada is included.

Does Sex Education Work?   No. 34

🌐 http://chanane.ucsf.edu/capsweb/sexedtext.html

The Center for AIDS Prevention Studies at the University of California at San Francisco presents this text-only page. The page is a research article evaluating the merits of sex education.

Dr. Feelgood   No. 35

🌐 http://Feelgood.msn.aus.com/quickfeel/newdefault.htm

Dr. Feelgood, Australia's answer to Dr. Ruth, provides online information concerning a variety of sexual issues. Data and opinions are presented in a fun, playful style.

E

Electronic Gay Community Magazine   No. 36

🌐 http://www.zzapp.org/awes/egcm

This is the oldest online service for gays and lesbians. Information and references on gay issues ranging from entertainment to political activism are presented. Links are provided to various topics, including quotes, lifestyle issues, politics issues, editorials, and more.

The English Server: Gender and Sexuality   No. 37

🌐 http://eserver.org/gender/

"This page publishes texts which address gender studies and queer studies, with a particular focus upon discussion of sex, gender, sexual identity and sexuality in cultural practices." Human sexuality as a cultural phenomenon is the focus of most of the writings posted here. The page, which is a links only page, is part of the English Server Web site, a members-run cooperative of graduate students started at Carnegie Mellon University in 1990 to encourage the "public distribution of research, criticism, novels, hypertext, and miscellaneous writings from humanities disciplines." Written mostly by and for those pursuing graduate studies in the humanities.

Equal Employment Opportunity Commission   No. 38

🌐 http://www.eeoc.gov/

The Equal Employment Opportunity Commission presents data and resources on sexual harassment, discrimination, and government policies. Links are provided.

Equal Marriage Rights Home Page   No. 39

🌐 http://www.ucc.gu.uwa.edu.au/~rod/gay/ marriage.html

A multitude of links leads visitors to topics on same-sex marriages and domestic partnerships. News, references, and E-mail addresses are provided. A list of states and their current policies is included.

F

The Female Genital Mutilation Research Homepage   No. 40

🌐 http://www.hollyfeld.org/fgm/

An excellent resource, this site is dedicated to research pertaining to Female Genital Mutilation (FGM). It presents this practice from a variety of perspectives: psychological, cultural, sexual, human rights, etc. With extensive information and a definitive list of links on this subject, this site provides access to a wide range of information and resources.

Female Sexual Disorder Screening   No. 41

🌐 http://www.med.nyu.edu/Psych/screens/sdsf.html

This site is presented by New York University. Visitors can learn about female sexual disorders, take a quiz, and get therapist information. Links are provided.

Feminism and Women's Resources   No. 42

🌐 http://www.ibd.nrc.ca/~mansfield/feminism/

This site is a listing of many of the women's studies or women-related sources on the Internet, which has recently added hundreds of new links. Find listings of Internet resources for women and feminists divided into several categories, with a short description of each link: click on *Women's Organizations, Women's Resources, Other Collections of Links,* and *Other Organizations and Links of Interest.* This site is the recipient of a Three Star Site designation from Magellan, an online directory of reviewed and rated Internet sites. Also rated as having "no content intended only for mature audiences," and is Clearinghouse Approved.

Feminist.com   No. 43

🌐 http://feminist.com/health.htm

This is a definitive site for women's health issues, which includes a multitude of links under such subjects as: *General Women's Health, Breast Cancer, Reproductive Health, Women and AIDS,* and *Do-It-Yourself Breast Exam.* An excellent place from which to start investigating women's issues.

Feminist Internet Gateway   No. 44

🌐 http://www.feminist.org/gateway/master2.html

A large collection of women's issues and feminist sites, which are organized by subject. Visitors can link to resources and information on topics such as global issues and abortion.

Forum on Women's Health   No. 45

🌐 http://www.womenshealth.org/

A female physician offers suggestions and answers on health matters. The forum also provides facts and information on wellness issues. Links are provided to related sites.

G

Gay, Lesbian, Bisexual, and Transgender Links   No. 46

🌐 http://www.indiana.edu/~glbserv/global.html

The University of Indiana's Gay, Lesbian, Bisexual, and Trans page. This site provides information, resources, and links to a global network concerned with GLBT-related issues.

Gender Equity in Sports   No. 47

🌐 http://www.arcade.uiowa.edu/proj/ge/

This site serves as a resource on gender equity in intercollegiate and other levels of sports. Research conducted at the University of Iowa is presented. Links are provided to information on the history of Title IX, an index of lawsuits, and a list of Civil Rights findings.

Gender Integrated Training   No. 48

🌐 http://www.defenselink.mil/pubs/git

This site highlights the Report of the Federal Advisory Committee on Gender-Integrated Training and Related Issues to the Secretary of Defense (December 16, 1997). Related information

includes links to the *Federal Advisory Committee on Gender-Integrated Training and Related Issues, a News Release* (December 16, 1997), *Defense Secretary's Press Conference Announcing Gender-Integrated Training Panel* (June 27, 1997), and *Background Briefing Gender-Integrated Training* (June 3, 1997). For primary sources on the integration of men and women in the military from the military's point-of-view, this is current information.

Gender Issues in Online Communication   No. 49

🌐 http://eserver.org/feminism/gender-issues-onlin.txt

This text-only page, principally written by Hoai-An Truong, in conjunction with Member of the Bay Area Women in Telecommunications, explores the experiences of women online. The 1993 copyright means that some of the specifics on the technology of the Internet have changed, but the issues raised and questions considered are relevant to any discussion of gender and media.

Go Ask Alice: Sexuality   No. 50

🌐 http://kwaziwai.cc.columbia.edu/cu/healthwise/Cat6.html

Go Ask Alice is the award-winning interactive Q&A health site from Healthwise, Columbia University's Health Education and Wellness program. In addition to examining the answers posted, visitors to this comprehensive site can review details on a variety of sexual topics.

H

Hawaii (State of) Report of the Commission on Sexual Orientation and the Law   No. 51

🌐 http://www.hawaii.gov/lrb/solcvr.html

The full text of all studies and reports relating to Hawaii's landmark gay marriage bill is presented. Details on legislative sessions and other legal information are included.

HealthGate   No. 52

🌐 http://www.healthgate.com

Health, wellness, and biomedical information are discussed at this subscriber-based source. A page explores the landmark book in women's health, *Our Bodies Ourselves,* and includes access to online databases. Many links are provided to various medical topics, including breast cancer and allergies.

J

JAMA HIV/AIDS Information Center   No. 53

🌐 http://www.ama-assn.org/special/hiv/hivhome.htm

The *Journal of the American Medical Association* offers information and resources on HIV/AIDS. This page covers a range of subjects, from clinical and treatment updates to legal and policy issues. Links are provided to a newsline, ethics updates, and expert advice.

Johns Hopkins University STD Research Group   No. 54

🌐 http://www.clark.net/pub/jhustd/

Epidemiology and the prevention and control of sexually transmitted diseases (STDs) are explored. This site is maintained by the Johns Hopkins University School of Medicine STD Research Group.

K

The Kinsey Institute for Research in Sex, Gender, and Reproduction — No. 55

🌐 http://www.indiana.edu/~kinsey/

The purpose of The Kinsey Institute's WWW site is to support interdisciplinary research and study of human sexuality. The Institute was founded by Dr. Alfred Kinsey (1894–1956) and this year celebrates its 50th Anniversary. Frequent updates and links to the institute's library and special collections, research and publications, clinics and training, special events and exhibitions, and other resources are highlights.

L

Lifelines @ Work: Resources for Improvement of Health, Productivity and Effectiveness — No. 56

🌐 http://www.lifelines.com/

Improving fitness and nutrition can improve sexual relations and responses. Lifelines' site presents links on topics such as eating healthy, stress, and smoking. A library and a list of related sites are included. The site was honored as a Top 5% Web Site.

M

Male Infertility — No. 57

🌐 http://www.ivf.com/male.html

The Atlanta Reproductive Health Centre explores Male Factor Infertility. Links provide education on donor insemination, the British Andrology Society's Lab Manual for Semen Analysis, how anti-oxidants may benefit male fertility and treat impotence.

Male Sexual Disorder Screening — No. 58

🌐 http://www.med.nyu.edu/Psych/screens/sdsm.html

Sexual disorders in men are explored at this site maintained by New York University. A survey and details on therapists are included.

Man's Guide to Sexuality — No. 59

🌐 http://www.igc.org/ppfa/manguide_section2.html

Relationships and male versus female issues are explored at this site. A Perfect Partner Quiz is included.

Marriage Encounter — No. 60

🌐 http://www.wwme.org/

Worldwide Marriage Encounter, an organization devoted to strengthening marriages and preserving families, maintains this home page. Links are provided to related information and resources. Valuable web site with scores of links.

Medic's Impotence Information Center — No. 61

🌐 http://medic-drug.com/impotence/impotence.html

Presented by Medic Drug, visitors can learn more about impotence, current treatments, and penile implants. Tips on picking a doctor and what to expect from an examination are explored. An E-mail service and related links are provided for further information.

Men Against Domestic Violence — No. 62

🌐 http://www.silcom.com/~paladin/madv/

Men Against Domestic Violence is a cyber-based organization of men and women sponsored by The Paladin Group and Correctional Systems, Inc. This site is dedicated to addressing the issue of domestic violence against women. Links are included to statistics, related sites, and addresses for more information. The comprehensive site also includes a list of crisis lines for urgent concerns.

Men Assisting Leading Education (M.A.L.E.) — No. 63

🌐 http://www.malesurvivor.org/

The Men Assisting Leading Education (M.A.L.E.) site contains extensive information concerning male survivors of sexual abuse. A detailed manifesto on male survivors, resources on how to help victims, and suggestions on how to treat offenders are included. Links are provided to press releases, men's issues, and services for male survivors.

Menopause Matters — No. 64

🌐 http://world.std.com/~susan207/

This site provides information on the treatment of menopausal symptoms. It seeks to empower women to make conscious decisions about health by disseminating state of the art information on the treatment of problems arising at menopause. Addresses such topics as: *What Can I Do About Hot Flashes And Night Sweats?*; *Other Resources on the Internet*; *Non-Internet Resources*; *What's New!*; and *What Your Doctor May Not Tell You About Menopause*. There are plans to establish a Directory of Physicians and Pharmacists sympathetic to alternative approaches to menopause.

Men's Health: Premature Ejaculation — No. 65

🌐 http://h-devil-www.mc.duke.edu/h-devil/men/men.htm

This site provides information about the causes and treatment of premature ejaculation, and addresses such subjects as: Erectile Disfunction, Premature Ejaculation, Testicular Self-Exam, and Urinary Tract Infection in Men. Also has links to a suggestions page and invites further questions.

Men's Health Issues — No. 66

🌐 http://www.vix.com/pub/men/health/health.html

Information on health, diet, HIV/AIDS, and sexual addiction is provided at this site. Links are provided to related articles and other resources.

Men's Health Page — No. 67

🌐 http://www.healthtouch.com/level1/leaflets/101529/101529.htm

Details are provided on a variety of men's health issues. The site, maintained by Healthtouch Online, focuses on topics such as sexual and reproductive health, prostrate and urologic problems, physical addictions, and cancer. Links are included to related sites, including a health resource directory.

Men's Issues — No. 68

🌐 http://www.vix.com/pub/men/index.html

Issues from a male perspective are the focus of this site. Domestic violence, child support, rape and sexual assault, and reproductive health are some of the subjects explored. Related information and resources on men's health are included.

Minnesota Center Against Violence and Abuse: Domestic Violence and Violence Against Women   No. 69

🌐 http://www.umn.edu.mincava/vaw.htm

Here you will find articles, fact sheets, informative resources, organizations, legal resources, regional service providers, and *National 24-Hour Domestic Violence Hotline.*

Minnesota Center Against Violence and Abuse: Rape, Sexual Assault, & Harassment   No. 70

🌐 http://www.umn.edu/mincava/sah.htm

A site with information on rape, sexual assault, and sexual harassment. Links to fact sheets on rape and guides to dealing with date rape, as well as articles from the *National Criminal Justice Reference Service* and access to direct services for sexual assault survivors.

N

National Abortion Rights League   No. 71

🌐 http://www.naral.org/

Federal abortion initiatives, fact sheets, and press releases are included at this site from the National Abortion and Reproductive Rights Action League. Lots of links lead visitors to publications, campus information, and related subjects.

National Cancer Institute   No. 72

🌐 http://www.nci.nih.gov

This site presents comprehensive information on all forms of cancer, including breast, cervical, and testicular. Statistics research, and information on support services are explored. Links are provided to related sites from this page maintained by the National Cancer Institute of the National Institutes of Health.

National Gay and Lesbian Task Force   No. 73

🌐 http://www.ngltf.org/

Current information on gay and lesbian issues is presented at this site from the National Gay and Lesbian Task Force. Links are included to general information, press releases, articles, and upcoming events.

The National Institute of Diabetes and Digestive and Kidney Diseases of the National Institutes of Health   No. 74

🌐 http://www.niddk.nih.gov/

This site is maintained by the National Institute of Diabetes and Digestive and Kidney Diseases of the National Institutes of Health. An informational overview of impotency and details on endocrine and urologic diseases is presented.

National Institute on Mental Health   No. 75

🌐 http://www.nimh.nih.gov/

The National Institute on Mental Health of the National Institute of Health presents this award-winning site. General information on mental health and links to the latest news and research are provided.

National Organization for Women (NOW)   No. 76

🌐 http://www.now.org/

Links are listed to key women's issues, news and other resources at this site from the National Organization for Women. The thorough site also includes chapter information and other resources.

National Right to Life   No. 77

🌐 http://www.nrlc.org/

This home page for the National Right to Life has resources and information on a variety of abortion and right to life issues, such as abortion alternatives, NRL news, will to live, and euthanasia. Provides links to outreach programs and other relevant pro-life sites.

National Task Force on Prostitution   No. 78

🌐 http://www.bayswan.org/NTFP.html

All-text page describes the position endorsed by the National Task Force on Prostitution, an organization that supports the rights of sex workers. Visitors can send E-mail or review the prostitutes education network.

National Women's Health Organization   No. 79

🌐 http://gynpages.com/nwho/

Information on women's health issues are presented by the National Women's Health Organization. An 800 number, details on the association and a list of offices are included.

Natural Family Planning   No. 80

🌐 http://www.missionnet.com/

Mission Net, a Christian Internet resource, provides information for couples interested in natural family planning. Related resources and support are included.

The New Male Sexuality   No. 81

🌐 http://www.thriveonline.com/@@lniu2wQAd17TsNnf/thrive/sex/malesex.intro.html

This is Thrive@Sex's site dedicated to male sexuality issues. It provides information and resources about the biomedical and psychosocial aspects of male sexuality.

NIAID DAIDS   No. 82

🌐 http://www.niaid.nih.gov/research/Daids.htm

This is the Division of Acquired Immunodeficiency Syndrome (DAIDS) page from the National Institute of Allergy and Infectious Diseases (NIAID) of the National Institute of Health. Information and resources on HIV/AIDS are provided on this page. Statistics on morbidity and mortality as well as details on current research are included.

Northeast Florida Potency Restoration Center   No. 83

🌐 http://www.impotency.com/index.html

Fact sheets about impotence—its causes and treatments—are presented by the Northeast Florida Potency Restoration Center. Answers to FAQs, discussions of new products, and information on seminars are available. Links are included.

Northeastern Centre Against Sexual Assault   No. 84

🌐 http://www.northern.casa.org.au/

Presents informative links to the issues of: what is sexual assault, what is its impact, what are the legal issues, and what resources are available. An excellent site to start from.

P

Pap Test
No. 85

🌐 http://www.erinet.com/fnadoc/pap.htm

The cervical pap smear is the only cancer screening test in the world which has decreased the incidence and mortality (numbers and deaths) of a cancer. This site contains articles and information, including statistics and graphs, about the pap test and has good Hot Links to other informative, related sites.

People for the American Way
No. 86

🌐 http://www.pfaw.org/

People for the American Way is one of the nation's anti-censorship watchdog organizations. This site describes what can be done to prevent censorship of sexually-oriented materials. Visitors can link to pages on free expression, building democracy, equal rights, education, and religious liberty.

The Physical Activity and Health Network
No. 87

🌐 http://www.pitt.edu/~pahnet/

A dynamic list of Internet sites that examine the relationship of physical activity and exercise to health is presented by the University of Pittsburgh. A variety of links lead visitors to related topics, including online journals, cutting edge research, and health issues in the news.

Planned Parenthood Federation of America
No. 88

🌐 http://www.plannedparenthood.org/

Founded in 1916, Planned Parenthood is "the oldest voluntary family planning organization." Its nationwide centers provide a variety of services, both medical and educational, related to sexual and reproductive health. At this easy to navigate and comprehensive site, you can find information on the organization, as well as on topics related to sexual and reproductive health: for example, from the home page, you can click on *Women's Health, Birth Control, Pro-Choice Advocacy, Fact Sheets, Products, Library,* or *Links* for detailed information.

A Primer on Natural Family Planning
No. 89

🌐 http://www.usc.edu/hsc/info/newman/resources/
primer.html

Text-only page provides information on fertility awareness. Current details and statistics are included.

Prostitution Issues: Student Home Page
No. 90

🌐 http://www.bayswan.org/student.html

An information site for students researching the decriminalization of prostitution. Provides links to a report from The San Francisco Task Force on Prostitution, with *Executive Summary* and *Summary of Recommendations,* which explores decriminalization or legalization of prostitution and reviews statistics. Also lists resource links for more information that include a bibliography of books findable at a library or bookstore, a story from one prostitutes' perspective, and information about prostitutes and law enforcement.

Q

The Queer Resources Directory
No. 91

🌐 http://qrd.tcp.com/qrd

This clearinghouse provides full-text articles, reference lists, political action updates, and current news pertaining to sexual minorities. Topics include family life, youth, health and business and legal issues. Links are offered to related organizations and sites. A well-documented site with a clear vision/mission statement and good information on who operates and maintains it.

R

Rape, Abuse, and Incest National Network (RAINN)
No. 92

🌐 http://feminist.com/rainn.htm

The Rape, Abuse and Incest National Network (RAINN) is a non-profit organization based in Washington, D.C. that operates a national toll-free hotline for victims of sexual assault. There are statistics, well-researched information, and links to resources, articles, speeches, and recovery support groups. A site that addresses the recent statistics that show that rape is still all too prevalent in America.

Ruth Westheimer's (Dr. Ruth's) Home Page
No. 93

🌐 http://www.drruth.com

Dr. Ruth is online. This fun page reveals Dr. Ruth's sex question of the day, sex tips, favorite Web Sites and more. Visitors can review answers to FAQs or pose questions to the sex therapist.

S

The Safer Sex Page
No. 94

🌐 http://www.safersex.org/

Safe sex issues and sexually transmitted diseases are discussed at this site. Links are provided to a variety of sites for health education and promotion.

Selected Women and Gender Resources on the World Wide Web
No. 95

🌐 http://www.library.wise.edu/libraries/WomensStudies/
others.htm

This index site offers well-focused links to: a subject listing of women and gender resources; women-centered magazines and newsletters on the Web; courses; feminist bookstores; organizations; women's studies programs and research centers; archives and libraries. Equipped with a *How To* section with instructions on conducting Web-based searches on these topics.

Sex, Censorship and the Internet
No. 96

🌐 http://www.eff.org/CAF/cafuiuc.html

This site describes threats to academic freedom and the use of the Internet to disseminate sexual material. An outline of topics links visitors directly to an *Introduction* and text on *Current Policies and Experience, Academic Freedom, Two Types of Acceptable Use Policies,* and *Top Library Intellectual Freedom Policies.*

Sex Directory   No. 97

🌐 http://www.u-net.com/~healthdv/sexweb/

Condoms are the focus at this site from the United Kingdom. Links provide visitors with tips on talking about condom use and important rules to remember.

Sexual Assault Information   No. 98

🌐 http://www.cs.utk.edu/~bartley/saInfoPage.html

Information and referrals on rape, sexual abuse, and domestic violence are found on this page. Statistics and text on acquaintance rape, child sexual abuse, counseling, and victims compensation are included. A search engine and links to many related sites, including WWWomen's WebRing's, are provided at this comprehensive site.

Sexual Compulsives Anonymous   No. 99

🌐 http://www.sca-recovery.org/

Sexual Compulsives Anonymous International Service Organization's home page presents details about the program, which is similar to the 12-step Alcoholics Anonymous program, that helps members overcome sexual compulsiveness. Links lead visitors to information on tools to get better, Q&As, suggestions to avoid slip-ups, and obstacles to success.

Sexual Health Advocate Peer Education (SHAPE)   No. 100

🌐 http://www.hsc.missouri.edu/shc/helthed4.htm

This student-authored site from the University of Missouri at Columbia campus provides information about sexuality from a peer-perspective. An E-mail address and phone numbers are included for more details.

Sexuality in Later Life   No. 101

🌐 http://www.nih.gov/nia/health/pubpub/sexual.htm

The National Institute on Aging (NIA), one of the federal government's National Institutes of Health (NIH), has posted a brief article on the aging process and sexuality. This is a text only page, which links back to the NIA and the Health Information Page.

Sexuality Information and Education Council (SIECUS)   No. 102

🌐 http://www.siecus.org

Details on sexuality, contraception, and sexual abuse and assault are presented by the Sexuality Information and Education Council, a nonprofit organization. A description of programs and a list of publications are included. Links are provided to related sites.

STD Home Page   No. 103

🌐 http://www.bu.edu/people/sycamore/std/std.htm

This site is dedicated to providing information about STDs. It features an interactive STD quiz, graphic pictures of sexually transmitted disease's signs and symptoms, and references for further reading.

The Student Counseling Virtual Pamphlet Collection   No. 104

🌐 http://uhs.bsd.uchicago.edu/scrs/vpc/virtulets.html #Relationships

A service of The University of Chicago and its Student Counseling and Resource Service, this page offers links (and only links) to a variety of online pamphlets written specifically for students and posted by colleges and universities across the United States and Canada. Particularly relevant for a course in human sexuality are the links to pamphlets on *Cultural Issues*, *Relationships*, *Sexual Assault*, *Sexual Harassment*, and *Sexual Orientation*. A good index site.

Suggestions for Improving Communication Skills in Relationships   No. 105

🌐 http://www.mancol.edu/stnlife/relcom.html

Text only page with a description of the communication skills necessary for developing relationships. Good, authoritative advice written for students. Page links back to The Manhattan College Counseling Center home page, which in turn offers links to articles on additional topics of interest for college students.

Survey: Informed Consent   No. 106

🌐 http://psych.fullerton.edu/throck/

For an interesting look at how a research survey on social attitudes and human sexuality is conducted, check out the Informed Consent Form and review the questionnaire at this address. A team of researchers at California State University-Fullerton is conducting a study on human sexuality, and at this address they have posted a questionnaire that is part of their research. You can participate in the survey by completing the questionnaire. After completing the survey, the researchers will give you an overview of the study.

T

Testicular Cancer   No. 107

🌐 http://vax2.jmu.edu/~taylorbw/

Information on testicular cancer and the importance of self-examination is presented on this page. Specific instructions and graphic pictures illustrate how to perform a testicular self-examination.

Thrive@Sex   No. 108

🌐 http://www.thriveonline.com/@@HhAjoAUAHCbM5p0x/ thrive/index.html

Sex, health, and nutrition are among the topics explored at this site from Thrive@Healthy Living. Updates on contraceptive technology and links to related sites are included.

Trojan: HIV/AIDS/STDs   No. 109

🌐 http://www.linkmag.com

Sponsored by The Trojan Company, manufacturers of condoms, this site offers useful information and illustrations about the role of condoms in the prevention of sexually transmitted diseases and HIV/AIDS. Links are provided.

U

University of California at San Francisco Center for AIDS Prevention Studies — No. 110

 http://chanane.ucsf.edu/capsweb/index.html

This page offers high quality, comprehensive information on HIV/AIDs. Details on prevention and current research projects are included. Maintained by the Center for AIDS Prevention Studies at the University of California at San Francisco, this site provides many links.

V

Voice of the Shuttle: Gender Studies Page — No. 111

http://www.humanitas.ucsb.edu/shuttle/gender.html

Links, links, links. Use this page of links from Alan Lui, a professor in the Department of English at the University of California-Santa Barbara, to begin your search for online gender-related information. Professor Lui provides links to a broad range of sites (zines, chat rooms, libraries, journals, resources, etc.) on a broad range of topics (everything from "gay, lesbian & queer studies" to "men's movements").

W

Women and AIDS — No. 112

http://www.thebody.com/whatis/women.html

A collection of articles on women and AIDS/HIV infection. Articles come from a variety of sources, including the International Association of Physicians, the Harvard AIDS Institute, and various Federal agency reports. Also has links to getting help, what's news, political action alert pages, and a well-linked site where America's leading experts on HIV/AIDS answer questions.

Women's Health Resources On-line — No. 113

http://www.web.net/cwhn/resource/resmain.html

Maintained by the Canadian Women's Health Network, this is a listing of Internet resources related to women's health issues. An impressive Table of Contents including: Looking at Our Health, Controlling Our Reproductive Health and Fertility, The Medical System and Women, Childbearing, General Women's Health Resources, Medical and Health Conditions, and more. An extensive site with links to other search engines.

WWWomen — No. 114

http://www.wwwomen.com

WWWomen is the premier search engine for women's issues. Information on topics such as gender, sexual orientation, health and feminism are featured. Lots of links are included to related pages.

Web Journal

journal Notes

http:// _____ **Topic** _____

_____

_____

_____

_____

_____

_____

_____

_____

_____

_____

_____

_____

_____

_____

Name _____

Course # _____ Section _____

Date _____ Soc. Sec. # _____

Web Journal

Journal Notes

http:// _____ Topic _____

_____

_____

_____

_____

_____

_____

_____

_____

_____

_____

_____

_____

_____

_____

ReadingsPLUS with WebLinks

ReadingsPLUS Web Site Evaluation Form

Student Name _____

Date _____ Soc. Sec. # or Student I.D. # _____

Course Name & Number _____ Instructor Name _____

Web Site Name: _____

Site Number (if applicable) _____

Site Address/URL _____

Briefly describe your online experience. Were you able to access the site?

Identify the Source / Who runs site. Who is the person or what is the organization behind the site?

Is the site links-intensive or content-intensive? Or is it a combination of text and links to other sites?

Provide a brief overview of site. What resources and subjects or types of material are covered?

How would you rate the quality of content? Was the information useful to you? If yes, how so? If not, why not?

How would you rate the quality of the site's graphics and its navigability/ease-of-use?

When was the site last updated?

What does this site offer compared to other sources of information used in this course?

ReadingsPLUS Reading Review Form

Student Name _____

Date _____ Soc. Sec. # or Student I.D. # _____

Course Name & Number _____ Instructor Name _____

Reading Number: _____ Reading Title:_____

_____

Reading Summary
Describe the central idea or argument of this reading.

Key Terms
List two or three key terms used in the reading and briefly define them.

Compare and Contrast Information
Select one question from the following three questions and answer it.

(1) How does the information in this reading compare to what has been presented in class on this topic, or in your textbook (if you're using one)? For example, does it support or does it contradict what you have previously learned?

(2) How does the information in this reading compare to information you've encountered on this topic at a related Web site?

(3) How has this reading influenced or changed your opinion on the topic?

Index

Intimacy, 54–57, 65, 68–71,
74–75
psychological, 59, 61–62
sexual, 61, 68, 70

J
Jealousy, 170
Job performance, 30

K
Kahn, Axel, 10
Kilbourne, Jean, 34
Krasnegor, Dr. Norman, 19

L
Laumann, Edward O., 14–15
Lewontin, R. C., 15
Libido, 3, 5
Limbic system, 18
*Little League's Official How-to-
Play Baseball Book*, 22, 24
Love, 58–64

M
Magazines, 33
Magnetic resonance imaging, 18
Male dominance, 33–34
Marijuana, 81
Marriage, 65–66, 72, 74
arranged, 60
Masculinity, 38
Masturbation, 68, 70
Maturation, 59, 144
McClintock, Dr. Martha K., 2–4
Media, 33
McEwen, Dr. Bruce, 3, 4
Menstrual cycle, 6, 15
Menstruation, 5, 86–87
Mental health profession, 58,
62–63
Miscarriage, 82
Misogyny, 33, 66
Money, John, 11
Monogamy, 14–15, 65–66,
128–129, 140, 170
Morality, 164
Munson, Dr. Ronald, 17, 19
Mythology, 65

N
National Academy of Sciences
(NAS), 89
National Cancer Institute, 3
National Health and Social Life
Survey, 13
National Institute of Child
Health and Human Devel-
opment, 7, 13, 19
National Institutes of Health, 13
National Opinion Research Cen-
ter (NORC), 13
National Victim Center, 166
Navy Times, 28
Needle exchange programs, 122
New, Dr. Maria, 7
1991 National Survey of Men
(NSM), 45

Non-consensual sex, 31
Nonintimate sex, 74
Nonpsychotic delusion, 60
Normal marital sadism, 72
Nudity, 165
Nutrition, 84
Nymphomaniacs, 34

O
Obscenity, 152–153
Internet, 152–153, 170, 172
Objectification, 34
Obstacle courses, 29
Officer Candidate School, 28
Olympic Games, 22
Oral sex, 106, 140–141
Orchidometer, 87
Orgasm, 65, 71, 74, 144
Ovaries, 2–6
Ovulation, 5

P
Parenthood, 50
Parenting, 44
Patriarchal sexual system, 35
Pelvic inflammatory disease, 135
Persian Gulf War, 28
Photographs, 33
Physical abuse, 29
differences, 29
standards, 28
strength differences, 29
structure, 27
Plato, 59
Polycystic ovarian syndrome, 6
Pornography, 33–35, 169
Post-menopausal, 5–6, 84
Poverty, 157
Pregnancy, 30–31, 44, 50, 81,
96, 102, 104, 106, 121,
132
prevention, 110
Privacy, 61
Progesterone, 6
Prostitution, 154–157
Provocative body positions, 34
Pseudo-hermaphrodites, 11
Psychiatric, 63
Psychoanalysis, 58
Psychopathology, 58, 63
Psychotherapy, 171
Puberty, 2–4, 6, 84–85
Public Health Service, 13

R
Racism, 157, 159
Ramsey, Mimi, 158–163
Rape, 27–28, 31, 155, 166–168
date, 166–168
gang, 34
marital, 69
Rape and Criminal Justice, 166
Rationalization, 60
Redmond, Dr. Geoffrey P., 6
Reinfibulation, 161–162
Relationships, 61, 66, 74
Internet, 172

Richards, Bob, 24
Richards, Tammy, 24
Rite of passage, 160
Rittmaster, Dr. Roger S., 6
Romantic interactions, 38, 54
Rosenfield, Dr. Robert, 3
Russo, Joseph, 23

S
Saturated Self, The, 37
Seavers, Tom, 22
Self-affirmation, 69
Self-identification, 38
Semen, 77–78
Sentimentality, 60
Sex
differences, 27
education, 114–117
eyes-open, 74
intimate, 68
non-consensual, 31
nonintimate, 74
reproductive, 68
Sexism, 33–35, 157
Sexual
abuse, 29
activity, 3, 34
assault, 31
attraction, 35
behavior, 13–15, 19, 45
boredom, 74
characteristics, 6
desire, 68–69
development, 72
dysfunctions, 68–70
experience, 70
fantasy, 3
fidelity, 59, 62
function, 5, 68
happiness, 68
harassment, 27–28, 148–150,
155, 164
identification, 15
integration, 29
interactions, 38
intercourse, 65–66, 132, 166
liberation, 68
networks, 14
performance, 68
pleasure, 59–60, 62, 171
preferences, 15
prime, 72–73
potential, 71, 73–74
response, 70
social organization, 13–15
styles, 72
therapy, 69
Sexual Attitudes and Lifestyles,
14
Sexuality, 33–35, 65–66, 74, 171
human, 70
in advertising, 164–165
spiritual, 71
Sexualization, 34
Sexually transmitted disease
(STD), 14–15, 44, 50, 90,

93, 102, 105–106, 110,
114, 131–142, 164
awareness, 133
education, 13, 132–133
intervention, 13
prevention, 133
treatment, 138
Shaywitz, Dr. Sally, 17–20
Shaywitz, Dr. Bennett A., 17–20
Singer, Irving, 59
Skakkebæk, Niels E., 78–88
*Social Organization of Sexuality
Practices in the United
States*, 13–15
Socialization, 38
Socrates, 59
Softball for Girls & Women, 22
Soldierization skills, 29
Soldiers, 27–32
Sperm, 77–88
count, 82
production, 82, 95
Spermatogenesis, 82, 86–87
Spirituality, 55, 71–72, 75
Spouse abuse, 36
Stars and Stripes, 30–31
Studd, Dr. John, 6
Sublimation, 66
Submission, 33, 35
Subordinate body positions, 34
Suicide, 29, 170
Syphilis, 136–137

T
Tennis, 22
Testes, 2, 6
Testicles, 78, 81, 85, 87
undescended, 82
Testicular cancer, 78–79, 82
Testosterone, 5–7, 84
Testosterone replacement ther-
apy, 6
"Throwing like a girl", 21–24
Tobacco, 81

V
Vagina, 77, 86
Vaginal cancer, 82
Vasectomies, 78
Victimization, 170
Vietnam Syndrome, 28
Virtual love, 169–173

W
Wells, Linda, 23
Wild, Dr. Robert A., 5
Winnicott, D. W., 56
Witelson, Dr. Sandra, 18, 20
World Health Organization, 8,
78, 91, 93

Y
Young, Hugh H., 11–12

ReadingsPLUS with WebLinks